Contents

page **12**

page **05**

page **17**

Find thousands of plans on-line, visit our website
www.familyhomeplans.com

Design, Build and Decorate
Your New Home on Your Kitchen Table

Don't let the frustration of complicated home design software get between you and your dream. Visualize and test your ideas using our proven design systems.

HOME QUICK PLANNER

Design and Decorate Your New Home

Go ahead! Knock down walls and move cabinets, bathroom fixtures, furniture, windows and doors—even whole rooms. 700 pre-cut, reusable peel-and-stick furniture, fixture and architectural symbols. Includes 1/4-in. scale Floor Plan Grid, stairs, outlets, switches, lights, plus design ideas.

Regularly $22.95   **Special Offer: $19.95**

3-D HOME KIT

"Build" Your New Home

Construct a three-dimensional scale model home of up to 3,000 square feet. (For larger homes, order an extra kit.) A complete assortment of cardboard building materials—from brick, stone, clapboards, roofing and decking to windows, doors, skylights, stairs, bathroom fixtures, kitchen cabinets and more. Includes Floor Plan Grid, interior walls, special Scaled Ruler and Roof Slope Calculator, professional design notes and complete model building instructions.

Regularly $33.95   **Special Offer: $29.95**

the Garlinghouse company
Helping to build dreams since 1907

To order, call
1-800-235-5700
Monday - Friday 8 a.m. - 8 p.m. Eastern Time

532 Ranch Home Plans

An Active Interest Media Publication

GARLINGHOUSE, LLC

General Manager	Steve Culpepper
Art Director	Christopher Berrien
Managing Editor	Debra Cochran
Art Production Manager	Debra Novitch
Production Artist	Cindy King
Exec. Director of Operations	Wade Schmelter
Senior Accountant	Angela West
Director of Home Plan Sales	Sue Lavigne
Director of Sales	Tom Valentino
Architectural Plan Reviewer	Jeanne Devins
Accounts Receivable/Payable	Monika Jackson
Telesales Manager	Helene Crispino
Telesales Team	Julianna Blamire
	Randolph Hollingsworth
	Renee Johnson
	Barbara Neal
	Carol Patenaude
	Robert Rogala
	Alice Sonski
Fulfillment Supervisor	Audrey Sutton
Fulfillment Support	Javier Gonzalez

Advertising Sales
1-800-279-7361

For Plan Orders in Canada
The Garlinghouse Company
102 Ellis Street, Penticton, BC V2A 4L5
1-800-361-7526

For Designer's Submission Information,
e-mail us at dcochran@aimmedia.com

532 RANCH HOME PLANS
Library of Congress: 2004106496   ISBN: 1-893536-18-1

At Garlinghouse, you're buying more than a set of plans.

You're buying a history of exceptional customer service and understanding.

In addition to our experienced staff of sales professionals, The Garlinghouse Company maintains an expert staff of trained house design professionals to help guide you through the complex process of customizing your plans to meet all your needs and expectations.

We don't just want to sell you a plan, we want to partner with you in building your dream home. Some of the many services we offer our customers include:

Answers to Your Questions
If you have technical questions on any plan we sell, give us a call toll-free at 1-800-235-5700.

Customizing Your Stock Plan
Any plan we sell can be modified to become your custom home. For more information, see page 32 and page 407.

Information for Budgeting Your New Home's Construction
A very general cost of building your new home can be arrived at using the so-called National Average Cost to Build, which is $110 per square foot. Based on that average, a 2,400-square-foot home would cost $264,000, including labor and materials, but excluding land, site preparation, windows, doors, cabinets, appliances, etc.

For a more inclusive rough estimate, Garlinghouse offers a Zip Quote estimate for every plan we sell. Based on current prices in your zip code area, we can provide a rough estimate of material and labor costs for the plans you select. See page 409 to learn more.

However, for a more accurate estimate of what it will cost to build your new home, we offer a full materials list, which lists the quantities, dimensions, and specifications for the major materials needed to build your home including appliances. Available at a modest additional charge, the materials list will allow you to get faster, more accurate bids from your contractors and building suppliers—and help you avoid paying for unused materials and waste. Due to differences in regional requirements and homeowner or builder preferences, electrical, plumbing, and heating/air conditioning equipment specifications are not designed specifically for each plan. See page 406 for additional information.

Garlinghouse blueprints have helped create a nation of homeowners, beginning back in 1907. Over the past century, we've made keeping up with the latest trends in floor plan design for new house construction our business. We understand the business of home plans and the real needs and expectations of the home plan buyer. To contact us, call 1-800-235-5700, or visit us on the web at www.familyhomeplans.com.

the
Garlinghouse
company

For America's best home plans.
Trust, value, and experience. Since 1907.

Comfort & Light

Banks of windows define the public spaces within this large, comfortable plan. Once inside the entry, a wall of windows at the rear of the home draws you into the living room where the ceiling height soars above twelve feet. The long living room is at the physical center of the home but leads directly into the true heart of any home, the kitchen. In this case, the kitchen is big and open with plenty of nicely defined workspace flooded with natural light from the abundant windows and skylights. Off to one side of the kitchen, a utility room and a coat closet are conveniently located by the door to the three-car garage.

The right side of the home is reserved for the bedrooms. At the rear is the master suite, which includes a large bedroom, spacious master bath, and two large walk-in closets. A secondary bedroom at the front of the home has private access to a hall bath.

The lower level contains 2,752 square feet, some of which could be finished to include two or three additional bedrooms plus a large family room. The home is designed with a basement foundation.

Above: Stepped, front-facing gables add depth to the facade of this home while drawing attention to the curved arch leading to the covered entry.

Design 98365

Price Code	F
Total Finished	2,436 sq. ft.
Main Finished	2,436 sq. ft.
Basement Unfinished	2,572 sq. ft.
Garage Unfinished	713 sq. ft.
Porch Unfinished	136 sq. ft.
Dimensions	61'4"x70'
Foundation	Basement
Bedrooms	2
Full Baths	2

Please note: The photographed home may have been modified to suit homeowner preferences. If you order plans, have a builder or design professional check them against the photographs to confirm construction details.

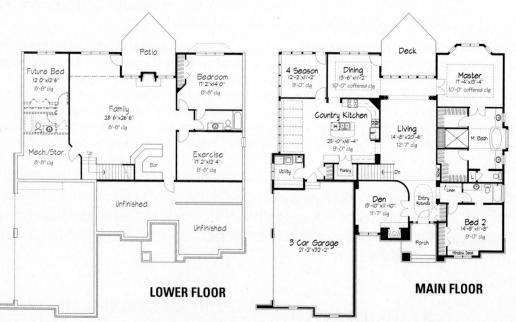

LOWER FLOOR

MAIN FLOOR

ABOVE: A double-pillared arched porch creates a stunning contrast to a trio of gables, giving this home classic curb appeal.

Design 50032

Price Code	C
Total Finished	1,860 sq. ft.
Main Finished	1,860 sq. ft.
Basement Unfinished	1,860 sq. ft.
Porch Unfinished	69 sq. ft.
Dimensions	64'2"x44'2"
Foundation	Basement
Bedrooms	3
Full Baths	2

Please note: The photographed home may have been modified to suit homeowner preferences. If you order plans, have a builder or design professional check them against the photographs to confirm construction details.

Elegance Throughout

An elegant porch leads directly into the foyer, designed with guests in mind. Immediately to the right, columns mark the boundaries of the formal dining room. The space opens into the vast great-room whose 11-foot ceiling makes it seem even larger than its actual dimensions. This space is ideal for formal and casual gatherings. Steps away, the breakfast room, with bay window nook, blends into the counter-lined kitchen, rounding out the common areas. A large laundry room, with closet and hanging space, and garage increase the efficiency of the plan. In the opposite wing, the three bedrooms are designed for maximum privacy. The master suite fills the rear, with its bedroom alcove, walk-in closet, and five-piece bath. The other rooms enjoy ample closet space and proximity to a full hall bath. A rear deck and porch allow outdoor living. This home is designed with a basement foundation.

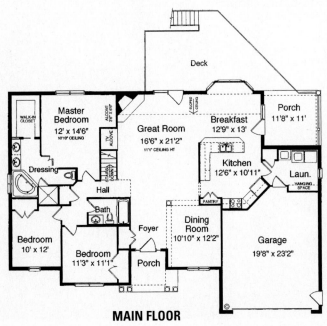

MAIN FLOOR

Courtyard Character

Above: Twin dormers that overlook the front courtyard also create a soft, high source of natural light in the open living area.

Built around twin courtyards, front and rear, this home carefully separates private and shared spaces into two main wings. To the left side of the 2,780-square-foot home, the bedroom wing includes the master suite and two secondary bedrooms; to the right and center, a large living area opens onto a dining area and turns left around the rear courtyard to enfold the kitchen/breakfast area and den.

Below: A rambling, light-filled and comfortable feeling reigns in the open spaces of this unique plan.

Among the shared spaces, the 462-square-foot living room dominates. French doors open onto both the front and rear courtyards, maximizing the room's sources of natural light. Twin columns separate the living from dining areas. French doors lead from the dining room to the kitchen/breakfast area. Here, a C-shape counter and a peninsula fireplace subtly distinguish the kitchen/breakfast area from the den. The two-car garage, which opens to the side of the home, defines the right boundary of the front courtyard. From the garage, one door leads to the courtyard, another into the home's living area, passing by the laundry.

The private wing of the home is carefully designed for maximum use. Two 270-square-foot secondary bedrooms share a full bath. A much larger bath is reserved for the master suite. Connecting the shared area with the master suite is a potting area with utility sink on one side and French doors onto the rear courtyard on the other. This home is designed with a slab foundation.

PHOTOGRAPHY: RICHARD SEXTON

Above: Courtyards fill in the open spaces on this home's H-shaped plan and create two main wings, one private, one shared. To the rear of home, generous use of window area creates light-filled interior.

Left: A peninsula fireplace forms a subtle separation between the den and the kitchen/breakfast area of the home's shared wing.

Design 32145

Price Code	G
Total Finished	2,780 sq. ft.
Main Finished	2,780 sq. ft.
Dimensions	67'x71'
Foundation	Slab
Bedrooms	3
Full Baths	2
Half Baths	1

Please note: The photographed home may have been modified to suit homeowner preferences. If you order plans, have a builder or design professional check them against the photographs to confirm construction details.

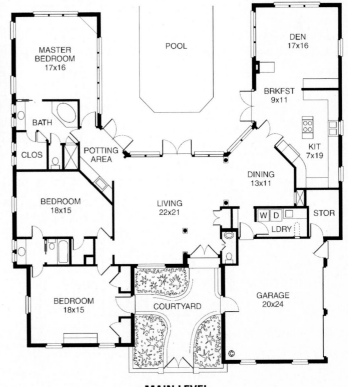

MAIN LEVEL

Country Comfort

Above: A series of low, gabled roofs give a rambling, vintage appeal to this classic country-style ranch.

This classic ranch home offers traditional comfort wrapped in a lovely country exterior. The long covered porch opens into a big living room that is accented by a fireplace. Straight ahead from the entry lies the dining room, which accesses the rear yard, while the kitchen—with every available wall space lined with counters and cabinets—opens to a side screen porch. The master bedroom includes a spacious private bath with a separate shower and a large walk-in-closet. Two secondary bedrooms share a full hall bath, which has the added convenience of a closet laundry centrally located to all the bedrooms—right where it's needed most. This home is designed with basement, slab, and crawlspace foundation options.

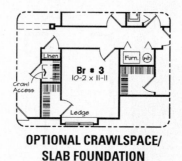

**OPTIONAL CRAWLSPACE/
SLAB FOUNDATION**

Design 24708

Price Code	B
Total Finished	1,576 sq. ft.
First Finished	1,576 sq. ft.
Basement Unfinished	1,454 sq. ft.
Garage Unfinished	576 sq. ft.
Porch Unfinished	391 sq. ft.
Dimensions	93'x36'
Foundation	Basement Crawlspace Slab
Bedrooms	3
Full Baths	2

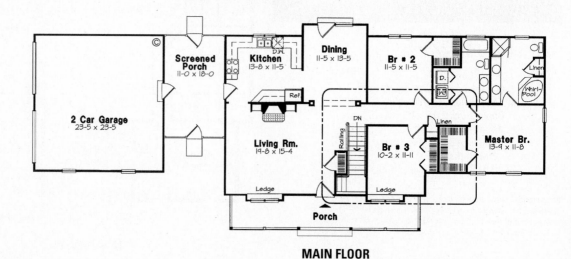

MAIN FLOOR

Above: This home's tall, keystoned sets of windows provide a glimpse of the detail found within.

Please note: The photographed home may have been modified to suit homeowner preferences. If you order plans, have a builder or design professional check them against the photographs to confirm construction details.

Perfect for Entertaining

Once inside the long foyer, guests are immediately ushered into the formal dining room or straight ahead to the living room, which, with its wetbar and access to the screen porch, is ideal for entertaining. Nearby, the family room is perfect for more casual gatherings, with its cozy fireplace and proximity to the breakfast area. Windows line the breakfast nook, which is separated from the kitchen by only a snack bar. The kitchen is almost completely surrounded by counters, a pantry adds even more storage. The three bedrooms are privately located in the left wing. This home is designed with basement, slab, and crawlspace foundation options. Alternate foundation options available at an additional charge. Please call 1-800-235-5700 for more information.

Design 68036

Price Code	D
Total Finished	2,120 sq. ft.
First Finished	2,120 sq. ft.
Garage Unfinished	548 sq. ft.
Dimensions	58'x68'
Foundation	Basement
	Crawlspace
	Slab
Bedrooms	3
Full Baths	2

Floor plan labels

SCREEN PORCH
$14^0 \times 11^8$
10'-0" CEILING
TRANSOMS

WHIRLPOOL

Mbr.
$13^0 \times 16^0$
9'-0" CLG.

Liv. rm.
$14^0 \times 17^0$
10'-0" CEILING
LIN.

Fam. rm.
$19^4 \times 14^0$

WET BAR

DN

Bfst.
$12^0 \times 10^0$
SNACK BAR

Din.
$11^0 \times 14^0$
9'-0" CLG.

Kit.
$12^0 \times 11^4$

E.

P.

B.

R.

Br. 3
$11^0 \times 12^7$

Br. 2
$12^0 \times 13^3$
9'-0" CEILING

COVERED PORCH

W./D.

Gar.
$21^4 \times 25^4$

MAIN FLOOR

Spacious Rooms

Careful planning makes the most of this charming plan. Tall windows flood the rooms with natural light, three porches extend the living area, and a secluded master bedroom provides the homeowner with a real retreat. A spacious living room, with a fireplace and access to a rear porch, serves as the central hub of this home. To the left, an octagonal dining room opens to an efficient kitchen. Here too are the utilitarian areas of the home, the utility/laundry room, the two-car garage and a storage room, all tucked away at the front of the home and out of the main traffic flow. At the rear of the home, the master bedroom, with it's compartmentalized bath, walk-in-closet, and cozy covered porch, offers amenity-laden privacy. On the right side of the home, two secondary bedrooms, buffered from the public areas by a short hall, share a full bath. This home is designed with slab and crawlspace foundation options.

Above: This elegant little home draws on Southern style to create a warm and welcoming appeal.

Design 65635

Price Code	B
Total Finished	1,655 sq. ft.
First Finished	1,655 sq. ft.
Dimensions	52'x66'
Foundation	Crawlspace Slab
Bedrooms	3
Full Baths	2

Please note: The photographed home may have been modified to suit homeowner preferences. If you order plans, have a builder or design professional check them against the photographs to confirm construction details.

Floor plan labels

lin
bath
shv
clo
shr

mbr 16 x 14
por 10x6
slope clg

ref
dining 14 x 14
porch
skylight
14 x 10
slope clg

clo   clo
br 2 12 x 12

kit 14x12
skylight
dw
ov
ct
pan
bar

sto 10x6
util
w
d
sto
clo
HEAT &AC
W.H.

living 18 x 18
lin
van
bath
clo
slope clg

garage 22 x 22

porch 18 x 6
br 3 12 x 12

MAIN FLOOR

PHOTOGRAPHY: COURTESY OF THE DESIGNER

Above: A mix of stone, brick and shingle siding, and square, tapered columns give an updated Craftsman-style appeal to the exterior of this plan.

Design 50043

Price Code	L
Total Finished	5,068 sq. ft.
Main Finished	3,171 sq. ft.
Lower Finished	1,897 sq. ft.
Basement Unfinished	3,171 sq. ft.
Garage Unfinished	828 sq. ft.
Porch Unfinished	333 sq. ft.
Dimensions	86'2"x63'8"
Foundation	Basement
Bedrooms	4
Full Baths	2
Half Baths	1

Plenty of Room

Large, open public spaces are the center point of the 3,171 square-foot main floor of this plan. Decorative box beams and columns separate the great room, foyer, and dining room. The kitchen features an angled eating bar that's open to the great room and to the bay windowed breakfast area. A large deck off the breakfast area includes an outdoor fireplace. To the right side of the home, a spacious master suite with an impressive walk-in-closet shares space with a secondary bedroom and a secluded library, which could serve as a third bedroom. The lower floor, designed to take advantage of a sloping lot, can be finished to include a large rec room and two additional bedrooms while retaining plenty of basement storage space. This home is designed with a basement foundation.

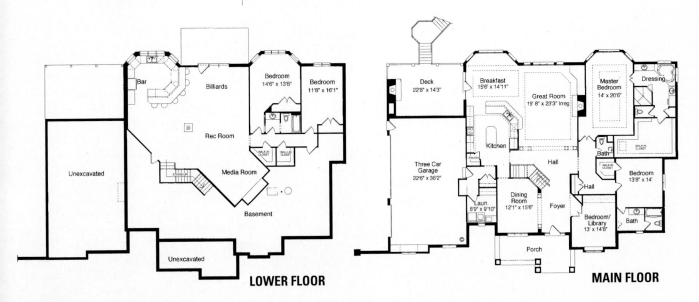

LOWER FLOOR

MAIN FLOOR

Please note: The photographed home may have been modified to suit homeowner preferences. If you order plans, have a builder or design professional check them against the photographs to confirm construction details.

Scenic Home

On the main level at the heart of the home is the kitchen, which receives morning sun through windows tucked into a small dormer over the front entry. The kitchen contains a walk-in pantry for extra storage space. Behind the kitchen is a small breakfast nook for casual meals. The layout of the home radiates out from the kitchen, and is designed for single-level living, with master suite and laundry on the main level. At one end of the home, the master suite includes a luxurious bath with fine built-ins and a relaxing corner tub. At the other end of the main level lies the great-room, which is separated from the kitchen by a raised counter. A large bank of transom-topped windows floods the room with light, while a vaulted ceiling lends a sense of space. The great-room features a fireplace with built-in cabinets that can be used for wood storage or an entertainment center. The lower level also contains lots of windows to keep it filled with light. Rather than having a basement walk-out, access to the backyard is through doors off the stair landing. The lower level is designed for fun and guests, and includes three bedrooms, a full bath, and a large recreation area with bar and fireplace. A doorway at the foot of the stairs can close off the lower level to keep noise to a minimum. This home is designed with a basement foundation.

Above: Natural colors in the stone, redwood siding, and shingles help the home blend with its environment. The low, sweeping roofline allows it to maintain an unobtrusive profile.

Below: Large windows flood the great room with sunlight to highlight the birch and cherry woodwork. A vaulted ceiling adds volume and detail without overpowering the room.

PHOTOGRAPHY: SUSAN GILLMORE

Left: Cherry wood cabinets and hardwood flooring glow in the abundant natural light that floods the kitchen. Contemporary fixtures and a coffered ceiling add detail to elegance.

Below left: Arts and Crafts-inspired details in the moldings, trim, and built-ins of the formal dining room create vintage appeal.

Below: Set into a sunny rear alcove just behind the kitchen, the breakfast nook has a wide-open feel thanks to transom-topped windows and open-railing stairs.

Above: Like the rest of the rooms in this light-filled design, the study receives plenty of natural light through its large windows—even while being shaded from the glare of direct sunlight by the covered porch that wraps around the front of the home.

Top Right: A built-in entertainment center in the recreation room blends with the fireplace mantel and surround.

Bottom Right: A small bump-out in the master bedroom creates space for a chest of drawers

Below: Finely crafted details and an abundance of natural light are the theme of this home, running through every space including the master bath.

Above: The home's design offers all types of views whether from the master suite, breakfast nook, or deck.

Design 32375

Price Code	L
Total Finished	4,022 sq. ft.
Main Finished	2,019 sq. ft.
Lower Finished	2,003 sq. ft.
Garage Unfinished	783 sq. ft.
Deck Unfinished	204 sq. ft.
Porch Unfinished	388 sq. ft.
Dimensions	73'8"x55'8"
Foundation	Basement
Bedrooms	4
Full Baths	2
Half Baths	1

Please note: The photographed home may have been modified to suit homeowner preferences. If you order plans, have a builder or design professional check them against the photographs to confirm construction details.

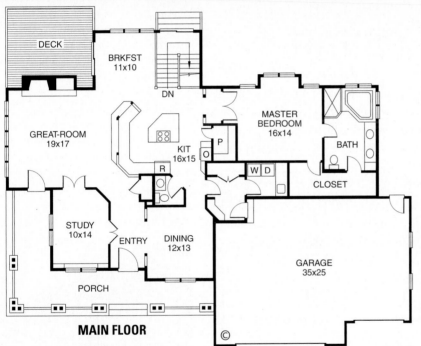

MAIN FLOOR

DECK

BRKFST
11x10

DN

MASTER
BEDROOM
16x14

BATH

GREAT-ROOM
19x17

KIT
16x15

P

CLOSET

W D

R

STUDY
10x14

ENTRY

DINING
12x13

GARAGE
35x25

PORCH

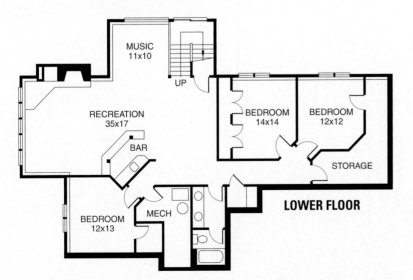

LOWER FLOOR

MUSIC
11x10

UP

RECREATION
35x17

BEDROOM
14x14

BEDROOM
12x12

BAR

STORAGE

BEDROOM
12x13

MECH

Casual Comfort

A sheltering entry leads into a long living room, which is the anchor of this inviting and efficient home. Exposed beams and a fireplace flanked by tall windows distinguish this room, which opens to the dining room, from which glass doors lead either onto an optional deck or to the backyard. A peninsula eating bar separates the dining room from the kitchen while adding a generous amount of workspace. A short hall leading to the garage offers access to a built-in pantry and the laundry room. On the opposite side of the 1,307-square-foot home, two secondary bedrooms share a full hall bath. The pleasantly proportioned master bedroom offers a full wall of closet space and a private full bath. This home is designed with basement, slab, and crawlspace foundation options.

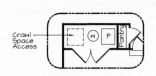

Crawl Space Access

OPTIONAL CRAWLSPACE/ SLAB FOUNDATION

Above: Clapboard and shingle siding mixed with stone facing create visual interest by highlighting the various shapes of the facade. Changing the orientation of the garage is a typical and simple modification.

Below: This view of the side and rear elevations shows how subtly the side-load garage blends with the profile of the home. Instead of a deck, this homeowner chose to have stairs descending to a patio. The bay window in the master bedroom has been replaced with sliders offering additional access to the patio.

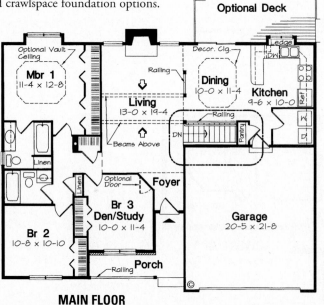

Optional Deck

Decor. Clg.

Optional Vault Ceiling

Mbr 1
11-4 x 12-8

Railing

Dining
10-0 x 11-4

Kitchen
9-6 x 10-0

Living
13-0 x 19-4

Railing

Beams Above

DN

Linen

Pantry

Optional Door

Foyer

Linen

**Br 3
Den/Study**
10-0 x 11-4

Garage
20-5 x 21-8

Br 2
10-8 x 10-10

Railing **Porch**

MAIN FLOOR

Design 20161

Price Code	A
Total Finished	1,307 sq. ft.
Main Finished	1,307 sq. ft.
Basement Unfinished	1,298 sq. ft.
Garage Unfinished	462 sq. ft.
Dimensions	50'x40'
Foundation	Basement Crawlspace Slab
Bedrooms	3
Full Baths	2

PHOTOGRAPHY: ROSS CHAPPLE, BOB GREENSPAN PHOTOGRAPHY

Above: Craftsman-inspired details such as low-pitched gabled roofs with wide overhanging eaves, square stone columns supporting the porch, and exposed ridge beams add traditional appeal to the exterior of this modern floor plan.

Design 32342

Price Code	L
Total Finished	5,725 sq. ft.
Main Finished	3,179 sq. ft.
Lower Finished	2,546 sq. ft.
Basement Unfinished	633 sq. ft.
Garage Unfinished	881 sq. ft.
Dimensions	78'x72'
Foundation	Basement
Bedrooms	4
Full Baths	2
3/4 Baths	2
Half Baths	1

Inside Garden

The traditional exterior of this home belies the surprises that await within its strikingly modern floor plan. A full wall separates the formal dining room from the entry, but half walls open it up to the great room. A balcony in the wide-open great room overlooks the dramatic two-story atrium, which brightens up the main public rooms on both levels. The dining and utility areas fill the left wing of the 3,179-square-foot main floor, while a private section houses bedrooms on the right. Stairs descend through the atrium's garden space to the family room in the 2,546-square-foot walk-out lower level. Additional bedrooms can be found on this level as well as a game area with bar. This home is designed with a basement foundation.

Above: The two-level atrium dominates the rear of the home.

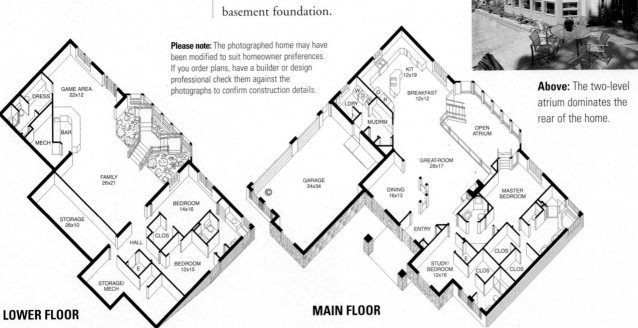

Please note: The photographed home may have been modified to suit homeowner preferences. If you order plans, have a builder or design professional check them against the photographs to confirm construction details.

LOWER FLOOR

MAIN FLOOR

European Charm

Above: Curved, copper-top dormers set into a richly tiled roof, Normandy-style windows inside a courtyard wall, and a decorative iron-work gate create a charming front facade.

Below: 12-foot high ceilings and 8-foot tall patio doors topped with transoms give a large-scale feel to the moderately sized dining room.

The courtyard entry, high-profile roofline, and arched French dormers create a slightly deceptive facade. Although it appears to be a large, one and a half-story home, a step through the gracious front door into the open living areas reveals a one-story design that's less than 2,600 square feet. Clever strategies give the moderately sized rooms a big feel. Ceilings in the living and dining rooms soar to great heights. Patio doors in each room are topped by transoms. The kitchen layout is equally suited for meal preparation for two or to large parties, when the island can serve as a buffet and gathering spot. Every wall in the nearby family room has a function: two walls filled with windows provide views into the backyard; a third wall holds built-ins. The master bedroom is separated from the secondary bedrooms and includes patio doors that open to the veranda. This home is designed with a slab foundation.

Left: In the living room, patio doors on exterior-mounted tracks slide open to create clean openings onto the veranda.

Below left: Maple cabinets in the kitchen take on the look of built-in furniture, with varying heights and depths and crown molding.

Below: French doors lead from the breakfast room to the long rear veranda. A niche in one wall frees floor space.

Above: The master bedroom features 10-foot ceilings and access to the rear veranda. Details in the room such as the built-up crown molding and operable plantation shutters contribute to the Old World charm found throughout the design.

Right: The master bath is at the front of the home. The courtyard wall that encloses the entrance to the home provides added privacy for the large window over the soaking tub.

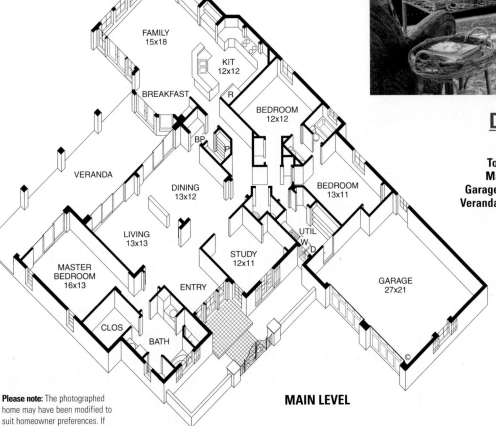

Left: A veranda along the back of the home overlooks the pool. Sliding doors open the home to the outdoor space. The doors to the left of the photo lead into the living room while the doors to the right lead into the master bedroom.

Below: Two walls of tall windows, arched built-ins for the entertainment center, and an open arrangement with the kitchen and breakfast nook contribute to the spacious feel of the family room.

Design 32380

Price Code	D
Total Finished	2,581 sq. ft.
Main Finished	2,581 sq. ft.
Garage Unfinished	602 sq. ft.
Veranda Unfinished	422 sq. ft.
Dimensions	62'x87'8"
Foundation	Slab
Bedrooms	3
Full Baths	2
Half Baths	1

FAMILY
15x18

KIT
12x12

BREAKFAST

R

BP P

VERANDA

DINING
13x12

BEDROOM
12x12

BEDROOM
13x11

LIVING
13x13

UTIL
W D

MASTER
BEDROOM
16x13

STUDY
12x11

CLOS

ENTRY

GARAGE
27x21

BATH

MAIN LEVEL

Please note: The photographed home may have been modified to suit homeowner preferences. If you order plans, have a builder or design professional check them against the photographs to confirm construction details.

Above: A simple facade is enlivened with traditional country detailing.

Dramatic Ranch

A deep front porch running the full width of the house adds to the sheltering appeal of this thoughtfully designed plan. A small, angled entry opens into a large living room with centrally located fireplace and decorative beamed ceiling. The beams continue into the kitchen and dining room, which open to the living room through doorways flanking the fireplace, creating an open and easy traffic flow through the public rooms of the home. Tucked away at the rear of the home, an oversize laundry room and pantry offer convenient storage. The bedrooms are grouped together on the right side of the home. Two secondary bedrooms at the front of the home, each featuring a generous closet, are separated from each other by a full bath. The master bedroom has a private bath with a big walk-in-closet. This home is designed with a basement foundation.

Design 20198

Price Code	C
Total Finished	1,792 sq. ft.
First Finished	1,792 sq. ft.
Basement Unfinished	818 sq. ft.
Garage Unfinished	857 sq. ft.
Porch Unfinished	336 sq. ft.
Dimensions	56'x32'
Foundation	Basement
Bedrooms	3
Full Baths	2

MAIN FLOOR

Above: Arched windows, keystone details, and a turned-post entry to a covered porch offer plenty of curb appeal in this top-selling plan.

Design 24700

Price Code	A
Total Finished	1,312 sq. ft.
First Finished	1,312 sq. ft.
Basement Unfinished	1,293 sq. ft.
Garage Unfinished	459 sq. ft.
Deck Unfinished	185 sq. ft.
Porch Unfinished	84 sq. ft.
Dimensions	50'x40'
Foundation	Basement
	Crawlspace
	Slab
Bedrooms	3
Full Baths	2

Small Wonder

With its charming details and convenient, practical floor plan, it's no wonder that this lovely, moderate-sized home is our best-selling ranch-style plan. The living room, dining room, and kitchen maintain a sense of separateness due to their careful arrangement within the plan and distinct ceiling treatments, yet remain open to one another to give the public rooms a feeling of spaciousness. The long living room features a fireplace flanked by windows. The dining room has glass doors opening it up to the outdoors. The kitchen includes a built-in pantry opposite the laundry room. The bedrooms are grouped together on the left side of the home. The careful placement of closets, bathrooms, and a short hallway within the bedroom wing offer added privacy by ensuring that none of the bedrooms share a common wall.

The master bedroom features a full wall of closet space serving as a buffer between it and the living room. This home is designed with basement, slab, and crawlspace foundation options.

MAIN FLOOR

**OPTIONAL CRAWLSPACE/
SLAB FOUNDATION**

Ranch Living

Guests enter the home through a long hallway that leads from the covered main entry directly into the living room. The location of the home's two bedrooms in the right wing of the home keeps private spaces separate from public spaces. Shared spaces include the living room with fireplace, large den (which could be converted into a third bedroom) the dining room, and kitchen. The den is just inside the foyer to the right and includes a vaulted ceiling and coat closet. At nearly 175 square feet, the living room provides plenty of room for large family gatherings or entertaining. It opens to the dining area, which is separated from the kitchen by an angled eating bar. Included in the kitchen and dining area are a built-in desk, pantry, closet, and laundry room. The master suite fills the rear of the bedroom wing. The master bedroom features an optional decorative ceiling and a bump-out window onto the backyard. The master bath is compartmentalized, allowing for for use by two people at once. A hall linen closet is between the two baths. A garage and rear deck complete the plan. This home is designed with basement, slab, and crawlspace foundation options.

Above: Small details, such as French doors and arched windows with keystone caps, add style to this traditional ranch design.

Design 20164

Price Code	A
Total Finished	1,456 sq. ft.
Main Finished	1,456 sq. ft.
Basement Unfinished	1,448 sq. ft.
Garage Unfinished	452 sq. ft.
Dimensions	50'x45'4"
Foundation	Basement Crawlspace Slab
Bedrooms	3
Full Baths	2

Please note: The photographed home may have been modified to suit homeowner preferences. If you order plans, have a builder or design professional check them against the photographs to confirm construction details.

OPTIONAL CRAWLSPACE/ SLAB FOUNDATION

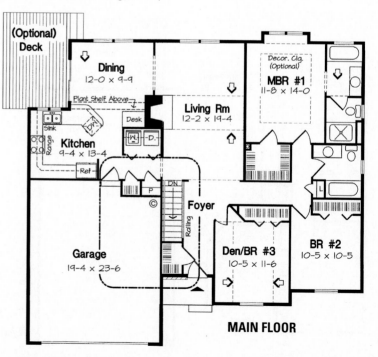

MAIN FLOOR

PHOTOGRAPHY: ROSS CHAPPLE, BOB GREENSPAN PHOTOGRAPHY

Above: An octagonal bay, wide porch, and brick and clapboard facing give this traditional design extra style.

Pretty & Practical

Design 34043

Price Code	B
Total Finished	1,583 sq. ft.
First Finished	1,583 sq. ft.
Basement Unfinished	1,573 sq. ft.
Garage Unfinished	484 sq. ft.
Dimensions	70'x46'
Foundation	Basement
	Crawlspace
	Slab
Bedrooms	3
Full Baths	2

This popular plan is perfect for the modern family with a taste for classic design. Traditional Victorian touches in this three-bedroom home include the front porch that covers the entrance and a polygonal breakfast bay just off the kitchen. The kitchen is centrally located in the common areas offering equal access to the foyer, breakfast room, dining room and the wide-open living room, which opens out to the deck. In the bedroom wing, the master suite enjoys a skylit, compartmentalized bath, while two secondary bedrooms boast ample closet space. A long hallway, leading to the two car garage, laundry room, and a full bath, separates the master bedroom from the secondary bedrooms. This home is designed with basement, slab, and crawlspace foundation options.

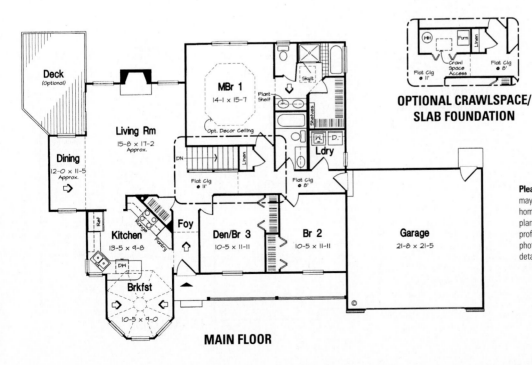

OPTIONAL CRAWLSPACE/ SLAB FOUNDATION

Please note: The photographed home may have been modified to suit homeowner preferences. If you order plans, have a builder or design professional check them against the photographs to confirm construction details.

MAIN FLOOR

Attractive and Economical

Above: Large rooms arranged in a U-shape design create an open and inviting atmosphere inside and out.

Design 10839

Price Code	A
Total Finished	1,456 sq. ft.
Main Finished	1,456 sq. ft.
Basement Unfinished	1,448 sq. ft.
Garage Unfinished	452 sq. ft.
Dimensions	50'x45'4"
Foundation	Basement Crawlspace Slab
Bedrooms	3
Full Baths	2

U-shape counters in the kitchen include a breakfast bar, allowing for casual meal service in the generous great-room. Across from the kitchen is a breakfast room, complete with a view of the porch from its shaded bay window. A sunken great-room lies in the back, and has twin sets of triple windows flanking its fireplace. Similar windows open the dining room to the screen porch in the corner. An optional deck can extend living space outdoors. A skylight graces the master bedroom, which includes access to a whirlpool and twin walk-in closets. This home is designed with basement, slab, and crawlspace foundation options.

OPTIONAL CRAWLSPACE/ SLAB FOUNDATION

Please note: The photographed home may have been modified to suit homeowner preferences. If you order plans, have a builder or design professional check them against the photographs to confirm construction details.

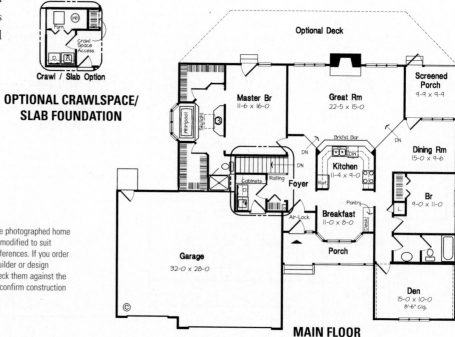

MAIN FLOOR

Above: Simple country lines with just the right touch of detail enliven this traditional design.

Design 99690

Price Code	I
Total Finished	5,755 sq. ft.
First Finished	2,442 sq. ft.
Garage Unfinished	935 sq. ft.
Porch Unfinished	442 sq. ft.
Dimensions	72'6"x76'10"
Foundation	Basement
Bedrooms	3
Full Baths	3
Half Baths	1

Well-Divided Space

A simple roof line and a basic rectangular footprint make this pretty little three-bedroom home very economical to build. A sheltering front porch extending the length of the facade provides a traditionally welcoming touch. The front door leads into a large living room, which, in turn, is open to the dining room. The dining room offers access to the back yard or a patio and is separated from the kitchen by an island. The open floor plan of the common areas makes the rooms seem larger and more spacious than their already generous proportions. A hall leads from the living room to the bedrooms. The master bedroom offers a real retreat to the homeowner with a private bath and large closet. Two secondary bedrooms at the front of the home share a full hall bath. An optional two-car garage can be built either attached or detached in whichever location best suits your property. This home is designed with basement, slab, and crawlspace foundation options.

Please note: The photographed home may have been modified to suit homeowner preferences. If you order plans, have a builder or design professional check them against the photographs to confirm construction details.

ALT GARAGE LOCATION
19'-6" X 20'-0"

PATIO

OPTIONAL BASEMENT STAIR LOCATION

PATIO

MSTR BDRM

MSTR BATH — DN — DINING

BATH — CL

CL

HALL

MAIN FLOOR

MSTR BEDRM
13'-0" X 15'-4"

MSTR BATH

UTIL RM

STEPPED CLG DINING
15'-0" X 13'-4"

KIT

DW — S

OPT TWO CAR GARAGE
22'-0" X 20'-0"

D

W

BATH

CL

P REF

UP

WIC

HALL

LIN

BEDRM #2
9'-0" X 11'-0"

BEDRM #3
9'-4" X 10'-0"

CL

TRAY CLG LIVING RM
15'-0" X 15'-4"

CL

PORCH

UP

Modifications Make it Right

Above: Stacked front-facing gables, a low, sheltering roof line, and a recessed covered entry present a traditionally welcoming facade to the street.

Below: Bobby and Wanda Carroll.

Bobby Carroll knew what he wanted from retirement and it wasn't sitting on the porch and watching the world go by. It wasn't even really retirement at all. When he left Chevron Oil after many years, he and his wife, Wanda, moved to Tennessee, where Bobby picked up a hammer and did something that had interested him since childhood: He became a licensed contractor.

After working with a contractor friend for about six month, Bobby set out on his own. He says he built more than 20 houses in the five years he plied his new trade, before eventually deciding to really retire. Along the way, he had picked up the skills he needed to do something else he'd wanted to do for a long time, which was to build himself and his wife their own dream home, on their own perfect lot, back home in Texas. The couple moved back to the Lone Star state, moved into an apartment, and began their search for the perfect lot and the perfect home plan.

They eventually found the perfect lot, which, by "no accident… was just steps away from the first fairway on the nearby golf course," says Bobby, an avid golfer who plays every day. All they needed now was the perfect plan. For that, they turned to a source they knew they could trust, a source with a huge selection of popular plans backed by a team of in-house experts in home design and customer service: The Garlinghouse Company.

When the Carrolls found their plan (number 92649), it was already fairly close to what they wanted. Bobby knew from experience, however, that a modification or two can turn a good stock home plan into the perfect custom home. Such modifications are usually slight, but they serve to customize a home to individual needs. And while Bobby knew that his professional experience would serve him well, he also knew that if he had any questions, he could turn to the Garlinghouse Design Team for help.

The Original Plan — #92649

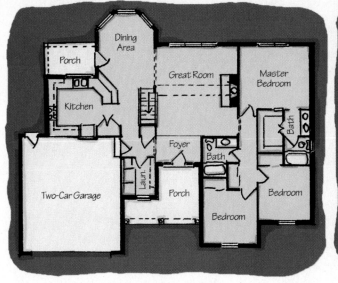

Carroll Residence

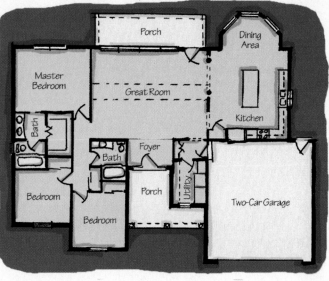

First, Bobby reversed the plan to better fit the lot then he increased the footprint of the house on both ends, "a foot on the left and a foot on the right." That gave him and Wanda a bigger master bedroom and master bath and it freed space elsewhere in the house for a few other changes he had in mind.

At the same time he expanded the house laterally, he also increased the garage by one foot to the left and one foot toward the street. And because he chose the slab foundation over the basement foundation, he could take advantage of the space where the stairway would have been to increase the size of the great-room from 16 feet 6 inches by 17 feet to 24 feet by 17 feet. He also eliminated the fireplace and replaced it with a "big screen high-definition television," the modern equivalent of the fireplace.

By increasing the great-room, he moved the dining bay and the kitchen together into one large space, which eliminated the small porch in the corner between the original L-shape kitchen/dining area. Instead of the small porch, he added a large porch, 7 feet by 22 feet, which runs nearly the full length

Below, Left & Right: Modifications to the great room included extending the length of the room, which allowed the addition of extra windows and a door to access a rear screen porch. A large screen TV took the place of the hearth.

Above and Right: In the modified plan, the dining bay is aligned with the kitchen in one large open space. Eliminating the stairs not only allowed Bobby and Wanda to increase the size of the great room, they were also able to add an arched doorway providing direct access from the great room to the kitchen.

Below Right: A secondary bedroom at the front of the house takes advantage of its location within a front facing gable to incorporate a cathedral ceiling. Volume ceilings like this help make a room appear larger and more spacious.

Below: Increasing the footprint of the house gave Bobby and Wanda a larger master bedroom and master bath.

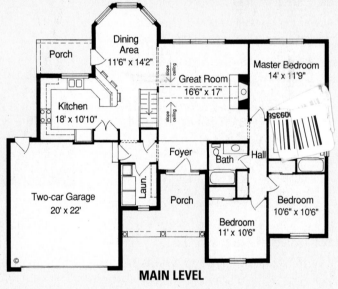

Above & Right: The original plan as available for purchase.

Design 92649

Price Code	B
Total Finished	1,508 sq. ft.
First Finished	1,508 sq. ft.
Basement Unfinished	1,439 sq. ft.
Garage Unfinished	440 sq. ft.
Dimensions	60'x47'
Foundation	Basement
Bedrooms	3
Full Baths	2

Please note: The photographed home was modified to suit homeowner preferences. If you order plans, you may wish to have a builder or design professional check them against the photographs to confirm construction details.

Porch

Dining Area
11'6" x 14'2"

Great Room
16'6" x 17'

Master Bedroom
14' x 11'9"

Kitchen
18' x 10'10"

Foyer

Bath

Hall

Two-car Garage
20' x 22'

Laun.

Porch

Bedroom
10'6" x 10'6"

Bedroom
11' x 10'6"

MAIN LEVEL

of the great-room out back. They also took out a foot of the front porch and gave that over to the laundry room.

Smaller changes inside included the creation of arched openings between the main spaces, which Bobby personally built. "I knew what I wanted and I wanted to make sure I got just that," he said. And increasing the size of the garage gave the couple a 12 foot by 22 foot bonus area above the garage, giving them 264 square feet of storage space, which is accessed by a "big, heavy-duty, pull-down staircase."

Today Bobby and Wanda Carroll couldn't be happier with their new home and the decisions they made in customizing it. Both will testify that a few careful modifications can turn the almost perfect plan into the ideal custom home.

As a builder and homeowner, Bobby does advise caution when choosing a contractor, a profession that doesn't require a license in some states. That's not to say you shouldn't use an unlicensed professional, it just means that you should be extra careful in your

search by checking references and seeing examples of recent work.

It's also very important that you find a company you can trust to help you decide on modifications, a company with people like the design team at Garlinghouse.

So if you think building your dream home is nothing but a pipe dream, look at Bobby and Wanda Carroll and think again. At Garlinghouse, we are here to help you build that dream, and we've been doing it for people like the Carrolls—and you—since 1907.

Quick and Easy Customizing
Make Changes to Your Home Plan in 4 Easy Steps

Here's an affordable and efficient way to make custom changes to your home plan.

1 Select the house plan that most closely meets your needs. Purchase of a reproducible master (vellum) is necessary to make changes to a plan.

2 Call 800-235-5700 to place your order. Tell the sales representative you're interested in customizing a plan. A $50 refundable consultation fee will be charged. Then you'll need to complete a customization checklist indicating all the changes you wish to make to your plan, attaching sketches if necessary. If you proceed with the custom changes, the $50 will be credited to the total amount charged.

3 Fax the completed customization checklist to our design consultant at 1-866-477-5173 or e-mail blarochelle@drummonddesigns.com. Within 24 to 48* business hours you will be provided with a written cost estimate to modify your plan. Our design consultant will contact you by phone if you wish to discuss any of your changes in greater detail.

4 Once you approve the estimate, a 75% retainer fee is collected and customization work gets underway. Preliminary drawings can usually be completed within 5 to10* business days. Following approval of these preliminary drawings, your design changes are completed within 5 to 10* business days. Your remaining 25% balance due is collected prior to shipment of your completed drawings. You will be shipped five sets of revised blueprints, or a reproducible master.

*Terms are subject to change without notice.

BEFORE

AFTER

Sample Modification Pricing Guide

CATEGORIES	AVERAGE COST
Adding or removing living space (square footage)	Quote required
Adding or removing a garage	$400—$680
Garage: Front entry to side load or vice versa	Starting at $300
Adding a screened porch	$280—$600
Adding a bonus room in the attic	$450—$780
Changing full basement to crawlspace or vice versa	Starting at $220
Changing full basement to slab or vice versa	Starting at $260
Changing exterior building material	Starting at $200
Changing roof lines	$360—$630
Adjusting ceiling height	$280—$500
Adding, moving, or removing an exterior opening	$55 per opening
Adding or removing a fireplace	$90—$200
Modifying a non-bearing wall or room	$55 per room
Changing exterior walls from 2"x4" to 2"x6"	Starting at $200
Redesigning a bathroom or a kitchen	$120—$280
Reverse plan right reading	Quote required
Adapting plans for local building code requirements	Quote required
Engineering stamping only	Quote required
Any other engineering services	Quote required
Adjust plan for handicapped accessibility	Quote required
Interactive Illustrations (choices of exterior materials)	Quote required
Metric conversion of home plan	$400

Note: Prices are subject to change according to plan size and style. Please remember that figures shown are average costs. Your quote may be higher or lower depending upon your specific requirements.

Design 65162

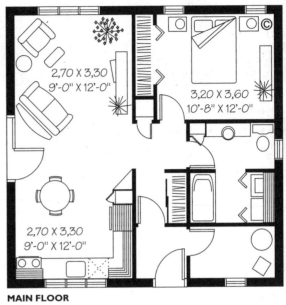

Units	Single
Price Code	A
Total Finished	784 sq. ft.
Main Finished	784 sq. ft.
Dimensions	28'x28'
Foundation	Slab
Bedrooms	1
Full Baths	1
Main Ceiling	8'
Max Ridge Height	18'
Roof Framing	Truss

2,70 X 3,30
9'-0" X 12'-0"

3,20 X 3,60
10'-8" X 12'-0"

2,70 X 3,30
9'-0" X 12'-0"

MAIN FLOOR

Design 99799

Units	Duplex
Price Code	G
Total Finished	828 sq. ft. (per unit)
Main Finished	828 sq. ft. (per unit)
Dimensions	56'x48'
Foundation	Crawlspace
Bedrooms	4
Full Baths	2
Max Ridge Height	15'
Roof Framing	Stick/Truss
Exterior Walls	2x6

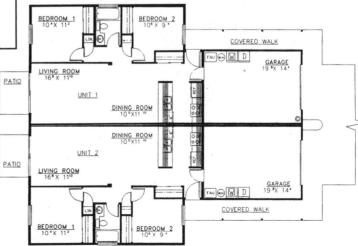

BEDROOM 1
10'4" X 11'2"

BEDROOM 2
10'6" X 9'4"

COVERED WALK

LIVING ROOM
16'8" X 11'10"

GARAGE
19'8" X 14'4"

PATIO

UNIT 1

DINING ROOM
10'6" X 11'10"

DINING ROOM
10'6" X 11'10"

PATIO

UNIT 2

LIVING ROOM
16'8" X 11'10"

GARAGE
19'8" X 14'4"

BEDROOM 1
10'4" X 11'2"

BEDROOM 2
10'6" X 9'4"

COVERED WALK

MAIN FLOOR

Units	Single
Price Code	A
Total Finished	832 sq. ft.
Main Finished	832 sq. ft.
Dimensions	26'x32'
Foundation	Basement
Bedrooms	2
Full Baths	1
Exterior Walls	2x4

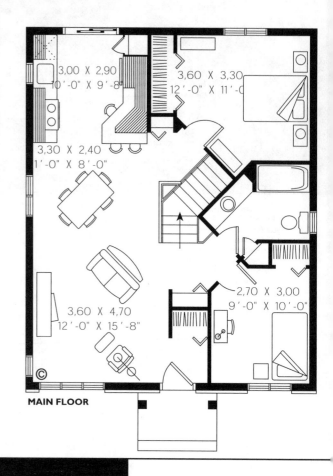

3,00 X 2,90
10'-0" X 9'-8"

3,60 X 3,30
12'-0" X 11'-0"

3,30 X 2,40
11'-0" X 8'-0"

3,60 X 4,70
12'-0" X 15'-8"

2,70 X 3,00
9'-0" X 10'-0"

MAIN FLOOR

Units	Single
Price Code	A
Total Finished	840 sq. ft.
Main Finished	840 sq. ft.
Porch Unfinished	466 sq. ft.
Dimensions	33'x31'
Foundation	Basement
Bedrooms	1
Full Baths	1
Main Ceiling	8'
Max Ridge Height	22'11"
Roof Framing	Truss
Exterior Walls	2x6

4,80 X 4,80
16'-0" X 16'-0"

4,40 X 3,30
14'-8" X 11'-0"

2,70 X 3,90
9'-0" X 13'-0"

2,40 X 3,90
8'-0" X 13'-0"

3,60 X 3,50
12'-0" X 11'-8"

MAIN FLOOR

---

34 To order blueprints, call **800-235-5700** or visit us on the web, **familyhomeplans.com**

Design 65045

Units	Single
Price Code	A
Total Finished	860 sq. ft.
Main Finished	860 sq. ft.
Dimensions	30'x30'
Foundation	Basement
Bedrooms	2
Full Baths	1
Roof Framing	Stick

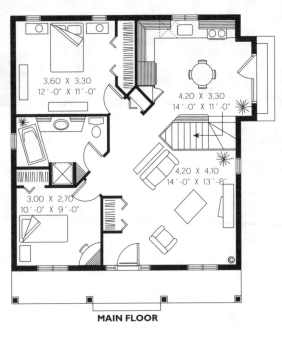

MAIN FLOOR

Design 90934

Units	Single
Price Code	A
Total Finished	884 sq. ft.
Main Finished	884 sq. ft.
Deck Finished	170 sq. ft.
Dimensions	34'x31'
Foundation	Crawlspace
Bedrooms	2
Full Baths	1
Main Ceiling	8'
Max Ridge Height	15'6"
Roof Framing	Truss
Exterior Walls	2x6

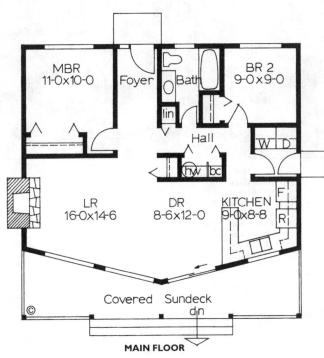

MAIN FLOOR

Design 65366

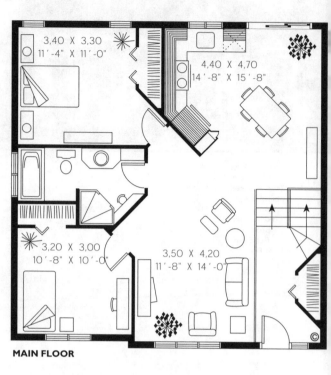

Units	Single
Price Code	A
Total Finished	923 sq. ft.
Main Finished	923 sq. ft.
Basement Unfinished	923 sq. ft.
Dimensions	30'x31'
Foundation	Basement
Bedrooms	2
Full Baths	I
Main Ceiling	8'
Max Ridge Height	22'1"

3,40 X 3,30
11'-4" X 11'-0"

4,40 X 4,70
14'-8" X 15'-8"

3,20 X 3,00
10'-8" X 10'-0"

3,50 X 4,20
11'-8" X 14'-0"

MAIN FLOOR

Design 65387

Units	Single
Price Code	A
Total Finished	948 sq. ft.
Main Finished	948 sq. ft.
Dimensions	30'x34'
Foundation	Basement
Bedrooms	2
Full Baths	I
Roof Framing	Stick

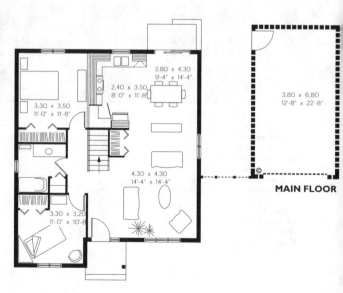

3,30 x 3,50
11'-0" x 11'-8"

2,40 x 3,50
8'-0" x 11'-8

2,80 x 4,30
9'-4" x 14'-4"

3,80 x 6,80
12'-8" x 22'-8"

4,30 x 4,30
14'-4" x 14'-4"

3,30 x 3,20
11'-0" x 10'-8

MAIN FLOOR

Design 65005

Units	Single
Price Code	A
Total Finished	972 sq. ft.
Main Finished	972 sq. ft.
Basement Unfinished	972 sq. ft.
Dimensions	30'x35'
Foundation	Basement
Bedrooms	2
Full Baths	1
Main Ceiling	8'2"
Max Ridge Height	17'6"
Exterior Walls	2x6

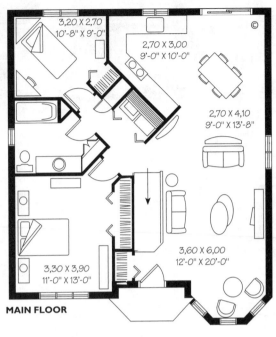

3,20 X 2,70
10'-8" X 9'-0"

2,70 X 3,00
9'-0" X 10'-0"

2,70 X 4,10
9'-0" X 13'-8"

3,30 X 3,90
11'-0" X 13'-0"

3,60 X 6,00
12'-0" X 20'-0"

MAIN FLOOR

Design 91147

Units	Single
Price Code	A
Total Finished	975 sq. ft.
Main Finished	975 sq. ft.
Dimensions	39'4"x31'2"
Foundation	Slab
Bedrooms	3
Full Baths	2

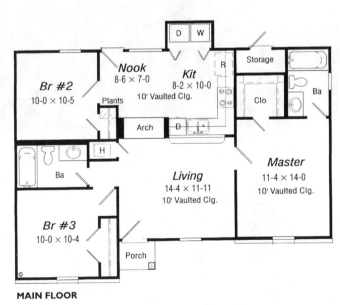

D W

Nook
8-6 × 7-0

Kit
8-2 × 10-0
10' Vaulted Clg.

R

Storage

Ba

Clo

Br #2
10-0 × 10-5

Plants

Arch

D

H

Ba

Master
11-4 × 14-0
10' Vaulted Clg.

Living
14-4 × 11-11
10' Vaulted Clg.

Br #3
10-0 × 10-4

Porch

MAIN FLOOR

Design 65643

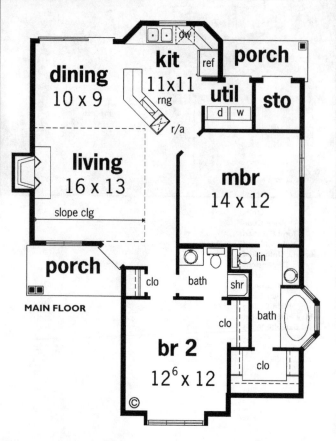

MAIN FLOOR

dining 10 x 9

kit 11x11 rng

porch

ref

util

sto

living 16 x 13

slope clg

mbr 14 x 12

porch

clo

bath

shr

lin

bath

clo

clo

br 2 12⁶ x 12

Units	Single
Price Code	A
Total Finished	984 sq. ft.
Main Finished	984 sq. ft.
Dimensions	33'9"×43'
Foundation	Crawlspace
	Slab
Bedrooms	2
Full Baths	1
3/4 Baths	1
Max Ridge Height	26'
Exterior Walls	2x6

Design 65260

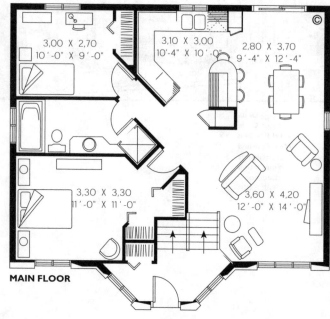

MAIN FLOOR

3,00 X 2,70 10'-0" X 9'-0"

3,10 X 3,00 10'-4" X 10'-0"

2,80 X 3,70 9'-4" X 12'-4"

3,30 X 3,30 11'-0" X 11'-0"

3,60 X 4,20 12'-0" X 14'-0"

Units	Single
Price Code	A
Total Finished	996 sq. ft.
Main Finished	996 sq. ft.
Dimensions	34'x32'4"
Foundation	Basement
Bedrooms	2
Full Baths	1
Exterior Walls	2x4

Design 65642

Units	Single
Price Code	A
Total Finished	998 sq. ft.
Main Finished	998 sq. ft.
Dimensions	48'x29'
Foundation	Crawlspace
	Slab
Bedrooms	3
Full Baths	I
Main Ceiling	8'
Max Ridge Height	26'
Roof Framing	Stick
Exterior Walls	2x4

patio

shvs clo

mbr 12 x 12

bath

lin

kit

ref

rng

clo

bar

dining 12 x 10

W.H.

wash

sto 12 x 7

divider

carport 20 x 12

HEAT & A/C

clo

br 2 13 x 10

clo

br 3 11 x 10

clo

living 15 x 13

MAIN FLOOR

Visit us at www.merillat.com

Merillat®

Design 98469

Units	Single
Price Code	A
Total Finished	1,042 sq. ft.
Main Finished	1,042 sq. ft.
Basement Unfinished	1,042 sq. ft.
Garage Unfinished	400 sq. ft.
Dimensions	60'x30'
Foundation	Basement Crawlspace
Bedrooms	3
Full Baths	2
Main Ceiling	9'
Max Ridge Height	22'
Roof Framing	Stick
Exterior Walls	2x4

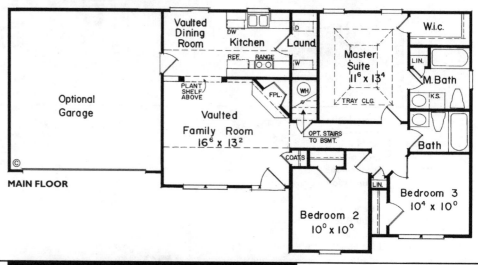

MAIN FLOOR

Optional Garage

Vaulted Dining Room

Kitchen

Laund.

W.i.c.

Master Suite 11⁶ x 13⁴

M. Bath

Vaulted Family Room 16⁶ x 13²

PLANT SHELF ABOVE

OPT. STAIRS TO BSMT.

TRAY CLG.

Bath

COATS

Bedroom 2 10⁰ x 10⁰

Bedroom 3 10⁴ x 10⁰

Design 65036

Units	Single
Price Code	A
Total Finished	1,052 sq. ft.
Main Finished	1,052 sq. ft.
Basement Unfinished	1,052 sq. ft.
Dimensions	32'8"x36'
Foundation	Basement
Bedrooms	2
Full Baths	1
Main Ceiling	8'
Max Ridge Height	17'6"
Roof Framing	Truss
Exterior Walls	2x6

3,30 X 2,40
11'-0" X 8'-0"

3,30 X 3,00
11'-0" X 10'-0"

3,90 X 3,60
13'-0" X 12'-0"

4,00 X 3,30
13'-4" X 11'-0"

MAIN FLOOR

Design 98413

FILES AVAILABLE
CAD For more information call
800-235-5700

Units	Single
Price Code	A
Total Finished	1,070 sq. ft.
Main Finished	1,070 sq. ft.
Basement Unfinished	1,090 sq. ft.
Garage Unfinished	400 sq. ft.
Dimensions	48'x36'
Foundation	Basement
	Crawlspace
	Slab
Bedrooms	3
Full Baths	2
Main Ceiling	9'
Max Ridge Height	22'
Roof Framing	Stick
Exterior Walls	2x4

MAIN FLOOR

Design 65149

Units	Single
Price Code	A
Total Finished	1,079 sq. ft.
Main Finished	1,079 sq. ft.
Dimensions	34'x34'
Foundation	Basement
Bedrooms	2
Full Baths	1
Max Ridge Height	22'6"
Roof Framing	Truss
Exterior Walls	2x6

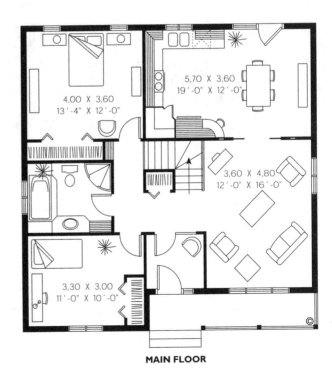

MAIN FLOOR

Design 92704

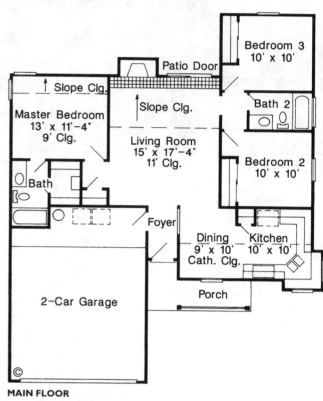

Units	Single
Price Code	A
Total Finished	1,078 sq. ft.
Main Finished	1,078 sq. ft.
Garage Unfinished	431 sq. ft.
Dimensions	41'8"x50'
Foundation	Slab
Bedrooms	3
Full Baths	2
Max Ridge Height	17'
Roof Framing	Stick
Exterior Walls	2x4

Bedroom 3 10' x 10'

Patio Door

↑ Slope Clg.

Master Bedroom 13' x 11'-4" 9' Clg.

↑ Slope Clg.

Bath 2

Living Room 15' x 17'-4" 11' Clg.

Bath

Bedroom 2 10' x 10'

Foyer

Dining 9' x 10' Cath. Clg.

Kitchen 10' x 10'

2-Car Garage

Porch

MAIN FLOOR

Design 65640

Units	Single
Price Code	A
Total Finished	1,088 sq. ft.
Main Finished	1,088 sq. ft.
Bonus Unfinished	580 sq. ft.
Dimensions	34'x44'
Foundation	Crawlspace
	Slab
Bedrooms	2
Full Baths	1
Main Ceiling	8'
Second Ceiling	8'
Max Ridge Height	30'
Roof Framing	Stick
Exterior Walls	2x6

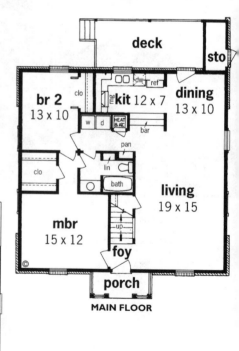

deck

sto

br 2 13 x 10

kit 12 x 7

dining 13 x 10

bar

pan

living 19 x 15

mbr 15 x 12

up

foy

porch

MAIN FLOOR

slope

SKY LITE

open to kitchen below

attic

bath

br 3 16 x 12

hall

br 4 16 x 12

clo

DOWN

clo

attic

attic

BONUS

To order blueprints, call **800-235-5700** or visit us on the web, **familyhomeplans.com**

Design 65383

Units	Single
Price Code	A
Total Finished	1,092 sq. ft.
Main Finished	1,092 sq. ft.
Dimensions	42'x26'
Foundation	Basement
Bedrooms	3
Full Baths	1

MAIN FLOOR

Design 24723

Units	Single
Price Code	A
Total Finished	1,112 sq. ft.
Main Finished	1,112 sq. ft.
Garage Unfinished	563 sq. ft.
Dimensions	64'x33'
Foundation	Crawlspace
	Slab
Bedrooms	3
Full Baths	2
Main Ceiling	8'-9'
Max Ridge Height	21'6"
Roof Framing	Stick
Exterior Walls	2x4

MAIN FLOOR

Design 65043

Hot New Design

Units	Single
Price Code	A
Total Finished	1,142 sq. ft.
Main Finished	1,142 sq. ft.
Dimensions	38'x34'
Foundation	Basement
Bedrooms	2
Full Baths	1

4,20 X 3,30
14'-0" X 11'-0"

3,60 X 3,30
12'-0" X 11'-0"

3,30 X 3,30
11'-0" X 11'-0"

4,20 X 6,30
14'-0" X 21'-0"

MAIN FLOOR

Design 65376

Units	Single
Price Code	A
Total Finished	1,142 sq. ft.
Main Finished	1,142 sq. ft.
Garage Unfinished	400 sq. ft.
Dimensions	46'x38'
Foundation	Basement
Bedrooms	2
Full Baths	1

3,70 X 3,00
12'-0" X 10'-0"

4,20 X 3,40
14'-0" X 11'-4"

4,20 X 3,30
14'-0" X 11'-0"

3,00 X 3,30
10'-0" X 11'-0"

3,60 X 4,50
12'-0" X 15'-0"

4,50 X 7,40
15'-0" X 24'-8"

MAIN FLOOR

Design 68093

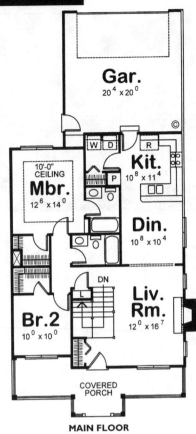

MAIN FLOOR

Units	Single
Price Code	A
Total Finished	1,142 sq. ft.
Main Finished	1,142 sq. ft.
Garage Unfinished	435 sq. ft.
Dimensions	30'4"x64'8"
Foundation	Basement
Bedrooms	2
Full Baths	2
Main Ceiling	9'
Max Ridge Height	20'3"
Roof Framing	Stick
Exterior Walls	2x4

* Alternate foundation options available at an additional charge.
Please call 1-800-235-5700 for more information.

Design 60112

Units	Single
Price Code	A
Total Finished	1,149 sq. ft.
Main Finished	1,149 sq. ft.
Basement Unfinished	1,166 sq. ft.
Garage Unfinished	422 sq. ft.
Dimensions	47'6"x42'4"
Foundation	Basement
Bedrooms	3
Full Baths	2
Main Ceiling	9'
Max Ridge Height	21'10"
Roof Framing	Stick
Exterior Walls	2x4

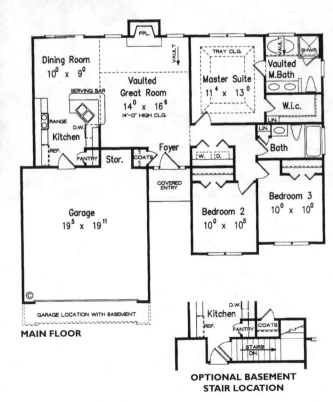

MAIN FLOOR

OPTIONAL BASEMENT STAIR LOCATION

Design 93006

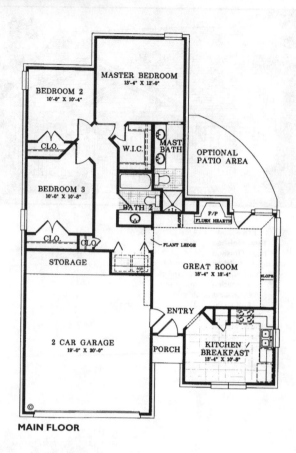

Units	Single
Price Code	A
Total Finished	1,163 sq. ft.
Main Finished	1,163 sq. ft.
Garage Unfinished	449 sq. ft.
Porch Unfinished	19 sq. ft.
Dimensions	39'2"x55'10"
Foundation	Slab
Bedrooms	3
Full Baths	1
3/4 Baths	1
Max Ridge Height	19'
Roof Framing	Stick
Exterior Walls	2x4

MAIN FLOOR

MASTER BEDROOM 15'-4" X 12'-0"
BEDROOM 2 10'-0" X 10'-4"
CLO.
W.I.C.
MAST BATH
OPTIONAL PATIO AREA
BEDROOM 3 10'-0" X 10'-8"
BATH 2
F/P FLUSH HEARTH
CLO.
CLO.
PLANT LEDGE
STORAGE
GREAT ROOM 15'-4" X 13'-4"
ENTRY
2 CAR GARAGE 19'-0" X 20'-0"
PORCH
KITCHEN / BREAKFAST 13'-4" X 10'-8"

Design 97296

Units	Single
Price Code	A
Total Finished	1,166 sq. ft.
Main Finished	1,166 sq. ft.
Basement Unfinished	1,166 sq. ft.
Dimensions	43'4"x34'
Foundation	Basement
Bedrooms	3
Full Baths	2
Max Ridge Height	22'3"
Roof Framing	Stick
Exterior Walls	2x4

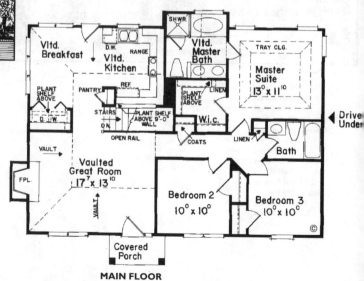

Vltd. Breakfast
D.W. RANGE
Vltd. Master Bath
SHWR.
TRAY CLG.
Master Suite 13° x 11¹⁰
Vltd. Kitchen
PLANT SHELF ABOVE
PANTRY
REF.
PLANT SHELF ABOVE
LINEN
Drive Under
STAIRS
PLANT SHELF ABOVE 9'-0" WALL
W.I.C.
LINEN
VAULT
DN
OPEN RAIL
COATS
Bath
Vaulted Great Room 17⁷ x 13¹⁰
FPL.
VAULT
Bedroom 2 10° x 10°
Bedroom 3 10° x 10°
Covered Porch

MAIN FLOOR

Design 98497

Units	Single
Price Code	A
Total Finished	1,169 sq. ft.
Main Finished	1,169 sq. ft.
Basement Unfinished	1,194 sq. ft.
Garage Unfinished	400 sq. ft.
Dimensions	40'x49'6"
Foundation	Basement
	Crawlspace
	Slab
Bedrooms	3
Full Baths	2
Main Ceiling	9'
Max Ridge Height	21'
Roof Framing	Stick
Exterior Walls	2x4

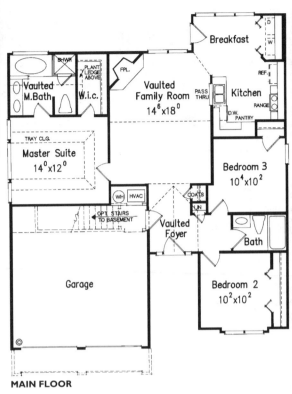

MAIN FLOOR

Design 97338

Units	Single
Price Code	A
Total Finished	1,186 sq. ft.
Main Finished	1,186 sq. ft.
Basement Unfinished	1,186 sq. ft.
Garage Unfinished	419 sq. ft.
Dimensions	66'4"x32'
Foundation	Basement
Bedrooms	3
Full Baths	1
Main Ceiling	9'
Max Ridge Height	20'8"
Roof Framing	Truss
Exterior Walls	2x6

MAIN FLOOR

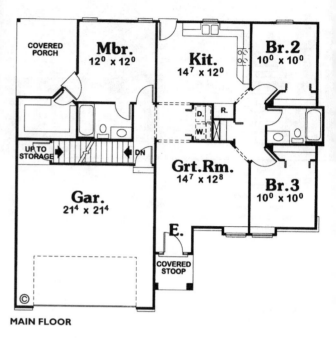

MAIN FLOOR

Units	Single
Price Code	A
Total Finished	1,191 sq. ft.
Main Finished	1,191 sq. ft.
Garage Unfinished	492 sq. ft.
Deck Unfinished	321 sq. ft.
Dimensions	48'4"x43'8"
Foundation	Basement
Bedrooms	3
Full Baths	2
Main Ceiling	9'
Max Ridge Height	23'3"
Roof Framing	Stick
Exterior Walls	2x4

* Alternate foundation options available at an additional charge.
Please call 1-800-235-5700 for more information.

MAIN FLOOR

Units	Single
Price Code	A
Total Finished	1,199 sq. ft.
Main Finished	1,199 sq. ft.
Garage Unfinished	484 sq. ft.
Porch Unfinished	34 sq. ft.
Dimensions	44'2"x42'6¾"
Foundation	Slab
Bedrooms	3
Full Baths	2
Main Ceiling	8'
Vaulted Ceiling	11'
Max Ridge Height	18'
Roof Framing	Stick
Exterior Walls	2x4

Design 97341

Units	Single
Price Code	A
Total Finished	1,206 sq. ft.
Main Finished	1,206 sq. ft.
Basement Unfinished	1,206 sq. ft.
Garage Unfinished	455 sq. ft.
Dimensions	56'4"x40'
Foundation	Basement
Bedrooms	3
Full Baths	1
Main Ceiling	9'
Max Ridge Height	21'4"
Roof Framing	Truss
Exterior Walls	2x4

MAIN FLOOR

Design 65084

Units	Single
Price Code	A
Total Finished	1,208 sq. ft.
Main Finished	1,208 sq. ft.
Garage Unfinished	278 sq. ft.
Dimensions	41'x45'
Foundation	Basement
Bedrooms	1
Full Baths	1
Main Ceiling	8'
Max Ridge Height	27'10"
Roof Framing	Truss
Exterior Walls	2x6

OPTIONAL
SECOND
BEDROOM

MAIN FLOOR

To order blueprints, call **800-235-5700** or visit us on the web, **familyhomeplans.com**   49

Design 98925

Units	Single
Price Code	A
Total Finished	1,208 sq. ft.
Main Finished	1,208 sq. ft.
Basement Unfinished	760 sq. ft.
Garage Unfinished	448 sq. ft.
Deck Unfinished	100 sq. ft.
Porch Unfinished	40 sq. ft.
Dimensions	50'4"x29'
Foundation	Basement
Bedrooms	3
Full Baths	2
Max Ridge Height	25'
Roof Framing	Truss
Exterior Walls	2x4

Sundeck 10-0 x 10-0

M.Bath

Bedroom 2

OPT. PLANT SHELF OPEN TO BDRM

Bath 2

W. D.

Kitchen 8-0 x 10-0

Dining 10-4 x 10-0

Ref.

Master Bedroom 11-6 x 14-6

Cts.

Down

Family Room 18-4 x 13-0

Entry

Bedroom 3 11-0 x 10-0

MAIN FLOOR

Design 97836

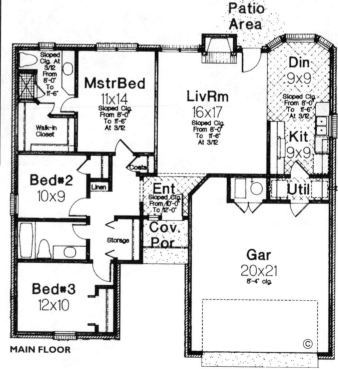

Units	Single
Price Code	A
Total Finished	1,225 sq. ft.
Main Finished	1,225 sq. ft.
Garage Unfinished	415 sq. ft.
Porch Unfinished	100 sq. ft.
Dimensions	45'x42'
Foundation	Slab
Bedrooms	3
Full Baths	1
3/4 Baths	1
Main Ceiling	8'
Max Ridge Height	17'
Roof Framing	Stick
Exterior Walls	2x4

Patio Area

Sloped Clg. At 3/12 From 8'-0 To 11'-6

MstrBed 11x14 Sloped Clg. From 8'-0 To 11'-6 At 3/12

Walk-In Closet

LivRm 16x17 Sloped Clg. From 8'-0 To 11'-6 At 3/12

Din 9x9 Sloped Clg. From 8'-0 To 11'-6 At 3/12

Kit 9x9

Bed#2 10x9

Linen

Coats

Ent Sloped Clg. From 10'-0 To 12'-0

Util

Storage

Cov. Por.

Gar 20x21 8'-4" clg.

Bed#3 12x10

MAIN FLOOR

Design 97339

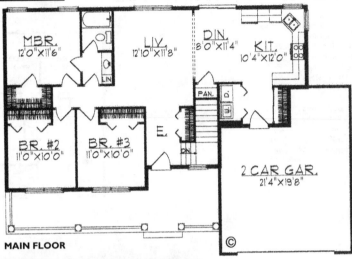

Units	Single
Price Code	A
Total Finished	1,233 sq. ft.
Main Finished	1,233 sq. ft.
Basement Unfinished	1,233 sq. ft.
Garage Unfinished	419 sq. ft.
Dimensions	57'x39'
Foundation	Basement
Bedrooms	3
Full Baths	1
Main Ceiling	9'
Max Ridge Height	23'1"
Roof Framing	Truss
Exterior Walls	2x6

MAIN FLOOR

Design 99428

Units	Duplex
Price Code	G
Total Finished	1,212 sq. ft. (unit A)
Total Finished	1,233 sq. ft. (unit B)
Main Finished	1,212 sq. ft. (unit A)
Main Finished	1,233 sq. ft. (unit B)
Basement Unfinished	1,212 sq. ft. (unit A)
Basement Unfinished	1,233 sq. ft. (unit B)
Garage Unfinished	448 sq. ft. (per unit)
Dimensions	80'x47'8"
Foundation	Basement
Bedrooms	2 (per unit)
Full Baths	1 (per unit)
3/4 Baths	1 (per unit)
Max Ridge Height	19'
Roof Framing	Stick
Exterior Walls	2x4

* Alternate foundation options available at an additional charge.
Please call 1-800-235-5700 for more information.

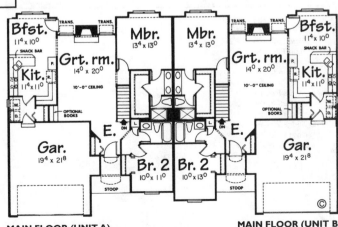

MAIN FLOOR (UNIT A)   **MAIN FLOOR (UNIT B)**

To order blueprints, call **800-235-5700** or visit us on the web, **family**homeplans.com   **51**

Design 90682

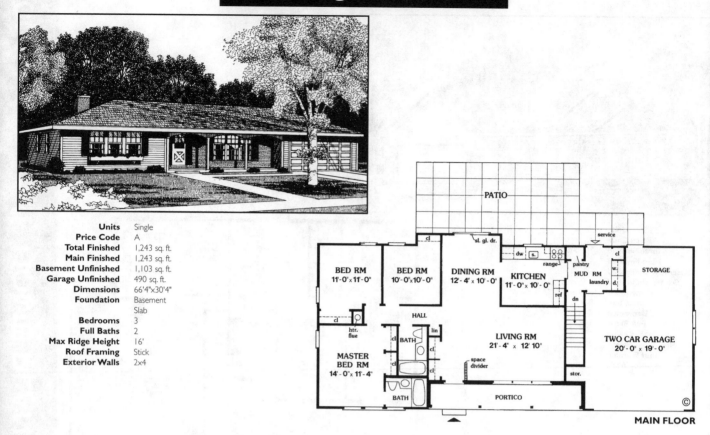

Units	Single
Price Code	A
Total Finished	1,243 sq. ft.
Main Finished	1,243 sq. ft.
Basement Unfinished	1,103 sq. ft.
Garage Unfinished	490 sq. ft.
Dimensions	66'4"x30'4"
Foundation	Basement
	Slab
Bedrooms	3
Full Baths	2
Max Ridge Height	16'
Roof Framing	Stick
Exterior Walls	2x4

PATIO

BED RM 11'-0" x 11'-0"

BED RM 10'-0"x10'-0"

DINING RM 12'-4" x 10'-0"

KITCHEN 11'-0" x 10'-0"

sl. gl. dr.

dw   s.

range

pantry

ref

MUD RM laundry

service

cl

w.

d.

STORAGE

HALL

lin

cl

cl

BATH

cl

LIVING RM 21'-4" x 12'10"

dn

TWO CAR GARAGE 20'-0" x 19'-0"

MASTER BED RM 14'-0" x 11'-4"

cl

space divider

stor.

BATH

PORTICO

htr. flue

MAIN FLOOR

Design 65638

Units	Single
Price Code	A
Total Finished	1,244 sq. ft.
Main Finished	1,244 sq. ft.
Dimensions	44'x62'
Foundation	Crawlspace
	Slab
Bedrooms	3
Full Baths	2
Main Ceiling	8'
Max Ridge Height	26'
Roof Framing	Stick
Exterior Walls	2x6

sto 11 x 6

sto 11 x 6

carport 22 x 22

dining 10 x 9

kit 9x9

p ref

rng

dw

lin

bath

bath

lin

shvs clo

mbr 14 x 13

shvs

W/A

shvs

living 19 x 17

wood box

shvs

clo

shvs

clo

clo

br 2 12 x 10

br 3 12 x 10

clo

porch 44 x 6

MAIN FLOOR

Design 96511

Units	Single
Price Code	A
Total Finished	1,247 sq. ft.
Main Finished	1,247 sq. ft.
Garage Unfinished	512 sq. ft.
Dimensions	43'x60'
Foundation	Crawlspace
	Slab
Bedrooms	3
Full Baths	2
Main Ceiling	8'
Max Ridge Height	19'
Roof Framing	Stick
Exterior Walls	2x4

GARAGE 19 × 22

DECK

PORCH

REFG   RNG

KITCHEN 11 × 11

DINING 11 × 11

BATH

MASTER SUITE 12 × 14

FAN

D/W   BAR

WASH   DRY

BATH

CLOSET

LIVING RM 15 × 18

FAN

F/P

LIN

CLOS

BEDRM 11 × 10

A/C

CLOS

BEDRM 11 × 12

CLO

PORCH

MAIN FLOOR

Design 91120

Units	Single
Price Code	A
Total Finished	1,249 sq. ft.
Main Finished	1,249 sq. ft.
Porch Unfinished	23 sq. ft.
Dimensions	29'x54'10"
Foundation	Slab
Bedrooms	2
Full Baths	2
Max Ridge Height	19'3"
Roof Framing	Truss
Exterior Walls	2x4

Storage

W   D

R

D

Closet

Pantry

Kit 14-0 × 11-0

Mbr 13-2 × 16-2

L

F

Bath

Din 10-4 × 11-0
11-0 Vault

Liv 15-0 × 17-6
11-0 Vault

Entry

Clo   Bath

Porch

Br #2 10-0 × 13-4

MAIN FLOOR

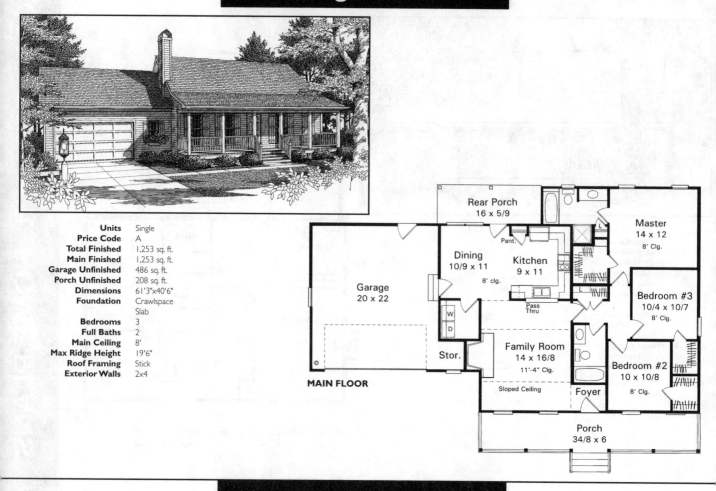

Units	Single
Price Code	A
Total Finished	1,253 sq. ft.
Main Finished	1,253 sq. ft.
Garage Unfinished	486 sq. ft.
Porch Unfinished	208 sq. ft.
Dimensions	61'3"x40'6"
Foundation	Crawlspace
	Slab
Bedrooms	3
Full Baths	2
Main Ceiling	8'
Max Ridge Height	19'6"
Roof Framing	Stick
Exterior Walls	2x4

MAIN FLOOR

- Rear Porch 16 x 5/9
- Master 14 x 12, 8' Clg.
- Dining 10/9 x 11
- Kitchen 9 x 11, 8' clg.
- Garage 20 x 22
- Bedroom #3 10/4 x 10/7, 8' Clg.
- Pant.
- Pass Thru
- W D
- Stor.
- Family Room 14 x 16/8, 11'-4" Clg.
- Bedroom #2 10 x 10/8, 8' Clg.
- Sloped Ceiling
- Foyer
- Porch 34/8 x 6

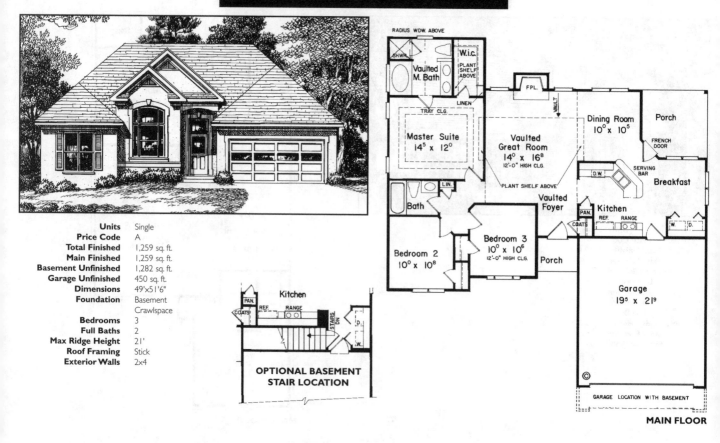

Units	Single
Price Code	A
Total Finished	1,259 sq. ft.
Main Finished	1,259 sq. ft.
Basement Unfinished	1,282 sq. ft.
Garage Unfinished	450 sq. ft.
Dimensions	49'x51'6"
Foundation	Basement
	Crawlspace
Bedrooms	3
Full Baths	2
Max Ridge Height	21'
Roof Framing	Stick
Exterior Walls	2x4

RADIUS WDW. ABOVE

- SHWR
- Vaulted M. Bath
- W.I.C.
- PLANT SHELF ABOVE
- FPL.
- LINEN
- TRAY CLG.
- Dining Room 10' x 10/5
- Porch
- FRENCH DOOR
- Master Suite 14/5 x 12/0
- Vaulted Great Room 14' x 16/8, 12'-0" HIGH CLG.
- SERVING BAR
- D.W.
- Breakfast
- Bath
- LIN.
- PLANT SHELF ABOVE
- Vaulted Foyer
- PAN.
- Kitchen
- REF. RANGE
- W. D.
- COATS
- Bedroom 3 10/0 x 10/6, 12'-0" HIGH CLG.
- Bedroom 2 10/0 x 10/8
- Porch
- Garage 19/5 x 21/9
- Porch

OPTIONAL BASEMENT STAIR LOCATION

- PAN.
- Kitchen
- COATS
- REF. RANGE
- STAIRS DN
- D.
- W.

GARAGE LOCATION WITH BASEMENT

MAIN FLOOR

Design 94927

Units	Single
Price Code	A
Total Finished	1,271 sq. ft.
Main Finished	1,271 sq. ft.
Garage Unfinished	433 sq. ft.
Dimensions	50'x46'
Foundation	Basement
	Slab
Bedrooms	3
Full Baths	1
3/4 Baths	1
Max Ridge Height	16'
Roof Framing	Stick
Exterior Walls	2x4

* Alternate foundation options available at an additional charge.
Please call 1-800-235-5700 for more information.

MAIN FLOOR

Design 97337

Units	Single
Price Code	A
Total Finished	1,274 sq. ft.
Main Finished	1,274 sq. ft.
Basement Unfinished	1,274 sq. ft.
Garage Unfinished	380 sq. ft.
Dimensions	51'x46'
Foundation	Basement
Bedrooms	3
Full Baths	2
Main Ceiling	9'
Second Ceiling	8'
Max Ridge Height	20'2"
Roof Framing	Truss
Exterior Walls	2x6

MAIN FLOOR

Design 97614

Units	Single
Price Code	A
Total Finished	1,287 sq. ft.
Main Finished	1,287 sq. ft.
Bonus Unfinished	312 sq. ft.
Basement Unfinished	1,287 sq. ft.
Garage Unfinished	516 sq. ft.
Dimensions	50'x55'10"
Foundation	Basement
	Crawlspace
Bedrooms	3
Full Baths	2
Max Ridge Height	24'
Roof Framing	Stick
Exterior Walls	2x4

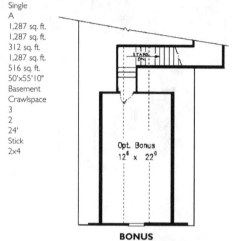

BONUS

MAIN FLOOR

CAD FILES AVAILABLE
For more information call
800-235-5700

Design 97334

Units	Single
Price Code	A
Total Finished	1,295 sq. ft.
Main Finished	1,295 sq. ft.
Basement Unfinished	1,295 sq. ft.
Garage Unfinished	386 sq. ft.
Dimensions	46'x47'4"
Foundation	Basement
Bedrooms	3
Full Baths	1
3/4 Baths	1
Main Ceiling	9'
Max Ridge Height	19'11"
Roof Framing	Truss
Exterior Walls	2x4

MAIN FLOOR

Design 63046

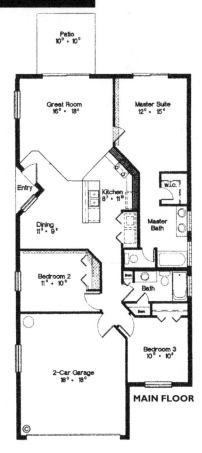

Units	Single
Price Code	A
Total Finished	1,309 sq. ft.
Main Finished	1,309 sq. ft.
Garage Unfinished	383 sq. ft.
Dimensions	30'x60'
Foundation	Slab
Bedrooms	3
Full Baths	2
Main Ceiling	8'
Vaulted Ceiling	11'10"
Max Ridge Height	15'11"
Roof Framing	Truss

MAIN FLOOR

Design 68096

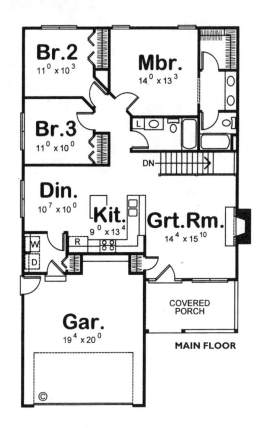

Units	Single
Price Code	A
Total Finished	1,311 sq. ft.
Main Finished	1,311 sq. ft.
Garage Unfinished	439 sq. ft.
Deck Unfinished	112 sq. ft.
Dimensions	34'8"x58'4"
Foundation	Crawlspace
	Slab
Bedrooms	3
Full Baths	2
Main Ceiling	9'
Max Ridge Height	22'6"
Exterior Walls	2x4

* Alternate foundation options available at an additional charge.
Please call 1-800-235-5700 for more information.

MAIN FLOOR

Design 97731

Units	Single
Price Code	A
Total Finished	1,315 sq. ft.
Main Finished	1,315 sq. ft.
Basement Unfinished	1,315 sq. ft.
Garage Unfinished	488 sq. ft.
Porch Unfinished	75 sq. ft.
Dimensions	50'x54'8"
Foundation	Basement
Bedrooms	3
Full Baths	2
Main Ceiling	8'
Max Ridge Height	18'
Roof Framing	Truss
Exterior Walls	2x4

Deck

Master Bedroom 12'-4" x 13'-0"

Great Room 18'-8" x 17'-4"

Bedroom 11'-4" x 10'-8"

Bath

Dining

Bath

Kitchen 13'-4" x 9'-11"

Foyer

Bedroom 12'-4" x 10'-10"

Laun.

Porch

MAIN FLOOR

Garage 20'-0" x 26'-2"

Design 82044

Units	Single
Price Code	A
Total Finished	1,317 sq. ft.
Main Finished	1,317 sq. ft.
Garage Unfinished	412 sq. ft.
Porch Unfinished	163 sq. ft.
Dimensions	46'x54'10"
Foundation	Basement
	Crawlspace
	Slab
Bedrooms	3
Full Baths	2
Main Ceiling	9'
Roof Framing	Stick
Exterior Walls	2x4

GRILLING PORCH

NOOK 7'-0" X 8'-0"

STORAGE

BED RM. 2 11'-0" X 13'-0"

REF.

GARAGE 17'-8" X 23'-4"

PAN.

KIT. 10'-4" X 14'-8"

BED RM. 3 10'-8" X 11'-6"

DW.

MAIN FLOOR

DINING 10'-0" X 9'-0"

OPT. GAS FIREPLACE

GREAT RM. 14'-0" X 16'-0"

MASTER SUITE 10' BOXED CEILING 13'-0" X 13'-0"

COVERED PORCH 14'-4" X 5'-0"

Design 93453

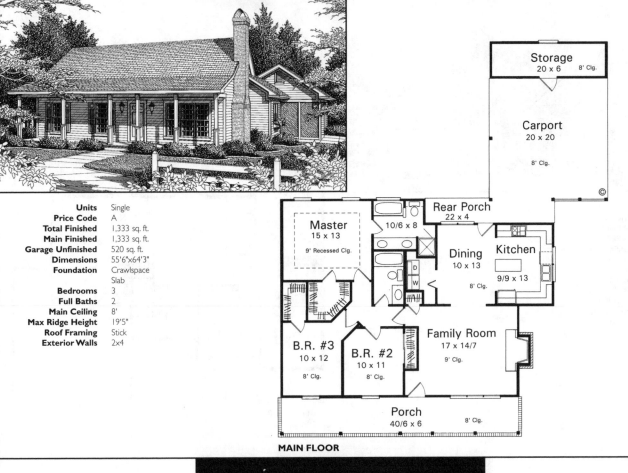

Units	Single
Price Code	A
Total Finished	1,333 sq. ft.
Main Finished	1,333 sq. ft.
Garage Unfinished	520 sq. ft.
Dimensions	55'6"x64'3"
Foundation	Crawlspace
	Slab
Bedrooms	3
Full Baths	2
Main Ceiling	8'
Max Ridge Height	19'5"
Roof Framing	Stick
Exterior Walls	2x4

Storage 20 x 6   8' Clg.

Carport 20 x 20   8' Clg.

Rear Porch 22 x 4

Master 15 x 13   9' Recessed Clg.

10/6 x 8

Dining 10 x 13   8' Clg.

Kitchen 9/9 x 13

Family Room 17 x 14/7   9' Clg.

B.R. #3 10 x 12   8' Clg.

B.R. #2 10 x 11   8' Clg.

Porch 40/6 x 6   8' Clg.

MAIN FLOOR

Design 97332

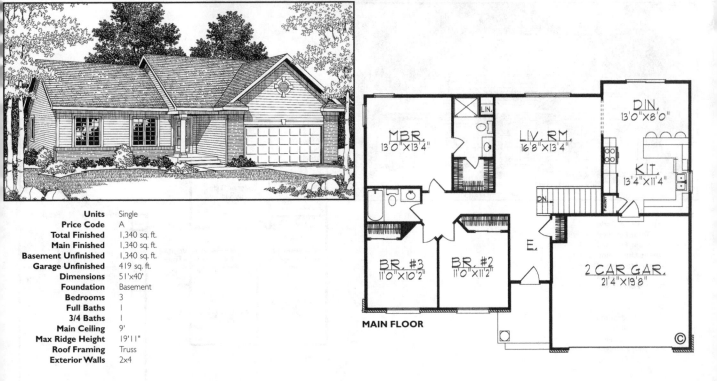

Units	Single
Price Code	A
Total Finished	1,340 sq. ft.
Main Finished	1,340 sq. ft.
Basement Unfinished	1,340 sq. ft.
Garage Unfinished	419 sq. ft.
Dimensions	51'x40'
Foundation	Basement
Bedrooms	3
Full Baths	1
3/4 Baths	1
Main Ceiling	9'
Max Ridge Height	19'11"
Roof Framing	Truss
Exterior Walls	2x4

MBR. 13'0"X13'4"

LIN.

LIV. RM. 16'8"X13'4"

DIN. 13'0"X8'0"

KIT. 13'4"X11'4"

DN.

BR. #3 11'0"X10'2"

BR. #2 11'0"X11'2"

E.

2 CAR GAR. 21'4"X19'8"

MAIN FLOOR

Design 97331

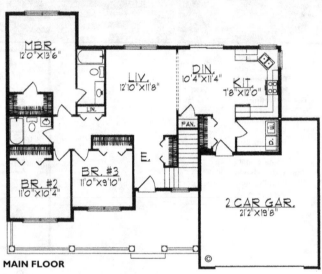

Units	Single
Price Code	A
Total Finished	1,342 sq. ft.
Main Finished	1,342 sq. ft.
Basement Unfinished	1,342 sq. ft.
Garage Unfinished	416 sq. ft.
Dimensions	57'x45'
Foundation	Basement
Bedrooms	3
Full Baths	2
Main Ceiling	9'
Max Ridge Height	23'5"
Roof Framing	Truss
Exterior Walls	2x6

MAIN FLOOR

Design 97202

Units	Single
Price Code	A
Total Finished	1,344 sq. ft.
Main Finished	1,344 sq. ft.
Basement Unfinished	1,363 sq. ft.
Garage Unfinished	409 sq. ft.
Dimensions	48'x44'10"
Foundation	Basement
	Crawlspace
	Slab
Bedrooms	3
Full Baths	2
Main Ceiling	9'
Max Ridge Height	22'6"
Roof Framing	Stick
Exterior Walls	2x4

MAIN FLOOR

Design 98912

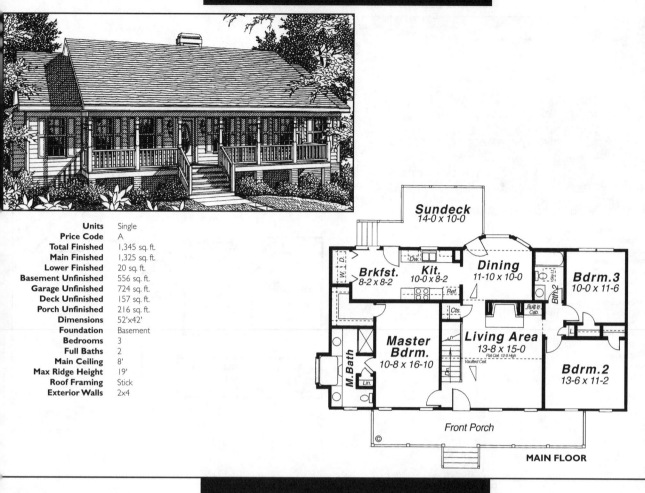

Units	Single
Price Code	A
Total Finished	1,345 sq. ft.
Main Finished	1,325 sq. ft.
Lower Finished	20 sq. ft.
Basement Unfinished	556 sq. ft.
Garage Unfinished	724 sq. ft.
Deck Unfinished	157 sq. ft.
Porch Unfinished	216 sq. ft.
Dimensions	52'x42'
Foundation	Basement
Bedrooms	3
Full Baths	2
Main Ceiling	8'
Max Ridge Height	19'
Roof Framing	Stick
Exterior Walls	2x4

Sundeck 14-0 x 10-0

Brkfst. 8-2 x 8-2

Kit. 10-0 x 8-2

Dining 11-10 x 10-0

Bdrm.3 10-0 x 11-6

Master Bdrm. 10-8 x 16-10

Living Area 13-8 x 15-0
Flat Ceil. 12-9 High
Vaulted Ceil.

Bdrm.2 13-6 x 11-2

M. Bath

Front Porch

MAIN FLOOR

Design 65644

Units	Single
Price Code	A
Total Finished	1,346 sq. ft.
Main Finished	1,346 sq. ft.
Dimensions	54'x44'6"
Foundation	Crawlspace
	Slab
Bedrooms	3
Full Baths	2
Main Ceiling	8'
Max Ridge Height	25'
Roof Framing	Stick
Exterior Walls	2x4

patio

mbr 15 x 13

dress rm

bath

bath

living 17⁶ x 17

dining 12 x 11
floor raised 8"
bar

turned wood post divider

false beams

kit 11⁶ x 11

clo

r/a

post

vault

br 2 12 x 11

br 3 12 x 11

clo

foy

sto 6⁹ x 6⁶

util

porch

ref

garage 21 x 21

MAIN FLOOR

Design 97272

Units	Single
Price Code	A
Total Finished	1,354 sq. ft.
Main Finished	1,354 sq. ft.
Basement Unfinished	1,390 sq. ft.
Garage Unfinished	434 sq. ft.
Dimensions	47'x46'
Foundation	Basement
	Crawlspace
Bedrooms	3
Full Baths	2
Main Ceiling	9'
Max Ridge Height	24'9"
Roof Framing	Stick
Exterior Walls	2x4

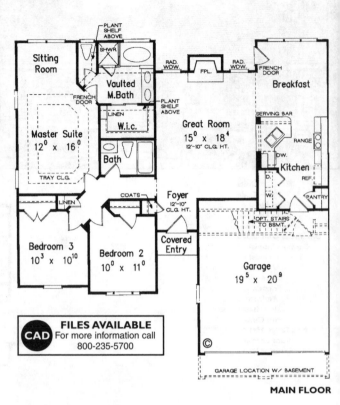

CAD FILES AVAILABLE
For more information call
800-235-5700

MAIN FLOOR

Design 97678

Units	Single
Price Code	A
Total Finished	1,354 sq. ft.
Main Finished	1,354 sq. ft.
Bonus Unfinished	246 sq. ft.
Basement Unfinished	1,354 sq. ft.
Garage Unfinished	450 sq. ft.
Dimensions	51'x48'4"
Foundation	Basement
	Crawlspace
Bedrooms	3
Full Baths	2
Main Ceiling	8'
Second Ceiling	8'
Max Ridge Height	22'
Roof Framing	Stick
Exterior Walls	2x4

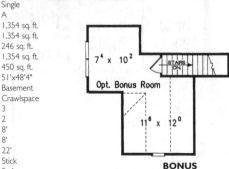

BONUS

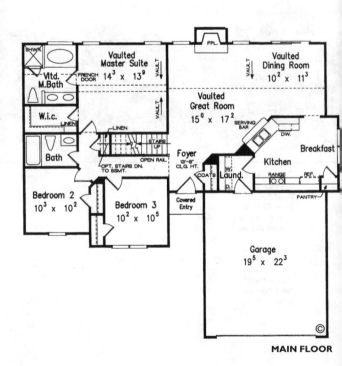

MAIN FLOOR

Design 97336

MAIN FLOOR

Units	Single
Price Code	A
Total Finished	1,356 sq. ft.
Main Finished	1,356 sq. ft.
Basement Unfinished	750 sq. ft.
Garage Unfinished	429 sq. ft.
Dimensions	48'x46'
Foundation	Basement
Bedrooms	2
Full Baths	1
3/4 Baths	1
Main Ceiling	9'
Max Ridge Height	23'2"
Roof Framing	Truss
Exterior Walls	2x6

BASEMENT

Design 94982

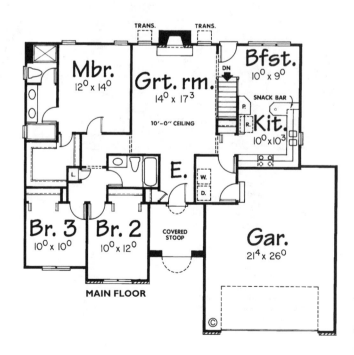

MAIN FLOOR

Units	Single
Price Code	A
Total Finished	1,360 sq. ft.
Main Finished	1,360 sq. ft.
Garage Unfinished	544 sq. ft.
Dimensions	52'x46'
Foundation	Basement
Bedrooms	3
Full Baths	2
Max Ridge Height	18'
Roof Framing	Stick
Exterior Walls	2x4

* Alternate foundation options available at an additional charge.
Please call 1-800-235-5700 for more information.

Design 99639

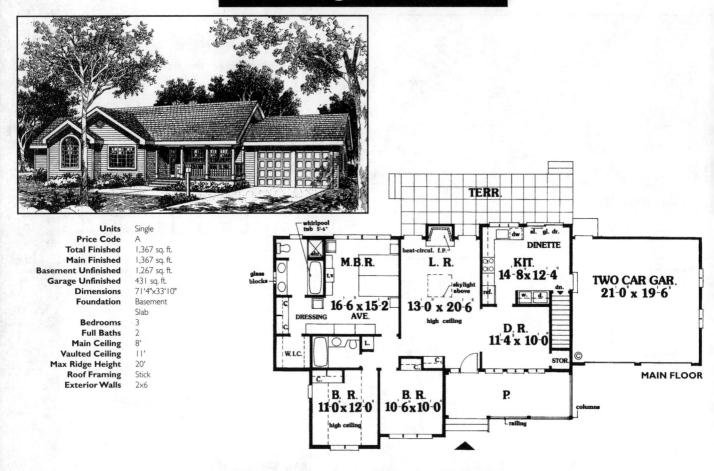

Units	Single
Price Code	A
Total Finished	1,367 sq. ft.
Main Finished	1,367 sq. ft.
Basement Unfinished	1,267 sq. ft.
Garage Unfinished	431 sq. ft.
Dimensions	71'4"x33'10"
Foundation	Basement
	Slab
Bedrooms	3
Full Baths	2
Main Ceiling	8'
Vaulted Ceiling	11'
Max Ridge Height	20'
Roof Framing	Stick
Exterior Walls	2x6

TERR.

whirlpool tub 5'-6"

glass blocks

M.B.R. 16-6 x 15-2 AVE.

DRESSING

W.I.C.

heat-circul. f.p.

L.R. 13-0 x 20-6 high ceiling

skylight above

sl. gl. dr.

DINETTE

KIT. 14-8 x 12-4

ref.

D.R. 11-4 x 10-0

STOR.

TWO CAR GAR. 21-0 x 19-6

MAIN FLOOR

B.R. 11-0 x 12-0 high ceiling

B.R. 10-6 x 10-0

P.

columns

railing

Design 99930

Units	Single
Price Code	A
Total Finished	1,368 sq. ft.
Main Finished	1,368 sq. ft.
Basement Unfinished	1,360 sq. ft.
Garage Unfinished	462 sq. ft.
Deck Unfinished	80 sq. ft.
Porch Unfinished	128 sq. ft.
Dimensions	46'x54'
Foundation	Basement
Bedrooms	3
Full Baths	2
Main Ceiling	8'
Tray Ceiling	11'6"
Max Ridge Height	19'
Roof Framing	Truss
Exterior Walls	2x6

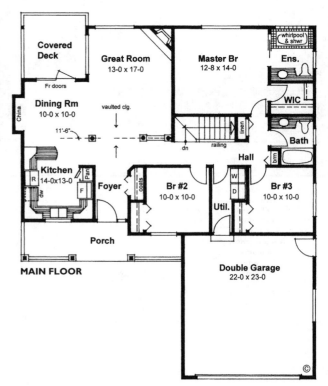

Covered Deck

Great Room 13-0 x 17-0

Master Br 12-8 x 14-0

whirlpool & shwr

Ens.

Fr doors

China

Dining Rm 10-0 x 10-0

vaulted clg.

WIC

11'-6"

dn   railing

linen

Bath

Kitchen 14-0x13-0

Pan

Foyer

coats

Br #2 10-0 x 10-0

Hall

Br #3 10-0 x 10-0

Util.

Porch

MAIN FLOOR

Double Garage 22-0 x 23-0

Design 96510

Units	Single
Price Code	A
Total Finished	1,372 sq. ft.
Main Finished	1,372 sq. ft.
Garage Unfinished	465 sq. ft.
Porch Unfinished	136 sq. ft.
Dimensions	38'x65'
Foundation	Crawlspace
	Slab
Bedrooms	3
Full Baths	2
Main Ceiling	8'
Max Ridge Height	19'
Roof Framing	Stick
Exterior Walls	2x4

MASTER SUITE 12 × 16
BATH
CLOSET
SHELVES
PORCH
BEDRM 11 × 12
DINING 10 × 9
LIVING RM 13 × 23
LIN
BATH
A/C
CLOS
KITCHEN 10 × 9
BEDRM 11 × 12
F/P
FOYER
DRY UTIL WASH STORAGE
PORCH
MAIN FLOOR
GARAGE 21 × 21

Design 97638

Units	Single
Price Code	A
Total Finished	1,374 sq. ft.
Main Finished	1,374 sq. ft.
Basement Unfinished	1,391 sq. ft.
Garage Unfinished	460 sq. ft.
Dimensions	50'4"x46'
Foundation	Basement
	Crawlspace
Bedrooms	3
Full Baths	2
Main Ceiling	9'
Max Ridge Height	24'
Roof Framing	Stick
Exterior Walls	2x4

CAD FILES AVAILABLE For more information call 800-235-5700

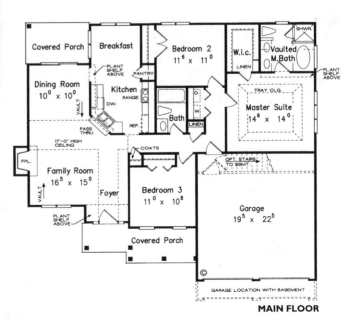

Covered Porch
Breakfast
Bedroom 2 11⁶ x 11⁰
W.i.c.
Vaulted M.Bath
Dining Room 10⁰ x 10⁰
Kitchen RANGE
PANTRY
LINEN
TRAY CLG
Master Suite 14⁶ x 14⁰
PLANT SHELF ABOVE
PASS THRU
Bath
17'-0" HIGH CEILING
FPL.
Family Room 16⁵ x 15⁰
COATS
OPT. STAIRS TO BSMT.
Foyer
Bedroom 3 11⁰ x 10⁸
Garage 19⁵ x 22⁵
PLANT SHELF ABOVE
Covered Porch
GARAGE LOCATION WITH BASEMENT
MAIN FLOOR

Design 65617

Units	Single
Price Code	A
Total Finished	1,375 sq. ft.
Main Finished	1,375 sq. ft.
Dimensions	61'x35'
Foundation	Crawlspace
	Slab
Bedrooms	3
Full Baths	2
Main Ceiling	8'
Max Ridge Height	24'
Roof Framing	Stick
Exterior Walls	2x4

patio

mbr 15 x 14

kit

dining 13 x 10

util

sto 9 x 10

living 20 x 15

carport 21 x 20

br 3 12 x 10

cathedral ceiling

beam

br 2 13 x 11

porch

MAIN FLOOR

Design 99673

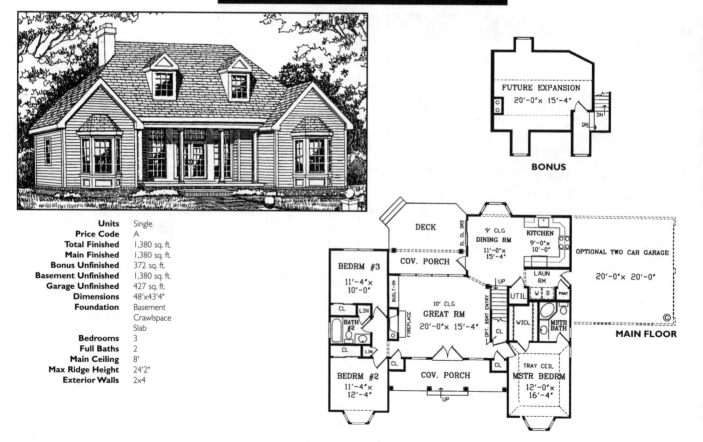

Units	Single
Price Code	A
Total Finished	1,380 sq. ft.
Main Finished	1,380 sq. ft.
Bonus Unfinished	372 sq. ft.
Basement Unfinished	1,380 sq. ft.
Garage Unfinished	427 sq. ft.
Dimensions	48'x43'4"
Foundation	Basement
	Crawlspace
	Slab
Bedrooms	3
Full Baths	2
Main Ceiling	8'
Max Ridge Height	24'2"
Exterior Walls	2x4

FUTURE EXPANSION 20'-0" x 15'-4"

BONUS

DECK

9' CLG DINING RM 11'-0"x 15'-4"

KITCHEN 9'-0"x 10'-0"

COV. PORCH

BEDRM #3 11'-4"x 10'-0"

OPTIONAL TWO CAR GARAGE 20'-0"x 20'-0"

LAUN RM

UTIL

10' CLG GREAT RM 20'-0"x 15'-4"

MSTR BATH

BEDRM #2 11'-4"x 12'-4"

COV. PORCH

TRAY CEIL MSTR BEDRM 12'-0"x 16'-4"

MAIN FLOOR

Design 96924

1,001-1,500 sq. ft. HOME PLANS

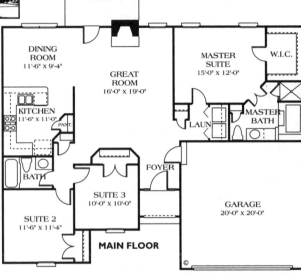

Units	Single
Price Code	A
Total Finished	1,383 sq. ft.
Main Finished	1,383 sq. ft.
Basement Unfinished	1,460 sq. ft.
Garage Unfinished	416 sq. ft.
Deck Unfinished	120 sq. ft.
Porch Unfinished	29 sq. ft.
Dimensions	50'x40'
Foundation	Basement
	Crawlspace
	Slab
Bedrooms	3
Full Baths	2
Main Ceiling	9'
Max Ridge Height	20'6"
Roof Framing	Truss
Exterior Walls	2x4

DECK/PATIO

DINING ROOM 11'-6" x 9'-4"

GREAT ROOM 16'-0" x 19'-0"

MASTER SUITE 15'-0" x 12'-0"

W.I.C.

KITCHEN 11'-6" x 11'-0"

PANT

MASTER BATH

LAUN

BATH

FOYER

SUITE 3 10'-0" x 10'-0"

GARAGE 20'-0" x 20'-0"

SUITE 2 11'-6" x 11'-4"

MAIN FLOOR

Design 94916

Units	Single
Price Code	A
Total Finished	1,392 sq. ft.
Main Finished	1,392 sq. ft.
Basement Unfinished	1,392 sq. ft.
Garage Unfinished	474 sq. ft.
Dimensions	42'x54'
Foundation	Basement
Bedrooms	3
Full Baths	2
Main Ceiling	8'
Max Ridge Height	19'3"
Roof Framing	Stick
Exterior Walls	2x4

*Alternate foundation options available at an additional charge.
Please call 1-800-235-5700 for more information.

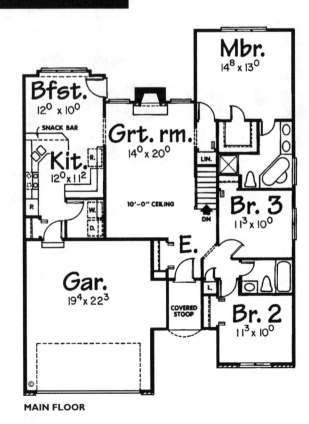

Bfst. 12⁰ x 10⁰

SNACK BAR

Mbr. 14⁸ x 13⁰

Grt. rm. 14⁰ x 20⁰

Kit. 12⁰ x 11²

10'-0" CEILING

LIN.

DN

Br. 3 11³ x 10⁰

E.

Gar. 19⁴ x 22³

COVERED STOOP

Br. 2 11³ x 10⁰

MAIN FLOOR

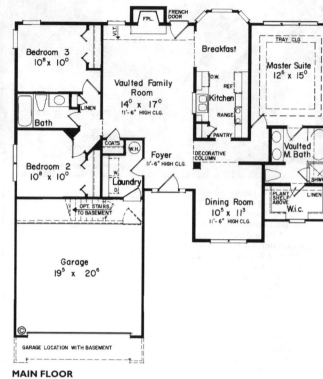

Units	Single
Price Code	A
Total Finished	1,392 sq. ft.
Main Finished	1,392 sq. ft.
Basement Unfinished	1,414 sq. ft.
Garage Unfinished	415 sq. ft.
Dimensions	49'x49'4"
Foundation	Basement
	Crawlspace
Bedrooms	3
Full Baths	2
Main Ceiling	9'
Max Ridge Height	23'
Roof Framing	Stick
Exterior Walls	2x4

MAIN FLOOR

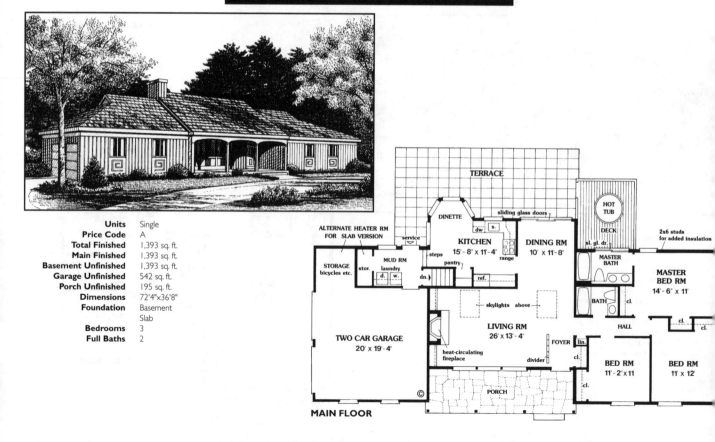

Units	Single
Price Code	A
Total Finished	1,393 sq. ft.
Main Finished	1,393 sq. ft.
Basement Unfinished	1,393 sq. ft.
Garage Unfinished	542 sq. ft.
Porch Unfinished	195 sq. ft.
Dimensions	72'4"x36'8"
Foundation	Basement
	Slab
Bedrooms	3
Full Baths	2

MAIN FLOOR

Design 34054

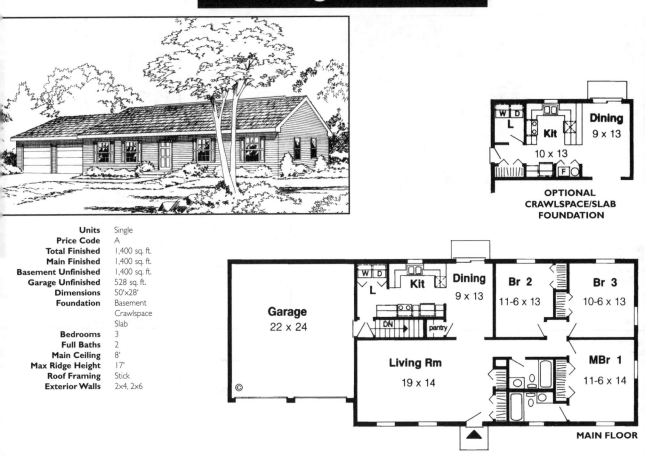

Units	Single
Price Code	A
Total Finished	1,400 sq. ft.
Main Finished	1,400 sq. ft.
Basement Unfinished	1,400 sq. ft.
Garage Unfinished	528 sq. ft.
Dimensions	50'x28'
Foundation	Basement
	Crawlspace
	Slab
Bedrooms	3
Full Baths	2
Main Ceiling	8'
Max Ridge Height	17'
Roof Framing	Stick
Exterior Walls	2x4, 2x6

OPTIONAL
CRAWLSPACE/SLAB
FOUNDATION

W D
L
Kit
10 x 13
Dining
9 x 13
F

Garage
22 x 24

W D
L
Kit
DN
pantry
Dining
9 x 13
Br 2
11-6 x 13
Br 3
10-6 x 13

Living Rm
19 x 14
MBr 1
11-6 x 14

MAIN FLOOR

Design 62024

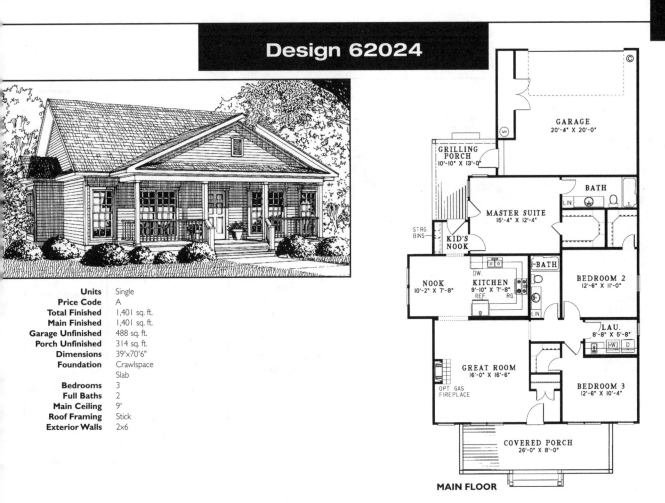

Units	Single
Price Code	A
Total Finished	1,401 sq. ft.
Main Finished	1,401 sq. ft.
Garage Unfinished	488 sq. ft.
Porch Unfinished	314 sq. ft.
Dimensions	39'x70'6"
Foundation	Crawlspace
	Slab
Bedrooms	3
Full Baths	2
Main Ceiling	9'
Roof Framing	Stick
Exterior Walls	2x6

GARAGE
20'-4" X 20'-0"

GRILLING
PORCH
10'-10" X 13'-0"

BATH

MASTER SUITE
15'-4" X 12'-4"

LIN

STRG
BINS

KID'S
NOOK

BATH

LIN

BEDROOM 2
12'-6" X 11'-0"

NOOK
10'-2" X 7'-8"

KITCHEN
9'-10" X 7'-8"
DW
REF
RG

LAU.
8'-8" X 5'-8"
W D

GREAT ROOM
16'-0" X 16'-6"

OPT GAS
FIREPLACE

BEDROOM 3
12'-6" X 10'-4"

COVERED PORCH
26'-0" X 8'-0"

MAIN FLOOR

Units	Single
Price Code	A
Total Finished	1,401 sq. ft.
Main Finished	1,401 sq. ft.
Porch Unfinished	137 sq. ft.
Dimensions	30'x59'10"
Foundation	Slab
Bedrooms	3
Full Baths	2
Main Ceiling	9'
Max Ridge Height	20'6"
Roof Framing	Stick
Exterior Walls	2x4

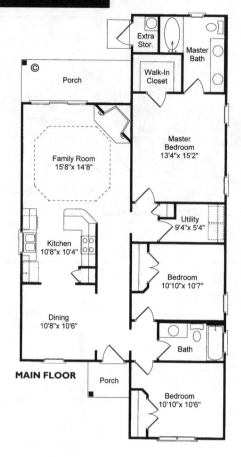

MAIN FLOOR

Design 94689

Units	Single
Price Code	A
Total Finished	1,405 sq. ft.
Main Finished	1,405 sq. ft.
Dimensions	42'x51'
Foundation	Slab
Bedrooms	3
Full Baths	2
Main Ceiling	8'
Max Ridge Height	19'4"
Roof Framing	Stick
Exterior Walls	2x4

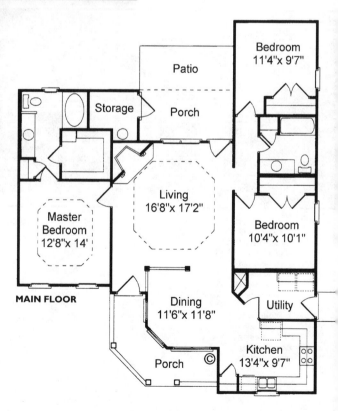

MAIN FLOOR

Design 98505

Units	Single
Price Code	A
Total Finished	1,405 sq. ft.
Main Finished	1,405 sq. ft.
Garage Unfinished	440 sq. ft.
Deck Unfinished	160 sq. ft.
Porch Unfinished	28 sq. ft.
Dimensions	40'x60'
Foundation	Slab
Bedrooms	3
Full Baths	2
Max Ridge Height	21'3"
Roof Framing	Stick
Exterior Walls	2x4

MAIN FLOOR

Design 98970

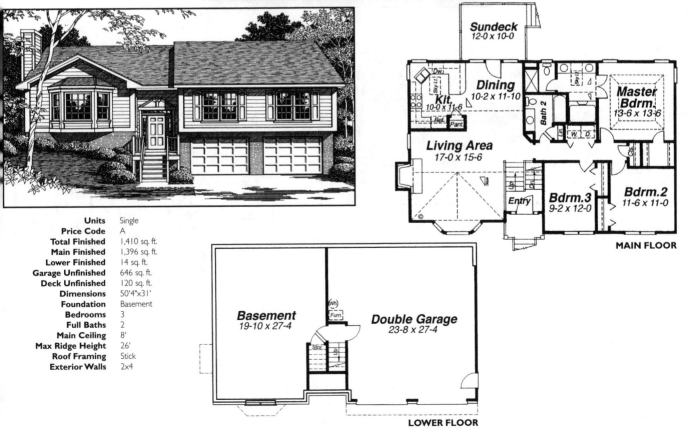

Units	Single
Price Code	A
Total Finished	1,410 sq. ft.
Main Finished	1,396 sq. ft.
Lower Finished	14 sq. ft.
Garage Unfinished	646 sq. ft.
Deck Unfinished	120 sq. ft.
Dimensions	50'4"x31'
Foundation	Basement
Bedrooms	3
Full Baths	2
Main Ceiling	8'
Max Ridge Height	26'
Roof Framing	Stick
Exterior Walls	2x4

MAIN FLOOR

LOWER FLOOR

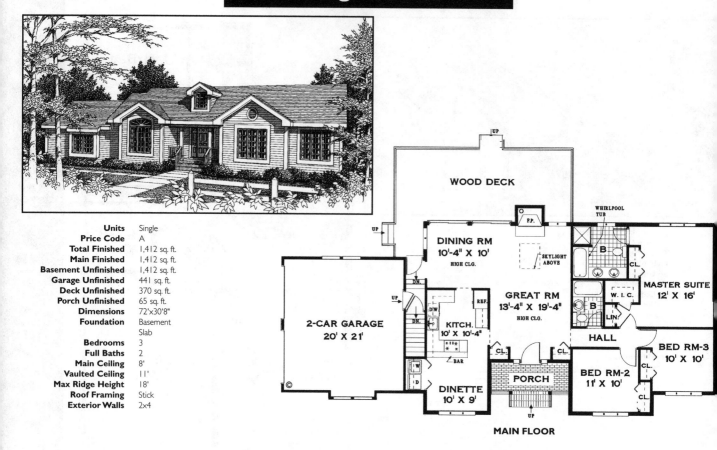

Units	Single
Price Code	A
Total Finished	1,412 sq. ft.
Main Finished	1,412 sq. ft.
Basement Unfinished	1,412 sq. ft.
Garage Unfinished	441 sq. ft.
Deck Unfinished	370 sq. ft.
Porch Unfinished	65 sq. ft.
Dimensions	72'x30'8"
Foundation	Basement
	Slab
Bedrooms	3
Full Baths	2
Main Ceiling	8'
Vaulted Ceiling	11'
Max Ridge Height	18'
Roof Framing	Stick
Exterior Walls	2x4

WOOD DECK

DINING RM 10'-4" X 10' HIGH CLG.

SKYLIGHT ABOVE

WHIRLPOOL TUB

MASTER SUITE 12' X 16'

2-CAR GARAGE 20' X 21'

KITCH. 10' X 10'-4"

GREAT RM 13'-4" X 19'-4" HIGH CLG.

W. I. C.

HALL

BED RM-3 10' X 10'

DINETTE 10' X 9'

PORCH

BED RM-2 11' X 10'

MAIN FLOOR

Units	Single
Price Code	A
Total Finished	1,415 sq. ft.
Main Finished	1,415 sq. ft.
Dimensions	56'x50'
Foundation	Crawlspace
	Slab
Bedrooms	3
Full Baths	2
Main Ceiling	8'
Max Ridge Height	26'
Roof Framing	Stick
Exterior Walls	2x6

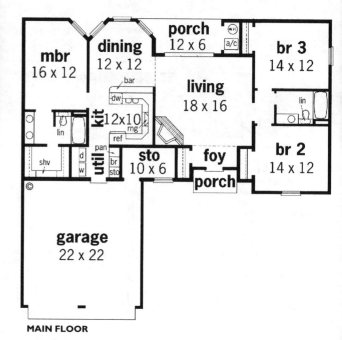

mbr 16 x 12

dining 12 x 12

porch 12 x 6

br 3 14 x 12

kit 12 x 10

living 18 x 16

util

sto 10 x 6

foy

br 2 14 x 12

porch

garage 22 x 22

MAIN FLOOR

Design 62106

Hot New Design

Units	Single
Price Code	A
Total Finished	1,422 sq. ft.
Main Finished	1,422 sq. ft.
Garage Unfinished	527 sq. ft.
Porch Unfinished	200 sq. ft.
Dimensions	43'x65'8"
Foundation	Basement
	Crawlspace
	Slab
Bedrooms	2
Full Baths	2
Main Ceiling	9'
Max Ridge Height	18'10"
Roof Framing	Stick
Exterior Walls	2x4, 2x6

MAIN FLOOR

Design 97113

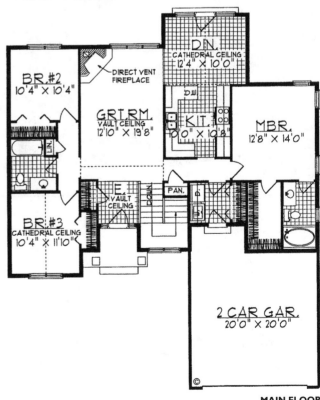

Units	Single
Price Code	A
Total Finished	1,416 sq. ft.
Main Finished	1,416 sq. ft.
Basement Unfinished	1,416 sq. ft.
Dimensions	48'x55'4"
Foundation	Basement
Bedrooms	3
Full Baths	2
Max Ridge Height	21'8"
Roof Framing	Truss
Exterior Walls	2x6

MAIN FLOOR

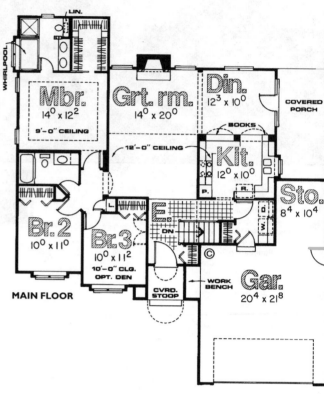

Units	Single
Price Code	A
Total Finished	1,422 sq. ft.
Main Finished	1,422 sq. ft.
Garage Unfinished	566 sq. ft.
Dimensions	50'x58'
Foundation	Basement
Bedrooms	3
Full Baths	2
Main Ceiling	8'
Max Ridge Height	21'3"
Roof Framing	Stick
Exterior Walls	2x4

* Alternate foundation options available at an additional charge.
Please call 1-800-235-5700 for more information.

MAIN FLOOR

Units	Single
Price Code	A
Total Finished	1,425 sq. ft.
Main Finished	1,425 sq. ft.
Garage Unfinished	353 sq. ft.
Porch Unfinished	137 sq. ft.
Dimensions	45'x64'10"
Foundation	Basement
	Crawlspace
	Slab
Bedrooms	3
Full Baths	2
Main Ceiling	9'
Roof Framing	Stick
Exterior Walls	2x4

MAIN FLOOR

Design 92056

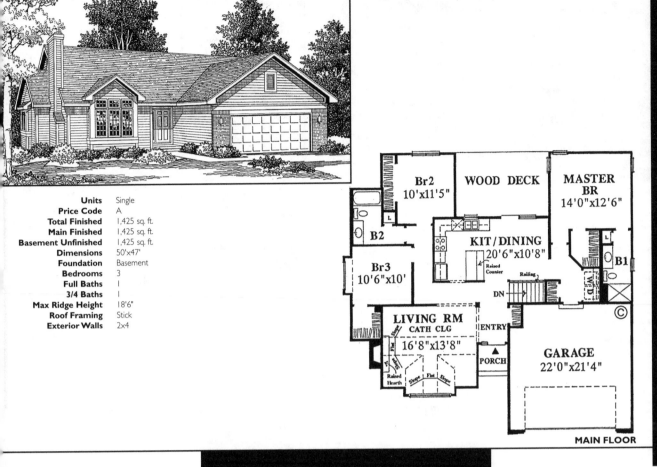

Units	Single
Price Code	A
Total Finished	1,425 sq. ft.
Main Finished	1,425 sq. ft.
Basement Unfinished	1,425 sq. ft.
Dimensions	50'x47'
Foundation	Basement
Bedrooms	3
Full Baths	1
3/4 Baths	1
Max Ridge Height	18'6"
Roof Framing	Stick
Exterior Walls	2x4

Floor plan labels: Br2 10'x11'5", WOOD DECK, MASTER BR 14'0"x12'6", B2, KIT/DINING 20'6"x10'8", Raised Counter, B1, Br3 10'6"x10', Railing, LIVING RM CATH CLG 16'8"x13'8", DN, ENTRY, Raised Hearth, Step Flat Step, PORCH, GARAGE 22'0"x21'4", W/D

MAIN FLOOR

Design 65059

Units	Single
Price Code	A
Total Finished	1,426 sq. ft.
Main Finished	1,426 sq. ft.
Dimensions	41'4"x42'
Foundation	Basement
Bedrooms	3
Full Baths	1
Main Ceiling	8'
Exterior Walls	2x6

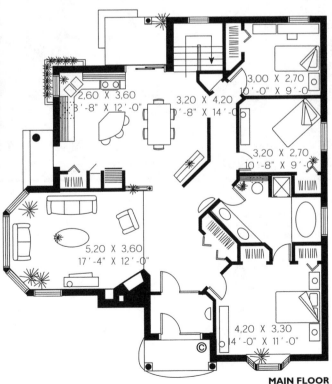

Floor plan labels: 2,60 X 3,60 8'-8" X 12'-0", 3,20 X 4,20 10'-8" X 14'-0", 3,00 X 2,70 10'-0" X 9'-0", 3,20 X 2,70 10'-8" X 9'-0", 5,20 X 3,60 17'-4" X 12'-0", 4,20 X 3,30 14'-0" X 11'-0"

MAIN FLOOR

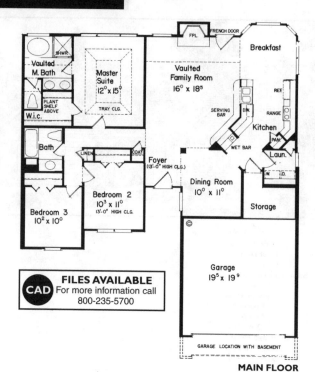

Units	Single
Price Code	A
Total Finished	1,430 sq. ft.
Main Finished	1,430 sq. ft.
Basement Unfinished	1,510 sq. ft.
Garage Unfinished	400 sq. ft.
Dimensions	47'x52'4"
Foundation	Basement
	Crawlspace
	Slab
Bedrooms	3
Full Baths	2
Max Ridge Height	23'6"
Roof Framing	Stick
Exterior Walls	2x4

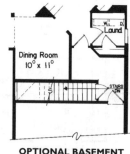

OPTIONAL BASEMENT STAIR LOCATION

CAD FILES AVAILABLE For more information call 800-235-5700

MAIN FLOOR

Units	Single
Price Code	A
Total Finished	1,431 sq. ft.
Main Finished	1,431 sq. ft.
Basement Unfinished	1,431 sq. ft.
Garage Unfinished	410 sq. ft.
Dimensions	53'x43'8"
Foundation	Basement
Bedrooms	3
Full Baths	2
Main Ceiling	8'
Max Ridge Height	21'
Roof Framing	Truss
Exterior Walls	2x6

MAIN FLOOR

Design 98549

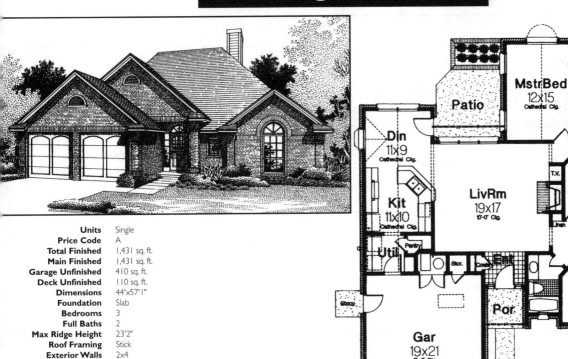

Units	Single
Price Code	A
Total Finished	1,431 sq. ft.
Main Finished	1,431 sq. ft.
Garage Unfinished	410 sq. ft.
Deck Unfinished	110 sq. ft.
Dimensions	44'x57'1"
Foundation	Slab
Bedrooms	3
Full Baths	2
Max Ridge Height	23'2"
Roof Framing	Stick
Exterior Walls	2x4

MAIN FLOOR

Design 92259

Units	Single
Price Code	A
Total Finished	1,432 sq. ft.
Main Finished	1,432 sq. ft.
Garage Unfinished	409 sq. ft.
Porch Unfinished	42 sq. ft.
Dimensions	50'x49'2"
Foundation	Slab
Bedrooms	3
Full Baths	2
Max Ridge Height	21'
Roof Framing	Stick
Exterior Walls	2x4

MAIN FLOOR

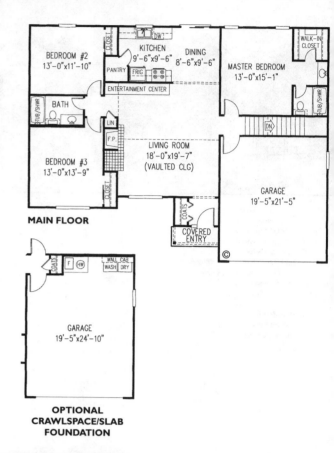

MAIN FLOOR

BEDROOM #2
13'-0"x11'-10"

KITCHEN
9'-6"x9'-6"

DINING
8'-6"x9'-6"

MASTER BEDROOM
13'-0"x15'-1"

PANTRY

ENTERTAINMENT CENTER

BATH

LIN

F.P.

BEDROOM #3
13'-0"x13'-9"

LIVING ROOM
18'-0"x19'-7"
(VAULTED CLG)

GARAGE
19'-5"x21'-5"

COATS

COVERED
ENTRY

Units	Single
Price Code	A
Total Finished	1,433 sq. ft.
Main Finished	1,433 sq. ft.
Basement Unfinished	1,433 sq. ft.
Garage Unfinished	456 sq. ft.
Dimensions	54'x41'
Foundation	Basement
	Crawlspace
	Slab
Bedrooms	3
Full Baths	2
Main Ceiling	8'
Vaulted Ceiling	11'9"
Max Ridge Height	19'9"
Roof Framing	Truss
Exterior Walls	2x4

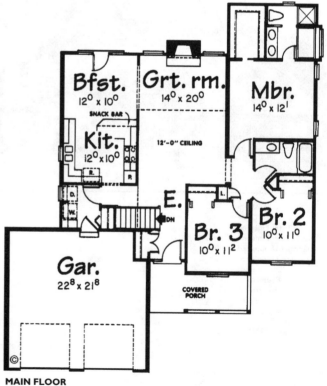

GARAGE
19'-5"x24'-10"

COATS

WALL CAB
WASH DRY

**OPTIONAL
CRAWLSPACE/SLAB
FOUNDATION**

Units	Single
Price Code	A
Total Finished	1,433 sq. ft.
Main Finished	1,433 sq. ft.
Garage Unfinished	504 sq. ft.
Dimensions	50'x58'
Foundation	Basement
Bedrooms	3
Full Baths	2
Main Ceiling	8'
Max Ridge Height	19'4"
Roof Framing	Stick
Exterior Walls	2x4

* Alternate foundation options available at an additional charge.
Please call 1-800-235-5700 for more information.

Bfst.
12⁰ x 10⁰

Grt. rm.
14⁰ x 20⁰

Mbr.
14⁰ x 12¹

SNACK BAR

Kit.
12⁰ x 10⁰

12'-0" CEILING

Gar.
22⁸ x 21⁸

Br. 3
10⁰ x 11²

Br. 2
10⁰ x 11⁰

COVERED
PORCH

MAIN FLOOR

Design 96509

Units	Single
Price Code	A
Total Finished	1,438 sq. ft.
Main Finished	1,438 sq. ft.
Garage Unfinished	486 sq. ft.
Deck Unfinished	282 sq. ft.
Porch Unfinished	126 sq. ft.
Dimensions	54'x57'
Foundation	Crawlspace
	Slab
Bedrooms	3
Full Baths	2
Max Ridge Height	19'
Roof Framing	Stick
Exterior Walls	2x4

GARAGE 22 × 22

DECK

MASTER SUITE 13 × 15

DINING 12 × 11

KITCHEN 12 × 10

BATH

BATH

GREAT RM 17 × 18

BEDRM 14 × 11

BEDRM 11 × 13

MAIN FLOOR

PORCH

Design 65095

Units	Single
Price Code	A
Total Finished	1,440 sq. ft.
Main Finished	1,440 sq. ft.
Basement Unfinished	1,440 sq. ft.
Garage Unfinished	332 sq. ft.
Dimensions	58'x36'
Foundation	Basement
Bedrooms	3
Full Baths	1
Main Ceiling	8'
Max Ridge Height	26'
Roof Framing	Truss
Exterior Walls	2x6

3.00 X 3.00 10'-0" X 10'-0"

3.00 X 3.00 10'-0" X 10'-0"

2.80 X 3.60 9'-4" X 12'-0"

3.60 X 4.60 12'-0" X 15'-4"

4.30 X 6.80 14'-4" X 22'-8"

3.60 X 5.00 12'-0" X 16'-8"

3.60 X 4.20 12'-0" X 14'-0"

MAIN FLOOR

Units	Single
Price Code	A
Total Finished	1,442 sq. ft.
Main Finished	1,442 sq. ft.
Garage Unfinished	417 sq. ft.
Porch Unfinished	172 sq. ft.
Dimensions	34'8"x71'
Foundation	Crawlspace
	Slab
Bedrooms	3
Full Baths	2
Main Ceiling	9'
Exterior Walls	2x4

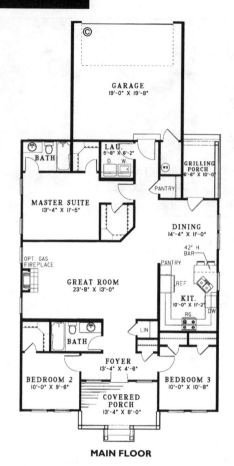

MAIN FLOOR

Units	Single
Price Code	A
Total Finished	1,447 sq. ft.
Main Finished	1,447 sq. ft.
Garage Unfinished	342 sq. ft.
Porch Unfinished	284 sq. ft.
Dimensions	44'x71'2"
Foundation	Crawlspace
	Slab
Bedrooms	3
Full Baths	2
Main Ceiling	9'
Roof Framing	Stick
Exterior Walls	2x4

MAIN FLOOR

Design 97172

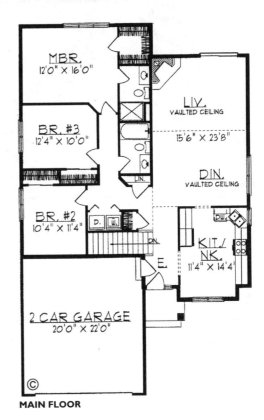

MAIN FLOOR

Units	Single
Price Code	A
Total Finished	1,448 sq. ft.
Main Finished	1,448 sq. ft.
Basement Unfinished	1,448 sq. ft.
Garage Unfinished	440 sq. ft.
Dimensions	38'x59'
Foundation	Basement
Bedrooms	3
Full Baths	1
3/4 Baths	1
Main Ceiling	8'
Roof Framing	Truss
Exterior Walls	2x6

Design 94914

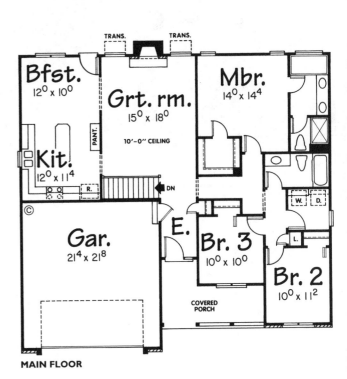

MAIN FLOOR

Units	Single
Price Code	A
Total Finished	1,453 sq. ft.
Main Finished	1,453 sq. ft.
Basement Unfinished	1,453 sq. ft.
Garage Unfinished	481 sq. ft.
Dimensions	48'8"x44'
Foundation	Basement
Bedrooms	3
Full Baths	2
Main Ceiling	8'
Max Ridge Height	18'6"
Roof Framing	Stick
Exterior Walls	2x4

* Alternate foundation options available at an additional charge.
Please call 1-800-235-5700 for more information.

MASTER BEDROOM OPTION

Design 97137

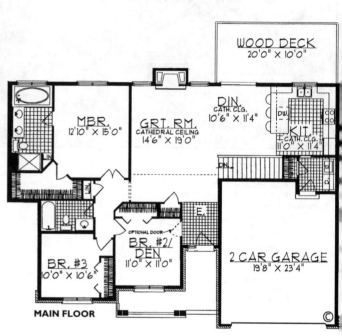

Units	Single
Price Code	A
Total Finished	1,461 sq. ft.
Main Finished	1,461 sq. ft.
Garage Unfinished	458 sq. ft.
Deck Unfinished	200 sq. ft.
Dimensions	56'x42'
Foundation	Basement
Bedrooms	3
Full Baths	2
Main Ceiling	8'
Max Ridge Height	21'5"
Roof Framing	Truss
Exterior Walls	2x6

Design 97176

Units	Single
Price Code	A
Total Finished	1,462 sq. ft.
Main Finished	1,462 sq. ft.
Basement Unfinished	1,462 sq. ft.
Garage Unfinished	400 sq. ft.
Dimensions	52'x46'
Foundation	Basement
Bedrooms	3
Full Baths	2
Main Ceiling	8'
Max Ridge Height	24'10"
Roof Framing	Truss
Exterior Walls	2x6

Design 99926

Units	Single
Price Code	A
Total Finished	1,463 sq. ft.
Main Finished	1,463 sq. ft.
Basement Unfinished	1,446 sq. ft.
Garage Unfinished	390 sq. ft.
Deck Unfinished	100 sq. ft.
Porch Unfinished	40 sq. ft.
Dimensions	40'x60'
Foundation	Basement
Bedrooms	3
Full Baths	2
Main Ceiling	8'
Vaulted Ceiling	11'
Max Ridge Height	18'6"
Roof Framing	Truss
Exterior Walls	2x6

Design 91554

Units	Single
Price Code	A
Total Finished	1,467 sq. ft.
Main Finished	1,467 sq. ft.
Garage Unfinished	400 sq. ft.
Dimensions	49'x43'
Foundation	Crawlspace
Bedrooms	3
Full Baths	2
Main Ceiling	8'1"
Vaulted Ceiling	13'
Max Ridge Height	20'6"
Roof Framing	Truss
Exterior Walls	2x6

Design 60084

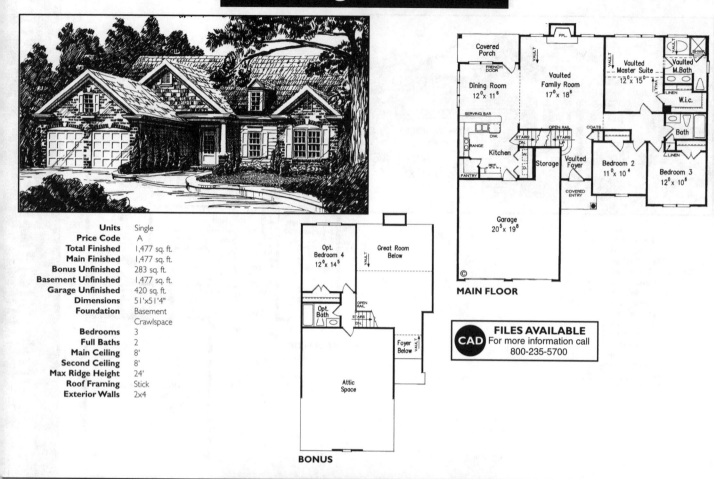

Units	Single
Price Code	A
Total Finished	1,477 sq. ft.
Main Finished	1,477 sq. ft.
Bonus Unfinished	283 sq. ft.
Basement Unfinished	1,477 sq. ft.
Garage Unfinished	420 sq. ft.
Dimensions	51'x51'4"
Foundation	Basement
	Crawlspace
Bedrooms	3
Full Baths	2
Main Ceiling	8'
Second Ceiling	8'
Max Ridge Height	24'
Roof Framing	Stick
Exterior Walls	2x4

MAIN FLOOR

BONUS

CAD FILES AVAILABLE
For more information call
800-235-5700

Design 91847

Units	Single
Price Code	A
Total Finished	1,479 sq. ft.
Main Finished	1,479 sq. ft.
Basement Unfinished	1,430 sq. ft.
Garage Unfinished	528 sq. ft.
Dimensions	56'x46'6"
Foundation	Basement
	Crawlspace
	Slab
Bedrooms	3
Full Baths	2
Main Ceiling	8'
Max Ridge Height	19'4"
Roof Framing	Truss
Exterior Walls	2x6

MAIN FLOOR

Design 99490

Units	Single
Price Code	A
Total Finished	1,479 sq. ft.
Main Finished	1,479 sq. ft.
Dimensions	48'x50'
Foundation	Basement
	Slab
Bedrooms	3
Full Baths	2
Max Ridge Height	21'6"
Roof Framing	Stick
Exterior Walls	2x4

* Alternate foundation options available at an additional charge.
Please call 1-800-235-5700 for more information.

THIRD BEDROOM OPTION

OPTIONAL
Br.3
10⁰ x 10⁰
10'-0" CLG.

Kit.
13⁰ x 11⁰
R. P.
SNACK BAR
Bfst.
11⁰ x 10⁰
DN
D. W.
TRANSOMS
Grt. rm.
14⁰ x 18⁰
11'-0" CEILING
WHIRLPOOL
GLASS SHELVES
Mbr.
13⁰ x 13⁰
9'-0" CLG.
Gar.
19⁸ x 22⁰
Den
10⁰ x 10⁰
OPTIONAL BEDROOM
10'-0" CLG.
TRANS.
COVERED PORCH
Br. 2
10⁸ x 10⁰
©

MAIN FLOOR

Design 61032

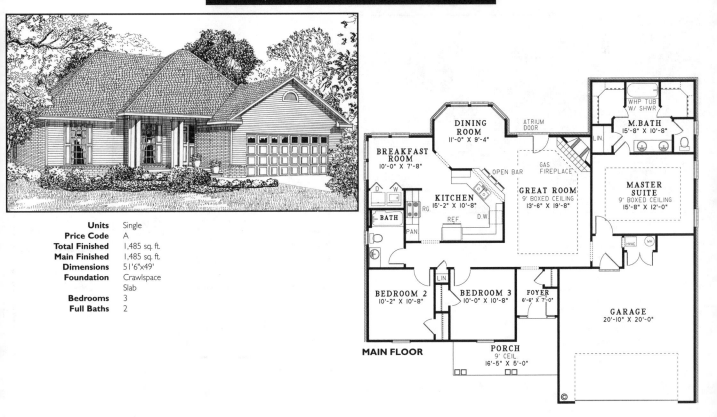

Units	Single
Price Code	A
Total Finished	1,485 sq. ft.
Main Finished	1,485 sq. ft.
Dimensions	51'6"x49'
Foundation	Crawlspace
	Slab
Bedrooms	3
Full Baths	2

DINING ROOM
11'-0" X 9'-4"
ATRIUM DOOR
WHP TUB W/ SHWR
M.BATH
15'-8" X 10'-8"
LIN
BREAKFAST ROOM
10'-0" X 7'-8"
OPEN BAR
GAS FIREPLACE
KITCHEN
15'-2" X 10'-8"
D W
BATH
RG.
REF.
D.W.
PAN.
GREAT ROOM
13'-6" X 19'-8"
9' BOXED CEILING
MASTER SUITE
15'-8" X 12'-0"
9' BOXED CEILING
HVAC WH
BEDROOM 2
10'-2" X 10'-8"
LIN
BEDROOM 3
10'-0" X 10'-8"
FOYER
6'-6" X 7'-0"
GARAGE
20'-10" X 20'-0"
PORCH
9' CEIL
16'-5" X 5'-0"
©

MAIN FLOOR

Units	Single
Price Code	A
Total Finished	1,485 sq. ft.
Main Finished	1,485 sq. ft.
Dimensions	51'6"x49'10"
Foundation	Crawlspace
	Slab
Bedrooms	3
Full Baths	2

MAIN FLOOR

Design 82026

Units	Single
Price Code	A
Total Finished	1,485 sq. ft.
Main Finished	1,485 sq. ft.
Garage Unfinished	415 sq. ft.
Porch Unfinished	180 sq. ft.
Dimensions	51'6"x49'10"
Foundation	Crawlspace
	Slab
Bedrooms	3
Full Baths	2
Main Ceiling	9'
Roof Framing	Stick
Exterior Walls	2x4

MAIN FLOOR

Design 61035

Units	Single
Price Code	A
Total Finished	1,490 sq. ft.
Main Finished	1,490 sq. ft.
Garage Unfinished	386 sq. ft.
Porch Unfinished	20 sq. ft.
Dimensions	31'6"x72'10"
Foundation	Crawlspace
	Slab
Bedrooms	3
Full Baths	2
Main Ceiling	9'
Exterior Walls	2x4

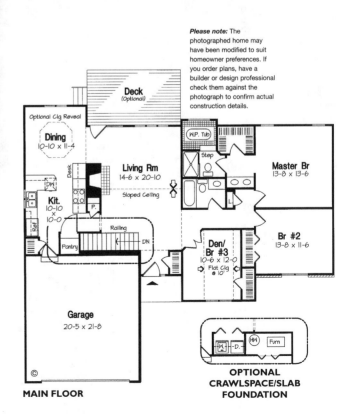

MAIN FLOOR

Design 34150

PHOTOGRAPHY: JOHN EHRENCLOU

Units	Single
Price Code	A
Total Finished	1,492 sq. ft.
Main Finished	1,492 sq. ft.
Basement Unfinished	1,486 sq. ft.
Garage Unfinished	462 sq. ft.
Dimensions	56'x48'
Foundation	Basement
	Crawlspace
	Slab
Bedrooms	3
Full Baths	2
Main Ceiling	8'
Vaulted Ceiling	13'
Max Ridge Height	19'
Roof Framing	Stick
Exterior Walls	2x4, 2x6

Please note: The photographed home may have been modified to suit homeowner preferences. If you order plans, have a builder or design professional check them against the photograph to confirm actual construction details.

MAIN FLOOR

OPTIONAL CRAWLSPACE/SLAB FOUNDATION

Design 90692

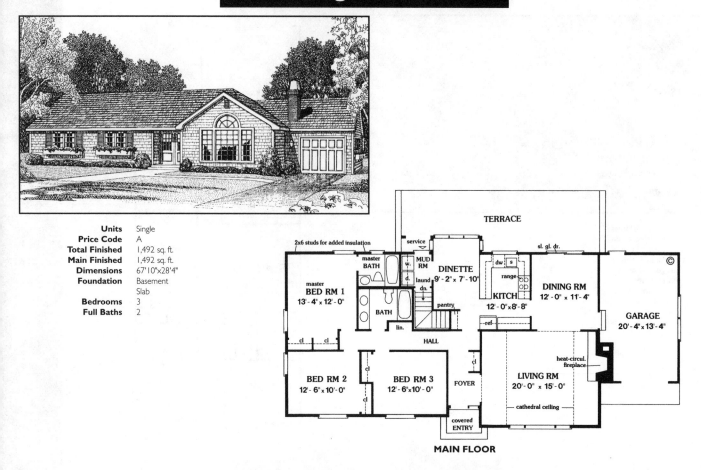

Units	Single
Price Code	A
Total Finished	1,492 sq. ft.
Main Finished	1,492 sq. ft.
Dimensions	67'10"x28'4"
Foundation	Basement
	Slab
Bedrooms	3
Full Baths	2

TERRACE

2x6 studs for added insulation

service

sl. gl. dr.

master
BATH

MUD
RM

DINETTE
9'-2" x 7'-10"

dw   s

range

DINING RM
12'-0" x 11'-4"

master
BED RM 1
13'-4" x 12'-0"

w.
d.

laund.
dn.

KITCH
12'-0"x8-8"

ref.

GARAGE
20'-4" x 13'-4"

BATH

pantry

lin.

cl   cl

HALL

heat-circul.
fireplace

BED RM 2
12'-6" x 10'-0"

cl

BED RM 3
12'-6"x10'-0"

cl

FOYER

LIVING RM
20'-0" x 15'-0"

cathedral ceiling

cl

covered
ENTRY

MAIN FLOOR

Design 98472

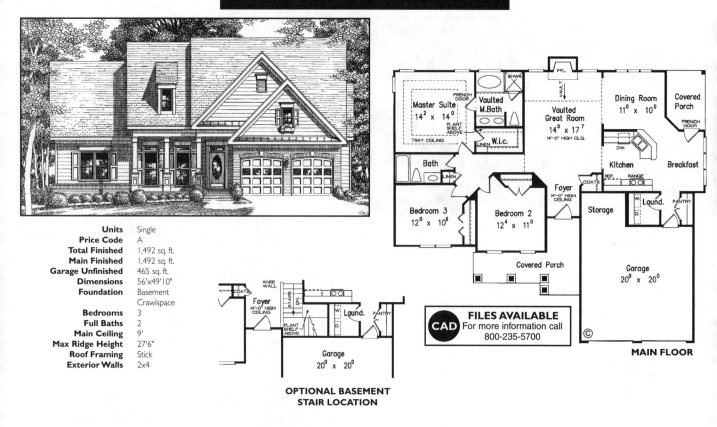

Units	Single
Price Code	A
Total Finished	1,492 sq. ft.
Main Finished	1,492 sq. ft.
Garage Unfinished	465 sq. ft.
Dimensions	56'x49'10"
Foundation	Basement
	Crawlspace
Bedrooms	3
Full Baths	2
Main Ceiling	9'
Max Ridge Height	27'6"
Roof Framing	Stick
Exterior Walls	2x4

SHWR

FPL

FRENCH
DOOR

Master Suite
14² x 14⁰

Vaulted
M.Bath

VAULT

Dining Room
11⁰ x 10⁰

Covered
Porch

PLANT
SHELF
ABOVE

TRAY CEILING

Vaulted
Great Room
14⁰ x 17⁷
14'-0" HIGH CLG.

W.i.c.

LINEN

FRENCH
DOOR

Bath

LINEN

Kitchen

DW.

Breakfast

REF.   RANGE

Bedroom 3
12⁰ x 10⁸

Bedroom 2
12⁴ x 11⁰

Foyer
14'-0" HIGH
CEILING

COATS

Storage

W.   Laund.
D.

PANTRY

Covered Porch

Garage
20⁰ x 20⁰

CAD **FILES AVAILABLE**
For more information call
800-235-5700

MAIN FLOOR

KNEE
WALL

COATS

Foyer
14'-0" HIGH
CEILING

STAIRS

DN.

W.
D.

Laund.

PANTRY

PLANT
SHELF
ABOVE

Garage
20⁰ x 20⁰

**OPTIONAL BASEMENT
STAIR LOCATION**

Design 99922

Units	Single
Price Code	A
Total Finished	1,493 sq. ft.
Main Finished	1,493 sq. ft.
Basement Unfinished	1,493 sq. ft.
Garage Unfinished	441 sq. ft.
Deck Unfinished	140 sq. ft.
Porch Unfinished	30 sq. ft.
Dimensions	48'x58'
Foundation	Basement
Bedrooms	3
Full Baths	2
Main Ceiling	8'
Vaulted Ceiling	10'6"
Max Ridge Height	20'
Roof Framing	Truss
Exterior Walls	2x6

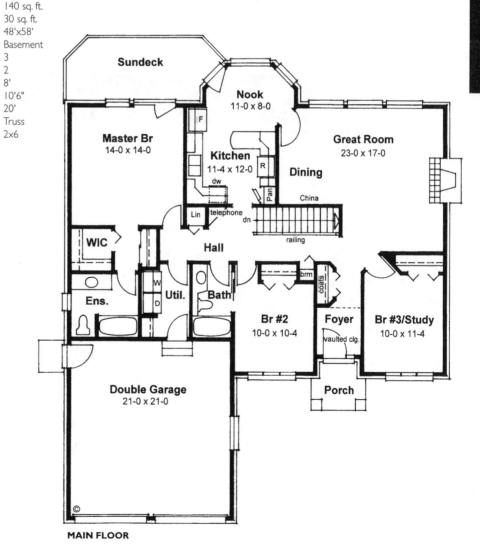

MAIN FLOOR

Design 98441

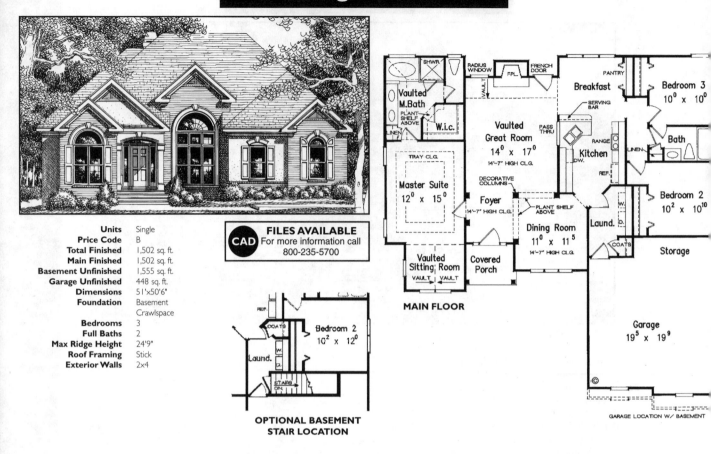

Units	Single
Price Code	B
Total Finished	1,502 sq. ft.
Main Finished	1,502 sq. ft.
Basement Unfinished	1,555 sq. ft.
Garage Unfinished	448 sq. ft.
Dimensions	51'x50'6"
Foundation	Basement
	Crawlspace
Bedrooms	3
Full Baths	2
Max Ridge Height	24'9"
Roof Framing	Stick
Exterior Walls	2x4

CAD FILES AVAILABLE
For more information call
800-235-5700

OPTIONAL BASEMENT STAIR LOCATION

Design 99936

Units	Single
Price Code	B
Total Finished	1,506 sq. ft.
Main Finished	1,506 sq. ft.
Basement Unfinished	1,506 sq. ft.
Garage Unfinished	440 sq. ft.
Deck Unfinished	448 sq. ft.
Porch Unfinished	30 sq. ft.
Dimensions	48'x58'
Foundation	Basement
Bedrooms	3
Full Baths	2
Main Ceiling	9'
Max Ridge Height	25'3"
Roof Framing	Truss
Exterior Walls	2x6

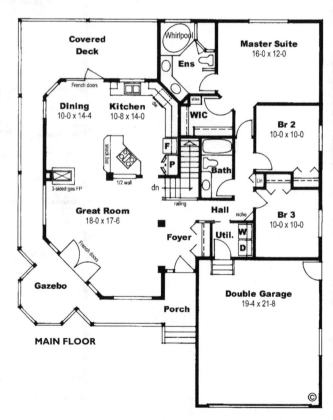

Design 94650

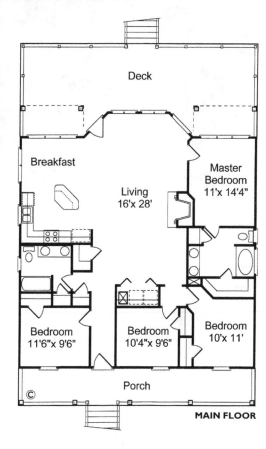

Deck

Breakfast

Living
16'x 28'

Master
Bedroom
11'x 14'4"

Bedroom
11'6"x 9'6"

Bedroom
10'4"x 9'6"

Bedroom
10'x 11'

Porch

MAIN FLOOR

Units	Single
Price Code	B
Total Finished	1,520 sq. ft.
Main Finished	1,520 sq. ft.
Dimensions	40'x59'
Foundation	Pier/Post
Bedrooms	4
Full Baths	2
Main Ceiling	9'
Max Ridge Height	32'
Roof Framing	Stick
Exterior Walls	2x4

Design 97261

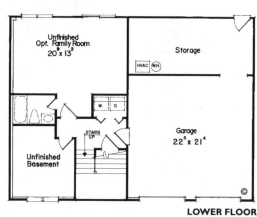

FPL.

Breakfast

FRENCH DOOR

M. Bath

TUB

Master Suite
12'3"x 16'0"

TRAY CLG.

SERVING BAR

Kitchen

RANGE

VAULT

Vaulted
Family Room
13'0"x 17'6"

Bath

D.W.

PANTRY

REF

LINEN

W.i.c.

Dining Room
11'x 12'8"

OPEN RAIL

COATS

LINEN

STAIRS DN

STAIRS UP

Foyer

Bedroom 2
11'0"x 10'0"

Bedroom 3
11'x 10'8"

MAIN FLOOR

Unfinished
Opt. Family Room
20'9"x 13'2"

Storage

HVAC

WH

Unfinished
Basement

W D

STAIRS UP

Garage
22'6"x 21'4"

LOWER FLOOR

Units	Single
Price Code	B
Total Finished	1,538 sq. ft.
Main Finished	1,466 sq. ft.
Lower Finished	72 sq. ft.
Basement Unfinished	902 sq. ft.
Garage Unfinished	495 sq. ft.
Dimensions	44'x36'6"
Foundation	Basement
Bedrooms	3
Full Baths	2
Main Ceiling	8'
Max Ridge Height	24'
Roof Framing	Stick
Exterior Walls	2x4

Design 24721

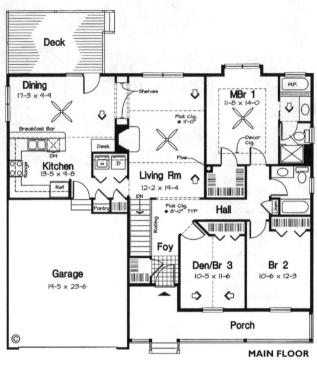

Deck

Dining
17-3 x 9-9

Breakfast Bar

Shelves

Flat Clg. @ 11'-0"

Decor Clg.

MBr 1
11-8 x 14-0

Kitchen
13-5 x 9-8

Desk

DW

Range

Ref.

Pantry

Living Rm
12-2 x 19-4

Flue

Flat Clg. @ 8'-0" TYP

Hall

DN

Railing

Foy

Linen

Garage
19-5 x 23-6

Den/Br 3
10-5 x 11-6

Br 2
10-6 x 12-3

Porch

MAIN FLOOR

Units	Single
Price Code	B
Total Finished	1,539 sq. ft.
Main Finished	1,539 sq. ft.
Basement Unfinished	1,530 sq. ft.
Garage Unfinished	460 sq. ft.
Deck Unfinished	160 sq. ft.
Porch Unfinished	182 sq. ft.
Dimensions	50'x45'4"
Foundation	Basement
	Crawlspace
	Slab
Bedrooms	3
Full Baths	2
Main Ceiling	8'
Max Ridge Height	21'
Roof Framing	Stick
Exterior Walls	2x6

Design 94920

Units	Single
Price Code	B
Total Finished	1,554 sq. ft.
Main Finished	1,554 sq. ft.
Basement Unfinished	1,554 sq. ft.
Garage Unfinished	464 sq. ft.
Dimensions	50'x52'8"
Foundation	Basement
Bedrooms	3
Full Baths	2
Main Ceiling	8'
Max Ridge Height	24'
Roof Framing	Stick
Exterior Walls	2x4

* Alternate foundation options available at an additional charge.
Please call 1-800-235-5700 for more information.

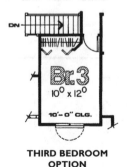

DN

Br.3
10⁰ x 12⁰

10'-0" CLG.

**THIRD BEDROOM
OPTION**

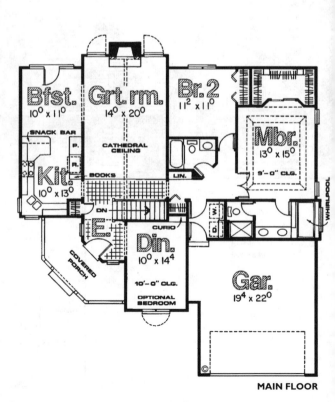

Bfst.
10⁰ x 11⁰

SNACK BAR

Grt. rm.
14⁰ x 20⁰

CATHEDRAL CEILING

Br. 2
11² x 11⁰

Kit.
10⁰ x 13⁰

BOOKS

LIN.

Mbr.
13⁰ x 15⁰

9'-0" CLG.

WHIRLPOOL

DN

CURIO

E.

COVERED PORCH

Din.
10⁰ x 14⁴

10'-0" CLG.

OPTIONAL BEDROOM

Gar.
19⁴ x 22⁰

MAIN FLOOR

Design 99152

Units	Single
Price Code	B
Total Finished	1,557 sq. ft.
Main Finished	1,557 sq. ft.
Basement Unfinished	1,557 sq. ft.
Garage Unfinished	440 sq. ft.
Dimensions	53'x49'
Foundation	Basement
Bedrooms	3
Full Baths	2
Max Ridge Height	21'
Roof Framing	Truss
Exterior Walls	2x4

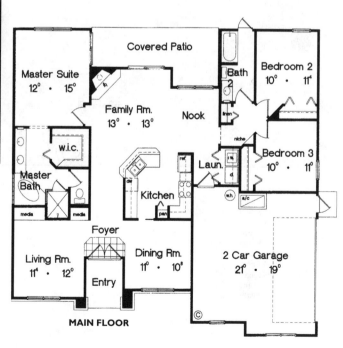

MAIN FLOOR

Design 63088

Units	Single
Price Code	B
Total Finished	1,558 sq. ft.
Main Finished	1,558 sq. ft.
Garage Unfinished	413 sq. ft.
Dimensions	50'x45'
Foundation	Slab
Bedrooms	3
Full Baths	2
Main Ceiling	10'-14'6"
Max Ridge Height	21'
Roof Framing	Truss
Exterior Walls	2x4

MAIN FLOOR

Design 63084

Units	Single
Price Code	B
Total Finished	1,571 sq. ft.
Main Finished	1,571 sq. ft.
Garage Unfinished	381 sq. ft.
Porch Unfinished	123 sq. ft.
Dimensions	40'x55'
Foundation	Slab
Bedrooms	3
Full Baths	2
Max Ridge Height	20'
Roof Framing	Truss
Exterior Walls	2x4

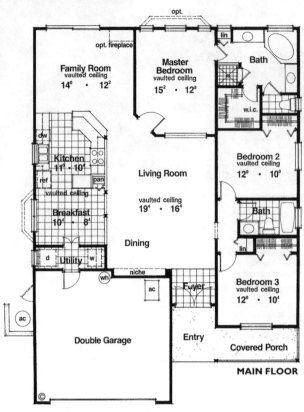

opt.

opt. fireplace

Family Room
vaulted ceiling
14⁰ · 12²

Master Bedroom
vaulted ceiling
15² · 12⁸

Bath

lin

w.i.c.

Kitchen
11⁰ · 10⁴

dw

ref

pan

Living Room
vaulted ceiling
19⁴ · 16⁴

vaulted ceiling

Breakfast
10⁴ · 8⁴

Bedroom 2
vaulted ceiling
12⁰ · 10⁰

Bath

Dining

d **Utility** w

wh

niche

ac

Foyer

lin

Bedroom 3
vaulted ceiling
12⁰ · 10⁴

ac

Double Garage

Entry

Covered Porch

MAIN FLOOR

©

Design 63089

Units	Single
Price Code	B
Total Finished	1,571 sq. ft.
Main Finished	1,571 sq. ft.
Garage Unfinished	381 sq. ft.
Dimensions	40'x55'
Foundation	Slab
Bedrooms	3
Full Baths	2
Max Ridge Height	20'
Roof Framing	Truss
Exterior Walls	2x4

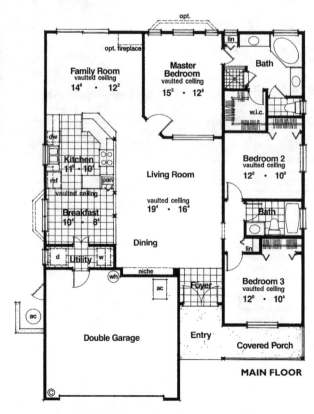

opt.

opt. fireplace

Family Room
vaulted ceiling
14⁰ · 12²

Master Bedroom
vaulted ceiling
15² · 12⁸

Bath

lin

w.i.c.

Kitchen
11⁰ · 10⁴

dw

ref

pan

Living Room

vaulted ceiling
19⁴ · 16⁴

vaulted ceiling

Breakfast
10⁴ · 8⁴

Bedroom 2
vaulted ceiling
12⁰ · 10⁰

Bath

Dining

d **Utility** w

wh

niche

ac

Foyer

lin

Bedroom 3
vaulted ceiling
12⁰ · 10⁴

ac

Double Garage

Entry

Covered Porch

MAIN FLOOR

©

Design 66044

Units	Single
Price Code	B
Total Finished	1,573 sq. ft.
Main Finished	1,573 sq. ft.
Dimensions	48'x51'
Foundation	Slab
Bedrooms	3
Full Baths	2
Main Ceiling	8'-10'
Max Ridge Height	24'
Roof Framing	Stick
Exterior Walls	2x4

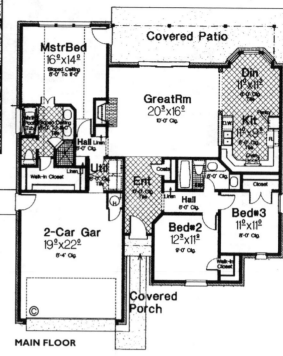

MAIN FLOOR

Design 93062

Units	Single
Price Code	B
Total Finished	1,575 sq. ft.
Main Finished	1,575 sq. ft.
Garage Unfinished	474 sq. ft.
Porch Unfinished	41 sq. ft.
Dimensions	55'6"x52'
Foundation	Crawlspace
	Slab
Bedrooms	3
Full Baths	2
Main Ceiling	10'
Max Ridge Height	20'
Roof Framing	Truss
Exterior Walls	2x4

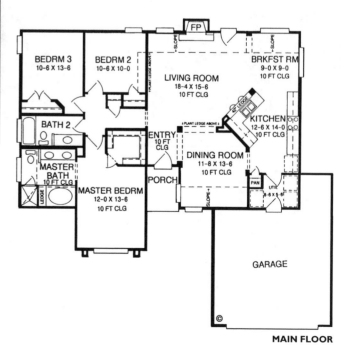

MAIN FLOOR

Units	Single
Price Code	B
Total Finished	1,575 sq. ft.
Main Finished	1,575 sq. ft.
Basement Unfinished	1,658 sq. ft.
Garage Unfinished	459 sq. ft.
Dimensions	50'x52'6"
Foundation	Basement
	Crawlspace
Bedrooms	3
Full Baths	2
Main Ceiling	9'
Max Ridge Height	23'6"
Roof Framing	Stick
Exterior Walls	2x4

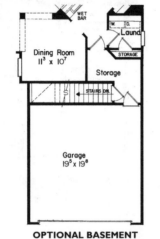

OPTIONAL BASEMENT STAIR LOCATION

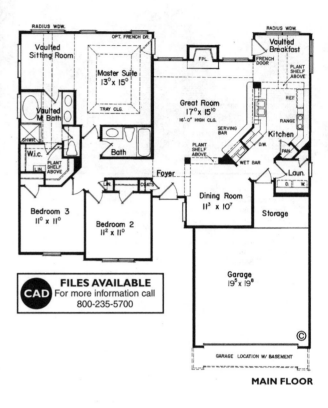

CAD **FILES AVAILABLE** For more information call 800-235-5700

MAIN FLOOR

Units	Single
Price Code	B
Total Finished	1,577 sq. ft.
Main Finished	1,577 sq. ft.
Garage Unfinished	489 sq. ft.
Deck Unfinished	28 sq. ft.
Dimensions	59'4"x49'4"
Foundation	Basement
Bedrooms	2
Full Baths	1
3/4 Baths	1
Half Baths	1
Max Ridge Height	22'3"
Roof Framing	Stick
Exterior Walls	2x4

* Alternate foundation options available at an additional charge.
Please call 1-800-235-5700 for more information.

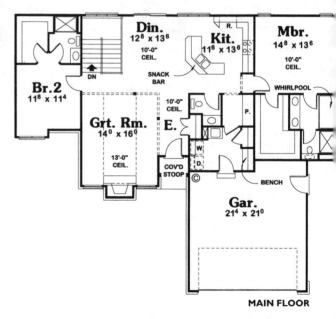

MAIN FLOOR

Design 20089

Units	Single
Price Code	B
Total Finished	1,588 sq. ft.
Main Finished	1,588 sq. ft.
Basement Unfinished	780 sq. ft.
Garage Unfinished	808 sq. ft.
Dimensions	52'x38'
Foundation	Basement
Bedrooms	3
Full Baths	2
Max Ridge Height	27'
Roof Framing	Stick
Exterior Walls	2x6

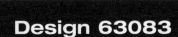

DECK

LIVING ROOM
15'-0" x 19'-4"

DINING RM.
10'-0" x 11'-0"

MASTER BEDROOM
13'-4" x 14'-0"

HALF WALL

C.

B.

B.

KITCH.
11'-0" x 11'-4"

LEDGE

SLOPE

HALL

RAILING

C.

FOYER

DN

REF.

P.

C.

W. D.

LAUNDRY

BEDROOM
11'-4" x 11'-4"

PORCH

BEDROOM
11'-4" x 11'-8"

DN

MAIN FLOOR

Design 63083

Units	Single
Price Code	B
Total Finished	1,589 sq. ft.
Main Finished	1,589 sq. ft.
Garage Unfinished	480 sq. ft.
Dimensions	43'x59'
Foundation	Slab
Bedrooms	3
Full Baths	2
Main Ceiling	11'
Vaulted Ceiling	13'
Max Ridge Height	19'
Roof Framing	Truss

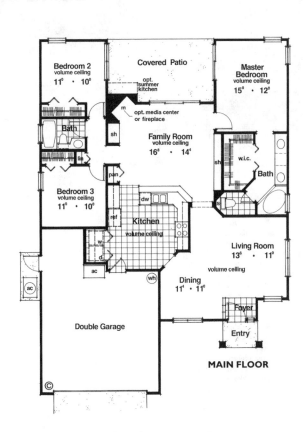

Covered Patio

Bedroom 2
volume ceiling
11⁰ · 10⁰

Master Bedroom
volume ceiling
15⁰ · 12⁰

opt. summer kitchen

opt. media center or fireplace

Bath

Family Room
volume ceiling
16⁸ · 14⁴

w.i.c.

Bath

Bedroom 3
volume ceiling
11⁰ · 10⁰

Kitchen
volume ceiling

ref

dw

pan

Living Room
13⁶ · 11⁰

volume ceiling

Dining
11⁴ · 11⁰

ac

wh

Foyer

Double Garage

Entry

MAIN FLOOR

Units	Single
Price Code	B
Total Finished	1,591 sq. ft.
Main Finished	1,591 sq. ft.
Garage Unfinished	480 sq. ft.
Deck Unfinished	280 sq. ft.
Dimensions	46'x64'
Foundation	Basement
	Crawlspace
	Slab
Bedrooms	3
Full Baths	2
Main Ceiling	9'
Max Ridge Height	20'
Roof Framing	Stick
Exterior Walls	2x4

Master Bdrm. 15-0 x 13-6 *Tray*
M. Bath
Patio / Deck 14-0 x 12-0
Bdrm.3 10-2 x 11-4
Bdrm.2 10-2 x 11-6
Lnd. W. D.
Bth.2
Living 13-2 x 17-8 *11' Ceiling*
Brkfst. 10-2 x 9-8
Kit. 10-2 x 13-8 *Ref.*
Foyer 6-0 x 9-8 *11' Ceiling*
Dining 11-4 x 13-8 *11' Ceiling*
Optional Basement Stairs Storage On Slab/Crawl Version
Double Garage 19-4 x 23-8

MAIN FLOOR

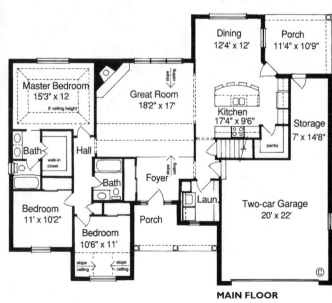

Units	Single
Price Code	B
Total Finished	1,593 sq. ft.
Main Finished	1,593 sq. ft.
Basement Unfinished	1,593 sq. ft.
Garage Unfinished	550 sq. ft.
Porch Unfinished	104 sq. ft.
Dimensions	60'x48'10"
Foundation	Basement
Bedrooms	3
Full Baths	2
Main Ceiling	8'
Vaulted Ceiling	11'6"
Tray Ceiling	9'
Max Ridge Height	21'6"
Roof Framing	Truss
Exterior Walls	2x4

Master Bedroom 15'3" x 12 *9' ceiling height*
Bath
Hall
walk-in closet
Great Room 18'2" x 17'
Dining 12'4" x 12'
Porch 11'4" x 10'9"
Kitchen 17'4" x 9'6' *pantry*
Storage 7' x 14'8"
Bath
Foyer
Bedroom 11' x 10'2"
Bedroom 10'6" x 11' *slope ceiling* *slope ceiling*
Laun.
Porch
Two-car Garage 20' x 22'

MAIN FLOOR

Design 93419

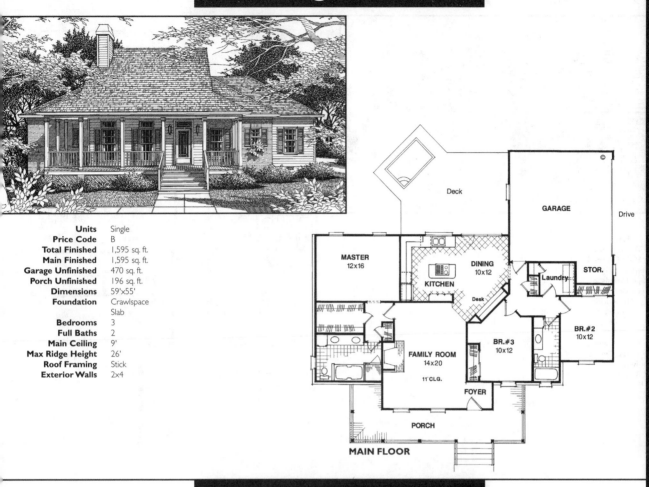

Units	Single
Price Code	B
Total Finished	1,595 sq. ft.
Main Finished	1,595 sq. ft.
Garage Unfinished	470 sq. ft.
Porch Unfinished	196 sq. ft.
Dimensions	59'x55'
Foundation	Crawlspace
	Slab
Bedrooms	3
Full Baths	2
Main Ceiling	9'
Max Ridge Height	26'
Roof Framing	Stick
Exterior Walls	2x4

Design 97489

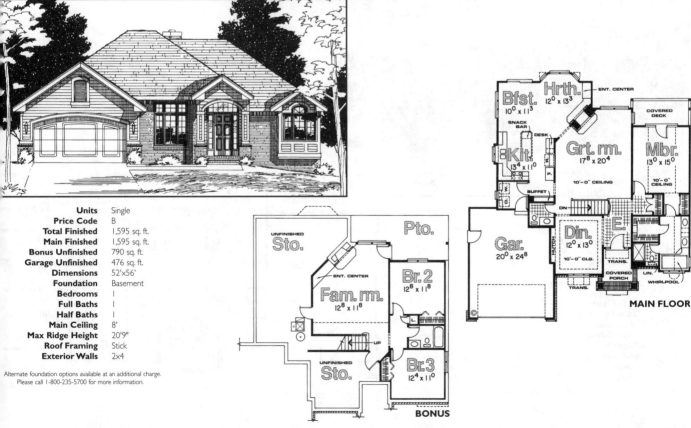

Units	Single
Price Code	B
Total Finished	1,595 sq. ft.
Main Finished	1,595 sq. ft.
Bonus Unfinished	790 sq. ft.
Garage Unfinished	476 sq. ft.
Dimensions	52'x56'
Foundation	Basement
Bedrooms	1
Full Baths	1
Half Baths	1
Main Ceiling	8'
Max Ridge Height	20'9"
Roof Framing	Stick
Exterior Walls	2x4

Alternate foundation options available at an additional charge.
Please call 1-800-235-5700 for more information.

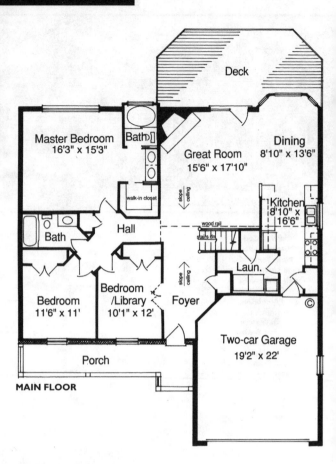

Units	Single
Price Code	B
Total Finished	1,595 sq. ft.
Main Finished	1,595 sq. ft.
Basement Unfinished	1,589 sq. ft.
Garage Unfinished	409 sq. ft.
Deck Unfinished	279 sq. ft.
Dimensions	48'x51'4"
Foundation	Basement
Bedrooms	3
Full Baths	2
Main Ceiling	8'
Vaulted Ceiling	14'
Max Ridge Height	24'6"
Roof Framing	Truss
Exterior Walls	2x4

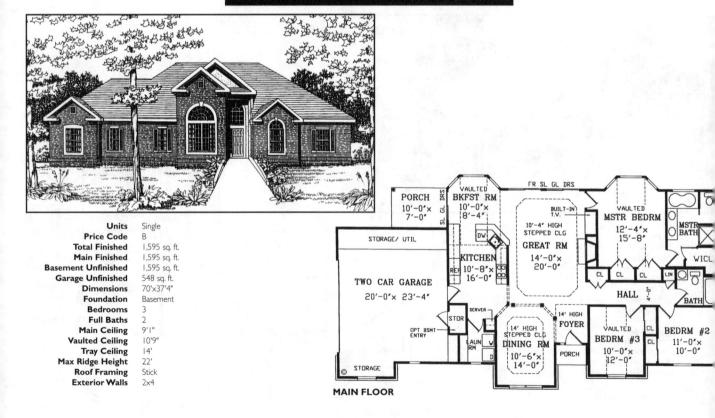

Units	Single
Price Code	B
Total Finished	1,595 sq. ft.
Main Finished	1,595 sq. ft.
Basement Unfinished	1,595 sq. ft.
Garage Unfinished	548 sq. ft.
Dimensions	70'x37'4"
Foundation	Basement
Bedrooms	3
Full Baths	2
Main Ceiling	9'1"
Vaulted Ceiling	10'9"
Tray Ceiling	14'
Max Ridge Height	22'
Roof Framing	Stick
Exterior Walls	2x4

Design 50007

1,501-2,000 sq. ft. HOME PLANS

Units	Single
Price Code	B
Total Finished	1,598 sq. ft.
Main Finished	1,598 sq. ft.
Basement Unfinished	1,598 sq. ft.
Garage Unfinished	478 sq. ft.
Porch Unfinished	161 sq. ft.
Dimensions	59'4"x45'6"
Foundation	Basement
Bedrooms	3
Full Baths	1
3/4 Baths	1
Main Ceiling	8'
Max Ridge Height	18'8"
Roof Framing	Truss
Exterior Walls	2x4

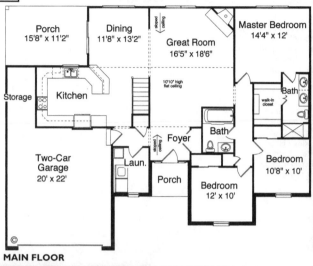

MAIN FLOOR

Design 99163

Units	Single
Price Code	B
Total Finished	1,600 sq. ft.
Main Finished	1,600 sq. ft.
Basement Unfinished	1,600 sq. ft.
Garage Unfinished	406 sq. ft.
Deck Unfinished	118 sq. ft.
Dimensions	54'8"x45'
Foundation	Basement
Bedrooms	3
Full Baths	2
Max Ridge Height	25'
Roof Framing	Truss
Exterior Walls	2x4

MAIN FLOOR

Design 62058

Units	Single
Price Code	C
Total Finished	1,601 sq. ft.
Main Finished	1,601 sq. ft.
Garage Unfinished	771 sq. ft.
Porch Unfinished	279 sq. ft.
Dimensions	39'x77'2"
Foundation	Crawlspace
	Slab
Bedrooms	3
Full Baths	2
Main Ceiling	9'
Max Ridge Height	22'
Roof Framing	Stick
Exterior Walls	2x4

MAIN FLOOR

Design 91115

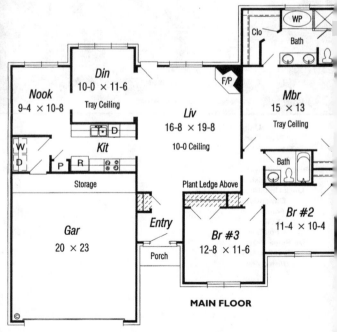

Units	Single
Price Code	B
Total Finished	1,611 sq. ft.
Main Finished	1,611 sq. ft.
Garage Unfinished	501 sq. ft.
Dimensions	53'10"x50'4"
Foundation	Slab
Bedrooms	3
Full Baths	2
Max Ridge Height	21'
Roof Framing	Stick
Exterior Walls	2x4

MAIN FLOOR

Design 97759

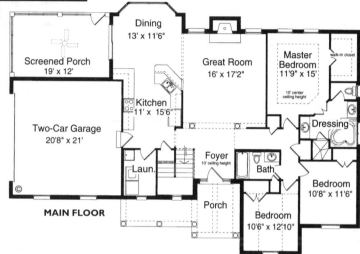

Units	Single
Price Code	B
Total Finished	1,611 sq. ft.
Main Finished	1,611 sq. ft.
Basement Unfinished	1,611 sq. ft.
Garage Unfinished	430 sq. ft.
Deck Unfinished	228 sq. ft.
Porch Unfinished	163 sq. ft.
Dimensions	67'x44'4"
Foundation	Basement
Bedrooms	3
Full Baths	2
Main Ceiling	8'
Vaulted Ceiling	10'
Tray Ceiling	10'
Max Ridge Height	22'6"
Roof Framing	Truss
Exterior Walls	2x4

MAIN FLOOR

Screened Porch 19' x 12'

Two-Car Garage 20'8" x 21'

Laun.

Kitchen 11' x 15'6"

Dining 13' x 11'6"

Great Room 16' x 17'2"

Master Bedroom 11'9" x 15'
walk-in closet
10' center ceiling height

Dressing

Foyer
10' ceiling height

Bath

Porch

Bedroom 10'6" x 12'10"

Bedroom 10'8" x 11'6"

Design 97495

Units	Single
Price Code	B
Total Finished	1,622 sq. ft.
Main Finished	1,622 sq. ft.
Garage Unfinished	469 sq. ft.
Dimensions	51'x52'
Foundation	Basement
Bedrooms	3
Full Baths	2
Main Ceiling	8'
Max Ridge Height	20'6"
Roof Framing	Stick
Exterior Walls	2x4

* Alternate foundation options available at an additional charge. Please call 1-800-235-5700 for more information.

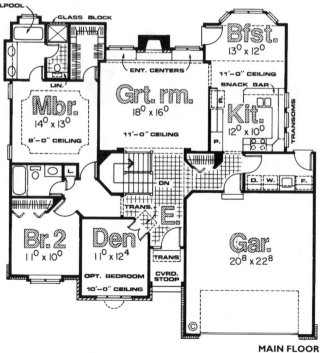

WHIRLPOOL

GLASS BLOCK

Bfst. 13⁰ x 12⁰
11'-0" CEILING

ENT. CENTERS

Grt. rm. 18⁰ x 16⁰
11'-0" CEILING

SNACK BAR

Kit. 12⁰ x 10⁰

TRANSOMS

Mbr. 14⁰ x 13⁰
8'-0" CEILING

LIN.

Br. 2 11⁰ x 10⁰

Den 11⁰ x 12⁴
OPT. BEDROOM 10'-0" CEILING

Gar. 20⁸ x 22⁸

TRANS.

CVRD. STOOP

MAIN FLOOR

OPTIONAL Br. 3 11⁰ x 10⁰
10'-0" CEILING

THIRD BEDROOM OPTION

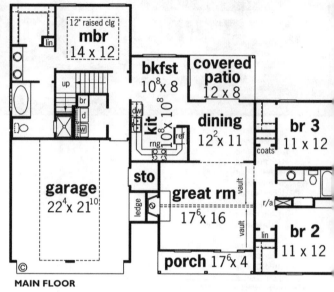

MAIN FLOOR

Units	Single
Price Code	B
Total Finished	1,624 sq. ft.
Main Finished	1,624 sq. ft.
Bonus Unfinished	142 sq. ft.
Garage Unfinished	462 sq. ft.
Dimensions	60'x48'
Foundation	Crawlspace
	Slab
Bedrooms	3
Full Baths	2
Main Ceiling	8'
Roof Framing	Stick
Exterior Walls	2x4

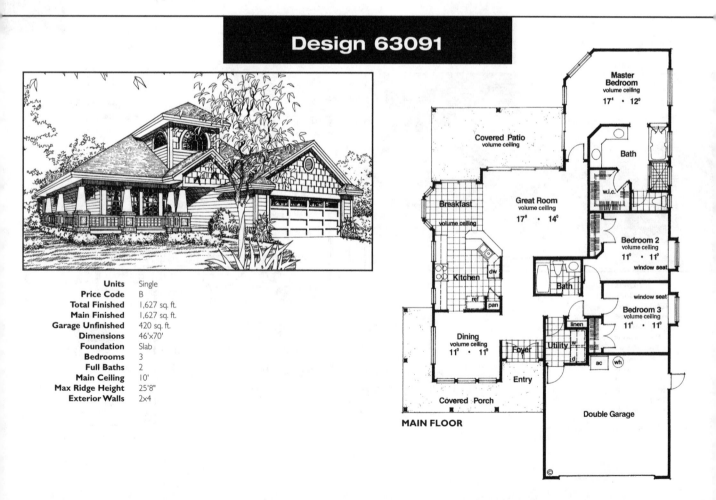

MAIN FLOOR

Units	Single
Price Code	B
Total Finished	1,627 sq. ft.
Main Finished	1,627 sq. ft.
Garage Unfinished	420 sq. ft.
Dimensions	46'x70'
Foundation	Slab
Bedrooms	3
Full Baths	2
Main Ceiling	10'
Max Ridge Height	25'8"
Exterior Walls	2x4

Design 96805

MAIN FLOOR

Units	Single
Price Code	B
Total Finished	1,627 sq. ft.
Main Finished	1,627 sq. ft.
Garage Unfinished	480 sq. ft.
Dimensions	52'x53'
Foundation	Crawlspace
	Slab
Bedrooms	3
Full Baths	2
Main Ceiling	8'2"
Vaulted Ceiling	13'9"
Max Ridge Height	20'8"
Roof Framing	Truss
Exterior Walls	2x4

Design 93418

MAIN FLOOR

Units	Single
Price Code	B
Total Finished	1,631 sq. ft.
Main Finished	1,631 sq. ft.
Basement Unfinished	1,015 sq. ft.
Garage Unfinished	616 sq. ft.
Porch Unfinished	115 sq. ft.
Dimensions	48'x44'
Foundation	Basement
Bedrooms	3
Full Baths	2
Max Ridge Height	26'
Roof Framing	Stick
Exterior Walls	2x4

Units	Single
Price Code	B
Total Finished	1,633 sq. ft.
Main Finished	1,633 sq. ft.
Basement Unfinished	1,633 sq. ft.
Dimensions	53'x52'
Foundation	Basement
Bedrooms	3
Full Baths	2
Max Ridge Height	20'
Roof Framing	Truss
Exterior Walls	2x6

MAIN FLOOR

MBR.
CATHEDRAL CEILING
12'8" X 15'8"

GRT. RM.
10'-1 1/8" CEILING
14'8" X 18'6"

NK.
10'6" X 10'0"

BR. #3
13'4" X 12'0"

KIT.
10'6" X 10'0"

BR. #2
10'0" X 11'4"

E.
10'-1 1/8"
CEILING

DIN.
11'0" X 11'4"

2 CAR GAR.
20'4" X 22'0"

DOWN

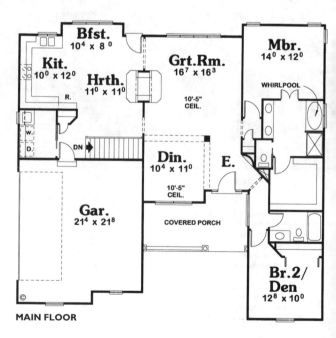

Units	Single
Price Code	B
Total Finished	1,636 sq. ft.
Main Finished	1,636 sq. ft.
Basement Unfinished	1,636 sq. ft.
Garage Unfinished	508 sq. ft.
Deck Unfinished	158 sq. ft.
Dimensions	53'4"x49'4"
Foundation	Basement
	Crawlspace
	Slab
Bedrooms	2
Full Baths	2
Main Ceiling	9'
Max Ridge Height	24'3"
Roof Framing	Stick
Exterior Walls	2x4

* Alternate foundation options available at an additional charge.
Please call 1-800-235-5700 for more information.

MAIN FLOOR

Bfst.
10⁴ x 8⁰

Kit.
10⁰ x 12⁰

Hrth.
11⁰ x 11⁰

Grt. Rm.
16⁷ x 16³
10'-5" CEIL.

Mbr.
14⁰ x 12⁰

WHIRLPOOL

Gar.
21⁴ x 21⁸

Din.
10⁴ x 11⁰
10'-5" CEIL.

E.

COVERED PORCH

Br. 2/
Den
12⁸ x 10⁰

DN

Design 97455

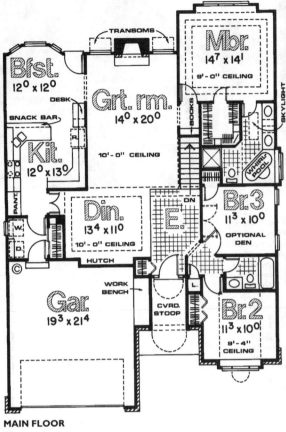

Units	Single
Price Code	B
Total Finished	1,636 sq. ft.
Main Finished	1,636 sq. ft.
Garage Unfinished	448 sq. ft.
Dimensions	42'x59'8"
Foundation	Basement
Bedrooms	3
Full Baths	2
Main Ceiling	8'
Max Ridge Height	21'
Roof Framing	Stick
Exterior Walls	2x4, 2x6

* Alternate foundation options available at an additional charge.
Please call 1-800-235-5700 for more information.

MAIN FLOOR

Plan labels: Bfst. 12⁰ x 12⁰; Grt. rm. 14⁰ x 20⁰ 10'-0" CEILING; TRANSOMS; DESK; SNACK BAR; Kit. 12⁰ x 13⁰; Din. 13⁴ x 11⁰ 10'-0" CEILING; HUTCH; PANT; W; D; Gar. 19³ x 21⁴; WORK BENCH; CVRD. STOOP; Mbr. 14⁷ x 14¹ 9'-0" CEILING; SKYLIGHT; WHIRL POOL; BOOKS; Br. 3 11³ x 10⁰ OPTIONAL DEN; DN; Br. 2 11³ x 10⁰ 9'-4" CEILING

Design 92242

Units	Single
Price Code	B
Total Finished	1,639 sq. ft.
Main Finished	1,639 sq. ft.
Garage Unfinished	442 sq. ft.
Deck Unfinished	145 sq. ft.
Porch Unfinished	52 sq. ft.
Dimensions	49'10"x57'1"
Foundation	Slab
Bedrooms	3
Full Baths	2
Main Ceiling	8'
Second Ceiling	10'
Vaulted Ceiling	10'
Max Ridge Height	24'6"
Roof Framing	Stick
Exterior Walls	2x4

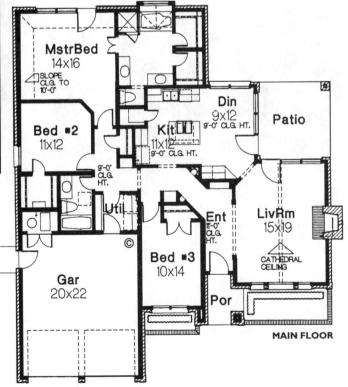

MAIN FLOOR

Plan labels: MstrBed 14x16 SLOPE CLG. TO 10'-0"; Bed #2 11x12 9'-0" CLG. HT.; Util; Kit 11x12 9'-0" CLG. HT.; Din 9x12 9'-0" CLG. HT.; Patio; Ent 11'-0" CLG. HT.; LivRm 15x19 CATHEDRAL CEILING; Bed #3 10x14; Gar 20x22; Por

Design 24717

OPTIONAL BASEMENT STAIR LOCATION

Units	Single
Price Code	B
Total Finished	1,642 sq. ft.
Main Finished	1,642 sq. ft.
Basement Unfinished	1,642 sq. ft.
Garage Unfinished	430 sq. ft.
Porch Unfinished	156 sq. ft.
Dimensions	59'x44'
Foundation	Basement
	Crawlspace
	Slab
Bedrooms	3
Full Baths	2
Main Ceiling	9'
Vaulted Ceiling	13'6"
Max Ridge Height	24'
Roof Framing	Stick
Exterior Walls	2x4

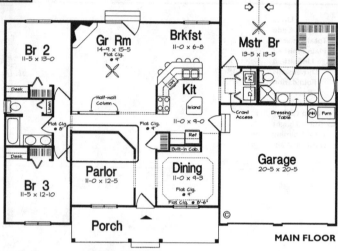

MAIN FLOOR

Design 96507

Units	Single
Price Code	B
Total Finished	1,647 sq. ft.
Main Finished	1,647 sq. ft.
Garage Unfinished	528 sq. ft.
Porch Unfinished	187 sq. ft.
Dimensions	51'x70'
Foundation	Crawlspace
	Slab
Bedrooms	3
Full Baths	2
Main Ceiling	9'
Max Ridge Height	23'
Roof Framing	Stick
Exterior Walls	2x4

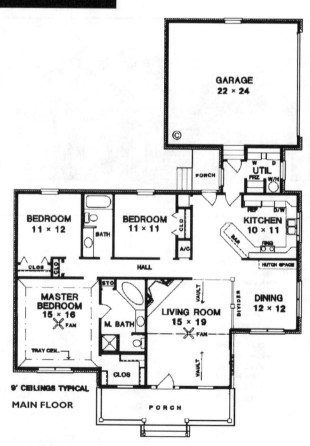

9' CEILINGS TYPICAL

MAIN FLOOR

Design 96513

Units	Single
Price Code	B
Total Finished	1,648 sq. ft.
Main Finished	1,648 sq. ft.
Garage Unfinished	479 sq. ft.
Dimensions	68'x50'
Foundation	Crawlspace
	Slab
Bedrooms	3
Full Baths	2
Half Baths	1
Main Ceiling	9'
Max Ridge Height	20'
Roof Framing	Stick
Exterior Walls	2x4

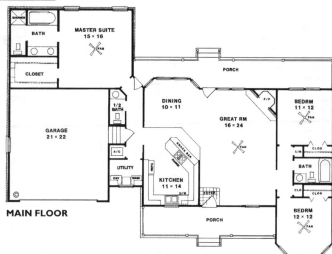

MAIN FLOOR

Design 94651

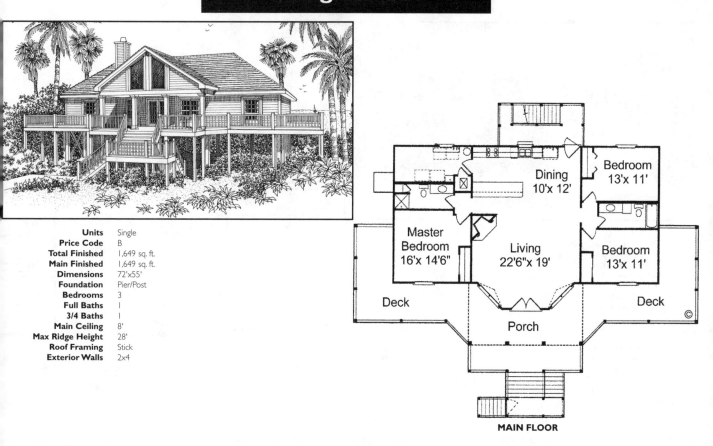

Units	Single
Price Code	B
Total Finished	1,649 sq. ft.
Main Finished	1,649 sq. ft.
Dimensions	72'x55'
Foundation	Pier/Post
Bedrooms	3
Full Baths	1
3/4 Baths	1
Main Ceiling	8'
Max Ridge Height	28'
Roof Framing	Stick
Exterior Walls	2x4

MAIN FLOOR

Design 94921

Units	Single
Price Code	B
Total Finished	1,651 sq. ft.
Main Finished	1,651 sq. ft.
Basement Unfinished	1,651 sq. ft.
Garage Unfinished	480 sq. ft.
Dimensions	62'x56'
Foundation	Basement
Bedrooms	2
Full Baths	2
Max Ridge Height	24'
Roof Framing	Stick
Exterior Walls	2x4

* Alternate foundation options available at an additional charge.
Please call 1-800-235-5700 for more information.

THIRD BEDROOM OPTION

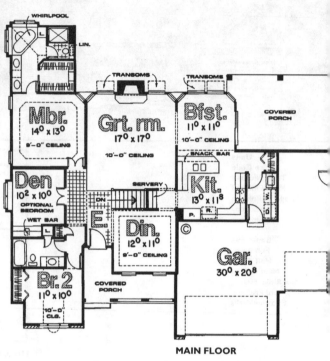

MAIN FLOOR

Design 96506

Units	Single
Price Code	B
Total Finished	1,654 sq. ft.
Main Finished	1,654 sq. ft.
Garage Unfinished	480 sq. ft.
Porch Unfinished	401 sq. ft.
Dimensions	68'x46'
Foundation	Crawlspace
	Slab
Bedrooms	3
Full Baths	2
Half Baths	1
Main Ceiling	9'
Max Ridge Height	21'
Roof Framing	Stick
Exterior Walls	2x4

MAIN FLOOR

Design 67007

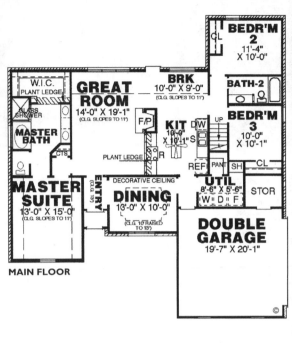

MAIN FLOOR

Units	Single
Price Code	B
Total Finished	1,670 sq. ft.
Main Finished	1,670 sq. ft.
Bonus Unfinished	350 sq. ft.
Garage Unfinished	474 sq. ft.
Porch Unfinished	10 sq. ft.
Dimensions	53'x55'9"
Foundation	Slab
Bedrooms	3
Full Baths	2
Main Ceiling	8'
Vaulted Ceiling	11'
Tray Ceiling	13'
Max Ridge Height	24'9"
Roof Framing	Truss

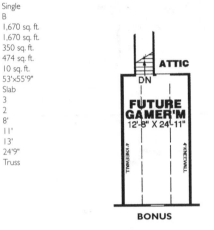

BONUS

Design 98423

Units	Single
Price Code	B
Total Finished	1,671 sq. ft.
Main Finished	1,671 sq. ft.
Basement Unfinished	1,685 sq. ft.
Garage Unfinished	400 sq. ft.
Dimensions	50'x51'
Foundation	Basement
	Crawlspace
	Slab
Bedrooms	3
Full Baths	2
Main Ceiling	9'
Max Ridge Height	22'6"
Roof Framing	Stick
Exterior Walls	2x4

CAD FILES AVAILABLE For more information call 800-235-5700

MAIN FLOOR

Design 90486

Units	Single
Price Code	B
Total Finished	1,672 sq. ft.
Main Finished	1,672 sq. ft.
Garage Unfinished	650 sq. ft.
Porch Unfinished	320 sq. ft.
Dimensions	52'10"x66'9"
Foundation	Crawlspace
	Slab
Bedrooms	3
Full Baths	2
Max Ridge Height	22'10"
Roof Framing	Stick
Exterior Walls	2x4

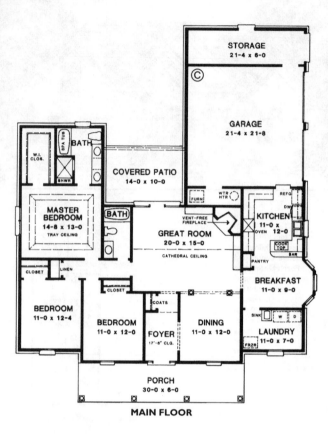

STORAGE 21-4 x 6-0

GARAGE 21-4 x 21-8

BATH

W.I. CLOS. SPA TUB SHWR

COVERED PATIO 14-0 x 10-0

FURN WTR HTR

REFG DW

KITCHEN 11-0 x OVEN 12-0

COOK TOP BAR

MASTER BEDROOM 14-8 x 13-0 TRAY CEILING

BATH

VENT-FREE FIREPLACE

GREAT ROOM 20-0 x 15-0 CATHEDRAL CEILING

PANTRY

BREAKFAST 11-0 x 9-0

CLOSET LINEN

CLOSET

COATS

SINK W D

BEDROOM 11-0 x 12-4

BEDROOM 11-0 x 12-0

FOYER 17'-8" CLG.

DINING 11-0 x 12-0

LAUNDRY 11-0 x 7-0

FRZR

PORCH 30-0 x 6-0

MAIN FLOOR

Design 97263

Units	Single
Price Code	B
Total Finished	1,674 sq. ft.
Main Finished	1,674 sq. ft.
Basement Unfinished	1,703 sq. ft.
Garage Unfinished	410 sq. ft.
Dimensions	45'6"x58'
Foundation	Basement
	Crawlspace
Bedrooms	3
Full Baths	2
Max Ridge Height	25'
Roof Framing	Stick
Exterior Walls	2x4

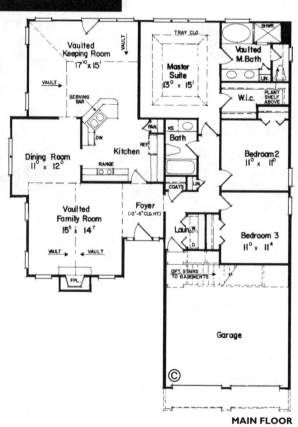

Vaulted Keeping Room 17¹⁰ x 15'

VAULT TRAY CLG. SHWR

Vaulted M.Bath

Master Suite 13⁰ x 15'

VAULT

SERVING BAR

W.i.c.

PLANT SHELF ABOVE

Dining Room 11⁰ x 12⁰

DW

Kitchen

RAN KS REF

Bath

Bedroom 2 11⁰ x 11⁰

RANGE

COATS LIN

LIN

Vaulted Family Room 15⁵ x 14⁷

Foyer (12'-6" CLG. HT)

Laun. W D

VAULT VAULT

FPL

OPT. STAIRS TO BASEMENT

Bedroom 3 11⁰ x 11⁴

Garage

MAIN FLOOR

Design 98960

MAIN FLOOR

Units	Single
Price Code	B
Total Finished	1,676 sq. ft.
Main Finished	1,676 sq. ft.
Garage Unfinished	552 sq. ft.
Deck Unfinished	192 sq. ft.
Porch Unfinished	89 sq. ft.
Dimensions	56'x62'
Foundation	Basement
Bedrooms	3
Full Baths	2
Main Ceiling	9'
Max Ridge Height	23'
Roof Framing	Stick
Exterior Walls	2x4

Design 98968

MAIN FLOOR

Units	Single
Price Code	B
Total Finished	1,676 sq. ft.
Main Finished	1,676 sq. ft.
Garage Unfinished	522 sq. ft.
Deck Unfinished	192 sq. ft.
Porch Unfinished	89 sq. ft.
Dimensions	56'x62'
Foundation	Crawlspace / Slab
Bedrooms	3
Full Baths	2
Main Ceiling	9'
Max Ridge Height	23'
Roof Framing	Stick
Exterior Walls	2x4

Design 99191

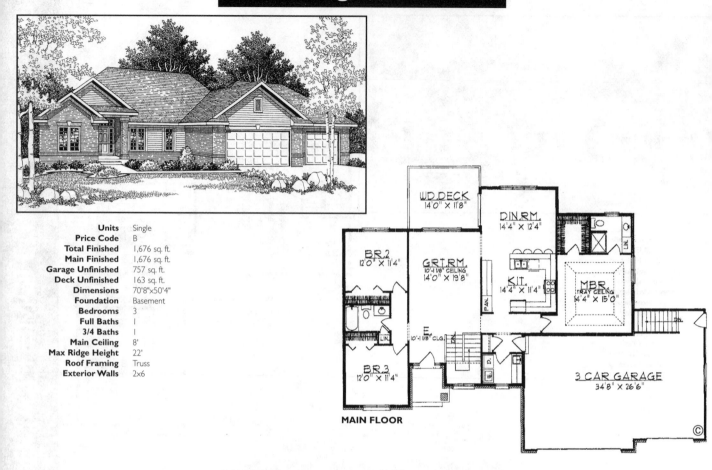

Units	Single
Price Code	B
Total Finished	1,676 sq. ft.
Main Finished	1,676 sq. ft.
Garage Unfinished	757 sq. ft.
Deck Unfinished	163 sq. ft.
Dimensions	70'8"×50'4"
Foundation	Basement
Bedrooms	3
Full Baths	1
3/4 Baths	1
Main Ceiling	8'
Max Ridge Height	22'
Roof Framing	Truss
Exterior Walls	2x6

WD. DECK 14'0" X 11'8"

DIN.RM. 14'4" X 12'4"

BR.2 12'0" X 11'4"

GR.RM. 10'4 1/8" CEILING 14'0" X 19'8"

KIT. 14'4" X 11'4"

MBR TRAY CEILING 14'4" X 15'0"

BR.3 12'0" X 11'4"

3 CAR GARAGE 34'8" X 26'6"

MAIN FLOOR

Design 92563

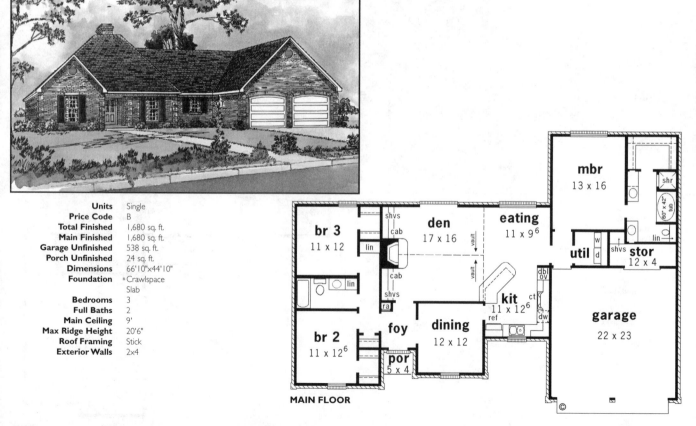

Units	Single
Price Code	B
Total Finished	1,680 sq. ft.
Main Finished	1,680 sq. ft.
Garage Unfinished	538 sq. ft.
Porch Unfinished	24 sq. ft.
Dimensions	66'10"×44'10"
Foundation	*Crawlspace
	Slab
Bedrooms	3
Full Baths	2
Main Ceiling	9'
Max Ridge Height	20'6"
Roof Framing	Stick
Exterior Walls	2x4

mbr 13 x 16

br 3 11 x 12

den 17 x 16

eating 11 x 9⁶

util

stor 12 x 4

kit 11 x 12⁶

br 2 11 x 12⁶

foy

dining 12 x 12

garage 22 x 23

por 5 x 4

MAIN FLOOR

Design 34029

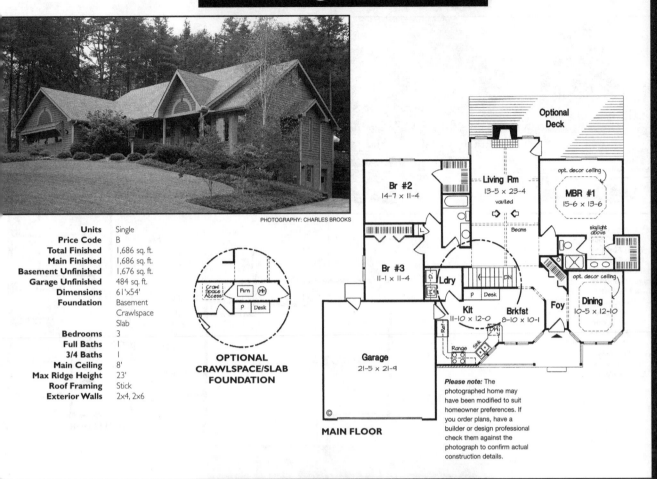

PHOTOGRAPHY: CHARLES BROOKS

Units	Single
Price Code	B
Total Finished	1,686 sq. ft.
Main Finished	1,686 sq. ft.
Basement Unfinished	1,676 sq. ft.
Garage Unfinished	484 sq. ft.
Dimensions	61'x54'
Foundation	Basement
	Crawlspace
	Slab
Bedrooms	3
Full Baths	1
3/4 Baths	1
Main Ceiling	8'
Max Ridge Height	23'
Roof Framing	Stick
Exterior Walls	2x4, 2x6

OPTIONAL CRAWLSPACE/SLAB FOUNDATION

Crawl Space Access — Furn — HH — P — Desk

Optional Deck

Living Rm 13-5 x 23-4 vaulted

opt. decor ceiling

MBR #1 15-6 x 13-6

skylight above

Br #2 14-7 x 11-4

Beams

opt. decor ceiling

Br #3 11-1 x 11-4

Ldry

Dining 10-5 x 12-10

Foy

Kit 11-10 x 12-0

Brkfst 8-10 x 10-1

Garage 21-5 x 21-4

MAIN FLOOR

Please note: The photographed home may have been modified to suit homeowner preferences. If you order plans, have a builder or design professional check them against the photograph to confirm actual construction details.

Design 97617

FILES AVAILABLE For more information call 800-235-5700

Units	Single
Price Code	B
Total Finished	1,688 sq. ft.
Main Finished	1,688 sq. ft.
Basement Unfinished	1,702 sq. ft.
Garage Unfinished	402 sq. ft.
Dimensions	50'x51'
Foundation	Basement
	Crawlspace
	Slab
Bedrooms	4
Full Baths	2
Max Ridge Height	24'6"
Roof Framing	Stick
Exterior Walls	2x4

Dining Room 11⁰x11⁰

TRAY CLG.

Master Suite 13⁰x16⁰

Vaulted M.Bath

W.i.c.

SERVING BAR

Vaulted Family Room 16³x17⁶

Kitchen

Bath

Bedroom 4 10⁴x10⁰

PLANT SHELF ABOVE

Breakfast

Laund.

Vaulted Foyer

Bedroom 3 10⁴x11¹⁰

OPT. STAIRS TO BASEMENT

Vaulted Bedroom 2 11⁰x11³

W.i.c.

WINDOW SEAT

Garage

MAIN FLOOR

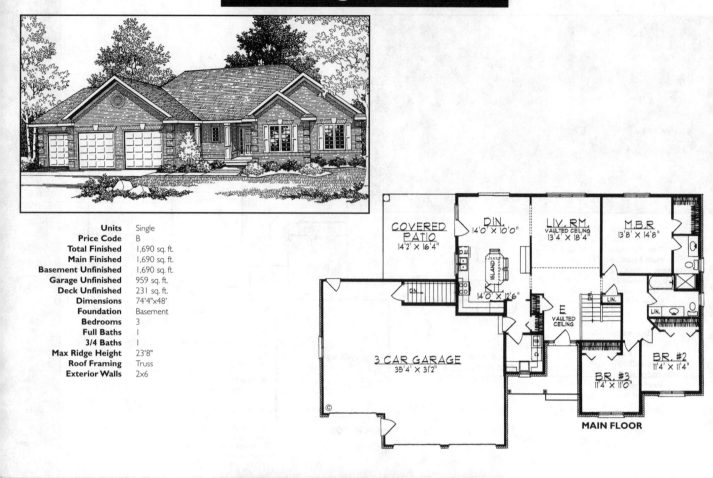

Units	Single
Price Code	B
Total Finished	1,690 sq. ft.
Main Finished	1,690 sq. ft.
Basement Unfinished	1,690 sq. ft.
Garage Unfinished	959 sq. ft.
Deck Unfinished	231 sq. ft.
Dimensions	74'4"x48'
Foundation	Basement
Bedrooms	3
Full Baths	1
3/4 Baths	1
Max Ridge Height	23'8"
Roof Framing	Truss
Exterior Walls	2x6

COVERED PATIO 14'2" X 16'4"

DIN. 14'0" X 10'0"

LIV. RM. VAULTED CEILING 13'4" X 18'4"

M.B.R 13'8" X 14'8"

ISLAND

14'0" X 12'6"

VAULTED CEILING

3 CAR GARAGE 35'4' X 31'2"

BR. #3 11'4" X 11'0"

BR. #2 11'4" X 11'4"

MAIN FLOOR

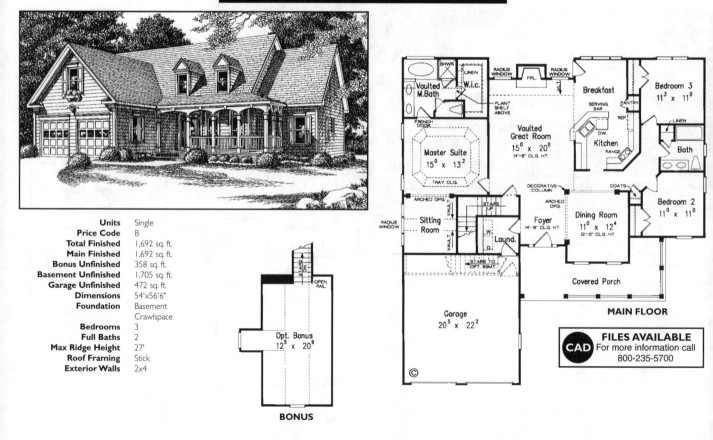

Units	Single
Price Code	B
Total Finished	1,692 sq. ft.
Main Finished	1,692 sq. ft.
Bonus Unfinished	358 sq. ft.
Basement Unfinished	1,705 sq. ft.
Garage Unfinished	472 sq. ft.
Dimensions	54'x56'6"
Foundation	Basement Crawlspace
Bedrooms	3
Full Baths	2
Max Ridge Height	27'
Roof Framing	Stick
Exterior Walls	2x4

Opt. Bonus 12⁵ x 20⁹

BONUS

Vaulted M.Bath

W.i.c.

LINEN

RADIUS WINDOW

FPL.

RADIUS WINDOW

Breakfast

Bedroom 3 11³ x 11⁰

SERVING BAR

PANTRY

REF.

LINEN

Vaulted Great Room 15⁰ x 20⁰ 14'-6" CLG. HT.

Kitchen

DW.

RANGE

Bath

Master Suite 15⁰ x 13²

TRAY CLG.

DECORATIVE COLUMN

COATS

Bedroom 2 11⁰ x 11⁰

ARCHED OPG.

STAIRS UP

ARCHED OPG.

Sitting Room

Foyer 14'-6" CLG. HT.

Dining Room 11⁰ x 12⁴ 12'-0" CLG. HT.

RADIUS WINDOW

W.

Laund.

STAIRS TO OPT. BSMT.

Covered Porch

Garage 20⁵ x 22²

MAIN FLOOR

Design 92290

MAIN FLOOR

Units	Single
Price Code	B
Total Finished	1,696 sq. ft.
Main Finished	1,696 sq. ft.
Garage Unfinished	389 sq. ft.
Deck Unfinished	200 sq. ft.
Porch Unfinished	30 sq. ft.
Dimensions	50'x62'2"
Foundation	Slab
Bedrooms	4
Full Baths	2
Max Ridge Height	22'
Roof Framing	Stick
Exterior Walls	2x4

Design 94925

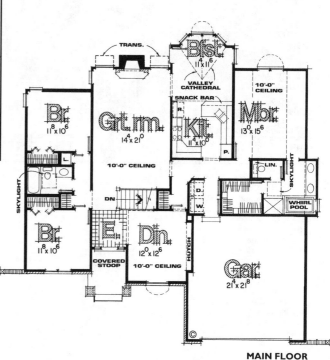

MAIN FLOOR

Units	Single
Price Code	B
Total Finished	1,697 sq. ft.
Main Finished	1,697 sq. ft.
Basement Unfinished	1,697 sq. ft.
Garage Unfinished	470 sq. ft.
Dimensions	54'x54'
Foundation	Basement
Bedrooms	3
Full Baths	2
Main Ceiling	8'-10'
Max Ridge Height	20'4"
Roof Framing	Stick
Exterior Walls	2x4

* Alternate foundation options available at an additional charge.
Please call 1-800-235-5700 for more information.

Design 94922

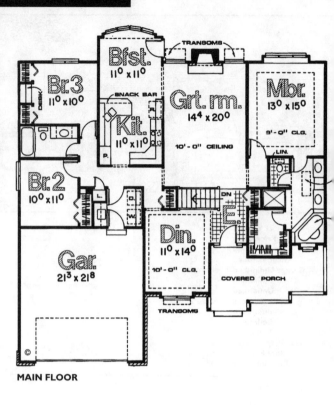

Units	Single
Price Code	B
Total Finished	1,710 sq. ft.
Main Finished	1,710 sq. ft.
Basement Unfinished	1,710 sq. ft.
Garage Unfinished	480 sq. ft.
Dimensions	53'4"x54'10"
Foundation	Basement
Bedrooms	3
Full Baths	2
Max Ridge Height	20'3"
Roof Framing	Stick
Exterior Walls	2x4

* Alternate foundation options available at an additional charge.
Please call 1-800-235-5700 for more information.

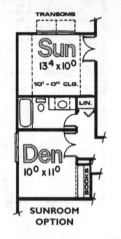

SUNROOM OPTION

MAIN FLOOR

Design 68080

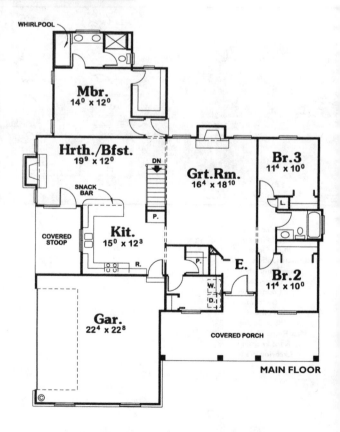

Units	Single
Price Code	B
Total Finished	1,712 sq. ft.
Main Finished	1,712 sq. ft.
Garage Unfinished	536 sq. ft.
Deck Unfinished	271 sq. ft.
Dimensions	52'x66'8"
Foundation	Basement
	Crawlspace
	Slab
Bedrooms	3
Full Baths	2
Main Ceiling	9'
Max Ridge Height	24'11"
Roof Framing	Stick
Exterior Walls	2x4

* Alternate foundation options available at an additional charge.
Please call 1-800-235-5700 for more information.

MAIN FLOOR

Design 98456

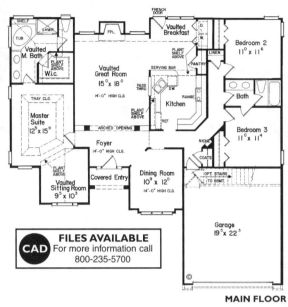

Units	Single
Price Code	B
Total Finished	1,715 sq. ft.
Main Finished	1,715 sq. ft.
Basement Unfinished	1,715 sq. ft.
Garage Unfinished	450 sq. ft.
Dimensions	55'x51'6"
Foundation	Basement
	Crawlspace
	Slab
Bedrooms	3
Full Baths	2
Main Ceiling	9'1"
Max Ridge Height	25'
Roof Framing	Stick
Exterior Walls	2x4

CAD FILES AVAILABLE For more information call 800-235-5700

MAIN FLOOR

Design 98981

Units	Single
Price Code	B
Total Finished	1,716 sq. ft.
Main Finished	1,716 sq. ft.
Dimensions	56'x55'
Foundation	Crawlspace
	Slab
Bedrooms	4
Full Baths	2
Main Ceiling	8'
Max Ridge Height	20'
Roof Framing	Stick
Exterior Walls	2x4

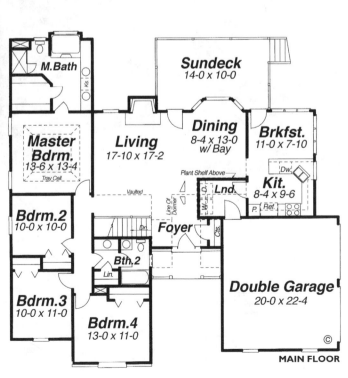

MAIN FLOOR

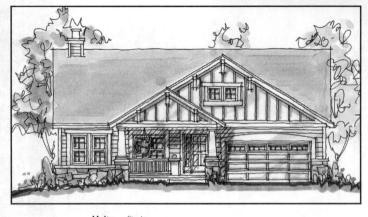

Units	Single
Price Code	B
Total Finished	1,724 sq. ft.
Main Finished	1,724 sq. ft.
Garage Unfinished	460 sq. ft.
Dimensions	50'x50'
Foundation	Basement
Bedrooms	3
Full Baths	2
Main Ceiling	9'
Max Ridge Height	24'4"
Roof Framing	Stick
Exterior Walls	2x4

* Alternate foundation options available at an additional charge.
Please call 1-800-235-5700 for more information.

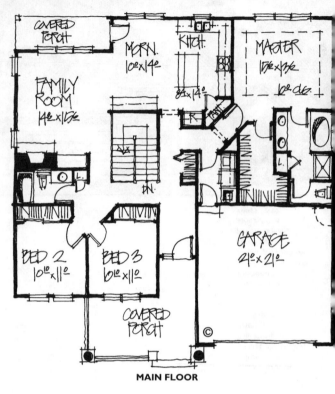

MAIN FLOOR

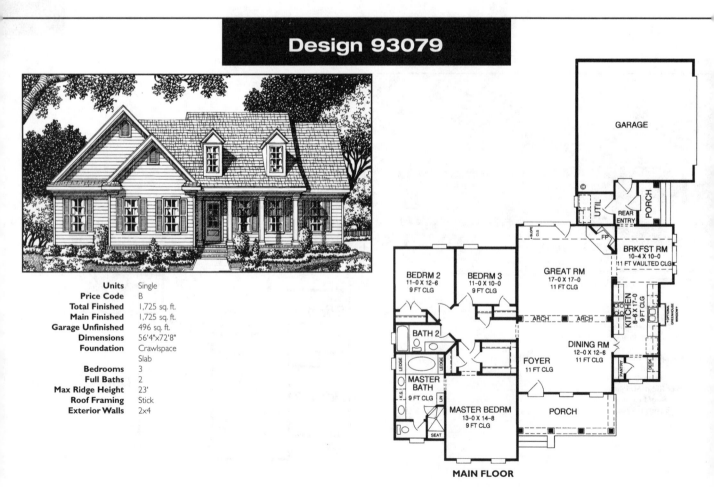

Units	Single
Price Code	B
Total Finished	1,725 sq. ft.
Main Finished	1,725 sq. ft.
Garage Unfinished	496 sq. ft.
Dimensions	56'4"x72'8"
Foundation	Crawlspace
	Slab
Bedrooms	3
Full Baths	2
Max Ridge Height	23'
Roof Framing	Stick
Exterior Walls	2x4

MAIN FLOOR

Design 99923

Units	Single
Price Code	B
Total Finished	1,734 sq. ft.
Main Finished	1,734 sq. ft.
Basement Unfinished	1,842 sq. ft.
Garage Unfinished	528 sq. ft.
Deck Unfinished	252 sq. ft.
Porch Unfinished	132 sq. ft.
Dimensions	66'x48'
Foundation	Basement
Bedrooms	3
Full Baths	2
Half Baths	1
Main Ceiling	8'
Vaulted Ceiling	10'
Max Ridge Height	22'
Roof Framing	Truss
Exterior Walls	2x6

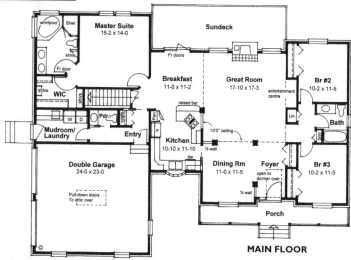

MAIN FLOOR

Design 93149

Units	Single
Price Code	B
Total Finished	1,739 sq. ft.
Main Finished	1,739 sq. ft.
Basement Unfinished	1,739 sq. ft.
Dimensions	54'x48'
Foundation	Basement
Bedrooms	3
Full Baths	2
Half Baths	1
Max Ridge Height	22'6"
Roof Framing	Stick
Exterior Walls	2x6

MAIN FLOOR

Design 93061

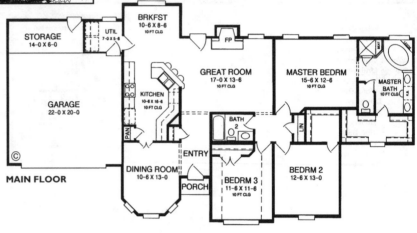

Units	Single
Price Code	B
Total Finished	1,742 sq. ft.
Main Finished	1,742 sq. ft.
Garage Unfinished	566 sq. ft.
Porch Unfinished	14 sq. ft.
Dimensions	78'10"x40'10"
Foundation	Crawlspace
	Slab
Bedrooms	3
Full Baths	2
Max Ridge Height	22'
Roof Framing	Truss
Exterior Walls	2x4

MAIN FLOOR

STORAGE 14-0 X 6-0

UTIL 7-0 X 5-6

BRKFST 10-6 X 8-6 10 FT CLG

FP

GARAGE 22-0 X 20-0

KITCHEN 10-6 X 16-6 10 FT CLG

PAN

GREAT ROOM 17-0 X 13-6 10 FT CLG

MASTER BEDRM 15-6 X 12-6 10 FT CLG

MASTER BATH 10 FT CLG

BATH 2

LIN

ENTRY

DINING ROOM 10-6 X 13-0

PORCH

BEDRM 3 11-6 X 11-6 10 FT CLG

BEDRM 2 12-6 X 13-0

Design 67006

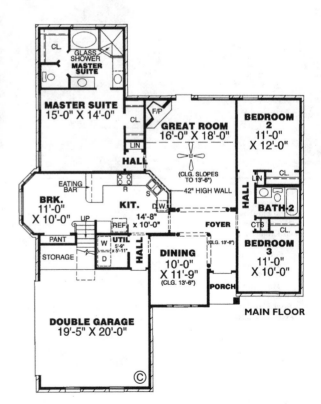

Units	Single
Price Code	B
Total Finished	1,744 sq. ft.
Main Finished	1,744 sq. ft.
Bonus Unfinished	264 sq. ft.
Garage Unfinished	487 sq. ft.
Porch Unfinished	24 sq. ft.
Dimensions	51'x63'
Foundation	Slab
Bedrooms	3
Full Baths	2
Main Ceiling	8'
Vaulted Ceiling	13'6"
Max Ridge Height	23'
Roof Framing	Stick
Exterior Walls	2x4

DN ATTIC

11'-6" X 18'-3"

4" KNEEWALL

4" KNEEWALL

FUTURE GAMEROOM

BONUS

CL.

GLASS SHOWER MASTER SUITE

MASTER SUITE 15'-0" X 14'-0"

CL.

F/P

LIN

HALL

GREAT ROOM 16'-0" X 18'-0"

(CLG. SLOPES TO 13'-6")

42" HIGH WALL

BEDROOM 2 11'-0" X 12'-0"

LIN

CL.

HALL

BATH-2

CTS

CL.

EATING BAR

R

S

BRK. 11'-0" X 10'-0"

KIT. 14'-8" x 10'-0"

DW

FOYER (CLG. 13'-6")

UP

REF

PANT

HALL

W D

UTIL 5'-9" x 5'-11"

DINING 10'-0" X 11'-9" (CLG. 13'-6")

BEDROOM 3 11'-0" X 10'-0"

STORAGE

DOUBLE GARAGE 19'-5" X 20'-0"

PORCH

MAIN FLOOR

Design 82050

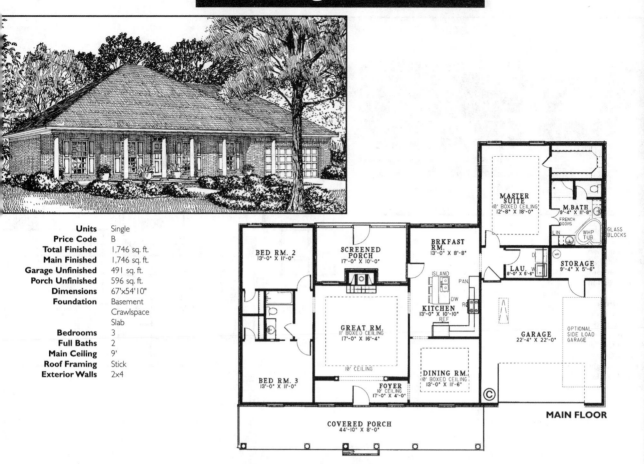

Units	Single
Price Code	B
Total Finished	1,746 sq. ft.
Main Finished	1,746 sq. ft.
Garage Unfinished	491 sq. ft.
Porch Unfinished	596 sq. ft.
Dimensions	67'x54'10"
Foundation	Basement
	Crawlspace
	Slab
Bedrooms	3
Full Baths	2
Main Ceiling	9'
Roof Framing	Stick
Exterior Walls	2x4

MASTER SUITE 10" BOXED CEILING 12'-8" X 18'-0"

M.BATH 9'-4" X 11'-8"

FRENCH DOORS

WHP TUB

GLASS BLOCKS

LAU. 8'-0" X 6'-6"

STORAGE 9'-4" X 5'-6"

BRKFAST RM. 13'-0" X 8'-8"

ISLAND

KITCHEN 13'-0" X 10'-10"

PAN.

DW

REF

GARAGE 22'-4" X 22'-0"

OPTIONAL SIDE LOAD GARAGE

BED RM. 2 13'-0" X 11'-0"

SCREENED PORCH 17'-0" X 10'-0"

GREAT RM. 11" BOXED CEILING 17'-0" X 16'-4"

10" CEILING

DINING RM. 10" BOXED CEILING 13'-0" X 11'-6"

BED RM. 3 13'-0" X 11'-0"

FOYER 10" CEILING 17'-0" X 4'-0"

COVERED PORCH 44'-10" X 8'-0"

MAIN FLOOR

Design 92655

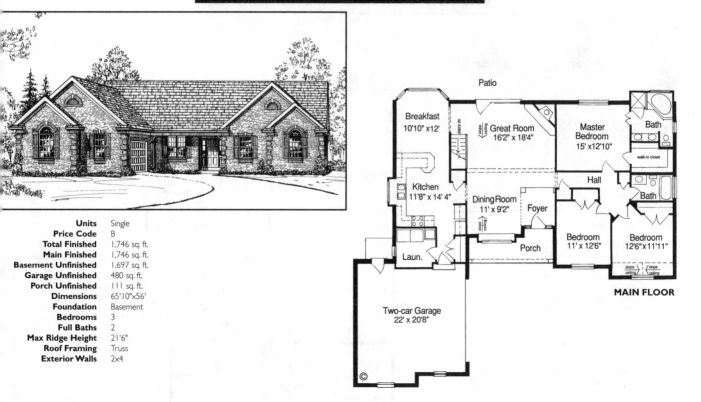

Units	Single
Price Code	B
Total Finished	1,746 sq. ft.
Main Finished	1,746 sq. ft.
Basement Unfinished	1,697 sq. ft.
Garage Unfinished	480 sq. ft.
Porch Unfinished	111 sq. ft.
Dimensions	65'10"x56'
Foundation	Basement
Bedrooms	3
Full Baths	2
Max Ridge Height	21'6"
Roof Framing	Truss
Exterior Walls	2x4

Patio

Breakfast 10'10" x12'

Great Room 16'2" x 18'4"

Master Bedroom 15' x12'10"

Bath

walk-in closet

Kitchen 11'8" x 14' 4"

Hall

Bath

Dining Room 11' x 9'2"

Foyer

Laun.

Porch

Bedroom 11' x 12'6"

Bedroom 12'6" x11'11"

slope ceiling

slope ceiling

Two-car Garage 22' x 20'8"

MAIN FLOOR

Design 98224

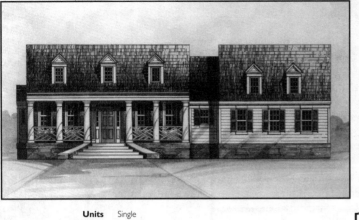

Units	Single
Price Code	C
Total Finished	1,751 sq. ft.
Main Finished	1,751 sq. ft.
Dimensions	64'x40'6"
Foundation	Basement
	Crawlspace
Bedrooms	3
Full Baths	2
Half Baths	1
Main Ceiling	9'
Vaulted Ceiling	12'
Tray Ceiling	12'
Max Ridge Height	16'
Roof Framing	Stick
Exterior Walls	2x4

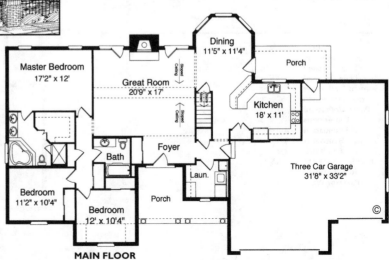

MAIN FLOOR

Design 97757

Units	Single
Price Code	B
Total Finished	1,755 sq. ft.
Main Finished	1,755 sq. ft.
Basement Unfinished	1,725 sq. ft.
Garage Unfinished	796 sq. ft.
Deck Unfinished	44 sq. ft.
Porch Unfinished	138 sq. ft.
Dimensions	78'6"x47'7"
Foundation	Basement
Bedrooms	3
Full Baths	2
Main Ceiling	8'
Max Ridge Height	22'
Roof Framing	Truss
Exterior Walls	2x4

MAIN FLOOR

Design 99185

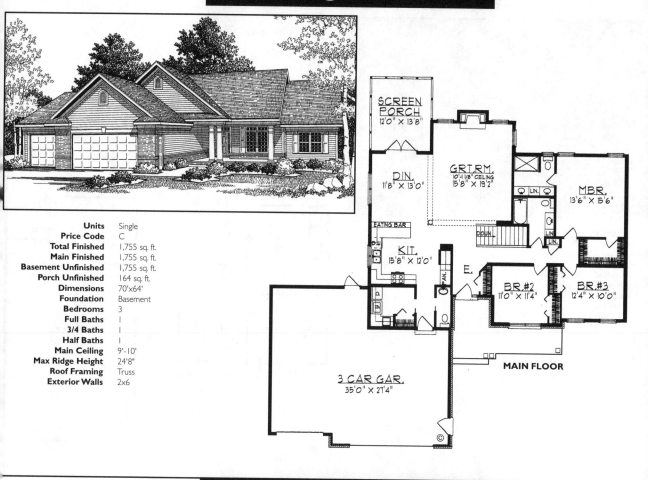

Units	Single
Price Code	C
Total Finished	1,755 sq. ft.
Main Finished	1,755 sq. ft.
Basement Unfinished	1,755 sq. ft.
Porch Unfinished	164 sq. ft.
Dimensions	70'x64'
Foundation	Basement
Bedrooms	3
Full Baths	1
3/4 Baths	1
Half Baths	1
Main Ceiling	9'-10'
Max Ridge Height	24'8"
Roof Framing	Truss
Exterior Walls	2x6

MAIN FLOOR

Design 63090

Units	Single
Price Code	C
Total Finished	1,758 sq. ft.
Main Finished	1,758 sq. ft.
Garage Unfinished	409 sq. ft.
Dimensions	60'x45'
Foundation	Slab
Bedrooms	3
Full Baths	2
Main Ceiling	10'
Max Ridge Height	20'8"
Roof Framing	Truss
Exterior Walls	2x4

OPTIONAL FOURTH BEDROOM

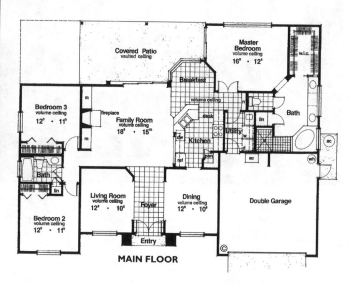

MAIN FLOOR

Design 97456

Units	Single
Price Code	C
Total Finished	1,758 sq. ft.
Main Finished	1,758 sq. ft.
Garage Unfinished	494 sq. ft.
Dimensions	55'4"x49'8"
Foundation	Basement
Bedrooms	3
Full Baths	2
Main Ceiling	9'
Max Ridge Height	26'
Roof Framing	Stick
Exterior Walls	2x4

* Alternate foundation options available at an additional charge. Please call 1-800-235-5700 for more information.

Mbr. 17⁰ x 12⁰

Grt. Rm 15⁰ x 21⁸ 11'-0" CEILING

Din. 11⁸ x 11⁰

COVERED STOOP

Bfst. 11² x 9¹⁰ SNACK BAR

Kit. 10⁹ x 12⁸

WHIRLPOOL

Br. 2 11⁰ x 11⁰

Br. 3 11² x 12⁰ 9'-8" CEILING

E.

Gar. 22⁰ x 24⁸

COVERED PORCH

MAIN FLOOR

Design 97755

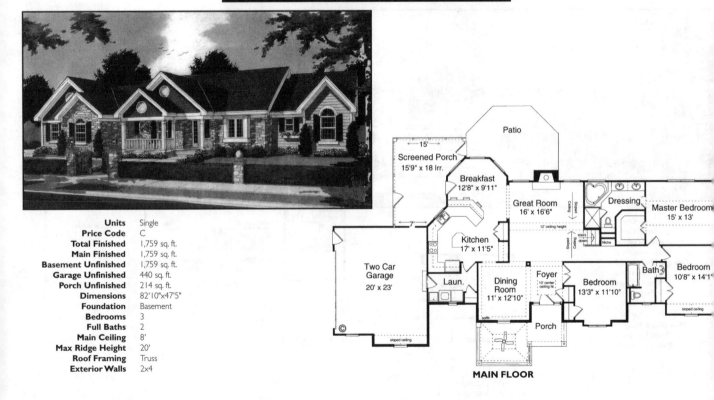

Units	Single
Price Code	C
Total Finished	1,759 sq. ft.
Main Finished	1,759 sq. ft.
Basement Unfinished	1,759 sq. ft.
Garage Unfinished	440 sq. ft.
Porch Unfinished	214 sq. ft.
Dimensions	82'10"x47'5"
Foundation	Basement
Bedrooms	3
Full Baths	2
Main Ceiling	8'
Max Ridge Height	20'
Roof Framing	Truss
Exterior Walls	2x4

Patio

Screened Porch 15'9" x 18 Irr.

Breakfast 12'8" x 9'11"

Great Room 16' x 16'6" 12' ceiling height

Dressing

Master Bedroom 15' x 13'

Kitchen 17' x 11'5"

Two Car Garage 20' x 23'

Laun.

Dining Room 11' x 12'10"

Foyer 10' center ceiling ht.

Bedroom 13'3" x 11'10"

Bath

Bedroom 10'8" x 14'1"

Porch

MAIN FLOOR

Design 93133

Units	Single
Price Code	C
Total Finished	1,763 sq. ft.
Main Finished	1,763 sq. ft.
Basement Unfinished	1,763 sq. ft.
Garage Unfinished	658 sq. ft.
Dimensions	67'8"x42'8"
Foundation	Basement
Bedrooms	3
Full Baths	2
Main Ceiling	8'
Vaulted Ceiling	14'
Max Ridge Height	22'
Roof Framing	Truss
Exterior Walls	2x6

MAIN FLOOR

Design 63048

Units	Single
Price Code	B
Total Finished	1,765 sq. ft.
Main Finished	1,765 sq. ft.
Deck Unfinished	90 sq. ft.
Porch Unfinished	130 sq. ft.
Dimensions	58'x54'
Foundation	Slab
Bedrooms	4
Full Baths	1
3/4 Baths	1
Main Ceiling	8'
Max Ridge Height	20'
Roof Framing	Truss

MAIN FLOOR

Design 63086

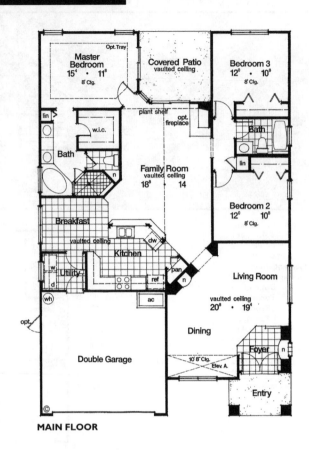

Units	Single
Price Code	C
Total Finished	1,768 sq. ft.
Main Finished	1,768 sq. ft.
Garage Unfinished	338 sq. ft.
Dimensions	40'x60'
Foundation	Slab
Bedrooms	3
Full Baths	2
Max Ridge Height	21'4"
Roof Framing	Truss
Exterior Walls	2x4

MAIN FLOOR

Design 65664

Units	Single
Price Code	C
Total Finished	1,770 sq. ft.
Main Finished	1,770 sq. ft.
Dimensions	64'x48'
Foundation	Crawlspace
	Slab
Bedrooms	3
Full Baths	2
Main Ceiling	8'-12'
Max Ridge Height	29'
Roof Framing	Stick
Exterior Walls	2x6

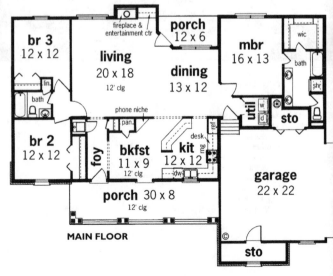

MAIN FLOOR

Design 98958

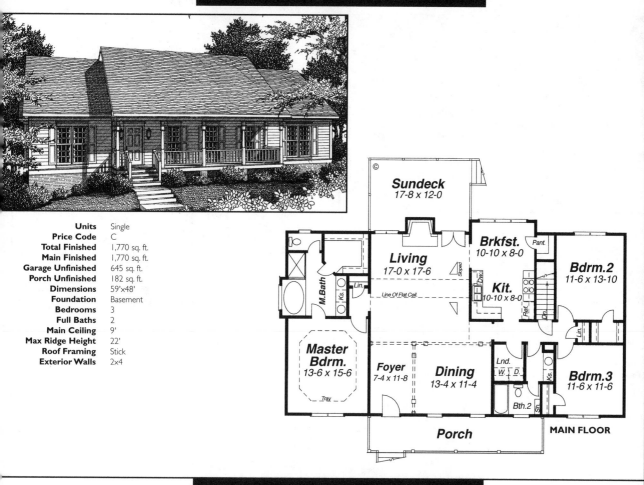

Units	Single
Price Code	C
Total Finished	1,770 sq. ft.
Main Finished	1,770 sq. ft.
Garage Unfinished	645 sq. ft.
Porch Unfinished	182 sq. ft.
Dimensions	59'x48'
Foundation	Basement
Bedrooms	3
Full Baths	2
Main Ceiling	9'
Max Ridge Height	22'
Roof Framing	Stick
Exterior Walls	2x4

Design 63087

Units	Single
Price Code	C
Total Finished	1,771 sq. ft.
Main Finished	1,771 sq. ft.
Garage Unfinished	394 sq. ft.
Dimensions	60'x54'4"
Foundation	Slab
Bedrooms	4
Full Baths	2
Max Ridge Height	18'2"
Roof Framing	Truss

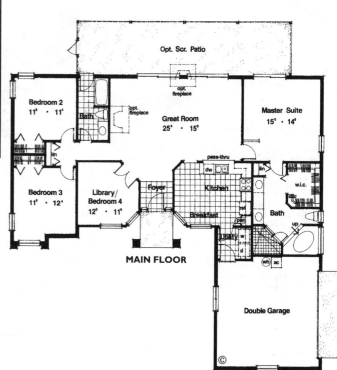

Design 98464

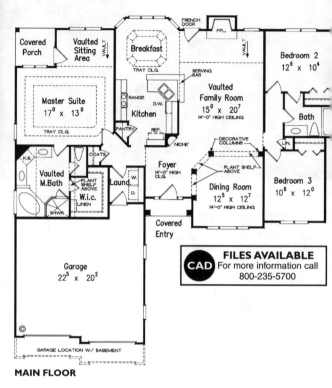

Units	Single
Price Code	C
Total Finished	1,779 sq. ft.
Main Finished	1,779 sq. ft.
Basement Unfinished	1,818 sq. ft.
Garage Unfinished	499 sq. ft.
Dimensions	57'x56'4"
Foundation	Basement
	Crawlspace
Bedrooms	3
Full Baths	2
Main Ceiling	9'
Max Ridge Height	24'6"
Roof Framing	Stick
Exterior Walls	2x4

OPTIONAL BASEMENT STAIR LOCATION

MAIN FLOOR

CAD FILES AVAILABLE For more information call 800-235-5700

Design 63111

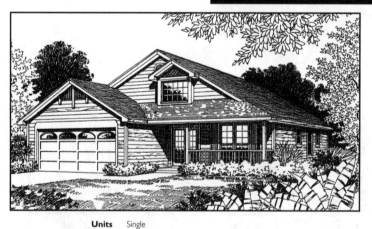

Units	Single
Price Code	C
Total Finished	1,782 sq. ft.
Main Finished	1,782 sq. ft.
Bonus Unfinished	262 sq. ft.
Garage Unfinished	394 sq. ft.
Dimensions	40'x61'
Foundation	Slab
Bedrooms	3
Full Baths	2
Main Ceiling	8'
Max Ridge Height	20'4"
Roof Framing	Truss

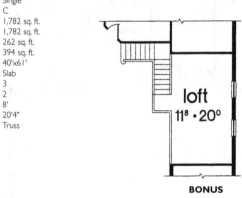

BONUS

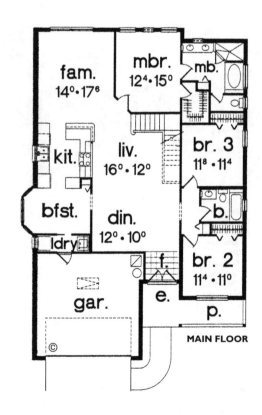

MAIN FLOOR

Design 92630

PHOTOGRAPHY: DONNA AND RON KOLB, EXPOSURES UNLIMITED

Units	Single
Price Code	C
Total Finished	1,782 sq. ft.
Main Finished	1,782 sq. ft.
Basement Unfinished	1,735 sq. ft.
Garage Unfinished	407 sq. ft.
Dimensions	67'2"×47'
Foundation	Basement
Bedrooms	3
Full Baths	2
Max Ridge Height	20'
Roof Framing	Truss
Exterior Walls	2x4

Please note: The photographed home may have been modified to suit homeowner preferences. If you order plans, have a builder or design professional check them against the photograph to confirm actual construction details.

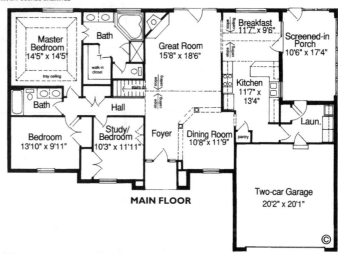

MAIN FLOOR

Design 94917

Units	Single
Price Code	C
Total Finished	1,782 sq. ft.
Main Finished	1,782 sq. ft.
Basement Unfinished	1,782 sq. ft.
Garage Unfinished	466 sq. ft.
Dimensions	52'x59'4"
Foundation	Basement
	Slab
Bedrooms	3
Full Baths	2
Max Ridge Height	21'
Roof Framing	Stick
Exterior Walls	2x4

Alternate foundation options available at an additional charge.
Please call 1-800-235-5700 for more information.

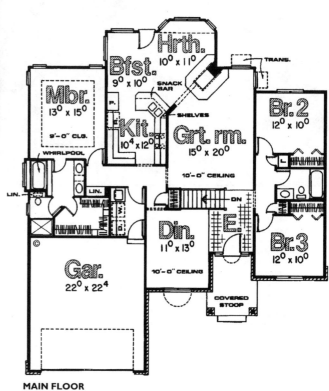

MAIN FLOOR

Design 93166

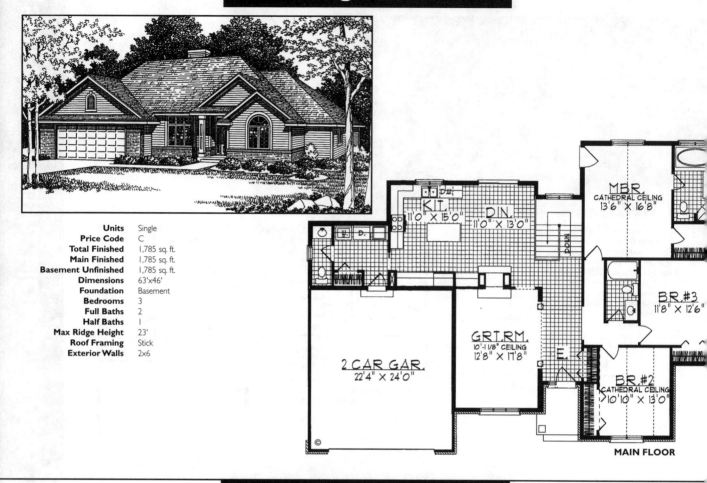

Units	Single
Price Code	C
Total Finished	1,785 sq. ft.
Main Finished	1,785 sq. ft.
Basement Unfinished	1,785 sq. ft.
Dimensions	63'x46'
Foundation	Basement
Bedrooms	3
Full Baths	2
Half Baths	1
Max Ridge Height	23'
Roof Framing	Stick
Exterior Walls	2x6

KIT. 11'0" X 15'0"
DIN. 11'0" X 13'0"
MBR. CATHEDRAL CEILING 13'6" X 16'8"
BR. #3 11'8" X 12'6"
GRT. RM. 10'-1 1/8" CEILING 12'8" X 17'8"
2 CAR GAR. 22'4" X 24'0"
BR. #2 CATHEDRAL CEILING 10'10" X 13'0"

MAIN FLOOR

Design 97466

Units	Single
Price Code	C
Total Finished	1,790 sq. ft.
Main Finished	1,790 sq. ft.
Garage Unfinished	546 sq. ft.
Deck Unfinished	170 sq. ft.
Dimensions	55'x57'
Foundation	Basement
Bedrooms	3
Full Baths	2
Main Ceiling	9'
Max Ridge Height	27'9"
Roof Framing	Stick
Exterior Walls	2x4

* Alternate foundation options available at an additional charge.
Please call 1-800-235-5700 for more information.

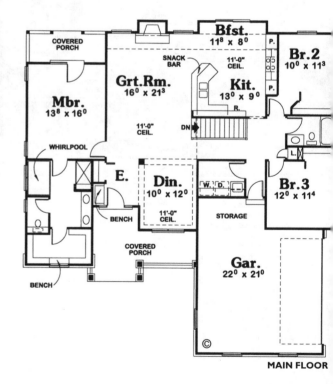

COVERED PORCH
Bfst. 11⁸ x 8⁰
Br. 2 10⁰ x 11³
SNACK BAR 11'-0" CEIL.
Grt. Rm. 16⁰ x 21³
Kit. 13⁰ x 9⁰
Mbr. 13⁸ x 16⁰
WHIRLPOOL
11'-0" CEIL.
E.
Din. 10⁰ x 12⁰ 11'-0" CEIL.
BENCH
W/D
STORAGE
Br. 3 12⁰ x 11⁴
COVERED PORCH
Gar. 22⁰ x 21⁰
BENCH

MAIN FLOOR

Design 98561

Units	Single
Price Code	C
Total Finished	1,794 sq. ft.
Main Finished	1,794 sq. ft.
Garage Unfinished	460 sq. ft.
Deck Unfinished	102 sq. ft.
Dimensions	60'x45'4"
Foundation	Crawlspace
	Slab
Bedrooms	3
Full Baths	2
Main Ceiling	8'-10'
Max Ridge Height	30'6"
Roof Framing	Stick
Exterior Walls	2x4

MAIN FLOOR

Design 93176

Units	Single
Price Code	C
Total Finished	1,795 sq. ft.
Main Finished	1,795 sq. ft.
Basement Unfinished	1,795 sq. ft.
Porch Unfinished	160 sq. ft.
Dimensions	68'x59'
Foundation	Basement
Bedrooms	3
Full Baths	2
Max Ridge Height	22'
Roof Framing	Stick
Exterior Walls	2x6

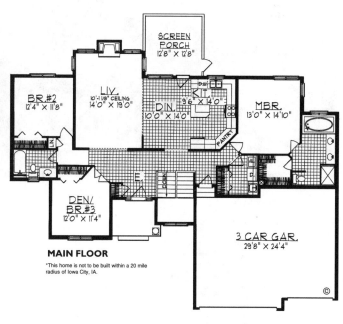

MAIN FLOOR

*This home is not to be built within a 20 mile radius of Iowa City, IA.

Units	Single
Price Code	C
Total Finished	1,800 sq. ft.
Main Finished	1,800 sq. ft.
Dimensions	80'x40'
Foundation	Crawlspace
	Slab
Bedrooms	3
Full Baths	2
Main Ceiling	8'
Vaulted Ceiling	12'
Max Ridge Height	25'
Roof Framing	Stick
Exterior Walls	2×4

Design 65622

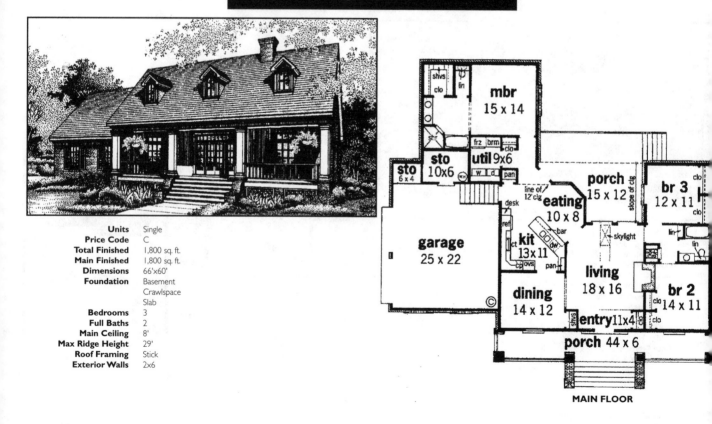

Units	Single
Price Code	C
Total Finished	1,800 sq. ft.
Main Finished	1,800 sq. ft.
Dimensions	66'x60'
Foundation	Basement
	Crawlspace
	Slab
Bedrooms	3
Full Baths	2
Main Ceiling	8'
Max Ridge Height	29'
Roof Framing	Stick
Exterior Walls	2×6

Design 65623

1,501-2,000 sq.ft. HOME PLANS

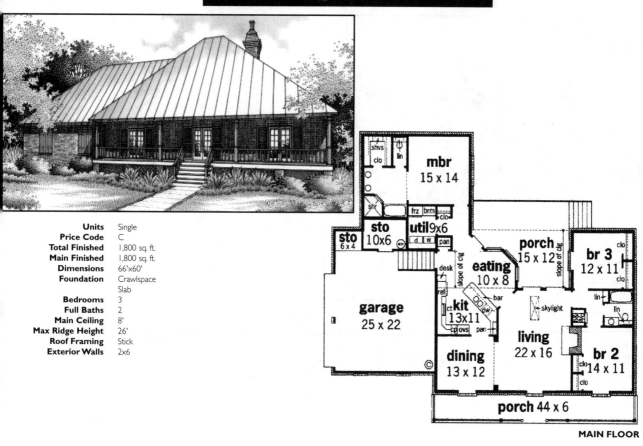

Units	Single
Price Code	C
Total Finished	1,800 sq. ft.
Main Finished	1,800 sq. ft.
Dimensions	66'x60'
Foundation	Crawlspace
	Slab
Bedrooms	3
Full Baths	2
Main Ceiling	8'
Max Ridge Height	26'
Roof Framing	Stick
Exterior Walls	2x6

MAIN FLOOR

Design 65625

Units	Single
Price Code	C
Total Finished	1,800 sq. ft.
Main Finished	1,800 sq. ft.
Dimensions	66'x60'
Foundation	Crawlspace
	Slab
Bedrooms	3
Full Baths	2
Main Ceiling	8'
Max Ridge Height	26'
Roof Framing	Stick
Exterior Walls	2x6

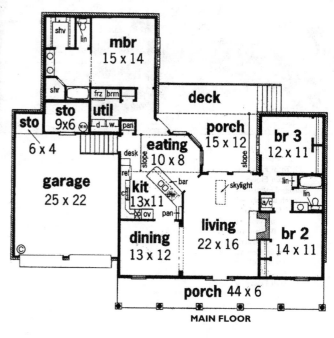

MAIN FLOOR

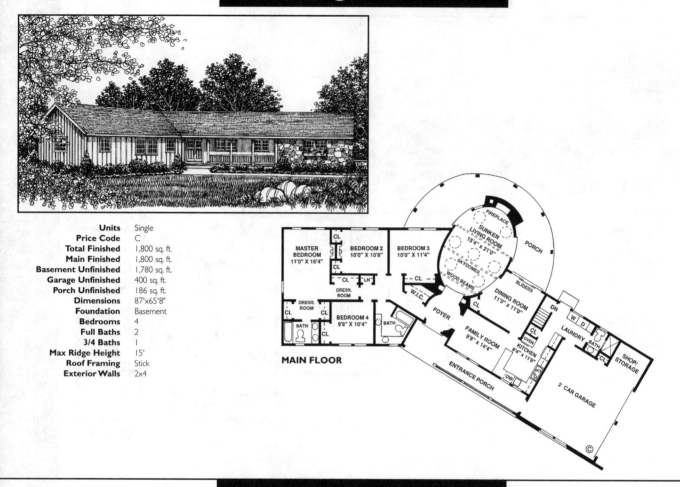

Units	Single
Price Code	C
Total Finished	1,800 sq. ft.
Main Finished	1,800 sq. ft.
Basement Unfinished	1,780 sq. ft.
Garage Unfinished	400 sq. ft.
Porch Unfinished	186 sq. ft.
Dimensions	87'x65'8"
Foundation	Basement
Bedrooms	4
Full Baths	2
3/4 Baths	1
Max Ridge Height	15'
Roof Framing	Stick
Exterior Walls	2x4

MAIN FLOOR

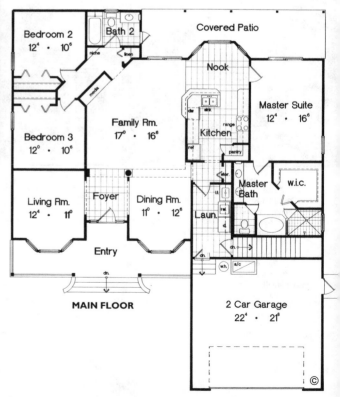

Units	Single
Price Code	C
Total Finished	1,806 sq. ft.
Main Finished	1,806 sq. ft.
Garage Unfinished	491 sq. ft.
Porch Unfinished	216 sq. ft.
Dimensions	54'x58'8"
Foundation	Slab
Bedrooms	3
Full Baths	2
Main Ceiling	8'
Vaulted Ceiling	13'6"
Max Ridge Height	18'
Roof Framing	Truss

MAIN FLOOR

Design 97462

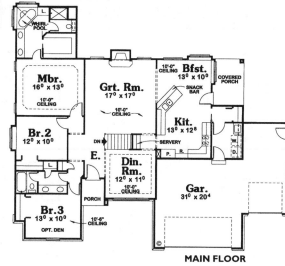

MAIN FLOOR

Units	Single
Price Code	B
Total Finished	1,806 sq. ft.
Main Finished	1,806 sq. ft.
Garage Unfinished	655 sq. ft.
Dimensions	65'4"x56'
Foundation	Basement
Bedrooms	3
Full Baths	2
Main Ceiling	9'
Max Ridge Height	21'
Roof Framing	Stick
Exterior Walls	2x4

* Alternate foundation options available at an additional charge.
Please call 1-800-235-5700 for more information.

Design 94928

MAIN FLOOR

Units	Single
Price Code	C
Total Finished	1,808 sq. ft.
Main Finished	1,808 sq. ft.
Basement Unfinished	1,808 sq. ft.
Garage Unfinished	551 sq. ft.
Dimensions	64'x44'
Foundation	Basement
Bedrooms	3
Full Baths	2
Main Ceiling	8'
Max Ridge Height	22'5"
Roof Framing	Stick
Exterior Walls	2x4

* Alternate foundation options available at an additional charge.
Please call 1-800-235-5700 for more information.

Design 90441

Units	Single
Price Code	C
Total Finished	1,811 sq. ft.
Main Finished	1,811 sq. ft.
Basement Unfinished	1,811 sq. ft.
Garage Unfinished	484 sq. ft.
Deck Unfinished	336 sq. ft.
Porch Unfinished	390 sq. ft.
Dimensions	89'6"x44'4"
Foundation	Basement
	Crawlspace
	Slab
Bedrooms	3
Full Baths	2
Main Ceiling	8'
Max Ridge Height	16'4"
Roof Framing	Stick
Exterior Walls	2x4

MAIN FLOOR

Design 97300

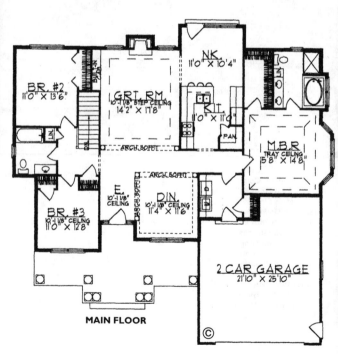

Units	Single
Price Code	C
Total Finished	1,814 sq. ft.
Main Finished	1,814 sq. ft.
Basement Unfinished	1,814 sq. ft.
Dimensions	58'x56'
Foundation	Basement
Bedrooms	3
Full Baths	2
Main Ceiling	9'1/8"
Max Ridge Height	27'8"
Roof Framing	Truss
Exterior Walls	2x6

MAIN FLOOR

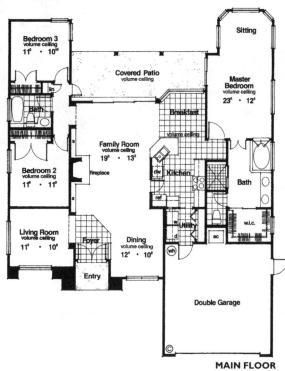

MAIN FLOOR

Units	Single
Price Code	C
Total Finished	1,817 sq. ft.
Main Finished	1,817 sq. ft.
Garage Unfinished	420 sq. ft.
Dimensions	50'x63'
Foundation	Slab
Bedrooms	3
Full Baths	2
Main Ceiling	10'
Max Ridge Height	26'5"
Roof Framing	Truss
Exterior Walls	2x4

Design 97123

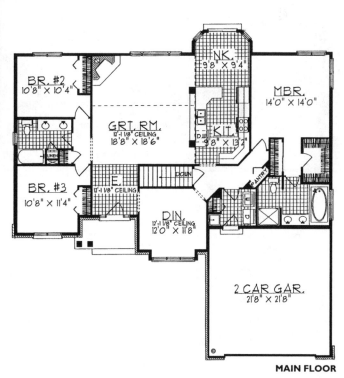

MAIN FLOOR

Units	Single
Price Code	C
Total Finished	1,817 sq. ft.
Main Finished	1,817 sq. ft.
Basement Unfinished	1,817 sq. ft.
Dimensions	57'x56'
Foundation	Basement
Bedrooms	3
Full Baths	2
Max Ridge Height	23'8"
Roof Framing	Truss
Exterior Walls	2x6

Design 92551

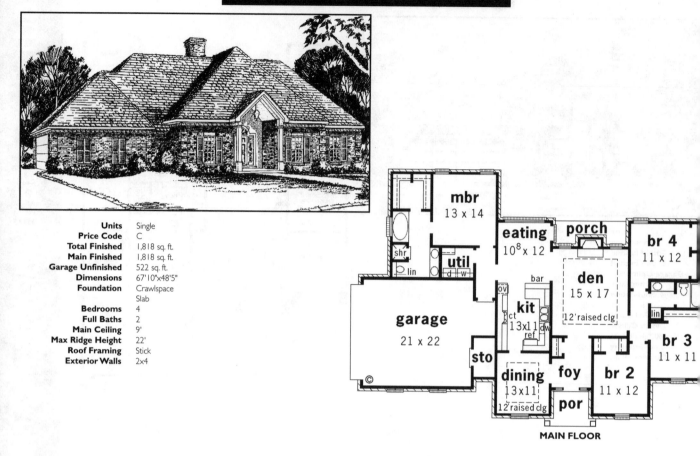

Units	Single
Price Code	C
Total Finished	1,818 sq. ft.
Main Finished	1,818 sq. ft.
Garage Unfinished	522 sq. ft.
Dimensions	67'10"x48'5"
Foundation	Crawlspace
	Slab
Bedrooms	4
Full Baths	2
Main Ceiling	9'
Max Ridge Height	22'
Roof Framing	Stick
Exterior Walls	2x4

Design 92220

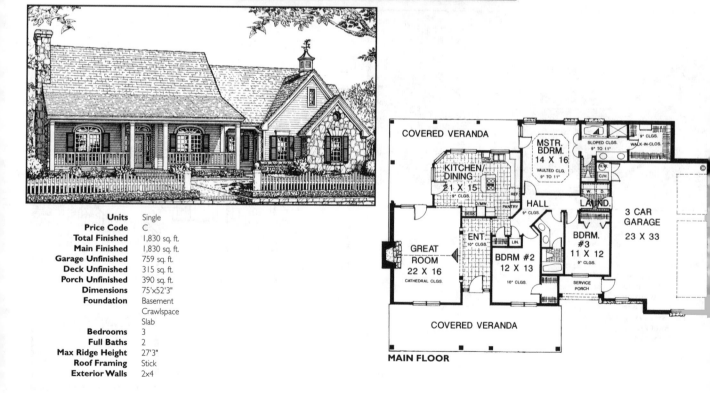

Units	Single
Price Code	C
Total Finished	1,830 sq. ft.
Main Finished	1,830 sq. ft.
Garage Unfinished	759 sq. ft.
Deck Unfinished	315 sq. ft.
Porch Unfinished	390 sq. ft.
Dimensions	75'x52'3"
Foundation	Basement
	Crawlspace
	Slab
Bedrooms	3
Full Baths	2
Max Ridge Height	27'3"
Roof Framing	Stick
Exterior Walls	2x4

Design 98957

Units	Single
Price Code	C
Total Finished	1,830 sq. ft.
Main Finished	1,830 sq. ft.
Garage Unfinished	390 sq. ft.
Dimensions	49'x64'
Foundation	Basement
	Crawlspace
	Slab
Bedrooms	3
Full Baths	2
Main Ceiling	8'
Max Ridge Height	21'
Roof Framing	Stick
Exterior Walls	2x4

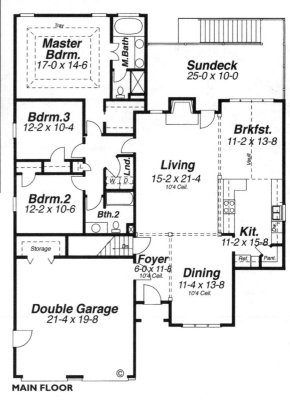

MAIN FLOOR

Design 63027

Units	Single
Price Code	C
Total Finished	1,833 sq. ft.
Main Finished	1,833 sq. ft.
Garage Unfinished	392 sq. ft.
Dimensions	59'4"x48'8"
Foundation	Slab
Bedrooms	3
Full Baths	2
Main Ceiling	10'
Max Ridge Height	19'6"
Roof Framing	Truss
Exterior Walls	2x4

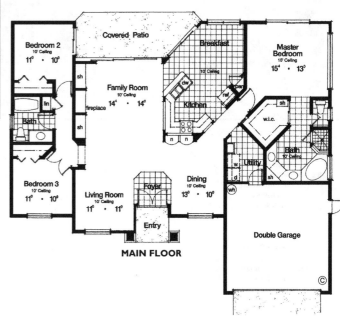

MAIN FLOOR

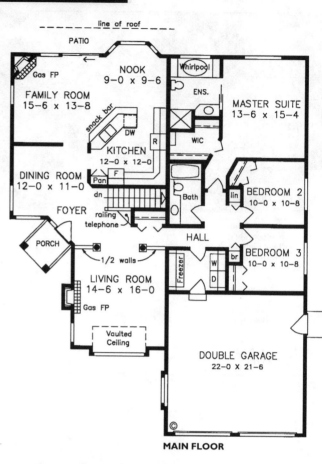

MAIN FLOOR

Units	Single
Price Code	C
Total Finished	1,833 sq. ft.
Main Finished	1,833 sq. ft.
Basement Unfinished	1,800 sq. ft.
Garage Unfinished	506 sq. ft.
Porch Unfinished	39 sq. ft.
Dimensions	48'x59'
Foundation	Basement
Bedrooms	3
Full Baths	2
Main Ceiling	8'
Vaulted Ceiling	11'
Max Ridge Height	20'
Roof Framing	Truss
Exterior Walls	2x6

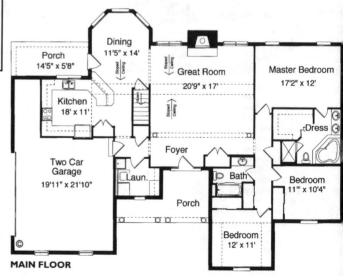

MAIN FLOOR

Unit	Single
Price Code	C
Total Finished	1,834 sq. ft.
Main Finished	1,834 sq. ft.
Basement Unfinished	1,834 sq. ft.
Garage Unfinished	485 sq. ft.
Porch Unfinished	140 sq. ft.
Dimensions	66'9"x50'7"
Foundation	Basement
Bedrooms	3
Full Baths	2
Main Ceiling	8'
Vaulted Ceiling	10'
Max Ridge Height	22'3"
Roof Framing	Truss
Exterior Walls	2x4

Design 91122

Units	Single
Price Code	C
Total Finished	1,838 sq. ft.
Main Finished	1,838 sq. ft.
Garage Unfinished	452 sq. ft.
Dimensions	48'6"x59'10"
Foundation	Slab
Bedrooms	3
Full Baths	2
Max Ridge Height	35'
Roof Framing	Stick
Exterior Walls	2x4

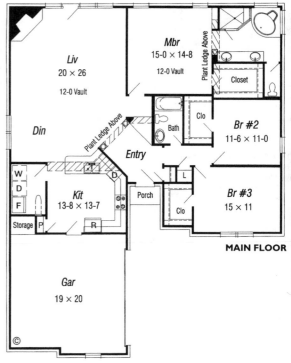

Liv 20 × 26 12-0 Vault

Mbr 15-0 × 14-8 12-0 Vault

Closet

Din

Plant Ledge Above

Entry

Bath

Clo

Br #2 11-6 × 11-0

W D F

Kit 13-8 × 13-7

Porch

Clo

Br #3 15 × 11

Storage P R

Gar 19 × 20

MAIN FLOOR

Design 93425

Units	Single
Price Code	C
Total Finished	1,842 sq. ft.
Main Finished	1,842 sq. ft.
Garage Unfinished	507 sq. ft.
Dimensions	56'4"x68'6"
Foundation	Crawlspace
	Slab
Bedrooms	3
Full Baths	2
Main Ceiling	9'
Vaulted Ceiling	12'
Max Ridge Height	20'6"
Roof Framing	Stick
Exterior Walls	2x4

Porch 11 x 6/10

Family Room 14 x 17/1 12' Vaulted Clg.

Breakfast 10/9 x 11/6 9' Ceiling

Bookcase

Skylight

Master 14 x 16 9' Ceiling

Kitchen 17/5 x 9

Br. #2 11 x 12/10 9' Ceiling

Skylight

Foyer 6 x 8 10' Ceiling

Dining 11 x 12

Utility W D

Br. #3 11 x12 9' Ceiling

Porch

MAIN FLOOR

Garage 22 x 22

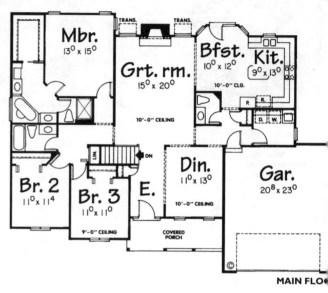

Units	Single
Price Code	C
Total Finished	1,842 sq. ft.
Main Finished	1,842 sq. ft.
Garage Unfinished	498 sq. ft.
Dimensions	62'x48'
Foundation	Basement
Bedrooms	3
Full Baths	2
Half Baths	I
Max Ridge Height	20'9"
Roof Framing	Stick

* Alternate foundation options available at an additional charge.
Please call 1-800-235-5700 for more information.

MAIN FLOO

Units	Single
Price Code	C
Total Finished	1,845 sq. ft.
Main Finished	1,845 sq. ft.
Garage Unfinished	512 sq. ft.
Deck Unfinished	216 sq. ft.
Porch Unfinished	38 sq. ft.
Dimensions	57'2"x54'10"
Foundation	Crawlspace
	Slab
Bedrooms	3
Full Baths	2
Half Baths	I
Main Ceiling	8'
Max Ridge Height	23'10"
Roof Framing	Stick
Exterior Walls	2x4

MAIN FLOOR

Design 98425

Units	Single
Price Code	C
Total Finished	1,845 sq. ft.
Main Finished	1,845 sq. ft.
Bonus Unfinished	409 sq. ft.
Basement Unfinished	1,845 sq. ft.
Garage Unfinished	529 sq. ft.
Dimensions	56'x60'
Foundation	Basement
	Crawlspace
Bedrooms	3
Full Baths	2
Half Baths	1
Main Ceiling	9'
Max Ridge Height	26'6"
Roof Framing	Stick
Exterior Walls	2x4

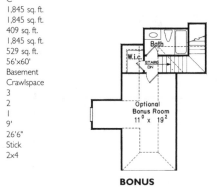

BONUS

CAD FILES AVAILABLE
For more information call
800-235-5700

MAIN FLOOR

Design 94692

Units	Single
Price Code	C
Total Finished	1,847 sq. ft.
Main Finished	1,847 sq. ft.
Garage Unfinished	593 sq. ft.
Porch Unfinished	528 sq. ft.
Dimensions	49'6"x72'5"
Foundation	Slab
Bedrooms	3
Full Baths	2
Max Ridge Height	24'8"
Roof Framing	Stick
Exterior Walls	2x4

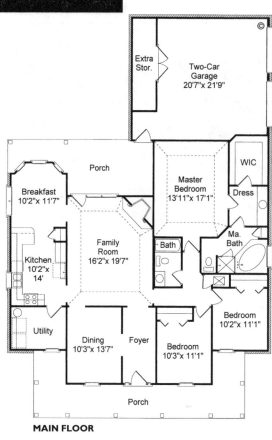

MAIN FLOOR

Design 99434

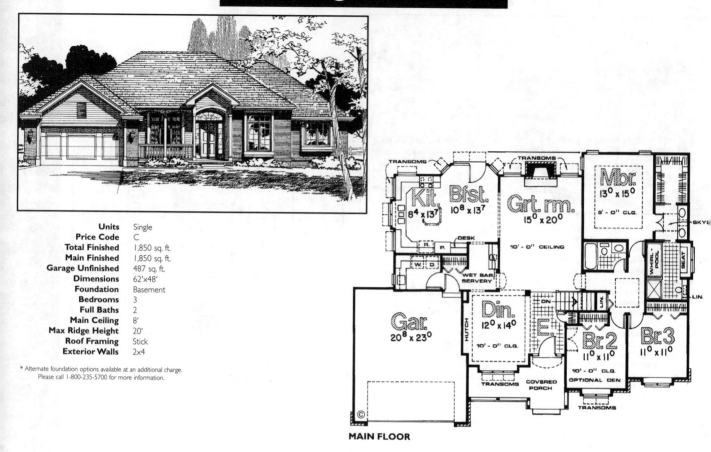

Units	Single
Price Code	C
Total Finished	1,850 sq. ft.
Main Finished	1,850 sq. ft.
Garage Unfinished	487 sq. ft.
Dimensions	62'x48'
Foundation	Basement
Bedrooms	3
Full Baths	2
Main Ceiling	8'
Max Ridge Height	20'
Roof Framing	Stick
Exterior Walls	2x4

* Alternate foundation options available at an additional charge.
Please call 1-800-235-5700 for more information.

TRANSOMS
TRANSOMS

Kit. 8⁴ x 13⁷

Bfst. 10⁸ x 13⁷

Grt. rm. 15⁰ x 20⁰
10'-0" CEILING

Mbr. 13⁰ x 15⁰
9'-0" CLG.

SKY

DESK

R. P.

W. D.

WET BAR
SERVERY

WHIRL-POOL

SEAT

LIN.

LIN.

Gar. 20⁸ x 23⁰

Din. 12⁰ x 14⁰
10'-0" CLG.

HUTCH

DN.

ON.

LIN.

Br. 2 11⁰ x 11⁰
10'-0" CLG.

Br. 3 11⁰ x 11⁰

OPTIONAL DEN

TRANSOMS

COVERED PORCH

TRANSOMS

©

MAIN FLOOR

Design 81008

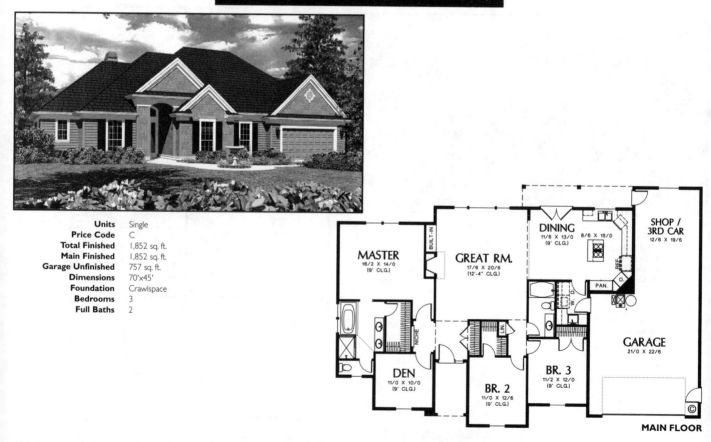

Units	Single
Price Code	C
Total Finished	1,852 sq. ft.
Main Finished	1,852 sq. ft.
Garage Unfinished	757 sq. ft.
Dimensions	70'x45'
Foundation	Crawlspace
Bedrooms	3
Full Baths	2

BUILT-IN

MASTER 16/2 X 14/0
(9' CLG.)

GREAT RM. 17/6 X 20/6
(12'-4" CLG.)

DINING 11/6 X 13/0
(9' CLG.)

8/6 X 15/0

SHOP / 3RD CAR 12/6 X 19/6

PAN.

NICHE

LIN.

W D

DEN 11/0 X 10/0
(9' CLG.)

BR. 2 11/0 X 12/6
(9' CLG.)

BR. 3 11/2 X 12/0
(9' CLG.)

GARAGE 21/0 X 22/6

©

MAIN FLOOR

Design 97719

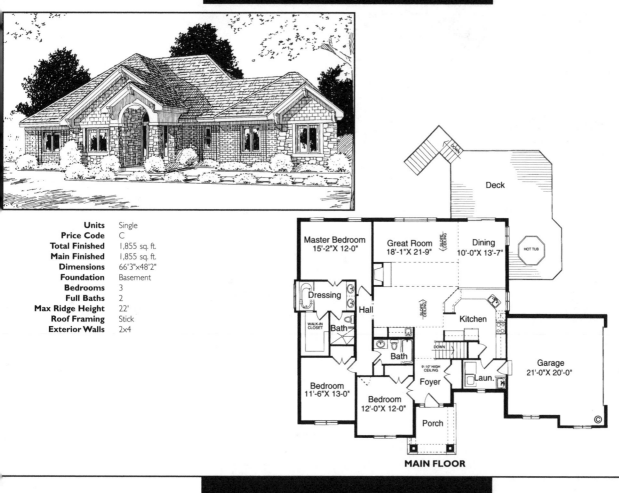

Units	Single
Price Code	C
Total Finished	1,855 sq. ft.
Main Finished	1,855 sq. ft.
Dimensions	66'3"x48'2"
Foundation	Basement
Bedrooms	3
Full Baths	2
Max Ridge Height	22'
Roof Framing	Stick
Exterior Walls	2x4

Deck

Master Bedroom 15'-2"X 12'-0"

Great Room 18'-1"X 21'-9"

Dining 10'-0"X 13'-7"

HOT TUB

Dressing

Hall

Kitchen

WALK-IN CLOSET

Bath

Bath

Garage 21'-0"X 20'-0"

Bedroom 11'-6" X 13'-0"

Bedroom 12'-0"X 12'-0"

Foyer

Laun.

9'-10" HIGH CEILING

Porch

MAIN FLOOR

Design 98408

Units	Single
Price Code	C
Total Finished	1,856 sq. ft.
Main Finished	1,856 sq. ft.
Basement Unfinished	1,856 sq. ft.
Garage Unfinished	429 sq. ft.
Dimensions	59'x54'6"
Foundation	Basement
	Crawlspace
	Slab
Bedrooms	3
Full Baths	2
Main Ceiling	9'
Max Ridge Height	25'6"
Roof Framing	Stick
Exterior Walls	2x4

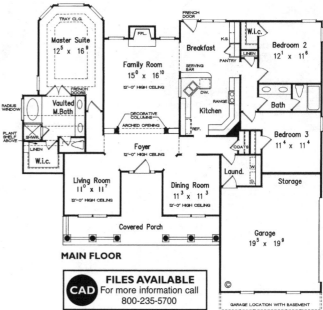

Bedroom 3 11'⁴ x 11'⁴

Coats

Laund.

STAIRS DN.

Garage 19'⁵ x 19'⁹

OPTIONAL BASEMENT STAIR LOCATION

TRAY CLG.

Master Suite 12'⁵ x 16'⁹

FPL.

FRENCH DOOR

W.i.c.

Breakfast

Bedroom 2 12'¹ x 11'⁶

Family Room 15'⁰ x 16'¹⁰ 12'-0" HIGH CEILING

SERVING BAR

K.S.

PANTRY

LINEN

RADIUS WINDOW

Vaulted M.Bath

FRENCH DOORS

DECORATIVE COLUMNS

DW.

Kitchen

RANGE

REF.

Bath

PLANT SHELF ABOVE

SHWR.

LINEN

ARCHED OPENING

Foyer 12'-0" HIGH CEILING

Bedroom 3 11'⁴ x 11'⁴

W.i.c.

COATS

Laund.

W D

Living Room 11'⁰ x 11'⁷ 12'-0" HIGH CEILING

Dining Room 11'³ x 11'³ 12'-0" HIGH CEILING

Storage

Covered Porch

Garage 19'⁵ x 19'⁹

MAIN FLOOR

CAD FILES AVAILABLE For more information call 800-235-5700

GARAGE LOCATION WITH BASEMENT

Design 99679

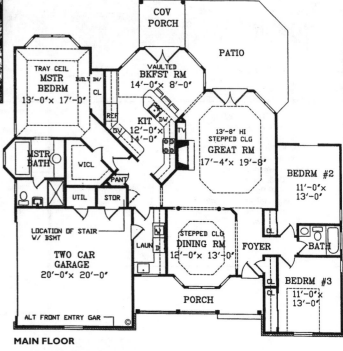

Units	Single
Price Code	C
Total Finished	1,860 sq. ft.
Main Finished	1,860 sq. ft.
Basement Unfinished	1,860 sq. ft.
Garage Unfinished	434 sq. ft.
Dimensions	57'4"x49'8"
Foundation	Basement
	Crawlspace
	Slab
Bedrooms	3
Full Baths	2
Main Ceiling	8'
Vaulted Ceiling	13'8"
Tray Ceiling	11'6"
Max Ridge Height	18'
Roof Framing	Stick
Exterior Walls	2x4

MAIN FLOOR

Design 97616

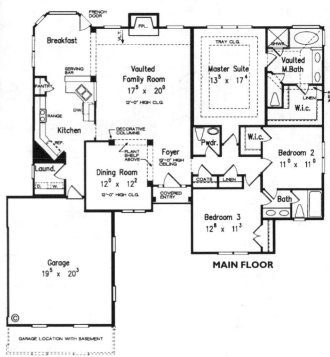

Units	Single
Price Code	C
Total Finished	1,861 sq. ft.
Main Finished	1,861 sq. ft.
Basement Unfinished	1,898 sq. ft.
Garage Unfinished	450 sq. ft.
Dimensions	58'6"x56'
Foundation	Basement
	Crawlspace
Bedrooms	3
Full Baths	2
Half Baths	1
Max Ridge Height	24'6"
Roof Framing	Stick
Exterior Walls	2x4

OPTIONAL BASEMENT STAIR LOCATION

MAIN FLOOR

Design 97777

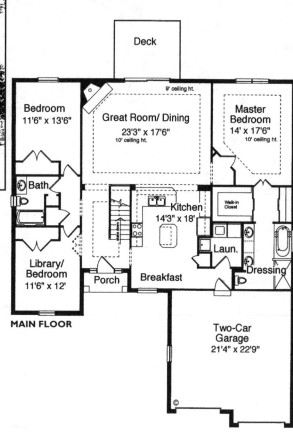

Deck

Bedroom
11'6" x 13'6"

Great Room/ Dining
23'3" x 17'6"
10' ceiling ht.

9' ceiling ht.

Master Bedroom
14' x 17'6"
10' ceiling ht.

Bath

Kitchen
14'3" x 18'

Walk-in Closet

Laun.

Library/ Bedroom
11'6" x 12'

Porch

Breakfast

Dressing

MAIN FLOOR

Two-Car Garage
21'4" x 22'9"

Units	Single
Price Code	C
Total Finished	1,861 sq. ft.
Main Finished	1,861 sq. ft.
Basement Unfinished	1,861 sq. ft.
Garage Unfinished	433 sq. ft.
Deck Unfinished	120 sq. ft.
Porch Unfinished	21 sq. ft.
Dimensions	50'8"x59'10"
Foundation	Basement
Bedrooms	3
Full Baths	2
Main Ceiling	9'
Tray Ceiling	10'
Max Ridge Height	23'
Roof Framing	Truss
Exterior Walls	2x4

Design 91157

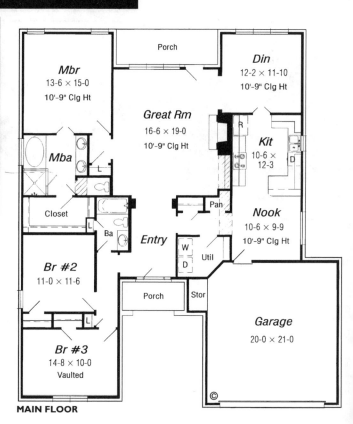

Porch

Mbr
13-6 × 15-0
10'-9" Clg Ht

Din
12-2 × 11-10
10'-9" Clg Ht

Great Rm
16-6 × 19-0
10'-9" Clg Ht

Mba

Kit
10-6 × 12-3

Closet

Ba

Pan

Nook
10-6 × 9-9
10'-9" Clg Ht

Entry

W D

Util

Br #2
11-0 × 11-6

Porch

Stor

Garage
20-0 × 21-0

Br #3
14-8 × 10-0
Vaulted

MAIN FLOOR

Units	Single
Price Code	C
Total Finished	1,862 sq. ft.
Main Finished	1,862 sq. ft.
Garage Unfinished	481 sq. ft.
Porch Unfinished	135 sq. ft.
Dimensions	50'4½"x56'11½"
Foundation	Crawlspace
Bedrooms	3
Full Baths	2

PHOTOGRAPHY: COURTESY OF THE DESIGNER

Please note: The photographed home may have been modified to suit homeowner preferences. If you order plans, have a builder or design professional check them against the photograph to confirm actual construction details.

Units	Single
Price Code	C
Total Finished	1,865 sq. ft.
Main Finished	1,865 sq. ft.
Dimensions	62'x64'
Foundation	Crawlspace
	Slab
Bedrooms	3
Full Baths	2
Main Ceiling	8'
Max Ridge Height	27'
Roof Framing	Stick
Exterior Walls	2x6

MAIN FLOOR

Design 65634

Units	Single
Price Code	C
Total Finished	1,868 sq. ft.
Main Finished	1,868 sq. ft.
Dimensions	62'x64'
Foundation	Crawlspace
	Slab
Bedrooms	3
Full Baths	2
Max Ridge Height	28'
Roof Framing	Stick
Exterior Walls	2x6

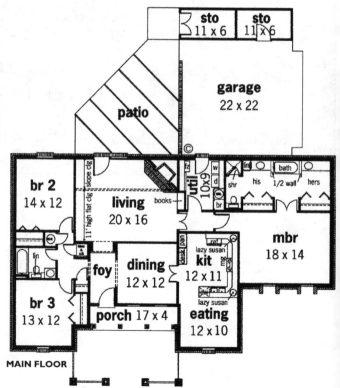

MAIN FLOOR

Design 63115

Units	Single
Price Code	C
Total Finished	1,869 sq. ft.
Main Finished	1,869 sq. ft.
Garage Unfinished	470 sq. ft.
Dimensions	61'8"x53'
Foundation	Slab
Bedrooms	3
Full Baths	2
Main Ceiling	10'
Max Ridge Height	20'
Roof Framing	Truss
Exterior Walls	2x4

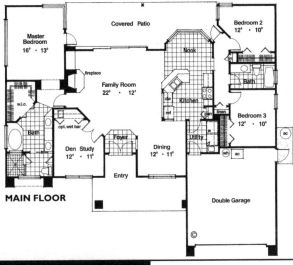

MAIN FLOOR

Design 98956

Units	Single
Price Code	C
Total Finished	1,869 sq. ft.
Main Finished	1,869 sq. ft.
Garage Unfinished	505 sq. ft.
Dimensions	54'x60'
Foundation	Basement
	Crawlspace
	Slab
Bedrooms	3
Full Baths	2
Main Ceiling	8'
Max Ridge Height	24'
Roof Framing	Stick
Exterior Walls	2x4

MAIN FLOOR

Design 63116

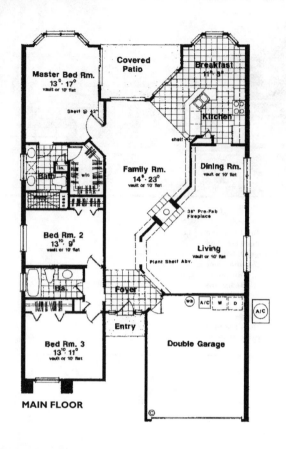

Units	Single
Price Code	C
Total Finished	1,872 sq. ft.
Main Finished	1,872 sq. ft.
Garage Unfinished	398 sq. ft.
Dimensions	40'x66'8"
Foundation	Slab
Bedrooms	3
Full Baths	1
3/4 Baths	1
Max Ridge Height	18'3"
Roof Framing	Truss

MAIN FLOOR

Design 93080

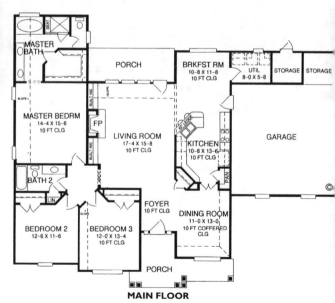

Units	Single
Price Code	C
Total Finished	1,890 sq. ft.
Main Finished	1,890 sq. ft.
Garage Unfinished	565 sq. ft.
Porch Unfinished	241 sq. ft.
Dimensions	65'10"x53'5"
Foundation	Crawlspace
	Slab
Bedrooms	3
Full Baths	2
Main Ceiling	10'
Max Ridge Height	21'6"
Roof Framing	Stick
Exterior Walls	2x4

MAIN FLOOR

Design 96601

Units	Single
Price Code	C
Total Finished	1,890 sq. ft.
Main Finished	1,890 sq. ft.
Garage Unfinished	565 sq. ft.
Porch Unfinished	241 sq. ft.
Dimensions	65'10"x53'5"
Foundation	Crawlspace
	Slab
Bedrooms	3
Full Baths	2
Max Ridge Height	21'4"
Roof Framing	Stick
Exterior Walls	2x4

MASTER BATH

PORCH

BRKFST RM
10-8 X 11-8
10 FT CLG

UTIL
d-0 X 5-8

STORAGE

STORAGE

MASTER BEDRM
14-4 X 15-6
10 FT CLG

LIVING ROOM
17-4 X 15-8
10 FT CLG

KITCHEN
10-8 X 13-6
10 FT CLG

GARAGE

BATH 2

BEDROOM 2
12-6 X 11-8

BEDROOM 3
12-0 X 13-4
10 FT CLG

FOYER
10 FT CLG

DINING ROOM
11-0 X 13-0
10 FT COFFERED CLG

PORCH

MAIN FLOOR

Design 65624

Units	Single
Price Code	C
Total Finished	1,891 sq. ft.
Main Finished	1,891 sq. ft.
Dimensions	49'x64'
Foundation	Crawlspace
	Slab
Bedrooms	2
Full Baths	2
Main Ceiling	9'
Vaulted Ceiling	12'
Max Ridge Height	24'
Roof Framing	Stick
Exterior Walls	2x4

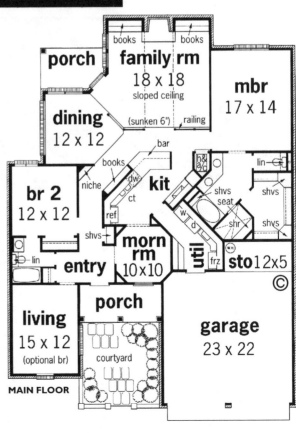

porch

books   books

family rm
18 x 18
sloped ceiling
(sunken 6")   railing

mbr
17 x 14

dining
12 x 12

bar

books

kit

lin

shvs

shvs
seat

shvs

shvs

br 2
12 x 12

niche

dw
ct

ref

w
d

shr

shvs

entry

shvs

lin

morn rm
10 x 10

util

frz

sto 12x5

living
15 x 12
(optional br)

porch

courtyard

garage
23 x 22

MAIN FLOOR

Units	Single
Price Code	C
Total Finished	1,901 sq. ft.
Main Finished	1,901 sq. ft.
Garage Unfinished	484 sq. ft.
Porch Unfinished	383 sq. ft.
Dimensions	62'x53'8"
Foundation	Slab
Bedrooms	3
Full Baths	2
Main Ceiling	8'
Max Ridge Height	20'
Roof Framing	Truss

MAIN FLOOR

Units	Single
Price Code	C
Total Finished	1,902 sq. ft.
Main Finished	1,902 sq. ft.
Garage Unfinished	636 sq. ft.
Deck Unfinished	210 sq. ft.
Porch Unfinished	185 sq. ft.
Dimensions	84'7"x34'5"
Foundation	Slab
Bedrooms	3
Full Baths	2
Half Baths	1
Roof Framing	Stick
Exterior Walls	2x4

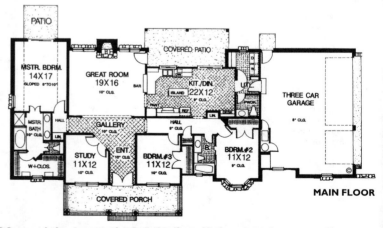

MAIN FLOOR

Design 97177

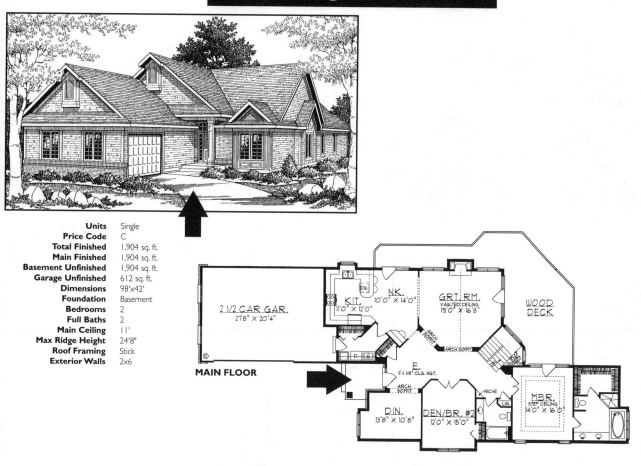

Units	Single
Price Code	C
Total Finished	1,904 sq. ft.
Main Finished	1,904 sq. ft.
Basement Unfinished	1,904 sq. ft.
Garage Unfinished	612 sq. ft.
Dimensions	98'x42'
Foundation	Basement
Bedrooms	2
Full Baths	2
Main Ceiling	11'
Max Ridge Height	24'8"
Roof Framing	Stick
Exterior Walls	2x6

MAIN FLOOR

Design 63141

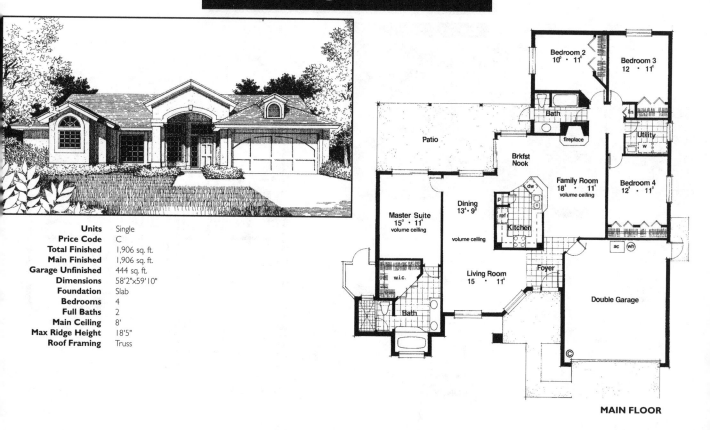

Units	Single
Price Code	C
Total Finished	1,906 sq. ft.
Main Finished	1,906 sq. ft.
Garage Unfinished	444 sq. ft.
Dimensions	58'2"x59'10"
Foundation	Slab
Bedrooms	4
Full Baths	2
Main Ceiling	8'
Max Ridge Height	18'5"
Roof Framing	Truss

MAIN FLOOR

Design 91839

MAIN FLOOR

Units	Single
Price Code	C
Total Finished	1,906 sq. ft.
Main Finished	1,224 sq. ft.
Lower Finished	682 sq. ft.
Basement Unfinished	520 sq. ft.
Dimensions	42'x32'
Foundation	Basement
Bedrooms	4
Full Baths	3
Max Ridge Height	21'4"
Roof Framing	Truss
Exterior Walls	2x6

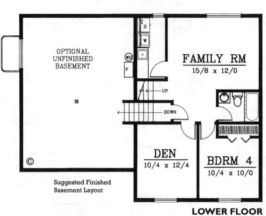

LOWER FLOOR

Design 66084

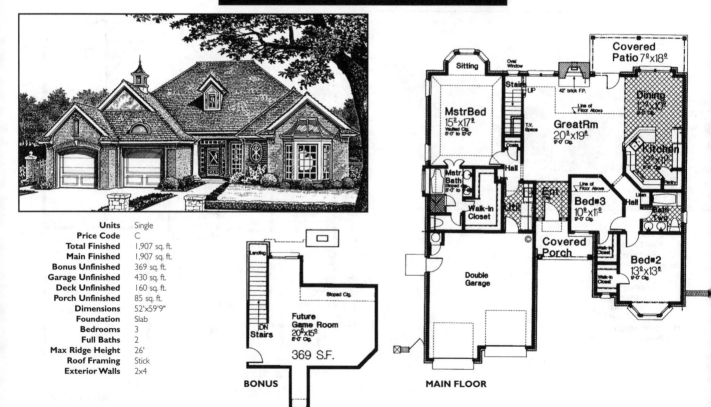

Units	Single
Price Code	C
Total Finished	1,907 sq. ft.
Main Finished	1,907 sq. ft.
Bonus Unfinished	369 sq. ft.
Garage Unfinished	430 sq. ft.
Deck Unfinished	160 sq. ft.
Porch Unfinished	85 sq. ft.
Dimensions	52'x59'9"
Foundation	Slab
Bedrooms	3
Full Baths	2
Max Ridge Height	26'
Roof Framing	Stick
Exterior Walls	2x4

BONUS

MAIN FLOOR

Design 94966

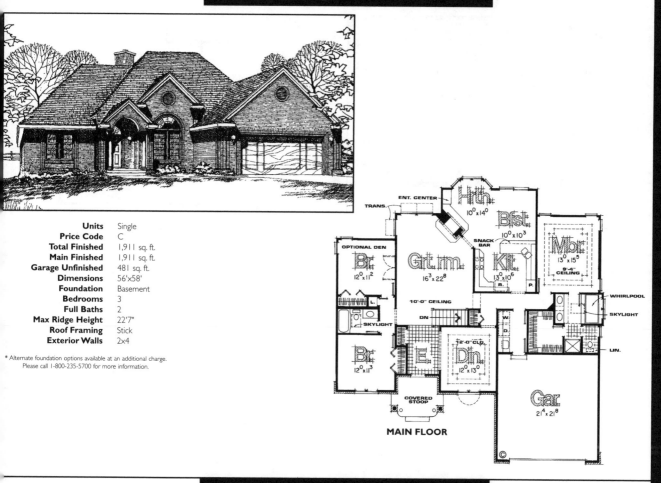

Units	Single
Price Code	C
Total Finished	1,911 sq. ft.
Main Finished	1,911 sq. ft.
Garage Unfinished	481 sq. ft.
Dimensions	56'x58'
Foundation	Basement
Bedrooms	3
Full Baths	2
Max Ridge Height	22'7"
Roof Framing	Stick
Exterior Walls	2x4

* Alternate foundation options available at an additional charge.
Please call 1-800-235-5700 for more information.

MAIN FLOOR

Design 97618

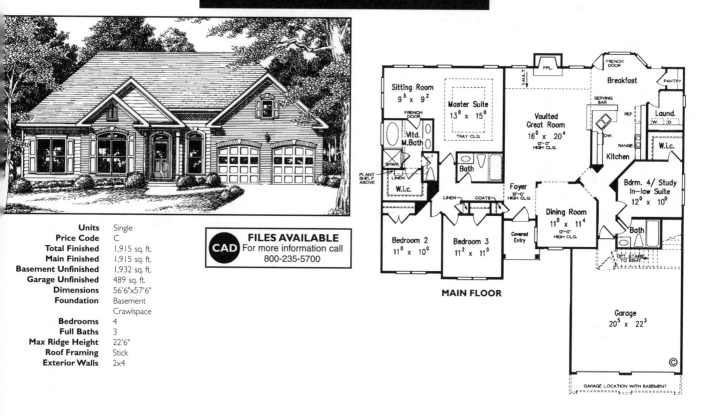

Units	Single
Price Code	C
Total Finished	1,915 sq. ft.
Main Finished	1,915 sq. ft.
Basement Unfinished	1,932 sq. ft.
Garage Unfinished	489 sq. ft.
Dimensions	56'6"x57'6"
Foundation	Basement
	Crawlspace
Bedrooms	4
Full Baths	3
Max Ridge Height	22'6"
Roof Framing	Stick
Exterior Walls	2x4

CAD FILES AVAILABLE
For more information call
800-235-5700

MAIN FLOOR

Design 82019

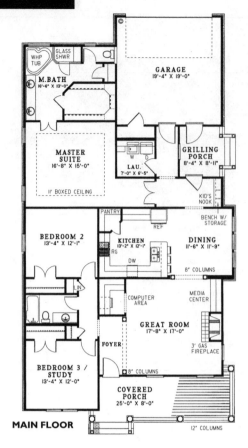

Units	Single
Price Code	C
Total Finished	1,915 sq. ft.
Main Finished	1,915 sq. ft.
Garage Unfinished	401 sq. ft.
Porch Unfinished	279 sq. ft.
Dimensions	39'x72'
Foundation	Crawlspace
	Slab
Bedrooms	3
Full Baths	2
Main Ceiling	10'
Roof Framing	Stick
Exterior Walls	2x4

MAIN FLOOR

Design 63001

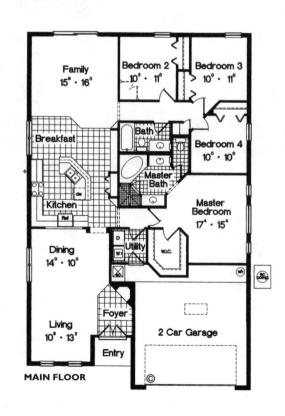

Units	Single
Price Code	C
Total Finished	1,919 sq. ft.
Main Finished	1,919 sq. ft.
Garage Unfinished	454 sq. ft.
Dimensions	40'x62'
Foundation	Slab
Bedrooms	4
Full Baths	2
Main Ceiling	8'
Max Ridge Height	18'6"
Roof Framing	Stick

MAIN FLOOR

Design 97870

Units	Single
Price Code	C
Total Finished	1,920 sq. ft.
Main Finished	1,920 sq. ft.
Garage Unfinished	483 sq. ft.
Deck Unfinished	150 sq. ft.
Porch Unfinished	42 sq. ft.
Dimensions	61'x48'7"
Foundation	Slab
Bedrooms	3
Full Baths	2
Half Baths	1
Main Ceiling	8'-10'
Max Ridge Height	30'
Roof Framing	Stick
Exterior Walls	2x4

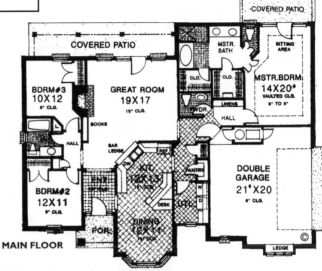

MAIN FLOOR

Design 99192

Units	Single
Price Code	C
Total Finished	1,921 sq. ft.
Main Finished	1,921 sq. ft.
Basement Unfinished	1,921 sq. ft.
Garage Unfinished	486 sq. ft.
Dimensions	53'8"x59'
Foundation	Basement
Bedrooms	3
Full Baths	2
Main Ceiling	9'
Tray Ceiling	11'
Max Ridge Height	25'3"
Roof Framing	Truss
Exterior Walls	2x4

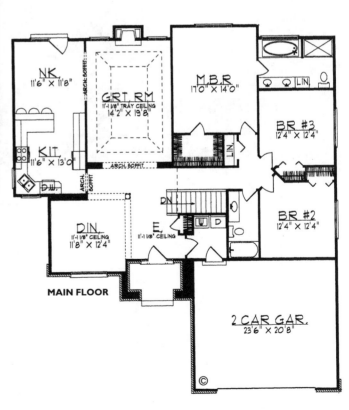

MAIN FLOOR

Design 97330

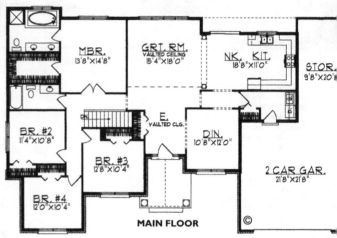

Units	Single
Price Code	C
Total Finished	1,923 sq. ft.
Main Finished	1,923 sq. ft.
Basement Unfinished	1,923 sq. ft.
Garage Unfinished	668 sq. ft.
Dimensions	70'8"x45'
Foundation	Basement
Bedrooms	4
Full Baths	2
Main Ceiling	21'4"
Max Ridge Height	21'4"
Roof Framing	Truss
Exterior Walls	2x6

MAIN FLOOR

Design 65672

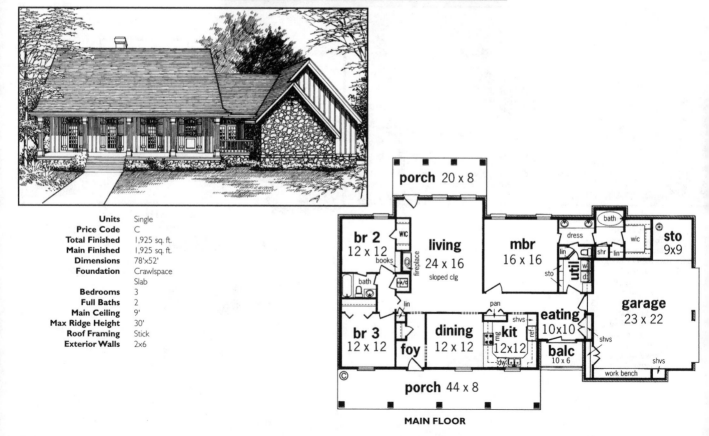

Units	Single
Price Code	C
Total Finished	1,925 sq. ft.
Main Finished	1,925 sq. ft.
Dimensions	78'x52'
Foundation	Crawlspace
	Slab
Bedrooms	3
Full Baths	2
Main Ceiling	9'
Max Ridge Height	30'
Roof Framing	Stick
Exterior Walls	2x6

MAIN FLOOR

Design 97277

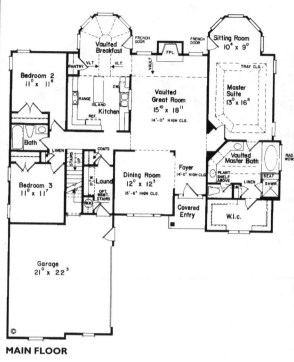

MAIN FLOOR

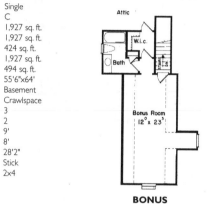

Attic

W.i.c.

Bath

Bonus Room
12⁰ x 23³

BONUS

Units	Single
Price Code	C
Total Finished	1,927 sq. ft.
Main Finished	1,927 sq. ft.
Bonus Unfinished	424 sq. ft.
Basement Unfinished	1,927 sq. ft.
Garage Unfinished	494 sq. ft.
Dimensions	55'6"x64'
Foundation	Basement
	Crawlspace
Bedrooms	3
Full Baths	2
Main Ceiling	9'
Second Ceiling	8'
Max Ridge Height	28'2"
Roof Framing	Stick
Exterior Walls	2x4

Design 97335

MAIN FLOOR

Units	Single
Price Code	C
Total Finished	1,927 sq. ft.
Main Finished	1,927 sq. ft.
Basement Unfinished	1,927 sq. ft.
Garage Unfinished	911 sq. ft.
Dimensions	62'x56'
Foundation	Basement
Bedrooms	3
Full Baths	2
Main Ceiling	9'
Max Ridge Height	22'11"
Roof Framing	Truss
Exterior Walls	2x6

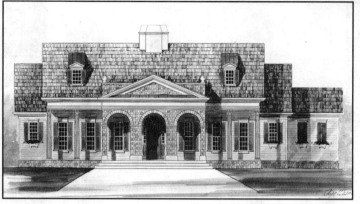

Units	Single
Price Code	C
Total Finished	1,928 sq. ft.
Main Finished	1,928 sq. ft.
Bonus Unfinished	160 sq. ft.
Garage Unfinished	400 sq. ft.
Porch Unfinished	315 sq. ft.
Dimensions	58'x47'
Foundation	Basement
Bedrooms	4
Full Baths	3
Main Ceiling	9'
Max Ridge Height	24'
Roof Framing	Stick
Exterior Walls	2x4

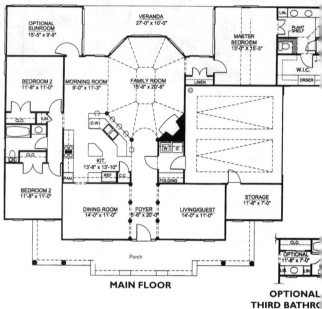

MAIN FLOOR

OPTIONAL THIRD BATHRO

Design 62053

Units	Single
Price Code	C
Total Finished	1,930 sq. ft.
Main Finished	1,930 sq. ft.
Garage Unfinished	509 sq. ft.
Porch Unfinished	357 sq. ft.
Dimensions	52'x71'6"
Foundation	Slab
Bedrooms	4
Full Baths	2
Main Ceiling	8'
Max Ridge Height	26'8"
Roof Framing	Truss
Exterior Walls	2x4, 2x6

MAIN FLOOR

Design 65647

Units	Single
Price Code	C
Total Finished	1,932 sq. ft.
Main Finished	1,932 sq. ft.
Bonus Unfinished	342 sq. ft.
Garage Unfinished	1,340 sq. ft.
Dimensions	66'x72'
Foundation	Crawlspace
	Slab
Bedrooms	3
Full Baths	2
Main Ceiling	9'
Second Ceiling	9'
Max Ridge Height	30'
Roof Framing	Stick
Exterior Walls	2x6

BONUS

bonus rm 22 x 14
future space 22 x 14
open to living rm below
future space 22 x 14

MAIN FLOOR

wic
bath
knee space
mbr 16 x 13
lin
frz
util 9x8
sto 10 x 9
pan
up
desk
3 car garage 32 x 22
kit
ref
ov
dining 14 x 12
eating
deck
porch 22 x 12
living 17 x 16
a/c
br 2 14 x 12
clo
bath
clo
br 3 13 x 11
clo
pan
foyer
clo
clo
porch 44 x 8

Design 93098

Units	Single
Price Code	C
Total Finished	1,932 sq. ft.
Main Finished	1,932 sq. ft.
Garage Unfinished	552 sq. ft.
Deck Unfinished	225 sq. ft.
Dimensions	65'10"x53'5"
Foundation	Crawlspace
	Slab
Bedrooms	3
Full Baths	2
Max Ridge Height	22'4"
Roof Framing	Stick
Exterior Walls	2x4

MASTER BATH
SLOPE CLG.
SLOPE CLG.
MASTER BEDRM 14-4 X 15-8 10 FT CLG
FP
BATH 2
LIN
BEDRM 2 12-6 X 13-0
BEDRM 3 12-0 X 15-6 10 FT CLG
SLOPE CLG.
PORCH
LIVING RM 17-4 X 20-6 10 FT CLG
FOYER 10 FT CLG
BRKFST RM 10-8 X 11-6 10 FT CLG
KITCHEN 10-8 X 15-0 10 FT CLG
PAN
DINING RM 12-8 X 13-0 10 FT CLG
UTIL 10-4 X 6-0
GARAGE
STORAGE
PORCH

MAIN FLOOR

Design 65670

Units	Single
Price Code	C
Total Finished	1,936 sq. ft.
Main Finished	1,936 sq. ft.
Dimensions	62'x68'
Foundation	Crawlspace
	Slab
Bedrooms	3
Full Baths	2
Main Ceiling	8'
Max Ridge Height	26'
Roof Framing	Stick
Exterior Walls	2x6

MAIN FLOOR

sto 11x6   sto 11x6

garage 22 x 22

deck

br 3 12 x 13

slope clg
skylights
living 20 x 20
12' clg

util

skylight

bath

wic

mbr 18 x 14
tray clg

bath lin

br 2 12 x 14

A/C

ref
desk
kit
pan
ct
ov

foy

dining 12x12
12' clg

eating 12 x 10

porch

Design 99115

Units	Single
Price Code	C
Total Finished	1,947 sq. ft.
Main Finished	1,947 sq. ft.
Basement Unfinished	1,947 sq. ft.
Dimensions	69'8"x46'
Foundation	Basement
Bedrooms	3
Full Baths	2
Half Baths	I
Main Ceiling	8'
Max Ridge Height	22'4"
Roof Framing	Truss
Exterior Walls	2x6

MAIN FLOOR

MBR. TRAY CEILING 13'8" X 18'4"

GRT. RM. VAULTED CEILING 15'0" X 20'4"

NK. 10'0" X 11'0"

KIT. 9'6" X 15'0"

DESK

E. VAULTED CEILING

DIN. 11'8" X 12'4"

3 CAR GAR. 24'4" X 44'0"

BR.#2 12'0" X 12'0"

BR.#3 10'0" X 12'8"

Design 97993

Units	Single
Price Code	C
Total Finished	1,948 sq. ft.
Main Finished	1,948 sq. ft.
Basement Unfinished	1,948 sq. ft.
Garage Unfinished	517 sq. ft.
Dimensions	64'x52'
Foundation	Basement
	Crawlspace
	Slab
Bedrooms	3
Full Baths	2
Half Baths	1
Main Ceiling	8'
Max Ridge Height	20'
Roof Framing	Stick
Exterior Walls	2x4

Alternate foundation options available at an additional charge.
Please call 1-800-235-5700 for more information.

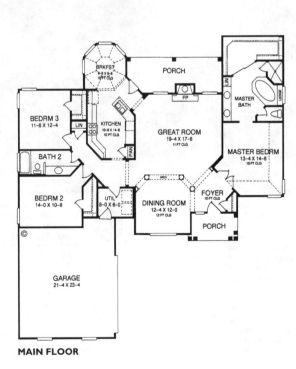

MAIN FLOOR

Design 93031

Units	Single
Price Code	C
Total Finished	1,955 sq. ft.
Main Finished	1,955 sq. ft.
Bonus Unfinished	240 sq. ft.
Garage Unfinished	561 sq. ft.
Porch Unfinished	215 sq. ft.
Dimensions	60'10"x65'
Foundation	Crawlspace
	Slab
Bedrooms	3
Full Baths	2
Max Ridge Height	24'
Roof Framing	Stick
Exterior Walls	2x4

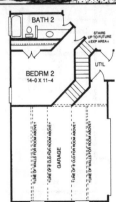

**BEDROOM/GARAGE OPTION
WITH STAIR TO BONUS**

MAIN FLOOR

Design 93085

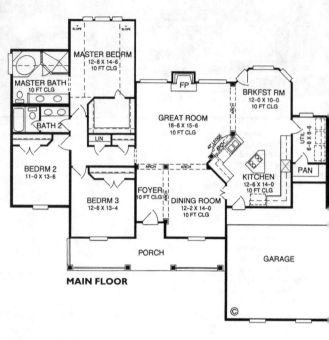

Units	Single
Price Code	C
Total Finished	1,955 sq. ft.
Main Finished	1,955 sq. ft.
Garage Unfinished	517 sq. ft.
Porch Unfinished	204 sq. ft.
Dimensions	65'x58'8"
Foundation	Crawlspace
	Slab
Bedrooms	3
Full Baths	2
Max Ridge Height	22'
Roof Framing	Stick
Exterior Walls	2x4

MAIN FLOOR

Design 97227

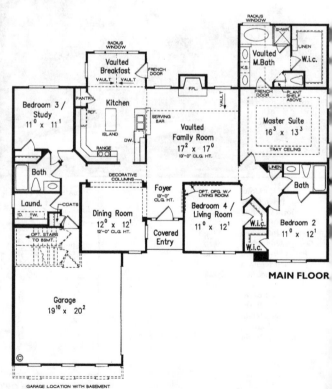

CAD FILES AVAILABLE
For more information call
800-235-5700

Units	Single
Price Code	C
Total Finished	1,960 sq. ft.
Main Finished	1,960 sq. ft.
Basement Unfinished	1,993 sq. ft.
Garage Unfinished	476 sq. ft.
Dimensions	59'x62'
Foundation	Basement
	Crawlspace
Bedrooms	4
Full Baths	3
Main Ceiling	9'1⅛"
Max Ridge Height	24'
Roof Framing	Stick
Exterior Walls	2x4

MAIN FLOOR

GARAGE LOCATION WITH BASEMENT

Design 69103

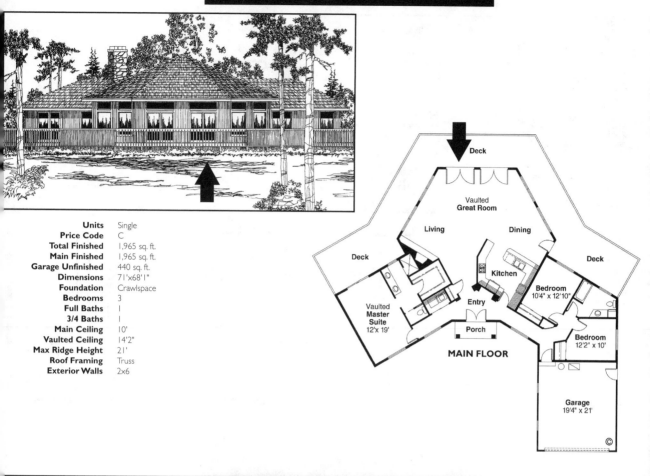

Units	Single
Price Code	C
Total Finished	1,965 sq. ft.
Main Finished	1,965 sq. ft.
Garage Unfinished	440 sq. ft.
Dimensions	71'x68'1"
Foundation	Crawlspace
Bedrooms	3
Full Baths	1
3/4 Baths	1
Main Ceiling	10'
Vaulted Ceiling	14'2"
Max Ridge Height	21'
Roof Framing	Truss
Exterior Walls	2x6

Design 93077

Units	Single
Price Code	C
Total Finished	1,971 sq. ft.
Main Finished	1,971 sq. ft.
Garage Unfinished	498 sq. ft.
Porch Unfinished	373 sq. ft.
Dimensions	66'2"x62'4"
Foundation	Crawlspace
Bedrooms	3
Full Baths	2
Max Ridge Height	20'
Roof Framing	Stick
Exterior Walls	2x4

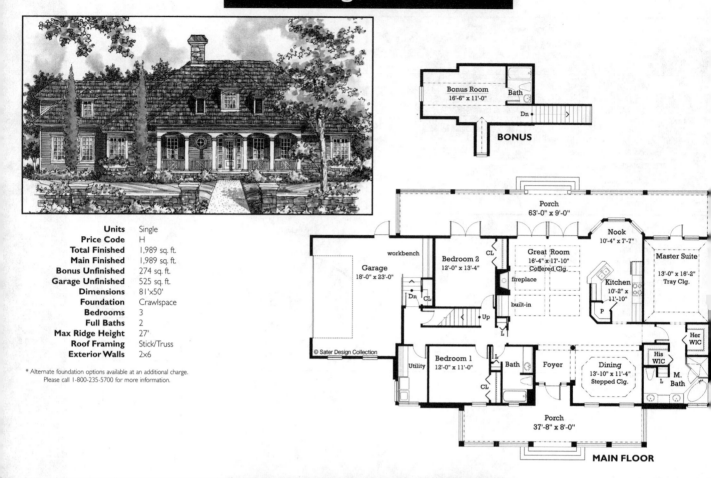

BONUS

Bonus Room 16'-6" x 11'-0"
Bath
Dn

Porch 63'-0" x 9'-0"

Nook 10'-4" x 7'-7"

workbench

Bedroom 2 12'-0" x 13'-4"

Great Room 16'-4" x17'-10" Coffered Clg.

Master Suite 13'-4" x 16'-2" Tray Clg.

Garage 18'-0" x 23'-0"

fireplace

Kitchen 10'-2" x 11'-10"

built-in

Up

Her WIC

© Sater Design Collection

Utility

Bedroom 1 12'-0" x 11'-0"

Bath

Foyer

Dining 13'-10" x 11'-4" Stepped Clg.

His WIC

M. Bath

Porch 37'-8" x 8'-0"

MAIN FLOOR

Units	Single
Price Code	H
Total Finished	1,989 sq. ft.
Main Finished	1,989 sq. ft.
Bonus Unfinished	274 sq. ft.
Garage Unfinished	525 sq. ft.
Dimensions	81'x50'
Foundation	Crawlspace
Bedrooms	3
Full Baths	2
Max Ridge Height	27'
Roof Framing	Stick/Truss
Exterior Walls	2x6

* Alternate foundation options available at an additional charge. Please call 1-800-235-5700 for more information.

BATH

BREAKFAST ROOM 12'-4" X 9'-6"

PORCH

MASTER SUITE TRAY CEILING 13'-4" X 15'-8"

KNEE SPACE

WHP TUB

GUEST ROOM/ BEDROOM 4 12'-8" X 11'-6"

BAR

GREAT ROOM 12' CEILING 15'-0" X 18'-4"

M.BATH 8'-10" X 21'-0"

KITCHEN 12'-4" X 13'-6"

BATH

LAU. 12'-8" X 5'-10"

REF PAN

8' BOX COL

FOYER 12' CEILING 7'-4" X 7'-10"

BEDROOM 2 11'-2" X 11'-8"

GARAGE 20'-10" X 25'-0"

DINING ROOM 10' BOX CEILING 12'-2" X 13'-4"

PORCH 7'-0" X 5'-6"

BEDROOM 3 11'-0" X 10'-4" VAULTED CEILING

MAIN FLOOR

Units	Single
Price Code	C
Total Finished	1,989 sq. ft.
Main Finished	1,989 sq. ft.
Garage Unfinished	521 sq. ft.
Porch Unfinished	105 sq. ft.
Dimensions	64'2"x49'
Foundation	Crawlspace
	Slab
Bedrooms	4
Full Baths	3
Main Ceiling	9'
Exterior Walls	2x4

Design 97912

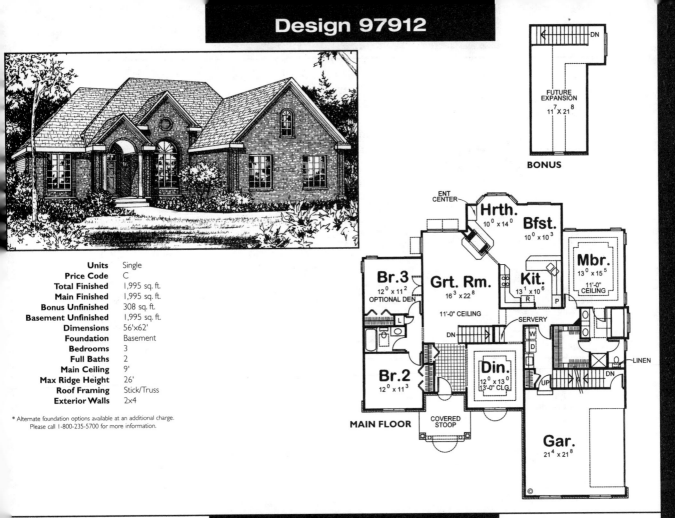

BONUS

FUTURE EXPANSION 11'⁷ X 21'⁸

Units	Single
Price Code	C
Total Finished	1,995 sq. ft.
Main Finished	1,995 sq. ft.
Bonus Unfinished	308 sq. ft.
Basement Unfinished	1,995 sq. ft.
Dimensions	56'x62'
Foundation	Basement
Bedrooms	3
Full Baths	2
Main Ceiling	9'
Max Ridge Height	26'
Roof Framing	Stick/Truss
Exterior Walls	2x4

* Alternate foundation options available at an additional charge.
Please call 1-800-235-5700 for more information.

MAIN FLOOR

Br.3 12'⁰ x 11'² OPTIONAL DEN
Br.2 12'⁰ x 11'³
Hrth. 10' x 14'
Grt. Rm. 16'³ x 22'⁸ 11'-0" CEILING
Bfst. 10' x 10'³
Kit. 13'¹ x 10'⁶
Mbr. 13'⁰ x 15'⁵ 11'-0" CEILING
Din. 12'⁰ x 13'⁰ 13'-0" CLG.
Gar. 21'⁴ x 21'⁸
COVERED STOOP
SERVERY
LINEN
ENT CENTER

Design 94926

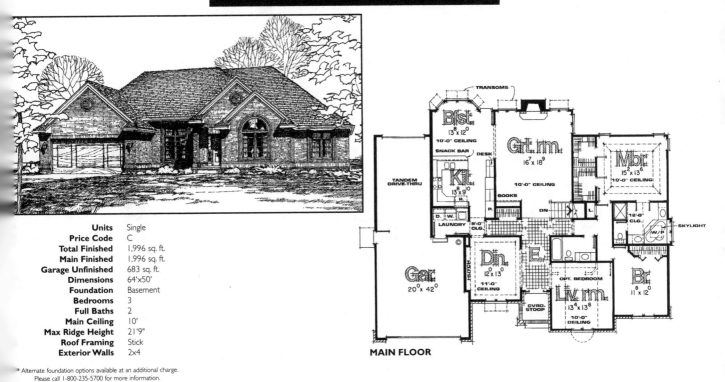

Units	Single
Price Code	C
Total Finished	1,996 sq. ft.
Main Finished	1,996 sq. ft.
Garage Unfinished	683 sq. ft.
Dimensions	64'x50'
Foundation	Basement
Bedrooms	3
Full Baths	2
Main Ceiling	10'
Max Ridge Height	21'9"
Roof Framing	Stick
Exterior Walls	2x4

* Alternate foundation options available at an additional charge.
Please call 1-800-235-5700 for more information.

MAIN FLOOR

Bfst. 13'⁸ x 12' 10'-0" CEILING
Grt. rm. 16' x 18'⁹ 10'-0" CEILING
Mbr. 15' x 13'⁶ 10'-0" CEILING
Kit. 13' x 9'
Din. 12' x 13' 11'-0" CEILING
Liv. rm. 13'⁴ x 13'⁸ 10'-0" CEILING
Br. 11' x 12'
Gar. 20' x 42'
SNACK BAR
DESK
BOOKS
LAUNDRY
TANDEM DRIVE-THRU
TRANSOMS
OPT. BEDROOM
CVRD. STOOP
SKYLIGHT

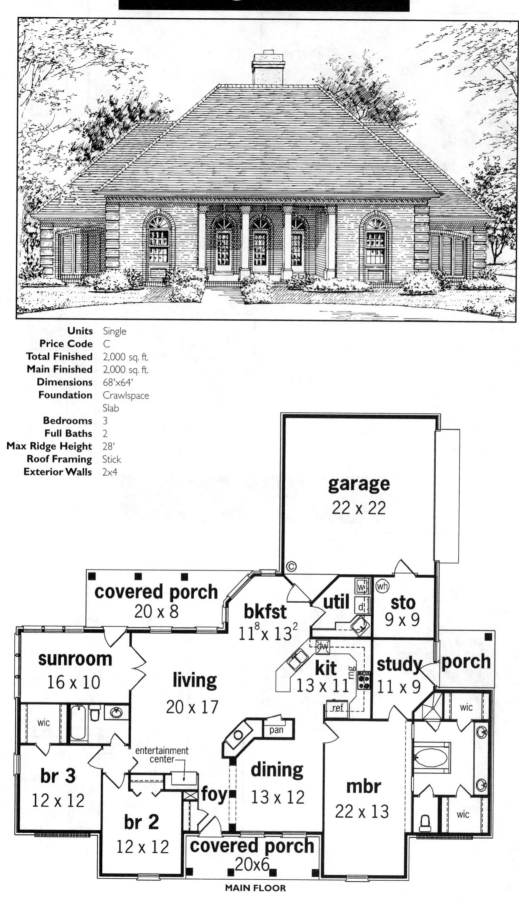

Units	Single
Price Code	C
Total Finished	2,000 sq. ft.
Main Finished	2,000 sq. ft.
Dimensions	68'x64'
Foundation	Crawlspace
	Slab
Bedrooms	3
Full Baths	2
Max Ridge Height	28'
Roof Framing	Stick
Exterior Walls	2x4

garage
22 x 22

covered porch
20 x 8

bkfst
11⁸ x 13²

util

sto
9 x 9

sunroom
16 x 10

living
20 x 17

kit
13 x 11

study
11 x 9

porch

wic

entertainment center

br 3
12 x 12

dining
13 x 12

mbr
22 x 13

wic

foy

br 2
12 x 12

covered porch
20x6

wic

MAIN FLOOR

Design 86019

Units	Single
Price Code	D
Total Finished	2,001 sq. ft.
Main Finished	2,001 sq. ft.
Basement Unfinished	979 sq. ft.
Garage Unfinished	455 sq. ft.
Deck Unfinished	220 sq. ft.
Porch Unfinished	21 sq. ft.
Dimensions	39'6"x84'10"
Foundation	Combo Basement/ Crawlspace
Bedrooms	3
Full Baths	2
Main Ceiling	8'
Max Ridge Height	27'7"
Roof Framing	Stick
Exterior Walls	2x4

MASTER BEDROOM 12'-0"x21'-0"

DECK 11'-8"x18'-0"

MR BATH

WIC

LIN

BEDROOM #2 12'-0"x10'-4"

FP

BOOKS

GREAT ROOM 19'-6"x 22'-8"

DINE

LINEN

BATH #2

W D

DN

KITCHEN 11'-4"x 11'-0"

LAUNDRY

FOYER

STUDY/ BEDROOM #3 12'-0"x10'-7"

NOOK 11'-4"x 7'-0" (+BAY)

GARAGE 20'-8"x 20'-8"

©

MAIN FLOOR

Design 65626

Units	Single
Price Code	D
Total Finished	2,002 sq. ft.
Main Finished	2,002 sq. ft.
Dimensions	66'x60'
Foundation	Crawlspace Slab
Bedrooms	3
Full Baths	2
Main Ceiling	8'
Max Ridge Height	29'
Roof Framing	Stick
Exterior Walls	2x6

hers

clo

lin

mbr 15 x 14

his

clo

frz brm

deck

desk

office 14 x 9

util 9x6

d w pan

br 3 12 x 11

clo

clo

storage

eating 10 x 8

porch 15 x 12

lin

garage 22 x 22

ref

kit 13x11

dw

DV

skylight

A/C

living 17 x 12

br 2 13 x 11

clo

clo

©

dining 14 x 12

shvs

entry clo

clo

porch 44 x 8

MAIN FLOOR

Design 63125

Units	Single
Price Code	D
Total Finished	2,005 sq. ft.
Main Finished	2,005 sq. ft.
Garage Unfinished	466 sq. ft.
Dimensions	58'x60'
Foundation	Slab
Bedrooms	3
Full Baths	2
Main Ceiling	10'
Max Ridge Height	20'10"
Roof Framing	Truss

MAIN FLOOR

Design 97308

Units	Single
Price Code	D
Total Finished	2,017 sq. ft.
Main Finished	2,017 sq. ft.
Garage Unfinished	912 sq. ft.
Dimensions	81'x51'4"
Foundation	Basement
Bedrooms	3
Full Baths	2
Half Baths	1
Main Ceiling	9'1⅛"
Max Ridge Height	24'8"
Roof Framing	Truss
Exterior Walls	2x6

MAIN FLOOR

Design 98361

MAIN FLOOR

Units	Single
Price Code	D
Total Finished	2,029 sq. ft.
Main Finished	2,029 sq. ft.
Basement Unfinished	2,029 sq. ft.
Garage Unfinished	704 sq. ft.
Dimensions	76'x71'4"
Foundation	Basement
Bedrooms	3
Full Baths	2
Half Baths	1
Max Ridge Height	24'
Roof Framing	Truss
Exterior Walls	2x6

Design 97619

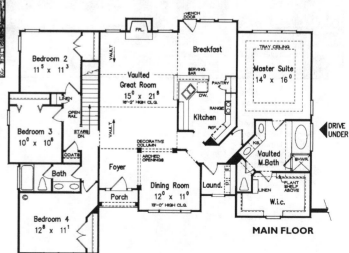

MAIN FLOOR

Units	Single
Price Code	D
Total Finished	2,032 sq. ft.
Main Finished	2,032 sq. ft.
Basement Unfinished	1,471 sq. ft.
Garage Unfinished	561 sq. ft.
Dimensions	58'6"x43'1"
Foundation	Basement
Bedrooms	4
Full Baths	2
Main Ceiling	9'
Max Ridge Height	24'
Roof Framing	Stick
Exterior Walls	2x4

Design 97406

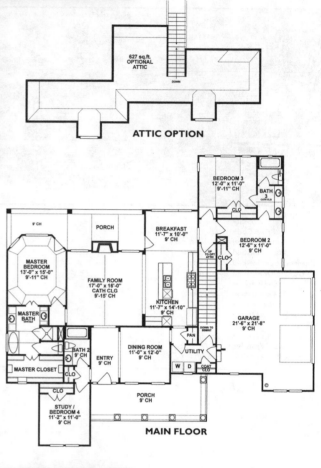

ATTIC OPTION

627 sq.ft. OPTIONAL ATTIC

Units	Single
Price Code	D
Total Finished	2,040 sq. ft.
Main Finished	2,040 sq. ft.
Dimensions	69'5"x63'6"
Foundation	Slab
Bedrooms	4
Full Baths	3
Max Ridge Height	28'
Roof Framing	Stick
Exterior Walls	2x4

* Alternate foundation options available at an additional charge. Please call 1-800-235-5700 for more information.

MAIN FLOOR

Design 63050

Units	Single
Price Code	D
Total Finished	2,041 sq. ft.
Main Finished	2,041 sq. ft.
Garage Unfinished	452 sq. ft.
Porch Unfinished	340 sq. ft.
Dimensions	60'4"x56'
Foundation	Slab
Bedrooms	4
Full Baths	2
Max Ridge Height	19'
Roof Framing	Truss
Exterior Walls	2x4

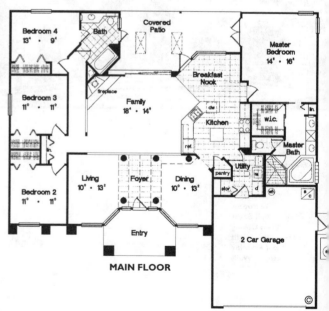

MAIN FLOOR

Design 92688

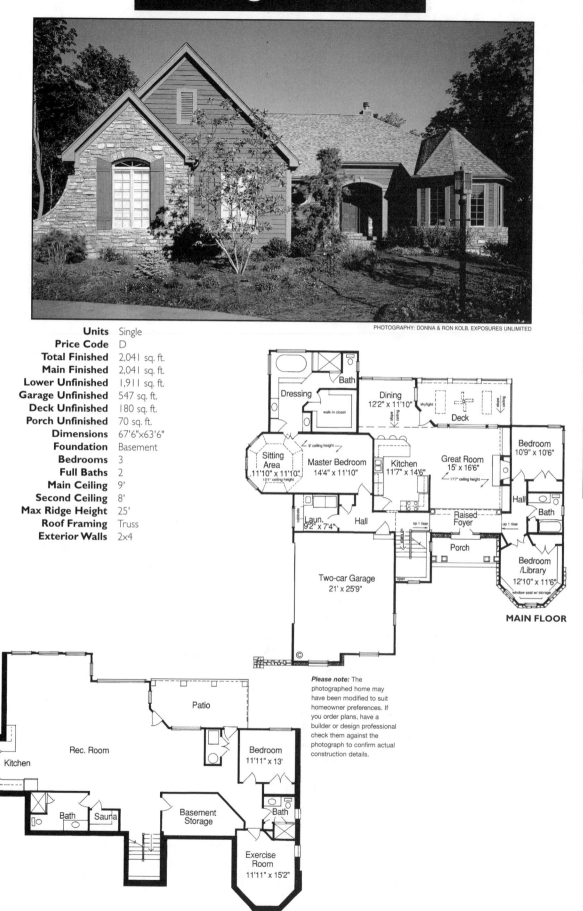

PHOTOGRAPHY: DONNA & RON KOLB, EXPOSURES UNLIMITED

Units	Single
Price Code	D
Total Finished	2,041 sq. ft.
Main Finished	2,041 sq. ft.
Lower Unfinished	1,911 sq. ft.
Garage Unfinished	547 sq. ft.
Deck Unfinished	180 sq. ft.
Porch Unfinished	70 sq. ft.
Dimensions	67'6"x63'6"
Foundation	Basement
Bedrooms	3
Full Baths	2
Main Ceiling	9'
Second Ceiling	8'
Max Ridge Height	25'
Roof Framing	Truss
Exterior Walls	2x4

MAIN FLOOR

LOWER FLOOR

Please note: The photographed home may have been modified to suit homeowner preferences. If you order plans, have a builder or design professional check them against the photograph to confirm actual construction details.

Units	Single
Price Code	D
Total Finished	2,042 sq. ft.
Main Finished	2,042 sq. ft.
Garage Unfinished	506 sq. ft.
Dimensions	65'4"x42'
Foundation	Basement
Bedrooms	3
Full Baths	2
Half Baths	I
Main Ceiling	8'
Max Ridge Height	19'
Roof Framing	Stick
Exterior Walls	2x4

* Alternate foundation options available at an additional charge.
  Please call 1-800-235-5700 for more information.

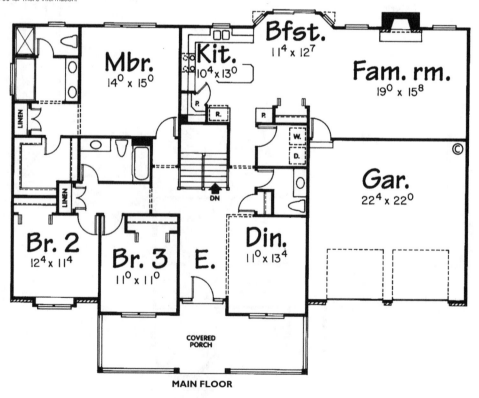

MAIN FLOOR

Design 68013

Units	Single
Price Code	D
Total Finished	2,047 sq. ft.
Main Finished	2,047 sq. ft.
Basement Unfinished	2,047 sq. ft.
Garage Unfinished	573 sq. ft.
Dimensions	66'x53'4"
Foundation	Basement
	Crawlspace
	Slab
Bedrooms	3
Full Baths	2
Half Baths	I
Main Ceiling	8'
Max Ridge Height	21'6"
Roof Framing	Stick
Exterior Walls	2x4

* Alternate foundation options available at an additional charge.
 Please call 1-800-235-5700 for more information.

THIRD BEDROOM OPTION

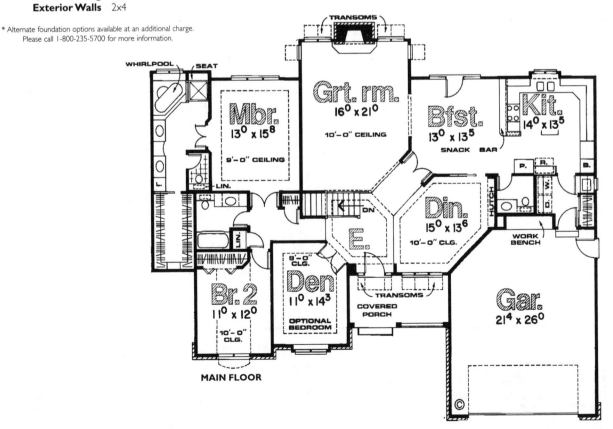

MAIN FLOOR

Units	Single
Price Code	D
Total Finished	2,060 sq. ft.
Main Finished	2,060 sq. ft.
Garage Unfinished	478 sq. ft.
Dimensions	60'4"x56'
Foundation	Slab
Bedrooms	4
Full Baths	2
Main Ceiling	10'
Max Ridge Height	24'
Roof Framing	Truss
Exterior Walls	2x4

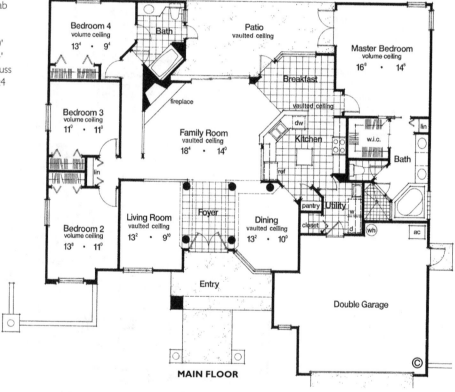

MAIN FLOOR

Design 99427

Units	Duplex
Price Code	G
Total Finished	1,908 sq. ft. (unit A)
Total Finished	2,060 sq. ft. (unit B)
Main Finished	1,908 sq. ft. (unit A)
Main Finished	2,060 sq. ft. (unit B)
Basement Unfinished	1,908 sq. ft. (unit A)
Basement Unfinished	2,060 sq. ft. (unit B)
Garage Unfinished	505 sq. ft. (unit A)
Garage Unfinished	530 sq. ft. (unit B)
Dimensions	82'8"x96'
Foundation	Basement
Bedrooms	2 or 3 (per unit)
Full Baths	2 (per unit)
Half Baths	1 (per unit)
Roof Framing	Stick
Exterior Walls	2x4

** Alternate foundation options available at an additional charge.
Please call 1-800-235-5700 for more information.*

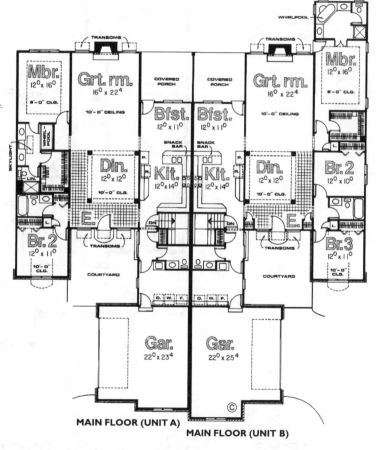

MAIN FLOOR (UNIT A)

MAIN FLOOR (UNIT B)

Units	Single
Price Code	D
Total Finished	2,062 sq. ft.
Main Finished	2,062 sq. ft.
Garage Unfinished	514 sq. ft.
Porch Unfinished	647 sq. ft.
Dimensions	63'x56'8"
Foundation	Slab
Bedrooms	3
Full Baths	I
3/4 Baths	I
Max Ridge Height	25'4"
Roof Framing	Truss

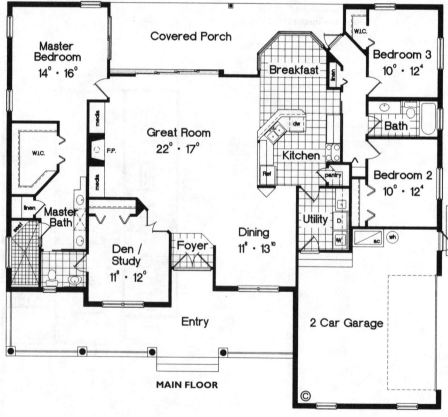

MAIN FLOOR

Merillat.

Visit us at www.merillat.com

Design 98583

2,001-2,500 sq. ft. HOME PLANS

Units	Single
Price Code	D
Total Finished	2,078 sq. ft.
Main Finished	2,078 sq. ft.
Garage Unfinished	734 sq. ft.
Deck Unfinished	140 sq. ft.
Porch Unfinished	240 sq. ft.
Dimensions	75'x47'10"
Foundation	Crawlspace
	Slab
Bedrooms	4
Full Baths	2
Max Ridge Height	27'
Roof Framing	Stick
Exterior Walls	2x4

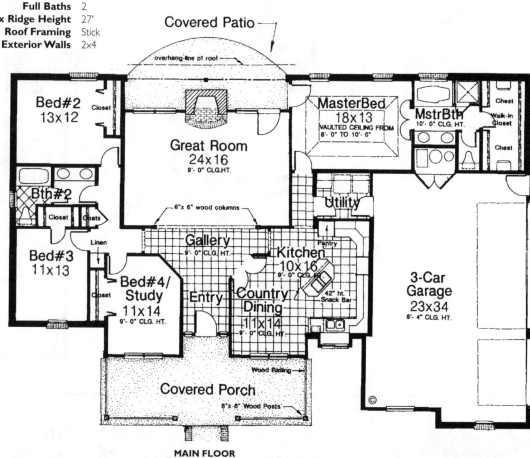

Covered Patio

Bed#2
13x12

Great Room
24x16
9'- 0" CLG. HT.

6"x 6" wood columns

MasterBed
18x13
VAULTED CEILING FROM
8'- 0" TO 10'- 0"

MstrBth
10'- 0" CLG. HT.

Chest

Walk-In Closet

Chest

Bth#2

Closet Coats

Utility

Gallery
9'- 0" CLG. HT.

Kitchen
10x16
9'- 0" CLG. HT.

Pantry

42" ht. Snack Bar

Bed#3
11x13

Linen

Bed#4/ Study
11x14
9'- 0" CLG. HT.

Entry

Country Dining
11x14
9'- 0" CLG. HT.

3-Car Garage
23x34
8'- 4" CLG. HT.

Wood Railing

Covered Porch

8"x 8" Wood Posts

©

MAIN FLOOR

Design 63052

Units	Single
Price Code	E
Total Finished	2,081 sq. ft.
Main Finished	2,081 sq. ft.
Garage Unfinished	559 sq. ft.
Porch Unfinished	219 sq. ft.
Dimensions	58'x66'8"
Foundation	Slab
Bedrooms	3
Full Baths	2
Main Ceiling	10'-12'
Max Ridge Height	24'
Roof Framing	Truss

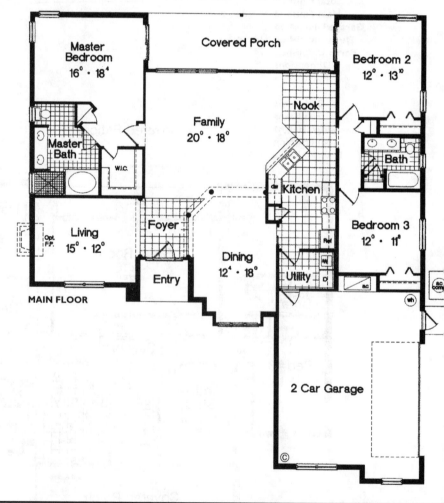

MAIN FLOOR

Design 98559

Units	Single
Price Code	D
Total Finished	2,081 sq. ft.
Main Finished	2,081 sq. ft.
Garage Unfinished	422 sq. ft.
Porch Unfinished	240 sq. ft.
Dimensions	55'x57'10"
Foundation	Slab
Bedrooms	3
Full Baths	2
3/4 Baths	1
Max Ridge Height	24'6"
Roof Framing	Stick
Exterior Walls	2x4

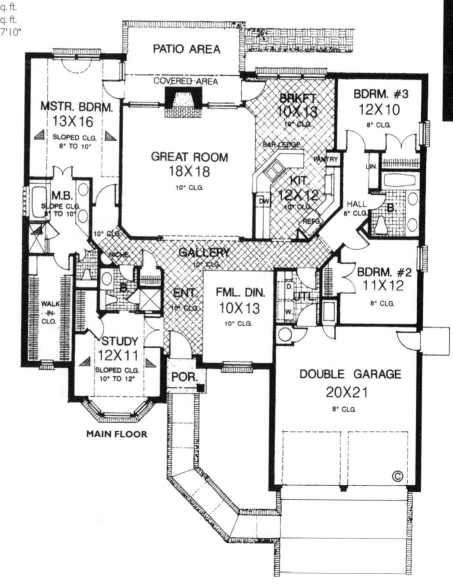

MAIN FLOOR

Units	Single
Price Code	D
Total Finished	2,083 sq. ft.
Main Finished	2,083 sq. ft.
Garage Unfinished	533 sq. ft.
Dimensions	84'x43'9"
Foundation	Crawlspace
Bedrooms	3
Full Baths	1
3/4 Baths	1
Main Ceiling	9'
Max Ridge Height	20'10"
Roof Framing	Truss
Exterior Walls	2x6

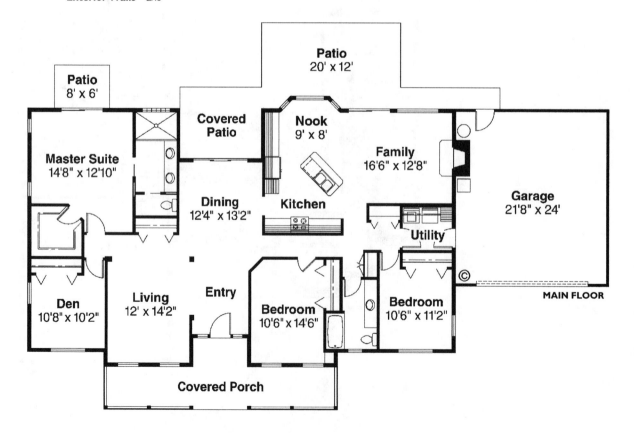

Design 63056

Units	Single
Price Code	C
Total Finished	2,089 sq. ft.
Main Finished	2,089 sq. ft.
Garage Unfinished	415 sq. ft.
Deck Unfinished	359 sq. ft.
Dimensions	61'8"x49'11"
Foundation	Slab
Bedrooms	4
Full Baths	3
Main Ceiling	10'
Max Ridge Height	20'10"
Exterior Walls	2x4

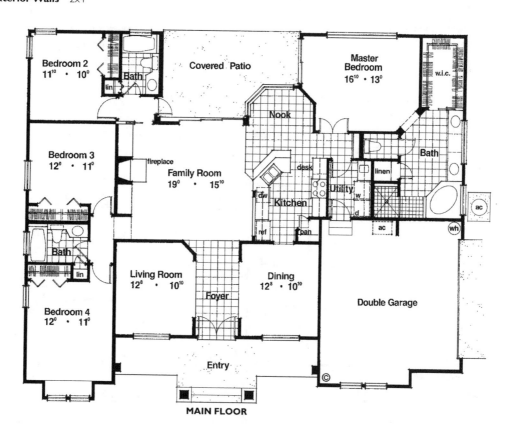

MAIN FLOOR

Design 96529

Units	Single
Price Code	D
Total Finished	2,089 sq. ft.
Main Finished	2,089 sq. ft.
Bonus Unfinished	497 sq. ft.
Garage Unfinished	541 sq. ft.
Dimensions	79'x52'
Foundation	Crawlspace
	Slab
Bedrooms	3
Full Baths	2
Half Baths	1
Main Ceiling	9'
Max Ridge Height	22'
Roof Framing	Stick
Exterior Walls	2x4

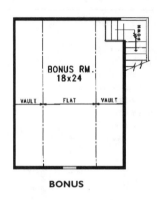

BONUS

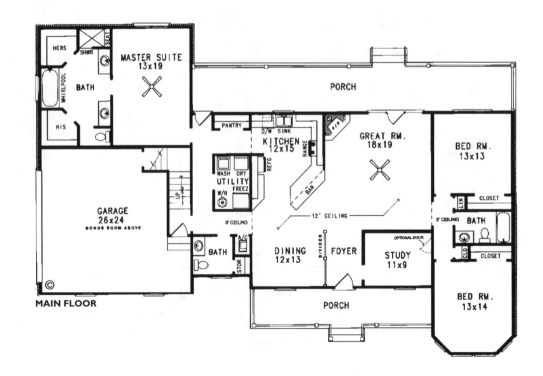

MAIN FLOOR

Design 93158

Units	Single
Price Code	D
Total Finished	2,095 sq. ft.
Main Finished	2,095 sq. ft.
Basement Unfinished	2,095 sq. ft.
Dimensions	67'x58'
Foundation	Basement
Bedrooms	3
Full Baths	2
Max Ridge Height	24'9"
Roof Framing	Stick
Exterior Walls	2x6

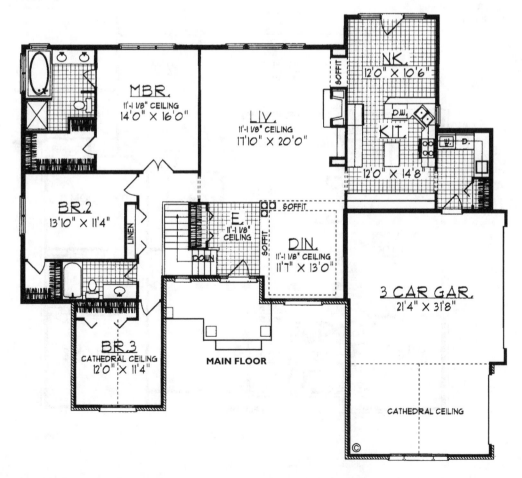

MBR.
11'-1 1/8" CEILING
14'0" X 16'0"

LIV.
11'-1 1/8" CEILING
17'10" X 20'0"

NK.
12'0" X 10'6"

KIT.
12'0" X 14'8"

BR.2
13'10" X 11'4"

E.
11'-1 1/8"
CEILING

DIN.
11'-1 1/8" CEILING
11'7" X 13'0"

SOFFIT

3 CAR GAR.
21'4" X 31'8"

BR.3
CATHEDRAL CEILING
12'0" X 11'4"

MAIN FLOOR

CATHEDRAL CEILING

Units	Single
Price Code	D
Total Finished	2,098 sq. ft.
Main Finished	2,098 sq. ft.
Garage Unfinished	590 sq. ft.
Porch Unfinished	292 sq. ft.
Dimensions	69'x64'
Foundation	Crawlspace
	Slab
Bedrooms	4
Full Baths	3
Max Ridge Height	26'
Roof Framing	Stick
Exterior Walls	2x4

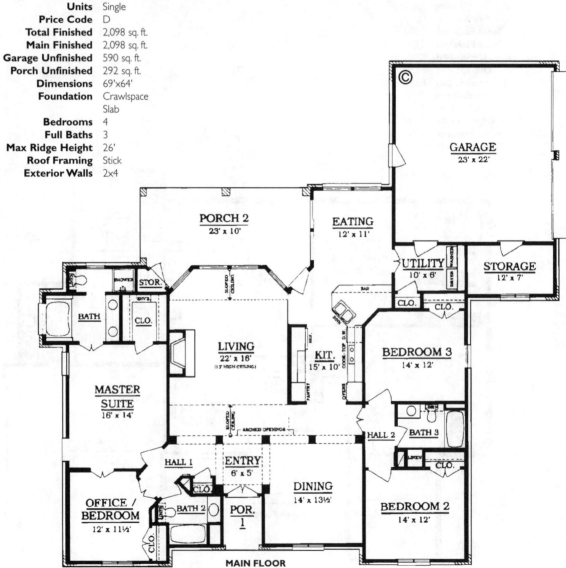

MAIN FLOOR

Design 24256

Units	Single
Price Code	D
Total Finished	2,108 sq. ft.
Main Finished	2,108 sq. ft.
Dimensions	50'x66'
Foundation	Basement
	Crawlspace
	Slab
Bedrooms	3
Full Baths	2
Max Ridge Height	23'
Roof Framing	Stick
Exterior Walls	2x4

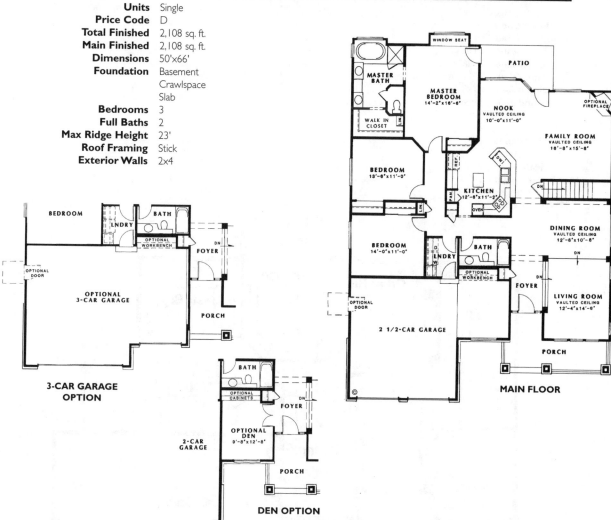

3-CAR GARAGE OPTION

DEN OPTION

MAIN FLOOR

Units	Single
Price Code	D
Total Finished	2,110 sq. ft.
Main Finished	2,110 sq. ft.
Basement Unfinished	2,096 sq. ft.
Garage Unfinished	724 sq. ft.
Dimensions	70'x56'
Foundation	Basement
	Crawlspace
	Slab
Bedrooms	3
Full Baths	2
Half Baths	1
Max Ridge Height	24'
Roof Framing	Stick
Exterior Walls	2x6

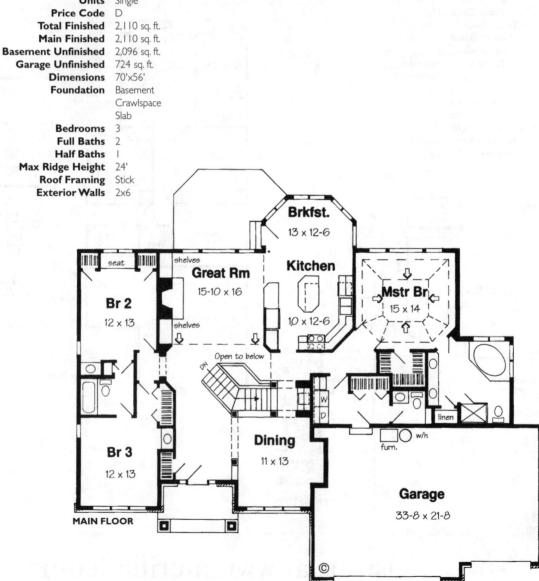

MAIN FLOOR

Design 63047

Units	Single
Price Code	D
Total Finished	2,118 sq. ft.
Main Finished	2,118 sq. ft.
Garage Unfinished	483 sq. ft.
Dimensions	58'x62'
Foundation	Slab
Bedrooms	3
Full Baths	2
Main Ceiling	9'4"
Max Ridge Height	20'9"
Roof Framing	Truss

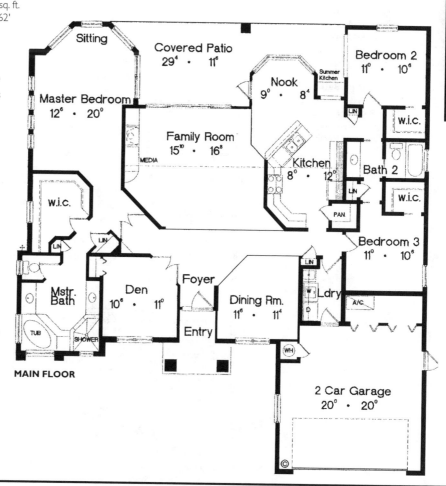

MAIN FLOOR

Units	Single
Price Code	D
Total Finished	2,132 sq. ft.
Main Finished	2,132 sq. ft.
Garage Unfinished	644 sq. ft.
Deck Unfinished	352 sq. ft.
Porch Unfinished	10 sq. ft.
Dimensions	60'x62'1"
Foundation	Slab
Bedrooms	4
Full Baths	3
Main Ceiling	8'-10'
Max Ridge Height	25'
Roof Framing	Stick
Exterior Walls	2x4

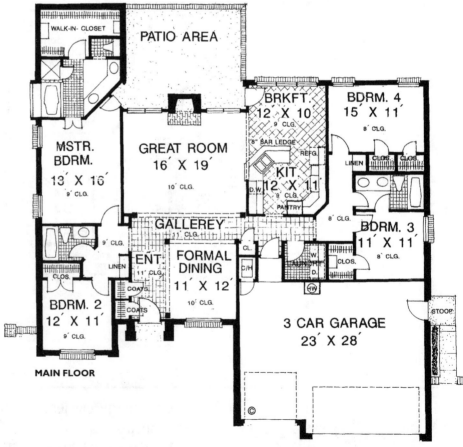

MAIN FLOOR

Design 97488

Units	Single
Price Code	D
Total Finished	2,132 sq. ft.
Main Finished	2,132 sq. ft.
Garage Unfinished	763 sq. ft.
Dimensions	72'x58'
Foundation	Basement
Bedrooms	3
Full Baths	2
Main Ceiling	8'
Max Ridge Height	22'
Exterior Walls	2x4

* Alternate foundation options available at an additional charge.
Please call 1-800-235-5700 for more information.

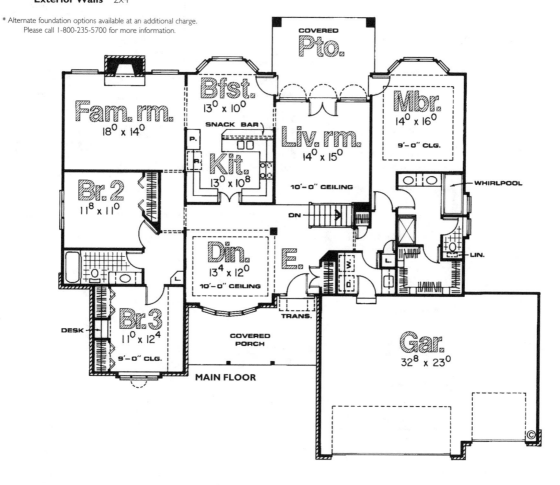

Units	Single
Price Code	F
Total Finished	2,137 sq. ft.
Main Finished	2,137 sq. ft.
Lower Unfinished	2,083 sq. ft.
Garage Unfinished	670 sq. ft.
Deck Unfinished	280 sq. ft.
Porch Unfinished	422 sq. ft.
Dimensions	44'x63'
Foundation	Basement
Bedrooms	3
Full Baths	2
Max Ridge Height	38'
Roof Framing	Truss
Exterior Walls	2x6

* Alternate foundation options available at an additional charge.
Please call 1-800-235-5700 for more information.

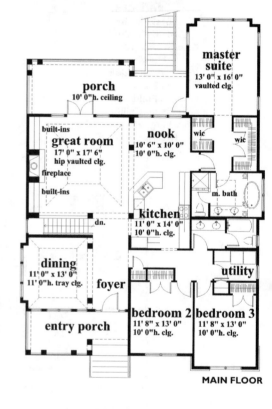

MAIN FLOOR

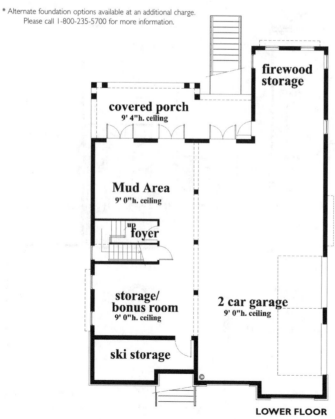

LOWER FLOOR

Design 61095

Units	Single
Price Code	D
Total Finished	2,140 sq. ft.
Main Finished	2,140 sq. ft.
Garage Unfinished	394 sq. ft.
Porch Unfinished	235 sq. ft.
Dimensions	40'x84'4"
Foundation	Basement
	Combo
	Basement/Crawlspace
Bedrooms	3
Full Baths	2
Main Ceiling	9'
Roof Framing	Stick
Exterior Walls	2x6

MAIN FLOOR

Design 92251

Units	Single
Price Code	D
Total Finished	2,140 sq. ft.
Main Finished	2,140 sq. ft.
Garage Unfinished	409 sq. ft.
Dimensions	65'x54'7"
Foundation	Crawlspace
	Slab
Bedrooms	3
Full Baths	2
Max Ridge Height	27'
Roof Framing	Stick
Exterior Walls	2x4

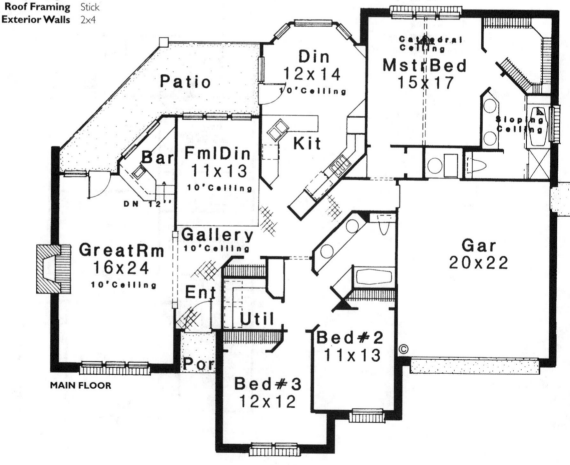

MAIN FLOOR

Design 94983

Units	Single
Price Code	D
Total Finished	2,144 sq. ft.
Main Finished	2,144 sq. ft.
Garage Unfinished	513 sq. ft.
Dimensions	60'8"x58'
Foundation	Basement
Bedrooms	3
Full Baths	2
Max Ridge Height	19'10"
Roof Framing	Stick
Exterior Walls	2x4

* Alternate foundation options available at an additional charge.
Please call 1-800-235-5700 for more information.

Mbr. 14⁰ x 16⁰

Liv. rm. 14⁰ x 14⁸
10'-0" CEILING

TRANSOMS

Bfst. 13⁰ x 10⁰

SNACK BAR

Kit. 13⁰ x 10⁸

Fam. rm. 18⁰ x 14⁰

Br. 2 11⁸ x 11⁰

Din. 13⁰ x 12⁰

E.

Gar. 21⁴ x 23⁰

COVERED PORCH

Br. 3 13⁴ x 10⁰

MAIN FLOOR

Units	Single
Price Code	D
Total Finished	2,145 sq. ft.
Main Finished	2,145 sq. ft.
Garage Unfinished	647 sq. ft.
Dimensions	60'11"x83'
Foundation	Crawlspace
Bedrooms	3
Full Baths	1
3/4 Baths	1
Main Ceiling	9'
Vaulted Ceiling	18'2"
Max Ridge Height	25'8"
Roof Framing	Truss
Exterior Walls	2x6

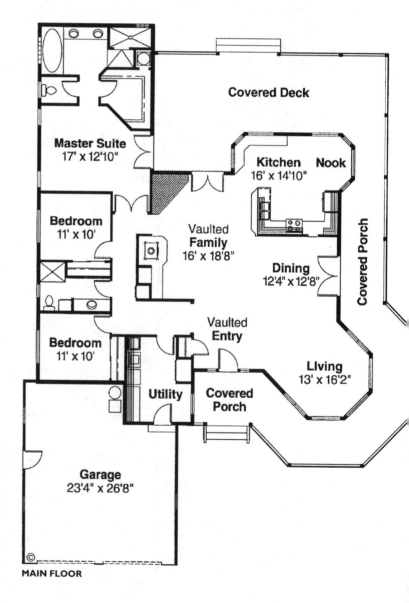

Covered Deck

Master Suite
17' x 12'10"

Kitchen 16' x 14'10" Nook

Bedroom 11' x 10'

Vaulted Family 16' x 18'8"

Covered Porch

Dining 12'4" x 12'8"

Bedroom 11' x 10'

Vaulted Entry

Living 13' x 16'2"

Utility

Covered Porch

Garage 23'4" x 26'8"

MAIN FLOOR

Design 61096

2,001-2,500 sq.ft. HOME PLANS

Units	Single
Price Code	D
Total Finished	2,148 sq. ft.
Main Finished	2,148 sq. ft.
Garage Unfinished	477 sq. ft.
Porch Unfinished	190 sq. ft.
Dimensions	63'x52'8"
Foundation	Crawlspace
	Slab
Bedrooms	4
Full Baths	2
Main Ceiling	9'
Roof Framing	Stick
Exterior Walls	2x4

MAIN FLOOR

BREAKFAST ROOM 11'-4" X 11'-2"

M. BATH 18'-2" X 9'-10"

WHP TUB

BEDROOM 2 11'-4" X 12'-0"

GREAT ROOM 20'-6" X 21'-0"

11' BOX

10' BOX

BAR

KIT. 10' BOX CEIL 11'-4" X 12'-6"

MASTER SUITE 10' BOXED CEILING 18'-2" X 13'-6"

BATH

LIN

HVAC

FRENCH FXD

FRENCH DOOR

LAU. 10'-0" X 5'-10"

STOR.

BEDROOM 3 11'-4" X 11'-10"

BEDROOM 4 9'-10" X 10'-6"

FOYER 7'-2" X 10'-4"

DINING ROOM 10' CEILING 11'-0" X 11'-3"

GARAGE 22'-0" X 21'-8"

10" COLUMNS

PORCH 20'-4" X 8'-6"

10" COLUMNS

Units	Single
Price Code	D
Total Finished	2,153 sq. ft.
Main Finished	2,153 sq. ft.
Garage Unfinished	434 sq. ft.
Dimensions	61'8"x62'
Foundation	Slab
Bedrooms	4
Full Baths	2
Main Ceiling	10'
Vaulted Ceiling	12'
Max Ridge Height	21'6"
Roof Framing	Truss
Exterior Walls	2x4

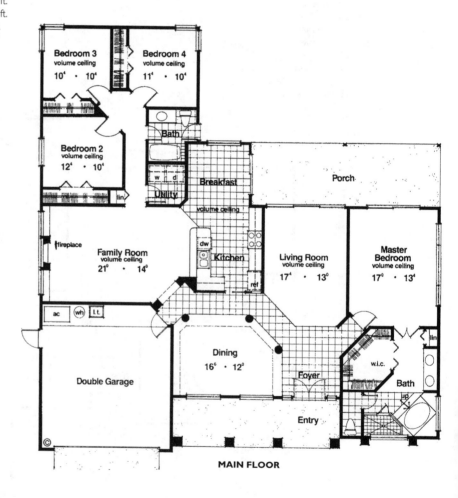

MAIN FLOOR

Design 97150

Units	Single
Price Code	D
Total Finished	2,153 sq. ft.
Main Finished	2,153 sq. ft.
Basement Unfinished	2,153 sq. ft.
Garage Unfinished	573 sq. ft.
Dimensions	65'x54'
Foundation	Basement
Bedrooms	3
Full Baths	2
Main Ceiling	9'1⅛"
Max Ridge Height	24'
Roof Framing	Truss
Exterior Walls	2x6

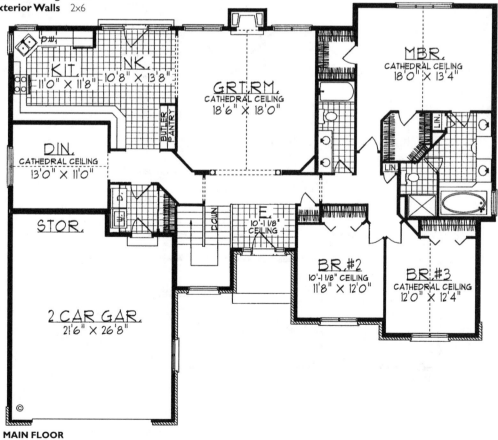

MAIN FLOOR

Units	Single
Price Code	D
Total Finished	2,155 sq. ft.
Main Finished	2,155 sq. ft.
Dimensions	60'x79'
Foundation	Crawlspace
Bedrooms	3
Full Baths	2
Half Baths	I
Max Ridge Height	22'
Roof Framing	Truss
Exterior Walls	2x6

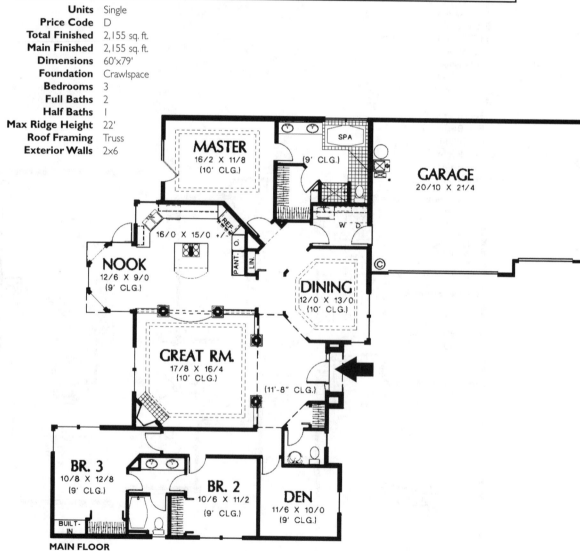

MASTER
16/2 X 11/8
(10' CLG.)

SPA

(9' CLG.)

GARAGE
20/10 X 21/4

16/0 X 15/0 +/-

REF.

PANT. LIN.

W   D

NOOK
12/6 X 9/0
(9' CLG.)

DINING
12/0 X 13/0
(10' CLG.)

GREAT RM.
17/8 X 16/4
(10' CLG.)

(11'-8" CLG.)

BR. 3
10/8 X 12/8
(9' CLG.)

BR. 2
10/6 X 11/2
(9' CLG.)

DEN
11/6 X 10/0
(9' CLG.)

BUILT-IN

MAIN FLOOR

Design 90484

Units	Single
Price Code	D
Total Finished	2,167 sq. ft.
Main Finished	2,167 sq. ft.
Basement Unfinished	2,167 sq. ft.
Garage Unfinished	491 sq. ft.
Deck Unfinished	184 sq. ft.
Dimensions	59'x59'10"
Foundation	Basement
	Crawlspace
	Slab
Bedrooms	3
Full Baths	2
Max Ridge Height	26'
Roof Framing	Stick
Exterior Walls	2x4

MAIN FLOOR

Units	Single
Price Code	D
Total Finished	2,167 sq. ft.
Main Finished	2,167 sq. ft.
Garage Unfinished	690 sq. ft.
Deck Unfinished	162 sq. ft.
Porch Unfinished	22 sq. ft.
Dimensions	64'x58'1"
Foundation	Slab
Bedrooms	3
Full Baths	2
Main Ceiling	8'-10'
Max Ridge Height	26'3"
Roof Framing	Stick
Exterior Walls	2x4

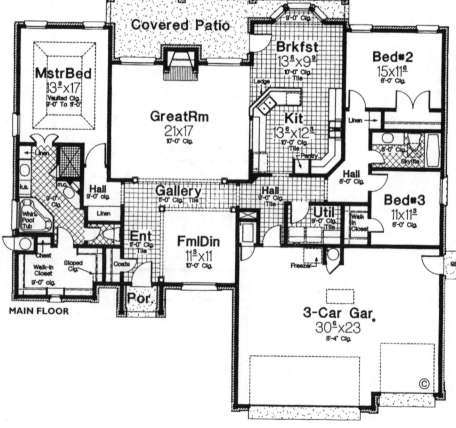

MAIN FLOOR

Design 98554

Units	Single
Price Code	D
Total Finished	2,169 sq. ft.
Main Finished	2,169 sq. ft.
Garage Unfinished	542 sq. ft.
Deck Unfinished	160 sq. ft.
Dimensions	76'6"x44'4"
Foundation	Slab
Bedrooms	4
Full Baths	3
Main Ceiling	8'-10'
Max Ridge Height	24'6"
Roof Framing	Stick
Exterior Walls	2x4

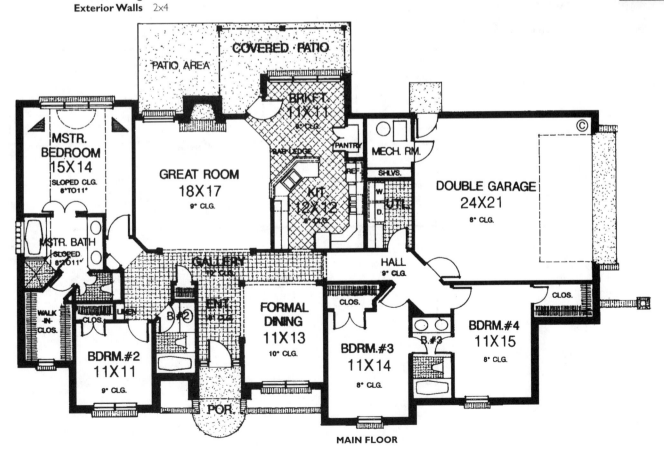

MAIN FLOOR

Units	Single
Price Code	D
Total Finished	2,170 sq. ft.
Main Finished	2,170 sq. ft.
Basement Unfinished	2,184 sq. ft.
Garage Unfinished	484 sq. ft.
Dimensions	63'6"x61'
Foundation	Basement
	Crawlspace
Bedrooms	3
Full Baths	2
Half Baths	1
Main Ceiling	9'
Max Ridge Height	27'
Roof Framing	Stick
Exterior Walls	2x4

CAD FILES AVAILABLE
For more information call
800-235-5700

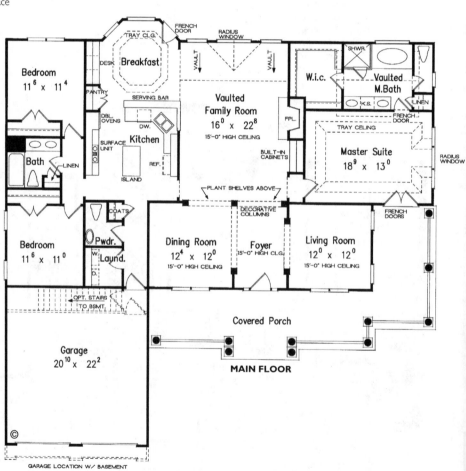

MAIN FLOOR

GARAGE LOCATION W/ BASEMENT

Units	Single
Price Code	D
Total Finished	2,180 sq. ft.
Main Finished	2,180 sq. ft.
Garage Unfinished	672 sq. ft.
Porch Unfinished	228 sq. ft.
Dimensions	58'4"x68'6"
Foundation	Basement
	Crawlspace
	Slab
Bedrooms	3
Full Baths	2
Half Baths	1
Exterior Walls	2x4

MAIN FLOOR

Merillat.

Visit us at www.merillat.com

Units	Single
Price Code	D
Total Finished	2,186 sq. ft.
Main Finished	2,186 sq. ft.
Garage Unfinished	720 sq. ft.
Dimensions	64'x66'
Foundation	Basement
Bedrooms	3
Full Baths	2
Half Baths	1
Main Ceiling	8'
Max Ridge Height	25'
Roof Framing	Stick
Exterior Walls	2x4

* Alternate foundation options available at an additional charge.
Please call 1-800-235-5700 for more information.

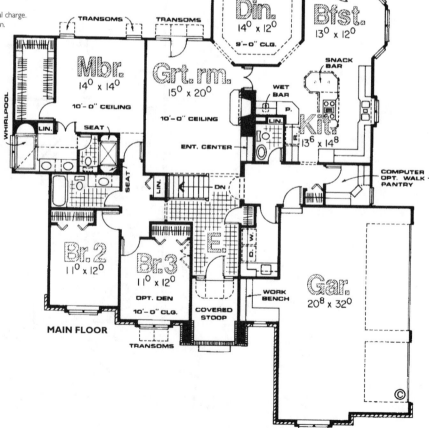

Design 97470

Units	Single
Price Code	D
Total Finished	2,188 sq. ft.
Main Finished	2,188 sq. ft.
Garage Unfinished	704 sq. ft.
Deck Unfinished	269 sq. ft.
Dimensions	74'x49'4"
Foundation	Basement
Bedrooms	3
Full Baths	2
Main Ceiling	9'
Max Ridge Height	28'10"
Roof Framing	Stick
Exterior Walls	2x4

*Alternate foundation options available at an additional charge.
Please call 1-800-235-5700 for more information.

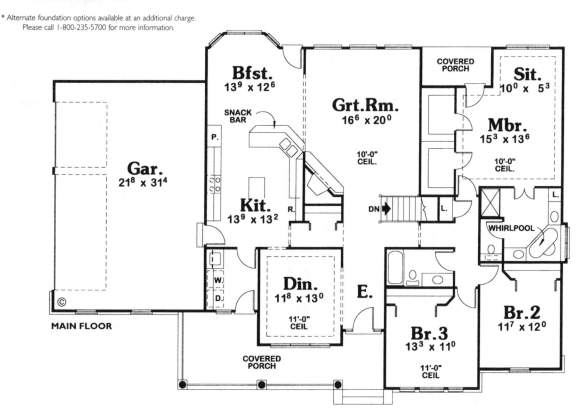

Units	Single
Price Code	D
Total Finished	2,190 sq. ft.
Main Finished	2,190 sq. ft.
Garage Unfinished	642 sq. ft.
Deck Unfinished	122 sq. ft.
Dimensions	65'×63'
Foundation	Slab
Bedrooms	4
Full Baths	2
Half Baths	1
Max Ridge Height	24'2"
Roof Framing	Stick
Exterior Walls	2x4

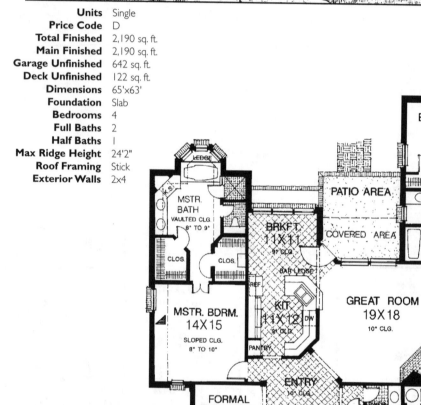

MAIN FLOOR

Design 97847

Units	Single
Price Code	D
Total Finished	2,192 sq. ft.
Main Finished	2,192 sq. ft.
Garage Unfinished	642 sq. ft.
Deck Unfinished	75 sq. ft.
Porch Unfinished	40 sq. ft.
Dimensions	54'10"x71'1"
Foundation	Slab
Bedrooms	4
Full Baths	3
Main Ceiling	8'-10'
Max Ridge Height	26'
Roof Framing	Stick
Exterior Walls	2x4

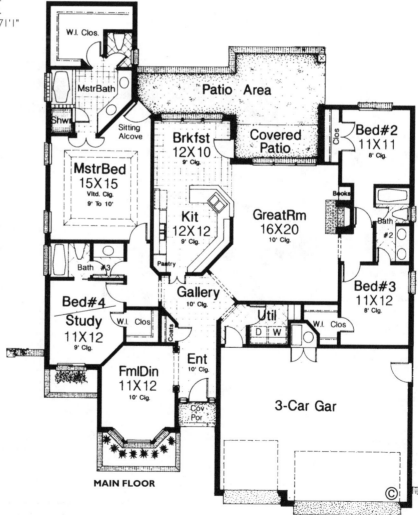

MAIN FLOOR

Design 98466

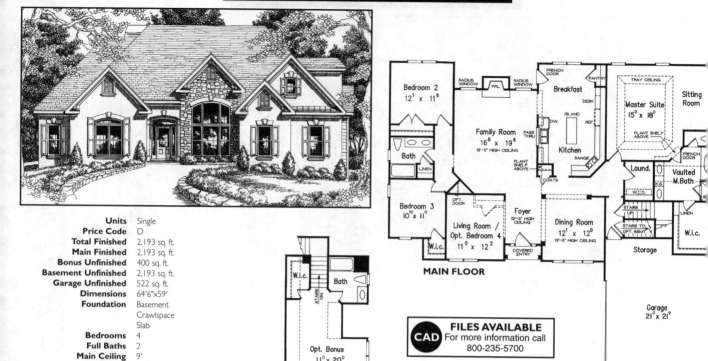

Units	Single
Price Code	D
Total Finished	2,193 sq. ft.
Main Finished	2,193 sq. ft.
Bonus Unfinished	400 sq. ft.
Basement Unfinished	2,193 sq. ft.
Garage Unfinished	522 sq. ft.
Dimensions	64'6"x59'
Foundation	Basement
	Crawlspace
	Slab
Bedrooms	4
Full Baths	2
Main Ceiling	9'
Second Ceiling	8'
Max Ridge Height	27'
Roof Framing	Stick
Exterior Walls	2x4

BONUS

MAIN FLOOR

CAD **FILES AVAILABLE**
For more information call
800-235-5700

Design 10507

Units	Single
Price Code	D
Total Finished	2,194 sq. ft.
Main Finished	2,194 sq. ft.
Garage Unfinished	576 sq. ft.
Dimensions	76'x75'
Foundation	Crawlspace
Bedrooms	3
Full Baths	1
3/4 Baths	1
Main Ceiling	8'
Max Ridge Height	15'
Roof Framing	Stick
Exterior Walls	2x6

MAIN FLOOR

Win free blueprints!

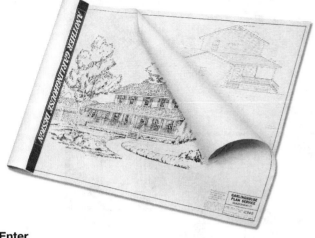

2 Easy Ways to Enter

1. Log on to www.garlinghouse.com and fill out our questionnaire on-line

—OR—

2. Fill out the questionnaire below and mail to:
   Free Home Plans Contest
   Garlinghouse, LLC
   4125 Lafayette Rd. Ste. 100
   Chantilly, VA 20151

Name: _____

the Garlinghouse company

Address: _____

City: _____ **State:** _____ **Zip:** _____

Daytime telephone number: (____) _____   **Email:** _____

Where did you buy this publication?

- ☐ Newsstand
- ☐ Grocery store
- ☐ Pharmacy/Conv. store
- ☐ Lumberyard/Home Center
- ☐ Bookstore
- ☐ Other _____

Please specify store: _____

Why did you buy this publication?

- ☐ Value
- ☐ Number of plans
- ☐ Appealing cover photo
- ☐ Impulse
- ☐ Other _____

What style are you most interested in?

- ☐ Farmhouse or Country
- ☐ Colonial
- ☐ Rustic Cottage or Cabin
- ☐ Victorian
- ☐ European
- ☐ Traditional
- ☐ Other _____

When are you planning to build?

- ☐ Within 6 months
- ☐ 6-12 months
- ☐ 1-2 years
- ☐ More than 2 years
- ☐ Undecided

What is the approximate size of the home?

- ☐ Under 1,000 square feet
- ☐ 1,000 to 2,000
- ☐ 2,000 to 3,000
- ☐ 3,000 to 4,000
- ☐ Over 4,000

What type of home?

- ☐ One level
- ☐ Two story with all bedrooms on second floor
- ☐ Two story with one or two bedrooms on first floor
- ☐ Other _____

Have you bought land? ☐ Yes ☐ No

Please provide any other comments.

Let us know if you have special requirements (e.g. you want a great-room but no living room) or specific property features (e.g. you have a sloped or narrow lot).

_____

_____

_____

Units	Single
Price Code	D
Total Finished	2,200 sq. ft.
Main Finished	2,200 sq. ft.
Dimensions	56'x74'
Foundation	Crawlspace
	Slab
Bedrooms	4
Full Baths	3
Main Ceiling	8'
Max Ridge Height	28'
Roof Framing	Stick
Exterior Walls	2x4

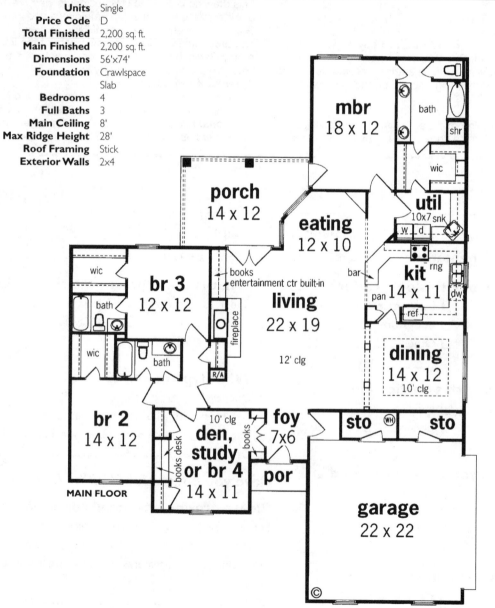

Design 97228

Units	Single
Price Code	D
Total Finished	2,201 sq. ft.
Main Finished	2,201 sq. ft.
Basement Unfinished	2,201 sq. ft.
Garage Unfinished	452 sq. ft.
Dimensions	59'6"x62'
Foundation	Basement
	Crawlspace
Bedrooms	3
Full Baths	2
Half Baths	1
Max Ridge Height	25'
Roof Framing	Stick
Exterior Walls	2x4

CAD FILES AVAILABLE
For more information call
800-235-5700

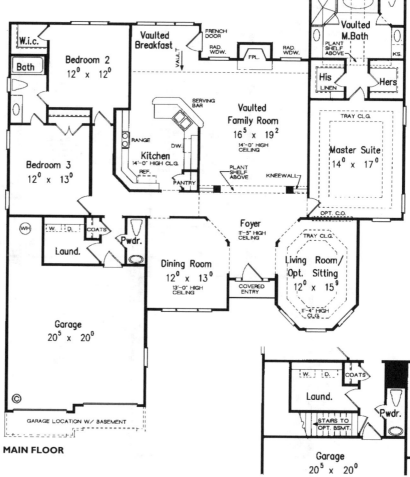

MAIN FLOOR

OPTIONAL BASEMENT STAIR LOCATION

Units	Single
Price Code	D
Total Finished	2,204 sq. ft.
Main Finished	2,204 sq. ft.
Basement Unfinished	2,204 sq. ft.
Dimensions	64'x56'
Foundation	Basement
Bedrooms	3
Full Baths	2
Max Ridge Height	23'8"
Roof Framing	Truss
Exterior Walls	2x6

NK.
12'4" X 13'0"

GRT. RM.
10'-1 1/8" CEILING
16'6" X 19'8"

MBR.
CATHEDRAL CEILING
18'0" X 16'0"

D.W.

KIT.
12'4" X 16'0"

PAN.

BR. #2
14'6" X 11'0"

W. D.

DESK

DOWN

LIN.

10'-1 1/8"
CEILING

SOFFIT

DIN.
10'-1 1/8" CEILING
13'4" X 12'6"

SOFFIT

SOFFIT

BR. #3
10'-1 1/8" CEILING
11'8" X 13'0"

2 CAR GAR.
22'0" X 22'0"

SOFFIT

©

MAIN FLOOR

Design 97858

Units	Single
Price Code	D
Total Finished	2,214 sq. ft.
Main Finished	2,214 sq. ft.
Garage Unfinished	599 sq. ft.
Deck Unfinished	136 sq. ft.
Porch Unfinished	42 sq. ft.
Dimensions	55'x77'11"
Foundation	Slab
Bedrooms	3
Full Baths	2
Half Baths	1
Main Ceiling	9'-10'
Max Ridge Height	27'
Roof Framing	Stick
Exterior Walls	2x4

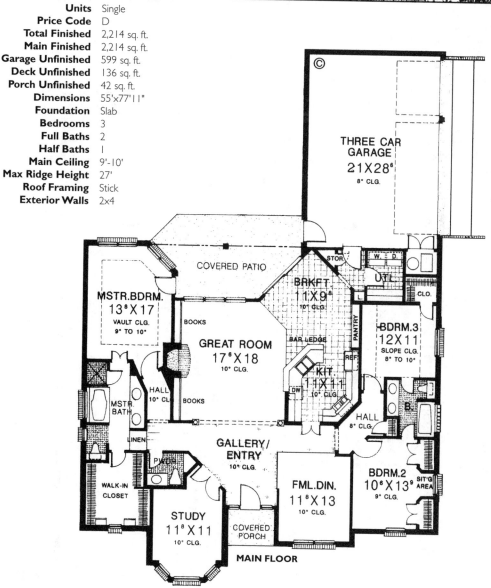

Units	Single
Price Code	D
Total Finished	2,224 sq. ft.
Main Finished	2,224 sq. ft.
Garage Unfinished	554 sq. ft.
Dimensions	58'6"x72'
Foundation	Slab
Bedrooms	4
Full Baths	2
3/4 Baths	1
Max Ridge Height	25'10"
Roof Framing	Truss

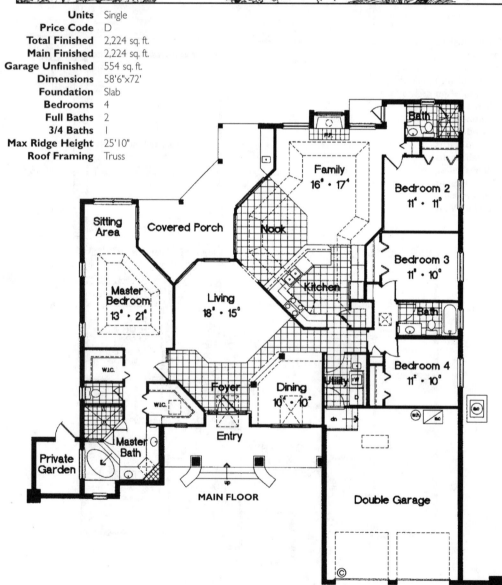

MAIN FLOOR

Design 91591

Units	Single
Price Code	D
Total Finished	2,225 sq. ft.
Main Finished	2,225 sq. ft.
Garage Unfinished	420 sq. ft.
Dimensions	45'x73'
Foundation	Crawlspace
Bedrooms	3
Full Baths	2
Max Ridge Height	28'
Roof Framing	Stick
Exterior Walls	2x6

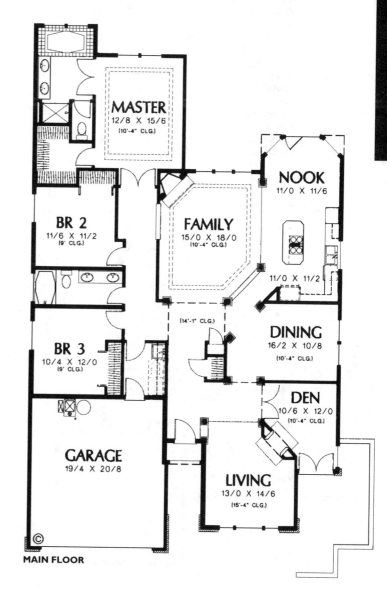

MAIN FLOOR

MASTER
12/8 X 15/6
(10'-4" CLG.)

NOOK
11/0 X 11/6

BR 2
11/6 X 11/2
(9' CLG.)

FAMILY
15/0 X 18/0
(10'-4" CLG.)

11/0 X 11/2

(14'-1" CLG.)

DINING
16/2 X 10/8
(10'-4" CLG.)

BR 3
10/4 X 12/0
(9' CLG.)

DEN
10/6 X 12/0
(10'-4" CLG.)

GARAGE
19/4 X 20/8

LIVING
13/0 X 14/6
(15'-4" CLG.)

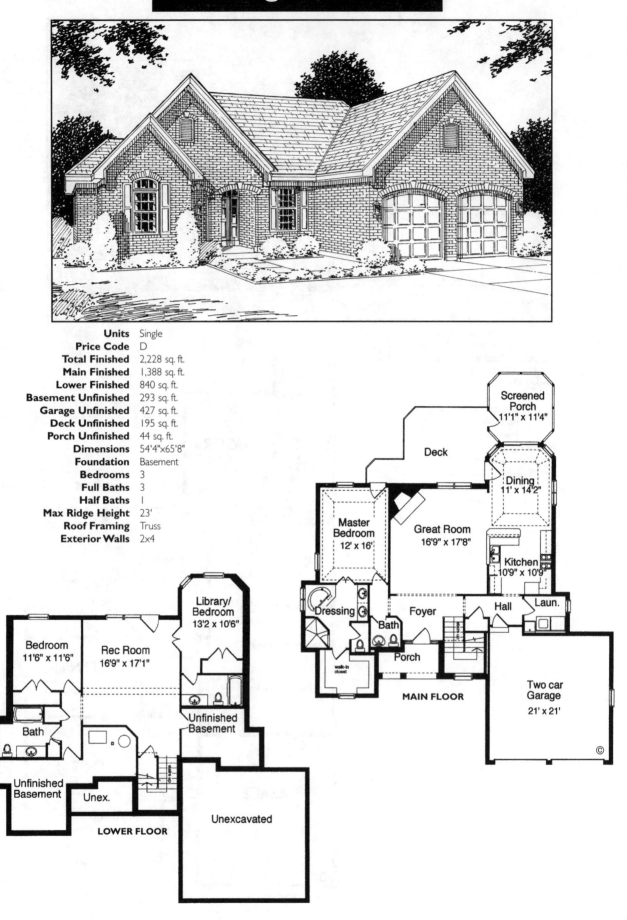

Units	Single
Price Code	D
Total Finished	2,228 sq. ft.
Main Finished	1,388 sq. ft.
Lower Finished	840 sq. ft.
Basement Unfinished	293 sq. ft.
Garage Unfinished	427 sq. ft.
Deck Unfinished	195 sq. ft.
Porch Unfinished	44 sq. ft.
Dimensions	54'4"x65'8"
Foundation	Basement
Bedrooms	3
Full Baths	3
Half Baths	1
Max Ridge Height	23'
Roof Framing	Truss
Exterior Walls	2x4

Screened Porch 11'1" x 11'4"

Deck

Dining 11' x 14'2"

Master Bedroom 12' x 16'

Great Room 16'9" x 17'8"

Kitchen 10'9" x 10'9"

Dressing

Bath

Foyer

Hall

Laun.

walk-in closet

Porch

MAIN FLOOR

Two car Garage 21' x 21'

Library/ Bedroom 13'2 x 10'6"

Bedroom 11'6" x 11'6"

Rec Room 16'9" x 17'1"

Unfinished Basement

Bath

Unfinished Basement

Unex.

Unexcavated

LOWER FLOOR

Design 98329

Units	Single
Price Code	D
Total Finished	2,228 sq. ft.
Main Finished	2,228 sq. ft.
Deck Unfinished	130 sq. ft.
Porch Unfinished	48 sq. ft.
Dimensions	58'4"x61'4"
Foundation	Slab
Bedrooms	3
Full Baths	2
Main Ceiling	10'
Max Ridge Height	22'6"
Roof Framing	Stick
Exterior Walls	2x6

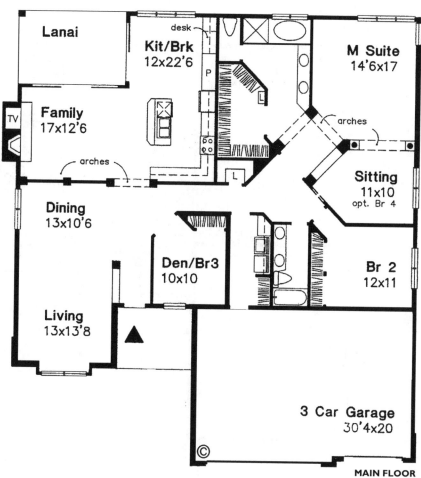

MAIN FLOOR

Units	Single
Price Code	D
Total Finished	2,229 sq. ft.
Main Finished	2,229 sq. ft.
Basement Unfinished	2,229 sq. ft.
Garage Unfinished	551 sq. ft.
Dimensions	65'x56'
Foundation	Basement
Bedrooms	3
Full Baths	2
Max Ridge Height	26'
Roof Framing	Truss
Exterior Walls	2x6

NK.
10'4" X 10'4"

DIN.
TRAY CEILING
11'4" X 12'6"

MBR.
CATHEDRAL CEILING
18'0" X 13'4"

GRT.RM.
CATHEDRAL CEILING
18'6" X 19'0"

KIT.
12'8" X 15'8"

PANTRY

OVEN

ARCH SOFFIT

11'-1 1/8" CEILING

LIN.

BR.2
11'2" X 12'8"

BR.3
12'8" X 12'4"

2 CAR GAR.
21'6" X 25'8"

MAIN FLOOR

Design 94673

Units	Single
Price Code	D
Total Finished	2,232 sq. ft.
Main Finished	1,944 sq. ft.
Bonus Unfinished	288 sq. ft.
Dimensions	58'x69'
Foundation	Slab
Bedrooms	3
Full Baths	2
Main Ceiling	8'
Max Ridge Height	25'
Roof Framing	Stick

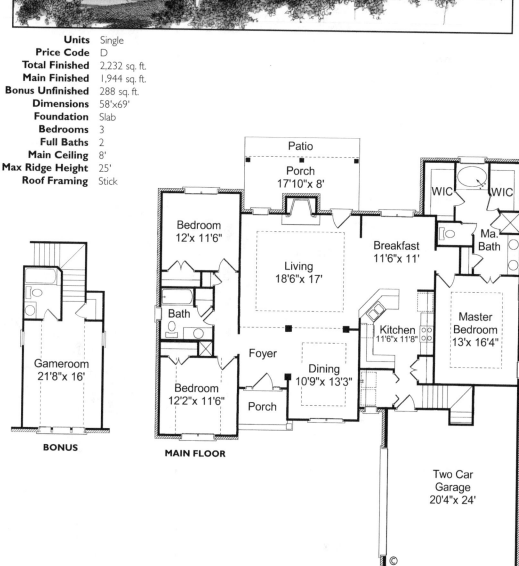

Patio

Porch 17'10"x 8'

Bedroom 12'x 11'6"

Living 18'6"x 17'

Breakfast 11'6"x 11'

WIC

WIC

Ma. Bath

Bath

Gameroom 21'8"x 16'

Kitchen 11'6"x 11'8"

Master Bedroom 13'x 16'4"

Foyer

Dining 10'9"x 13'3"

Bedroom 12'2"x 11'6"

Porch

Two Car Garage 20'4"x 24'

BONUS

MAIN FLOOR

Units	Single
Price Code	D
Total Finished	2,234 sq. ft.
Main Finished	2,234 sq. ft.
Bonus Unfinished	489 sq. ft.
Garage Unfinished	755 sq. ft.
Dimensions	76'x56'4"
Foundation	Crawlspace
Bedrooms	3
Full Baths	2
Main Ceiling	9'
Second Ceiling	8'
Vaulted Ceiling	18'
Max Ridge Height	26'
Roof Framing	Truss
Exterior Walls	2x6

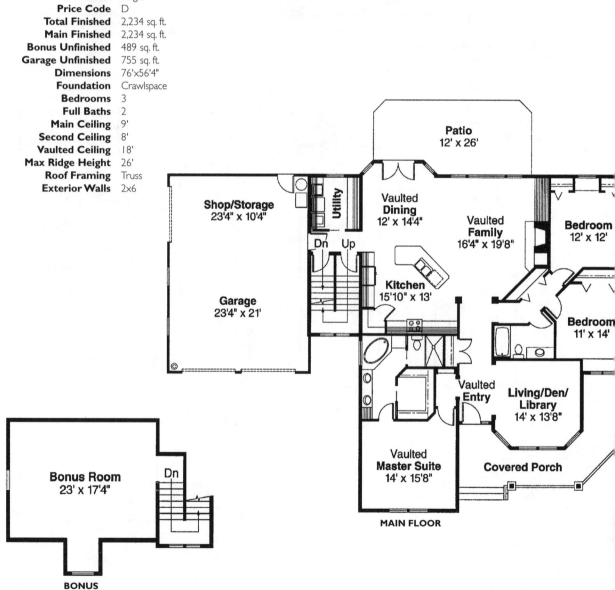

Design 98424

Units	Single
Price Code	D
Total Finished	2,236 sq. ft.
Main Finished	2,236 sq. ft.
Basement Unfinished	2,236 sq. ft.
Garage Unfinished	517 sq. ft.
Dimensions	63'x67'
Foundation	Basement
	Crawlspace
Bedrooms	3
Full Baths	2
Half Baths	1
Max Ridge Height	25'5"
Roof Framing	Stick
Exterior Walls	2x4

CAD FILES AVAILABLE
For more information call
800-235-5700

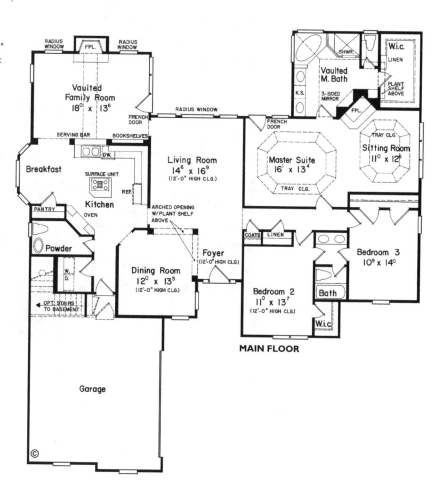

MAIN FLOOR

Design 98544

Units	Single
Price Code	D
Total Finished	2,238 sq. ft.
Main Finished	2,238 sq. ft.
Dimensions	60'x61'1"
Foundation	Slab
Bedrooms	4
Full Baths	3
Max Ridge Height	24'
Roof Framing	Stick
Exterior Walls	2x4

MAIN FLOOR

Design 68068

Units	Single
Price Code	D
Total Finished	2,242 sq. ft.
Main Finished	2,242 sq. ft.
Bonus Unfinished	613 sq. ft.
Garage Unfinished	525 sq. ft.
Dimensions	63'4"x60'
Foundation	Basement
	Crawlspace
	Slab
Bedrooms	2
Full Baths	2
Main Ceiling	9'
Max Ridge Height	26'
Roof Framing	Stick
Exterior Walls	2x4

Alternate foundation options available at an additional charge. Please call 1-800-235-5700 for more information.

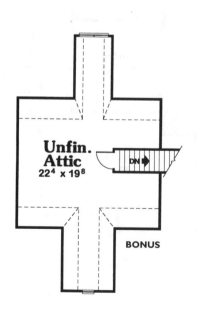

Unfin. Attic
22⁴ x 19⁸

BONUS

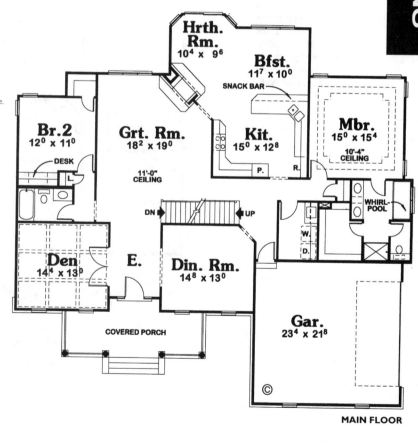

Hrth. Rm.
10⁴ x 9⁶

Bfst.
11⁷ x 10⁰

SNACK BAR

Mbr.
15⁰ x 15⁴

10'-4" CEILING

Br. 2
12⁰ x 11⁰

DESK

Grt. Rm.
18² x 19⁰

Kit.
15⁰ x 12⁸

11'-0" CEILING

WHIRL-POOL

W. D.

DN   UP

Den
14⁴ x 13⁰

E.

Din. Rm.
14⁸ x 13⁰

Gar.
23⁴ x 21⁸

COVERED PORCH

MAIN FLOOR

Units	Single
Price Code	D
Total Finished	2,246 sq. ft.
Main Finished	2,246 sq. ft.
Garage Unfinished	546 sq. ft.
Porch Unfinished	195 sq. ft.
Dimensions	61'10"x65'5"
Foundation	Crawlspace
	Slab
Bedrooms	4
Full Baths	2
Half Baths	1
Main Ceiling	9'
Max Ridge Height	24'
Roof Framing	Truss
Exterior Walls	2x4, 2x6

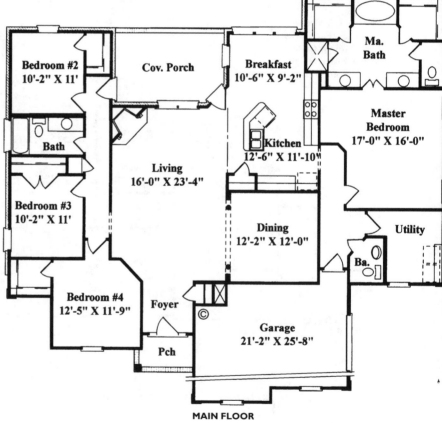

MAIN FLOOR

Design 65667

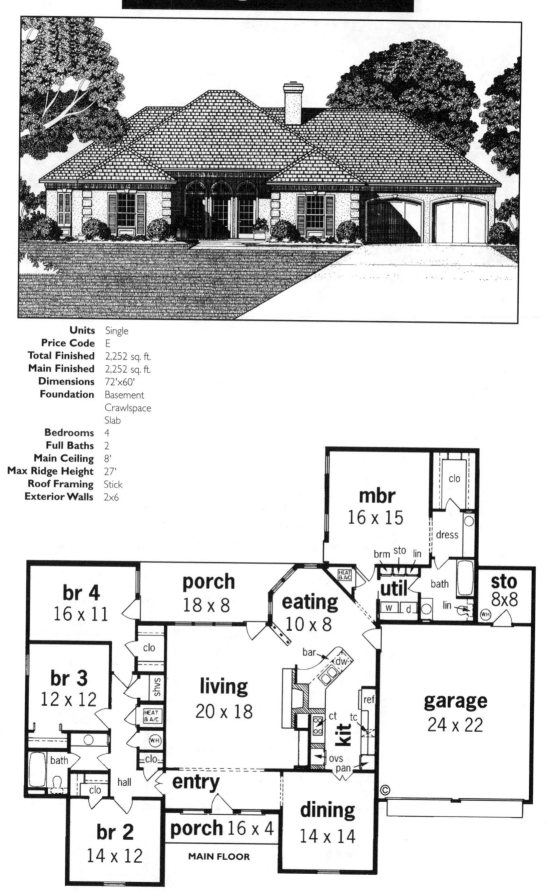

Units	Single
Price Code	E
Total Finished	2,252 sq. ft.
Main Finished	2,252 sq. ft.
Dimensions	72'x60'
Foundation	Basement
	Crawlspace
	Slab
Bedrooms	4
Full Baths	2
Main Ceiling	8'
Max Ridge Height	27'
Roof Framing	Stick
Exterior Walls	2x6

mbr 16 x 15

clo

dress

br 4 16 x 11

porch 18 x 8

eating 10 x 8

brm sto lin

util

w d

bath

lin

sto 8x8

clo

shvs

HEAT & A/C

br 3 12 x 12

living 20 x 18

bar

dw

ct tc

ref

garage 24 x 22

WH

bath

clo

clo

hall

entry

ovs pan

kit

br 2 14 x 12

porch 16 x 4

dining 14 x 14

MAIN FLOOR

Design 97850

Units	Single
Price Code	E
Total Finished	2,253 sq. ft.
Main Finished	2,253 sq. ft.
Garage Unfinished	602 sq. ft.
Deck Unfinished	205 sq. ft.
Porch Unfinished	110 sq. ft.
Dimensions	63'x60'3"
Foundation	Slab
Bedrooms	4
Full Baths	2
3/4 Baths	1
Main Ceiling	8'-10'
Max Ridge Height	26'
Roof Framing	Stick
Exterior Walls	2x4

MAIN FLOOR

Design 66090

Units	Single
Price Code	F
Total Finished	2,255 sq. ft.
Main Finished	2,255 sq. ft.
Bonus Unfinished	324 sq. ft.
Garage Unfinished	660 sq. ft.
Dimensions	55'x70'
Foundation	Slab
Bedrooms	4
Full Baths	2
3/4 Baths	1
Main Ceiling	8'
Max Ridge Height	24'6"
Roof Framing	Stick
Exterior Walls	2x4

Attic Storage

Future Bonus Rm
16 x 19
10'-0" Clg.

5'-0" Wall   5'-0" Wall

Ceiling Slope

BONUS

MstrBed
18 x 15
Pullman Clg.
9'-0" to 10'-6"

Sitting Area

Mstr. Bath

GreatRm
15 x 20
Cathedral Clg.
From 10'-0" PL
at 5/12 Pitch

36" Pre-Fab
w/ Gas Start

Brkfst
11 x 10
10'-0" Clg.

Cov'd Patio

Sliding Door

Kitchen
30" Drop-In
Unit w/ Oven

Bed#2
14 x 10
9'-0" Clg.

Bath 2
Walk-In Closet

Bed#3
11 x 11⁶
9'-0" Clg.

Stairs

Utility

Storage

Gallery

Walk-In Closet

Bath 3
5'-0" Tub w/ Shower

Coats

Entry
10'-0" Clg.

FmlDin
10 x 11
10'-0" Clg.

Study Bed#4
10 x 11
9'-0" Clg.

Closet

Cov'd Porch

Wing Wall

Planter

Planter

Three-Car Garage

Stoop

Wing Wall

MAIN FLOOR

Units	Single
Price Code	E
Total Finished	2,257 sq. ft.
Main Finished	2,257 sq. ft.
Garage Unfinished	528 sq. ft.
Dimensions	64'7"x77'10"
Foundation	Slab
Bedrooms	3
Full Baths	2
Half Baths	1
Main Ceiling	9'-10'
Max Ridge Height	26'6"
Roof Framing	Stick
Exterior Walls	2x4

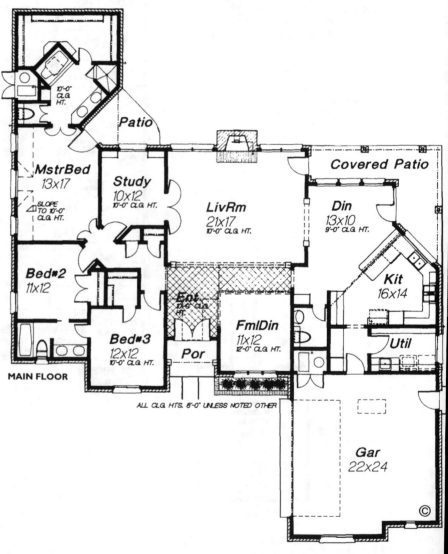

MAIN FLOOR

ALL CLG HTS. 8'-0" UNLESS NOTED OTHER

Design 65668

Units	Single
Price Code	E
Total Finished	2,259 sq. ft.
Main Finished	2,259 sq. ft.
Dimensions	56'x93'
Foundation	Crawlspace
	Slab
Bedrooms	3
Full Baths	2
Half Baths	1
Max Ridge Height	32'
Roof Framing	Stick
Exterior Walls	2x6

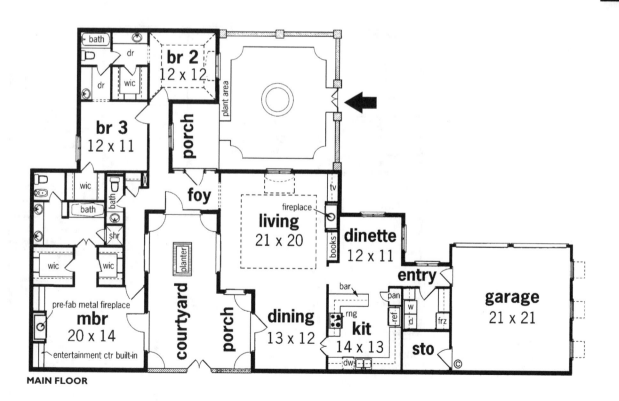

MAIN FLOOR

Units	Single
Price Code	E
Total Finished	2,271 sq. ft.
Main Finished	2,271 sq. ft.
Garage Unfinished	484 sq. ft.
Dimensions	61'6"x57'10"
Foundation	Basement
	Crawlspace
	Slab
Bedrooms	4
Full Baths	2
Max Ridge Height	25'4"
Roof Framing	Stick
Exterior Walls	2x4

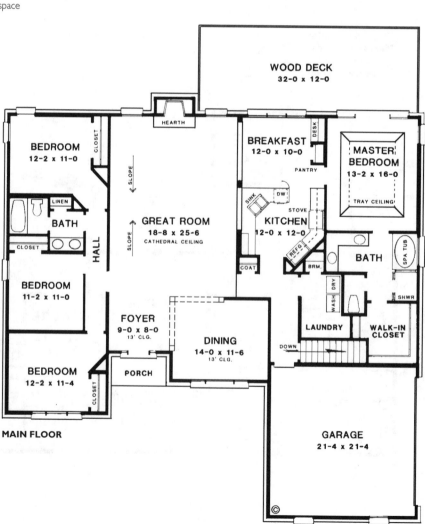

MAIN FLOOR

Design 93172

Units	Single
Price Code	E
Total Finished	2,274 sq. ft.
Main Finished	2,274 sq. ft.
Basement Unfinished	2,274 sq. ft.
Porch Unfinished	232 sq. ft.
Dimensions	77'8"x56'
Foundation	Basement
Bedrooms	3
Full Baths	2
Max Ridge Height	24'6"
Roof Framing	Stick
Exterior Walls	2x6

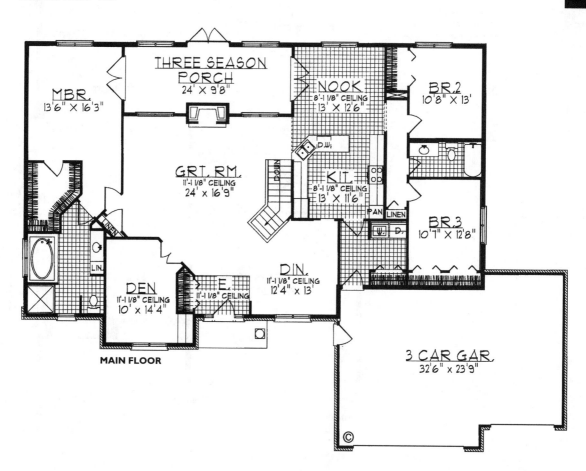

MAIN FLOOR

Units	Single
Price Code	E
Total Finished	2,278 sq. ft.
Main Finished	2,278 sq. ft.
Basement Unfinished	2,278 sq. ft.
Garage Unfinished	540 sq. ft.
Porch Unfinished	41 sq. ft.
Dimensions	59'×57'
Foundation	Basement
Bedrooms	3
Full Baths	1
3/4 Baths	1
Main Ceiling	9'
Max Ridge Height	25'
Roof Framing	Truss
Exterior Walls	2x4

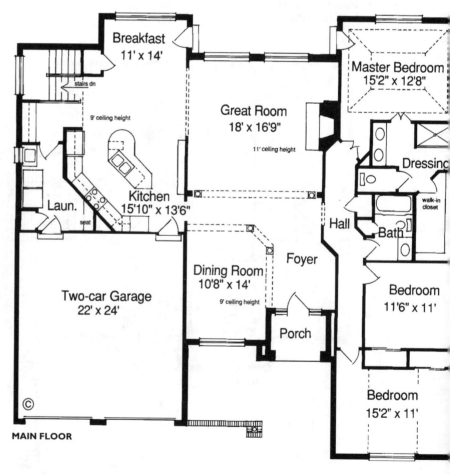

MAIN FLOOR

Design 91796

Units	Single
Price Code	E
Total Finished	2,280 sq. ft.
Main Finished	2,280 sq. ft.
Garage Unfinished	440 sq. ft.
Dimensions	99'6"x66'
Foundation	Basement
Bedrooms	3
Full Baths	1
3/4 Baths	1
Max Ridge Height	17'
Roof Framing	Stick/Truss
Exterior Walls	2x6

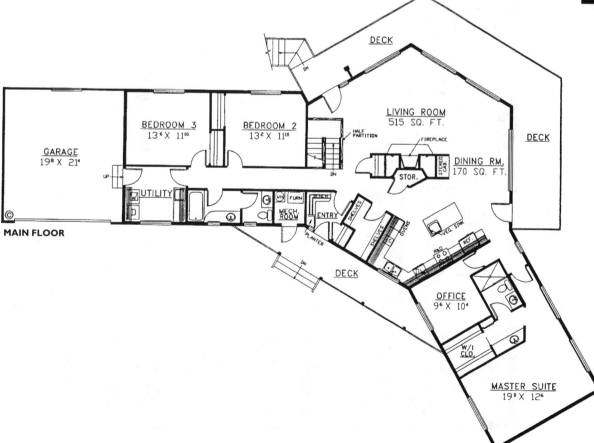

MAIN FLOOR

Units	Single
Price Code	E
Total Finished	2,285 sq. ft.
Main Finished	2,285 sq. ft.
Garage Unfinished	653 sq. ft.
Dimensions	74'10"x56'10"
Foundation	Slab
Bedrooms	4
Full Baths	3
Max Ridge Height	22'
Roof Framing	Stick
Exterior Walls	2x4

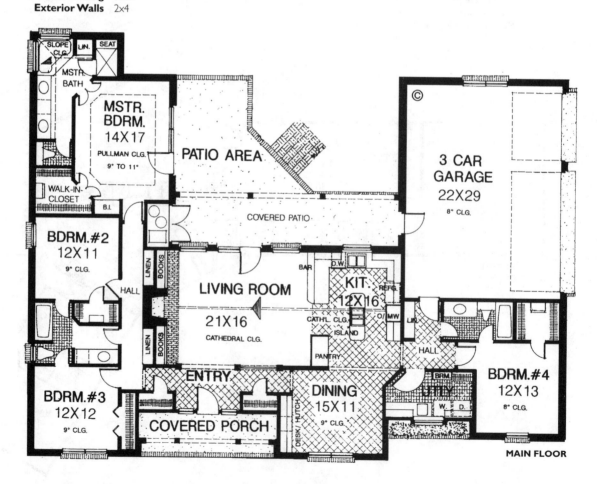

MAIN FLOOR

Design 96530

Units	Single
Price Code	E
Total Finished	2,289 sq. ft.
Main Finished	2,289 sq. ft.
Garage Unfinished	758 sq. ft.
Dimensions	66'x77'
Foundation	Crawlspace
	Slab
Bedrooms	3
Full Baths	3
Main Ceiling	8'
Max Ridge Height	22'
Roof Framing	Stick
Exterior Walls	2x4

DINING 12x14

VERANDA

LOUNGING 12x10

MASTER SUITE 16x14

12' CLG / VAULT

KITCHEN 12x12

GREAT RM 22x20
12' CEILING

SEE-THRU FIREPLACE

RECEIVING RM 23x10

CLOSET

CLOSET

WHIRLPOOL

BATH

SHOWER

UTILITY

BATH

LIN

CLOSET   STO

CLOSET   CLOS

PORCH

STUDY/BEDRM 12x11

CLOSET

BATH

PORCH

BEDRM 16x12

MAIN FLOOR

GARAGE 32x22

Design 93049

Units	Single
Price Code	E
Total Finished	2,292 sq. ft.
Main Finished	2,292 sq. ft.
Garage Unfinished	526 sq. ft.
Dimensions	80'7"x50'6"
Foundation	Crawlspace
	Slab
Bedrooms	4
Full Baths	2
Half Baths	1
Max Ridge Height	22'
Roof Framing	Stick
Exterior Walls	2x4

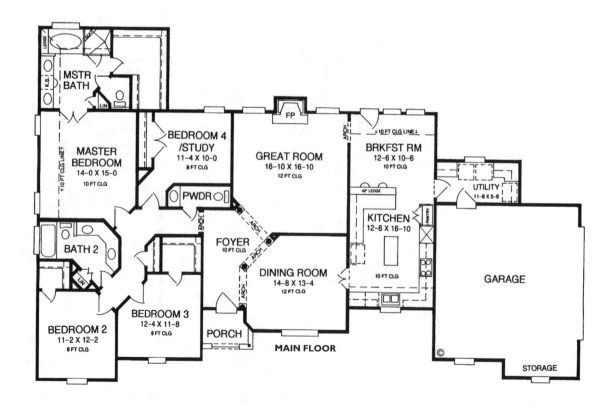

MAIN FLOOR

Design 97246

Units	Single
Price Code	E
Total Finished	2,311 sq. ft.
Main Finished	2,311 sq. ft.
Bonus Unfinished	425 sq. ft.
Basement Unfinished	2,311 sq. ft.
Garage Unfinished	500 sq. ft.
Dimensions	61'x65'4"
Foundation	Basement Crawlspace
Bedrooms	4
Full Baths	2
Half Baths	I
Main Ceiling	9'
Second Ceiling	8'
Max Ridge Height	26'8"
Roof Framing	Stick
Exterior Walls	2x4

MAIN FLOOR

CAD FILES AVAILABLE
For more information call
800-235-5700

BONUS

Units	Single
Price Code	E
Total Finished	2,313 sq. ft.
Main Finished	2,313 sq. ft.
Bonus Unfinished	433 sq. ft.
Garage Unfinished	448 sq. ft.
Deck Unfinished	198 sq. ft.
Porch Unfinished	48 sq. ft.
Dimensions	60'x60'1½"
Foundation	Slab
Bedrooms	3
Full Baths	2
Half Baths	1
Max Ridge Height	25'6"
Roof Framing	Stick
Exterior Walls	2x4

MAIN FLOOR

Optional PlayRm
433 Sq. Ft. Not Included In
Total Square Footage
10x21
Sloped Ceiling
4'-0" To 8'-0"

BONUS

Design 97504

Units	Single
Price Code	E
Total Finished	2,322 sq. ft.
Main Finished	2,322 sq. ft.
Garage Unfinished	484 sq. ft.
Porch Unfinished	100 sq. ft.
Dimensions	68'11"x74'
Foundation	Slab
Bedrooms	4
Full Baths	2
Half Baths	1
Main Ceiling	9'-12'
Max Ridge Height	30'
Roof Framing	Stick
Exterior Walls	2x4

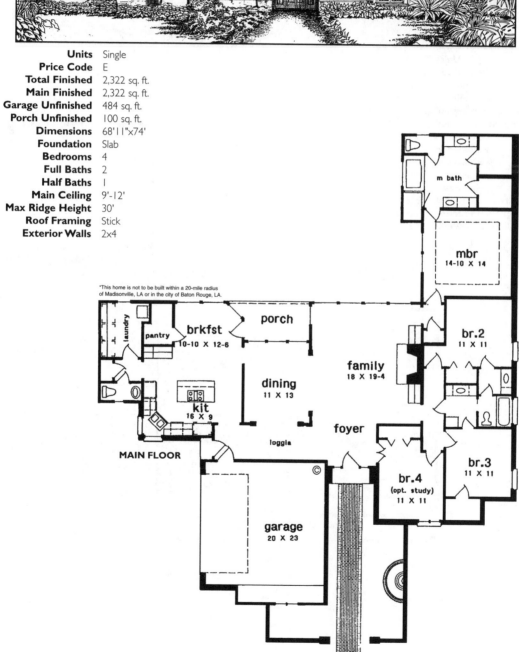

*This home is not to be built within a 20-mile radius of Madisonville, LA or in the city of Baton Rouge, LA.

MAIN FLOOR

laundry

pantry

brkfst
10-10 X 12-6

porch

m bath

mbr
14-10 X 14

family
18 X 19-4

br.2
11 X 11

dining
11 X 13

kit
16 X 9

loggia

foyer

br.3
11 X 11

br.4
(opt. study)
11 X 11

garage
20 X 23

Units	Single
Price Code	H
Total Finished	2,329 sq. ft.
Main Finished	2,329 sq. ft.
Garage Unfinished	528 sq. ft.
Porch Unfinished	215 sq. ft.
Dimensions	72'x73'
Foundation	Crawlspace
Bedrooms	3
Full Baths	2
Half Baths	1
Max Ridge Height	25'4"
Roof Framing	Stick/Truss
Exterior Walls	2x6

* Alternate foundation options available at an additional charge.
Please call 1-800-235-5700 for more information.

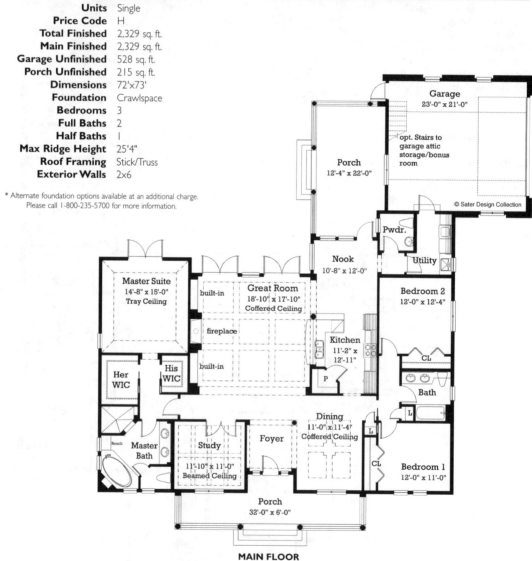

MAIN FLOOR

Design 97857

Units	Single
Price Code	E
Total Finished	2,332 sq. ft.
Main Finished	2,332 sq. ft.
Garage Unfinished	620 sq. ft.
Deck Unfinished	80 sq. ft.
Porch Unfinished	48 sq. ft.
Dimensions	82'3"x86'6"
Foundation	Slab
Bedrooms	3
Full Baths	2
Half Baths	1
Main Ceiling	9'-10'
Max Ridge Height	29'
Roof Framing	Stick
Exterior Walls	2x4

MAIN FLOOR

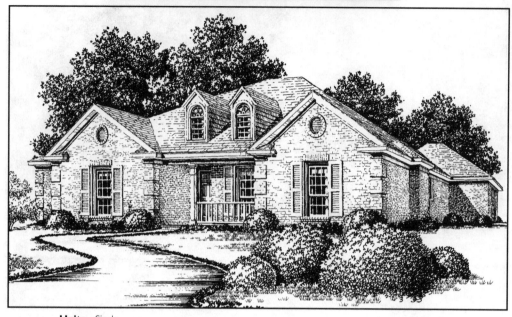

Units	Single
Price Code	E
Total Finished	2,345 sq. ft.
Main Finished	2,345 sq. ft.
Garage Unfinished	510 sq. ft.
Porch Unfinished	62 sq. ft.
Dimensions	59'10"x66'3"
Foundation	Slab
Bedrooms	3
Full Baths	3
Max Ridge Height	23'
Roof Framing	Stick
Exterior Walls	2x4

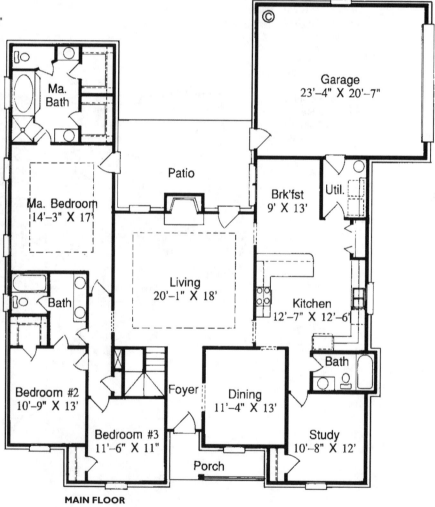

MAIN FLOOR

Design 66048

Units	Single
Price Code	E
Total Finished	2,352 sq. ft.
Main Finished	2,352 sq. ft.
Garage Unfinished	702 sq. ft.
Deck Unfinished	230 sq. ft.
Porch Unfinished	262 sq. ft.
Dimensions	76'x48'4"
Foundation	Slab
Bedrooms	3
Full Baths	2
Half Baths	1
Main Ceiling	9'-10'
Max Ridge Height	26'
Roof Framing	Stick
Exterior Walls	2x4

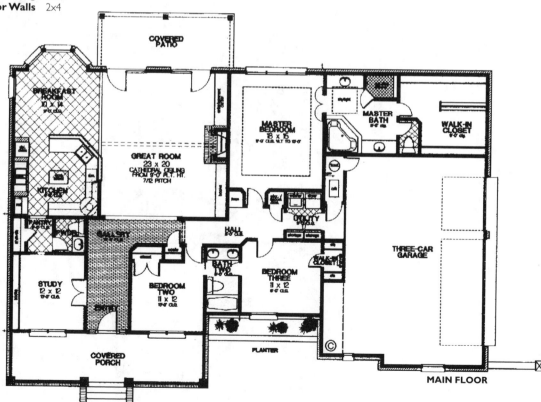

MAIN FLOOR

Units	Single
Price Code	E
Total Finished	2,353 sq. ft.
Main Finished	2,353 sq. ft.
Garage Unfinished	650 sq. ft.
Deck Unfinished	150 sq. ft.
Dimensions	55'x70'7¼"
Foundation	Slab
Bedrooms	4
Full Baths	3
Main Ceiling	9'
Max Ridge Height	27'6"
Roof Framing	Stick
Exterior Walls	2x4

MAIN FLOOR

Design 93440

Units	Single
Price Code	E
Total Finished	2,361 sq. ft.
Main Finished	2,361 sq. ft.
Basement Unfinished	2,361 sq. ft.
Garage Unfinished	490 sq. ft.
Porch Unfinished	168 sq. ft.
Dimensions	67'x69'6"
Foundation	Basement
Bedrooms	3
Full Baths	3
Main Ceiling	9'
Vaulted Ceiling	14'
Max Ridge Height	22'5"
Roof Framing	Stick
Exterior Walls	2x4

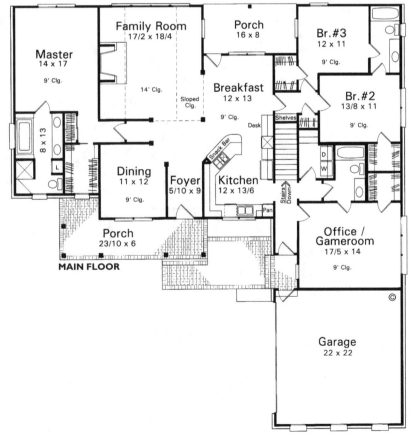

Units	Single
Price Code	E
Total Finished	2,365 sq. ft.
Main Finished	2,365 sq. ft.
Basement Unfinished	2,365 sq. ft.
Garage Unfinished	566 sq. ft.
Dimensions	79'x70'6"
Foundation	Crawlspace
Bedrooms	3
Full Baths	2
Main Ceiling	10'
Second Ceiling	8'
Vaulted Ceiling	21'
Max Ridge Height	24'
Roof Framing	Truss
Exterior Walls	2x6

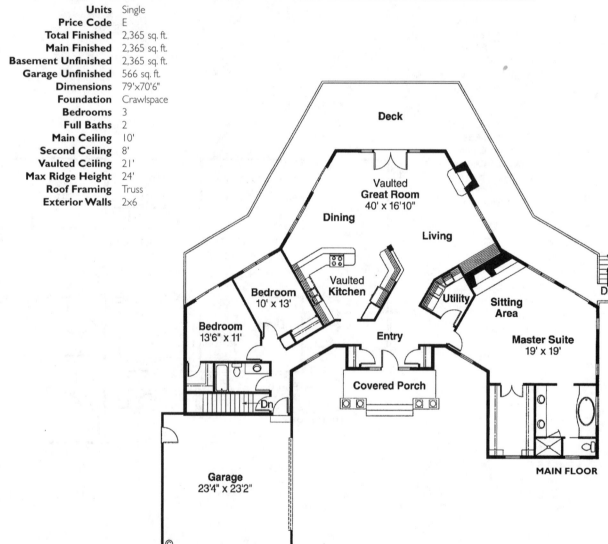

Design 94632

Units	Single
Price Code	E
Total Finished	2,365 sq. ft.
Main Finished	2,365 sq. ft.
Dimensions	67'6"x73'
Foundation	Crawlspace
	Slab
Bedrooms	4
Full Baths	2
Main Ceiling	9'
Max Ridge Height	31'6"
Roof Framing	Stick
Exterior Walls	2x4

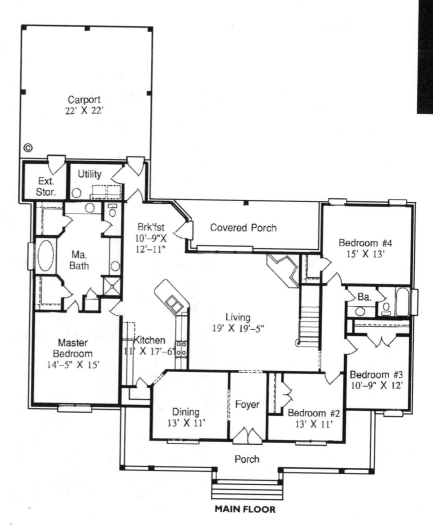

MAIN FLOOR

Units	Single
Price Code	E
Total Finished	2,370 sq. ft.
Main Finished	2,370 sq. ft.
Garage Unfinished	638 sq. ft.
Deck Unfinished	132 sq. ft.
Porch Unfinished	30 sq. ft.
Dimensions	55'x63'10"
Foundation	Slab
Bedrooms	4
Full Baths	2
Half Baths	1
Max Ridge Height	26'8"
Roof Framing	Stick
Exterior Walls	2x4

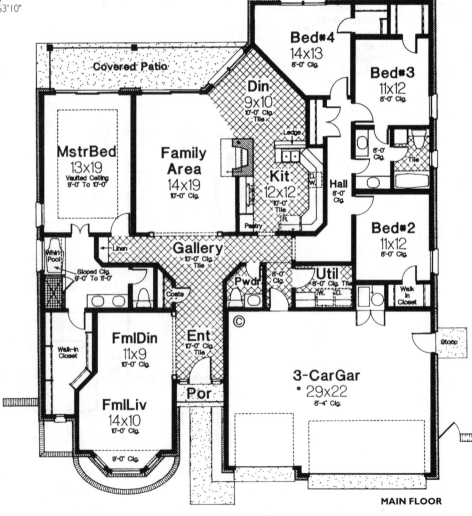

MAIN FLOOR

Design 66039

Units	Single
Price Code	E
Total Finished	2,390 sq. ft.
Main Finished	2,390 sq. ft.
Garage Unfinished	602 sq. ft.
Deck Unfinished	202 sq. ft.
Dimensions	60'x76'
Foundation	Slab
Bedrooms	3
Full Baths	2
Half Baths	1
Main Ceiling	9'-10'
Max Ridge Height	27'6"
Roof Framing	Stick
Exterior Walls	2x4

MAIN FLOOR

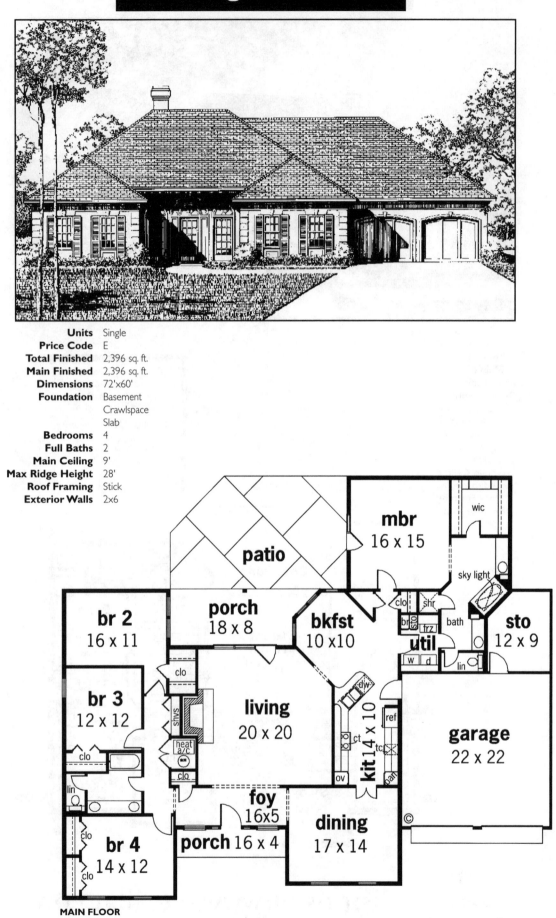

Units	Single
Price Code	E
Total Finished	2,396 sq. ft.
Main Finished	2,396 sq. ft.
Dimensions	72'x60'
Foundation	Basement
	Crawlspace
	Slab
Bedrooms	4
Full Baths	2
Main Ceiling	9'
Max Ridge Height	28'
Roof Framing	Stick
Exterior Walls	2x6

MAIN FLOOR

Units	Single
Price Code	E
Total Finished	2,397 sq. ft.
Main Finished	2,397 sq. ft.
Garage Unfinished	473 sq. ft.
Dimensions	73'2"x73'2"
Foundation	Slab
Bedrooms	3
Full Baths	2
Half Baths	1
Main Ceiling	10'
Tray Ceiling	13'4"
Max Ridge Height	22'8"
Roof Framing	Truss
Exterior Walls	2x4

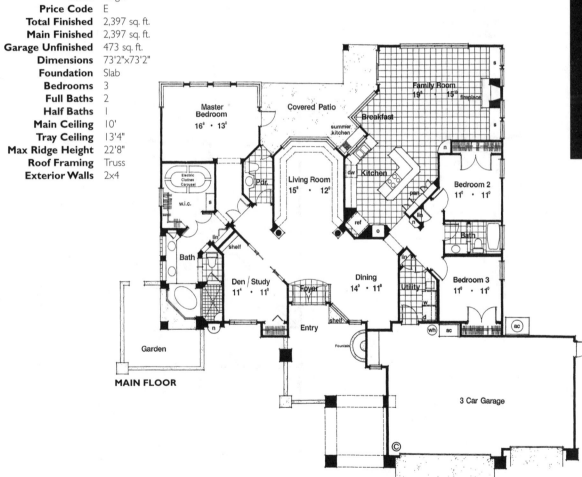

MAIN FLOOR

Visit us at www.merillat.com

Merillat

Design 97446

Units	Single
Price Code	E
Total Finished	2,404 sq. ft.
Main Finished	2,404 sq. ft.
Garage Unfinished	493 sq. ft.
Dimensions	50'4''x70'8''
Foundation	Slab
Bedrooms	3
Full Baths	2
Half Baths	1
Main Ceiling	9'
Max Ridge Height	25'
Roof Framing	Stick
Exterior Walls	2x4

* Alternate foundation options available at an additional charge.
Please call 1-800-235-5700 for more information.

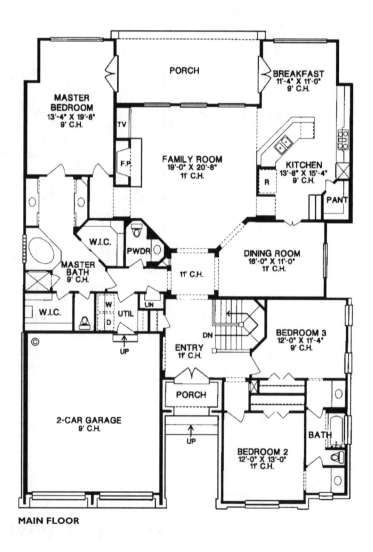

MAIN FLOOR

Design 93095

PHOTOGRAPHY: COURTESY OF THE DESIGNER

Units	Single
Price Code	E
Total Finished	2,409 sq. ft.
Main Finished	2,409 sq. ft.
Bonus Unfinished	709 sq. ft.
Garage Unfinished	644 sq. ft.
Porch Unfinished	392 sq. ft.
Dimensions	85'8"x68'4"
Foundation	Crawlspace Slab
Bedrooms	3
Full Baths	2
Half Baths	1
Max Ridge Height	25'8"
Roof Framing	Stick
Exterior Walls	2x4

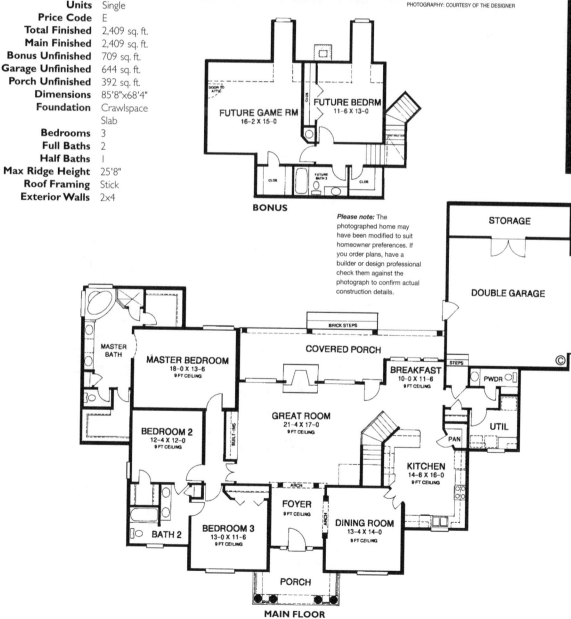

Please note: The photographed home may have been modified to suit homeowner preferences. If you order plans, have a builder or design professional check them against the photograph to confirm actual construction details.

BONUS

MAIN FLOOR

Units	Single
Price Code	E
Total Finished	2,421 sq. ft.
Main Finished	2,421 sq. ft.
Garage Unfinished	622 sq. ft.
Deck Unfinished	246 sq. ft.
Porch Unfinished	56 sq. ft.
Dimensions	65'x76'1"
Foundation	Slab
Bedrooms	4
Full Baths	3
Main Ceiling	9'
Max Ridge Height	28'
Exterior Walls	2x4

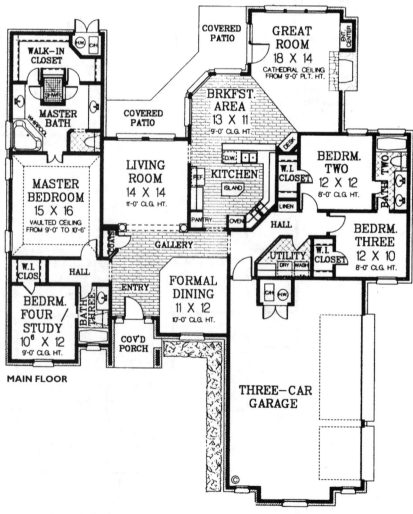

MAIN FLOOR

Design 63107

Units	Single
Price Code	E
Total Finished	2,431 sq. ft.
Main Finished	2,431 sq. ft.
Garage Unfinished	464 sq. ft.
Dimensions	61'4"x66'6"
Foundation	Slab
Bedrooms	4
Full Baths	2
3/4 Baths	1
Main Ceiling	10'
Tray Ceiling	13'4"
Max Ridge Height	22'3"
Roof Framing	Truss

MAIN FLOOR

Units	Single
Price Code	E
Total Finished	2,437 sq. ft.
Main Finished	2,437 sq. ft.
Garage Unfinished	646 sq. ft.
Porch Unfinished	213 sq. ft.
Dimensions	64'9"x59'
Foundation	Basement
	Crawlspace
	Slab
Bedrooms	3
Full Baths	2
Main Ceiling	9'
Max Ridge Height	26'
Roof Framing	Stick
Exterior Walls	2x4

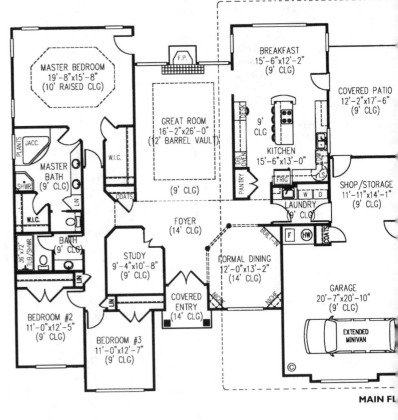

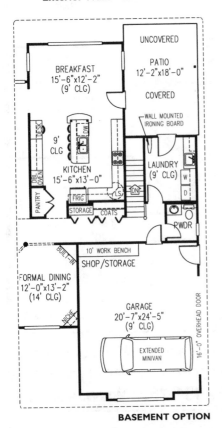

BASEMENT OPTION

Design 98511

2,001-2,500 sq. ft. HOME PLANS

Units	Single
Price Code	E
Total Finished	2,445 sq. ft.
Main Finished	2,445 sq. ft.
Garage Unfinished	630 sq. ft.
Deck Unfinished	234 sq. ft.
Porch Unfinished	32 sq. ft.
Dimensions	65'x68'8"
Foundation	Crawlspace
	Slab
Bedrooms	4
Full Baths	3
Half Baths	1
Main Ceiling	9'-12'
Max Ridge Height	32'
Roof Framing	Stick
Exterior Walls	2x4

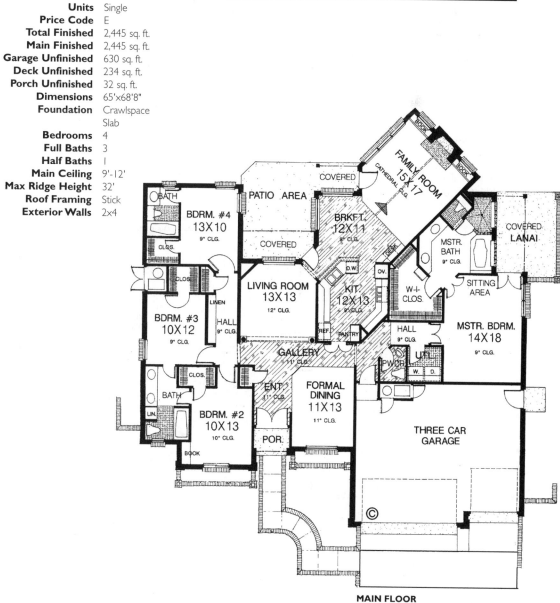

MAIN FLOOR

Units	Single
Price Code	E
Total Finished	2,451 sq. ft.
Main Finished	2,451 sq. ft.
Garage Unfinished	484 sq. ft.
Deck Unfinished	368 sq. ft.
Dimensions	66'x60'
Foundation	Basement
	Crawlspace
	Slab
Bedrooms	4
Full Baths	2
Half Baths	1
Main Ceiling	9'
Max Ridge Height	27'
Exterior Walls	2x4

* Alternate foundation options available at an additional charge.
Please call 1-800-235-5700 for more information.

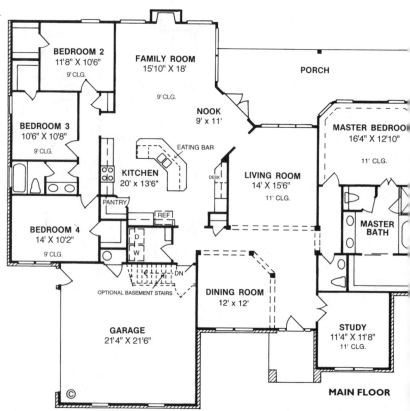

MAIN FLOOR

Design 96922

Units	Single
Price Code	E
Total Finished	2,452 sq. ft.
Main Finished	2,452 sq. ft.
Bonus Unfinished	427 sq. ft.
Basement Unfinished	2,426 sq. ft.
Garage Unfinished	474 sq. ft.
Deck Unfinished	176 sq. ft.
Porch Unfinished	36 sq. ft.
Dimensions	58'x76'
Foundation	Basement
	Crawlspace
Bedrooms	3
Full Baths	2
Half Baths	1
Main Ceiling	9'
Max Ridge Height	23'6"
Roof Framing	Stick
Exterior Walls	2x4

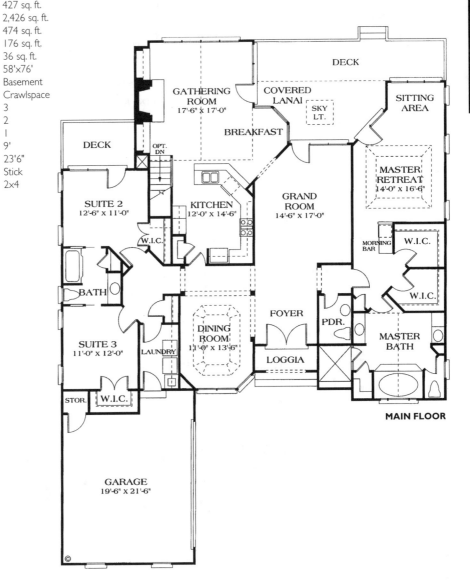

MAIN FLOOR

Units	Single
Price Code	H
Total Finished	2,454 sq. ft.
Main Finished	2,454 sq. ft.
Bonus Unfinished	256 sq. ft.
Porch Unfinished	165 sq. ft.
Dimensions	80'6"x66'6"
Foundation	Crawlspace
Bedrooms	3
Full Baths	2
Roof Framing	Stick/Truss
Exterior Walls	2x6

* Alternate foundation options available at an additional charge.
Please call 1-800-235-5700 for more information.

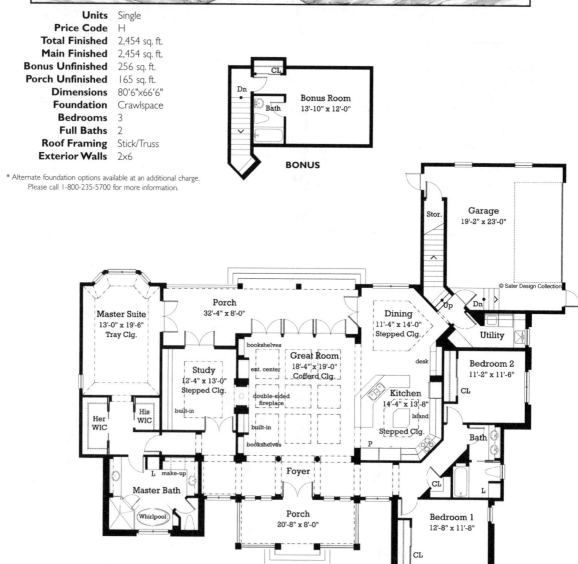

Design 97752

Units	Single
Price Code	E
Total Finished	2,469 sq. ft.
Main Finished	2,469 sq. ft.
Bonus Unfinished	1,671 sq. ft.
Basement Unfinished	798 sq. ft.
Garage Unfinished	491 sq. ft.
Deck Unfinished	299 sq. ft.
Dimensions	59'x59'6"
Foundation	Basement
Bedrooms	3
Full Baths	2
Main Ceiling	9'
Max Ridge Height	26'
Roof Framing	Stick
Exterior Walls	2x4, 2x6

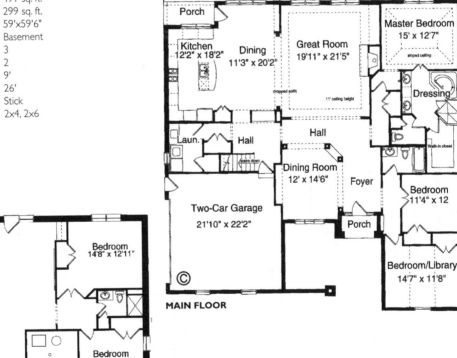

MAIN FLOOR

BONUS

Units	Single
Price Code	E
Total Finished	2,469 sq. ft.
Main Finished	1,462 sq. ft.
Lower Finished	1,007 sq. ft.
Basement Unfinished	455 sq. ft.
Garage Unfinished	528 sq. ft.
Deck Unfinished	142 sq. ft.
Porch Unfinished	47 sq. ft.
Dimensions	46'x59'4"
Foundation	Basement
Bedrooms	2
Full Baths	2
Half Baths	1
Main Ceiling	9'1"
Vaulted Ceiling	10'
Max Ridge Height	22'6"
Roof Framing	Truss
Exterior Walls	2x4

MAIN FLOOR

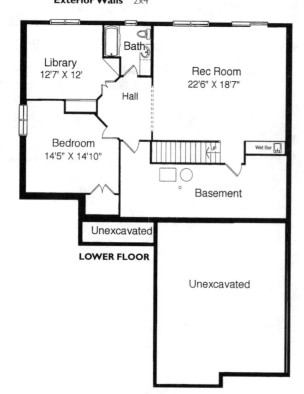

LOWER FLOOR

Design 64126

Units	Single
Price Code	H
Total Finished	2,477 sq. ft.
Main Finished	2,477 sq. ft.
Basement Unfinished	1,742 sq. ft.
Dimensions	70'x72'
Foundation	Basement
	Slab
Bedrooms	3
Full Baths	2
Max Ridge Height	29'
Roof Framing	Stick/Truss
Exterior Walls	2x6

* Alternate foundation options available at an additional charge.
Please call 1-800-235-5700 for more information.

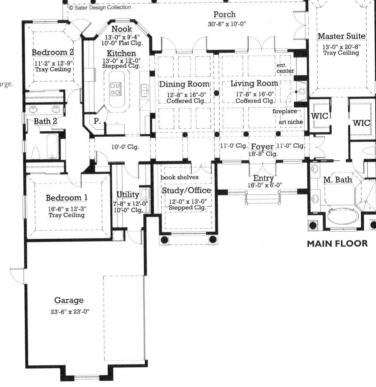

MAIN FLOOR

**OPTIONAL BASEMENT
STAIR LOCATION**

Visit us at www.merillat.com

Units	Single
Price Code	E
Total Finished	2,483 sq. ft.
Main Finished	2,483 sq. ft.
Garage Unfinished	504 sq. ft.
Dimensions	75'x61'8"
Foundation	Crawlspace
Bedrooms	4
Full Baths	3
Half Baths	I
Main Ceiling	9'
Vaulted Ceiling	II'
Max Ridge Height	23'
Roof Framing	Stick
Exterior Walls	2x4

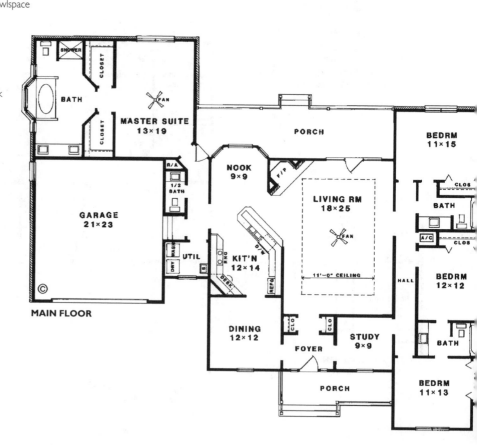

MASTER SUITE 13×19

GARAGE 21×23

MAIN FLOOR

PORCH

BEDRM 11×15

NOOK 9×9

LIVING RM 18×25

11'-0" CEILING

KIT'N 12×14

UTIL

1/2 BATH

BATH

HALL

BEDRM 12×12

DINING 12×12

STUDY 9×9

FOYER

PORCH

BEDRM 11×13

BATH

Design 64125

Units	Single
Price Code	H
Total Finished	2,487 sq. ft.
Main Finished	2,487 sq. ft.
Basement Unfinished	1,742 sq. ft.
Dimensions	70'x72'
Foundation	Basement
	Slab
Bedrooms	3
Full Baths	2
Max Ridge Height	27'4"
Roof Framing	Stick/Truss
Exterior Walls	2x6

* Alternate foundation options available at an additional charge.
Please call 1-800-235-5700 for more information.

OPTIONAL BASEMENT STAIR LOCATION

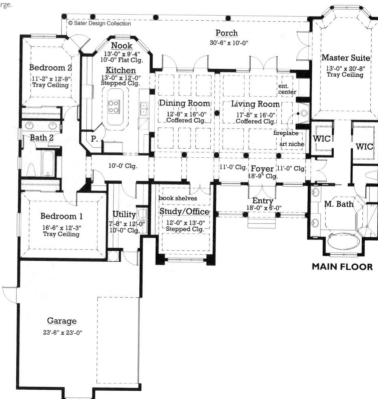

MAIN FLOOR

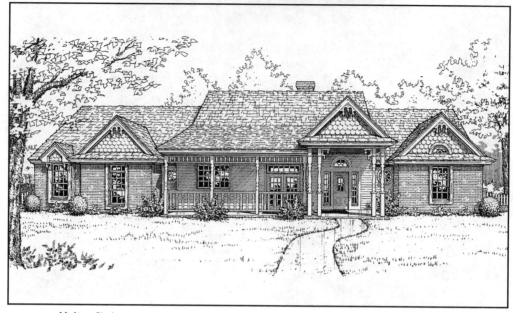

Units	Single
Price Code	E
Total Finished	2,495 sq. ft.
Main Finished	2,495 sq. ft.
Garage Unfinished	720 sq. ft.
Deck Unfinished	73 sq. ft.
Porch Unfinished	273 sq. ft.
Dimensions	87'10"x62'7"
Foundation	Crawlspace
	Slab
Bedrooms	4
Full Baths	2
Half Baths	1
Main Ceiling	9'-10'
Max Ridge Height	20'3"
Roof Framing	Stick
Exterior Walls	2x4

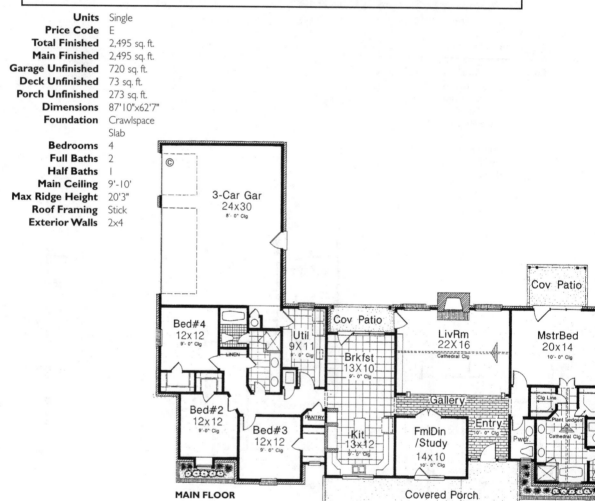

MAIN FLOOR

Design 98733

Units	Single
Price Code	E
Total Finished	2,496 sq. ft.
Main Finished	2,496 sq. ft.
Basement Unfinished	2,401 sq. ft.
Garage Unfinished	827 sq. ft.
Dimensions	96'x54'
Foundation	Basement
Bedrooms	3
Full Baths	2
Max Ridge Height	23'6"
Roof Framing	Stick/Truss
Exterior Walls	2x6

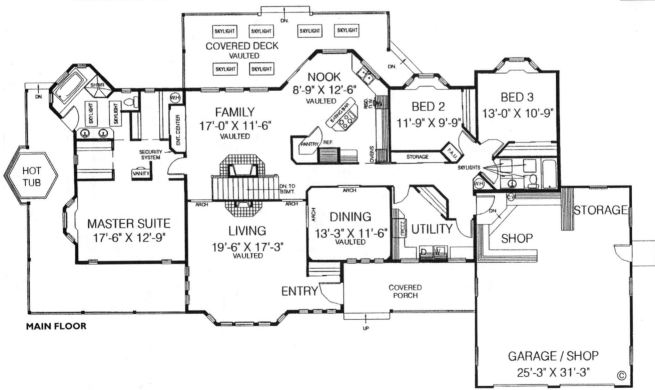

MAIN FLOOR

Units	Single
Price Code	F
Total Finished	2,504 sq. ft.
Main Finished	2,504 sq. ft.
Garage Unfinished	1,187 sq. ft.
Dimensions	84'x70'8"
Foundation	Basement
Bedrooms	3
Full Baths	2
Half Baths	1
Main Ceiling	9'
Max Ridge Height	22'
Roof Framing	Stick
Exterior Walls	2x4

* Alternate foundation options available at an additional charge.
Please call 1-800-235-5700 for more information.

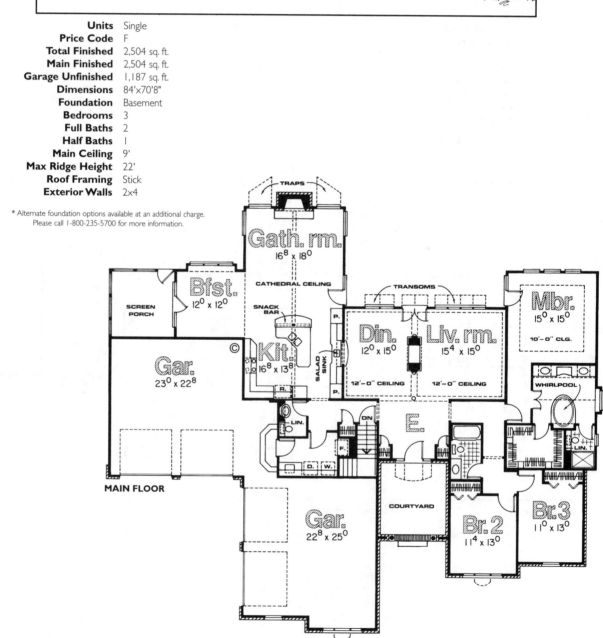

MAIN FLOOR

Design 66040

Units	Single
Price Code	F
Total Finished	2,508 sq. ft.
Main Finished	2,508 sq. ft.
Garage Unfinished	660 sq. ft.
Deck Unfinished	245 sq. ft.
Dimensions	68'x70'
Foundation	Slab
Bedrooms	4
Full Baths	2
3/4 Baths	1
Main Ceiling	9'-10'
Max Ridge Height	28'
Roof Framing	Stick
Exterior Walls	2x4

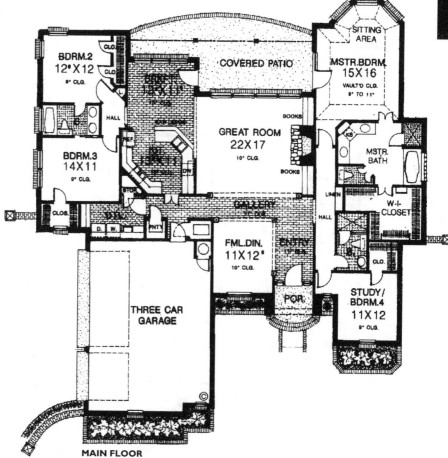

MAIN FLOOR

Units	Single
Price Code	F
Total Finished	2,510 sq. ft.
Main Finished	2,510 sq. ft.
Basement Unfinished	2,510 sq. ft.
Garage Unfinished	1,333 sq. ft.
Deck Unfinished	497 sq. ft.
Dimensions	93'8"x68'
Foundation	Basement
Bedrooms	3
Full Baths	2
Half Baths	1
Main Ceiling	9'-11'
Max Ridge Height	25'8"
Roof Framing	Truss
Exterior Walls	2x4

HEARTH ROOM
CATHEDRAL CEILING
15'4" X 17'0"

WD. DECK
16'10" X 29'6"

M.B.R.
16'2" X 14'8"

GRT. RM.
11'-1 1/8" CEILING
15'10" X 20'6"

NK.
9'0" X 10'8"

PAN.

KIT.
14'0" X 12'8"

BR #2
11'4" X 11'2"

2 CAR GARAGE
30'6" X 21'8"

SOFFIT

11'-1 1/8" CEILING

DIN. RM.
11'-1 1/8" CEILING
12'8" X 14'6"

SOFFIT

SOFFIT

SOFFIT

BR #3
12'4" X 12'8"

I CAR GARAGE
21'4" X 31'6"

MAIN FLOOR

Units	Single
Price Code	F
Total Finished	2,511 sq. ft.
Main Finished	2,511 sq. ft.
Garage Unfinished	469 sq. ft.
Dimensions	69'x63'6"
Foundation	Crawlspace
	Slab
Bedrooms	4
Full Baths	2
Half Baths	1
Max Ridge Height	21'4"
Roof Framing	Stick
Exterior Walls	2x4

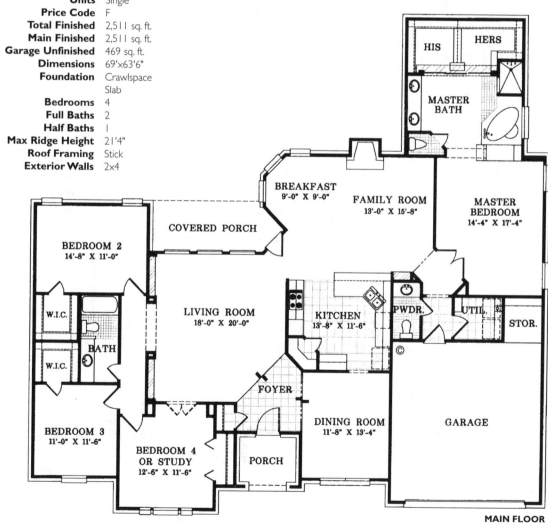

HIS   HERS

MASTER BATH

BREAKFAST
9'-0" X 9'-0"

FAMILY ROOM
13'-0" X 15'-8"

MASTER BEDROOM
14'-4" X 17'-4"

COVERED PORCH

BEDROOM 2
14'-8" X 11'-0"

W.I.C.

BATH

W.I.C.

LIVING ROOM
18'-0" X 20'-0"

KITCHEN
13'-8" X 11'-6"

PWDR.

UTIL.

STOR.

FOYER

BEDROOM 3
11'-0" X 11'-6"

BEDROOM 4
OR STUDY
12'-6" X 11'-6"

PORCH

DINING ROOM
11'-8" X 13'-4"

GARAGE

MAIN FLOOR

Merillat.   Visit us at www.merillat.com

Units	Single
Price Code	F
Total Finished	2,512 sq. ft.
Main Finished	2,512 sq. ft.
Garage Unfinished	783 sq. ft.
Dimensions	74'x67'8"
Foundation	Basement
Bedrooms	3
Full Baths	2
Half Baths	I
Main Ceiling	9'-10'
Max Ridge Height	25'5"
Roof Framing	Stick
Exterior Walls	2x4

* Alternate foundation options available at an additional charge.
Please call 1-800-235-5700 for more information.

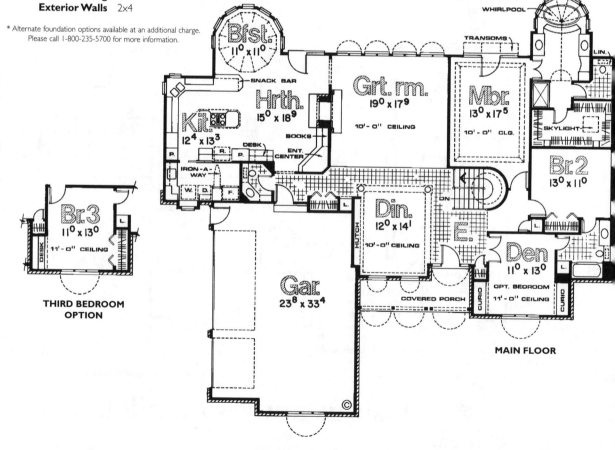

THIRD BEDROOM
OPTION

MAIN FLOOR

Design 97486

Units	Single
Price Code	F
Total Finished	2,517 sq. ft.
Main Finished	2,517 sq. ft.
Garage Unfinished	617 sq. ft.
Deck Unfinished	101 sq. ft.
Dimensions	77'x59'
Foundation	Slab
Bedrooms	3
Full Baths	2
Half Baths	1
Main Ceiling	9'
Max Ridge Height	27'4"
Exterior Walls	2x4

* Alternate foundation options available at an additional charge.
Please call 1-800-235-5700 for more information.

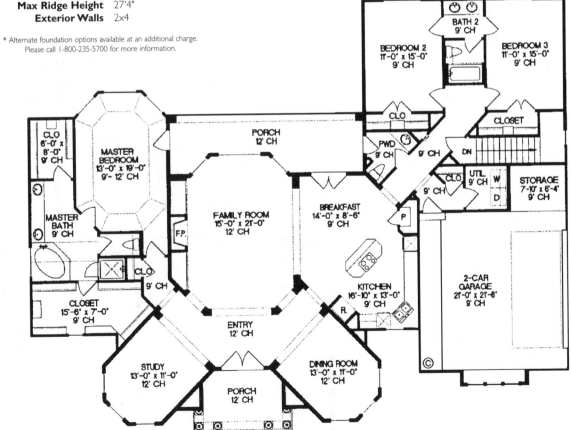

MAIN FLOOR

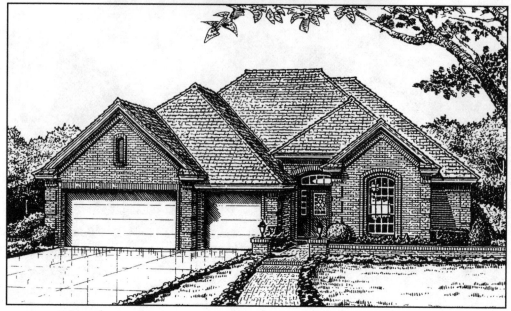

Units	Single
Price Code	F
Total Finished	2,518 sq. ft.
Main Finished	2,518 sq. ft.
Garage Unfinished	609 sq. ft.
Deck Unfinished	102 sq. ft.
Dimensions	59'7"x72'9"
Foundation	Slab
Bedrooms	4
Full Baths	3
Main Ceiling	9'-10'
Max Ridge Height	28'2"
Roof Framing	Stick
Exterior Walls	2x4

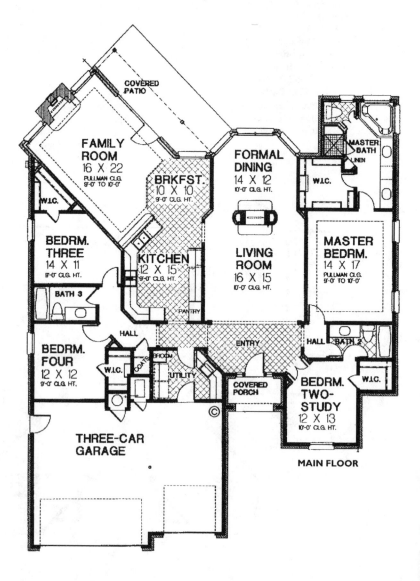

MAIN FLOOR

Design 86021

Units	Single
Price Code	F
Total Finished	2,529 sq. ft.
Main Finished	2,529 sq. ft.
Basement Unfinished	2,495 sq. ft.
Garage Unfinished	675 sq. ft.
Deck Unfinished	126 sq. ft.
Porch Unfinished	280 sq. ft.
Dimensions	77'4"x49'4"
Foundation	Basement
Bedrooms	3
Full Baths	2
Half Baths	1
Max Ridge Height	26'11½"
Roof Framing	Stick/Truss
Exterior Walls	2x6

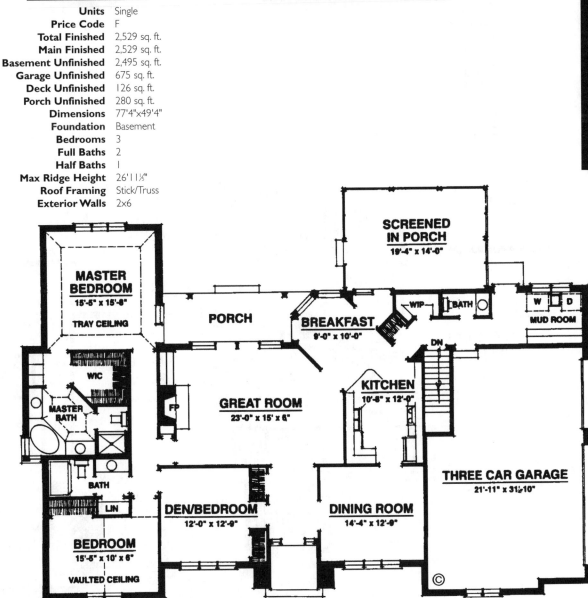

MAIN FLOOR

Units	Single
Price Code	E
Total Finished	2,531 sq. ft.
Main Finished	2,531 sq. ft.
Garage Unfinished	667 sq. ft.
Deck Unfinished	95 sq. ft.
Porch Unfinished	44 sq. ft.
Dimensions	84'7"x56'
Foundation	Crawlspace
Bedrooms	3
Full Baths	2
Half Baths	I
Main Ceiling	10'
Max Ridge Height	25'6"
Roof Framing	Stick
Exterior Walls	2x4

MAIN FLOOR

Design 97720

Units	Single
Price Code	F
Total Finished	2,535 sq. ft.
Main Finished	2,535 sq. ft.
Basement Unfinished	2,535 sq. ft.
Deck Unfinished	395 sq. ft.
Dimensions	72'x56'
Foundation	Basement
Bedrooms	3
Full Baths	2
Max Ridge Height	26'
Roof Framing	Truss
Exterior Walls	2x4

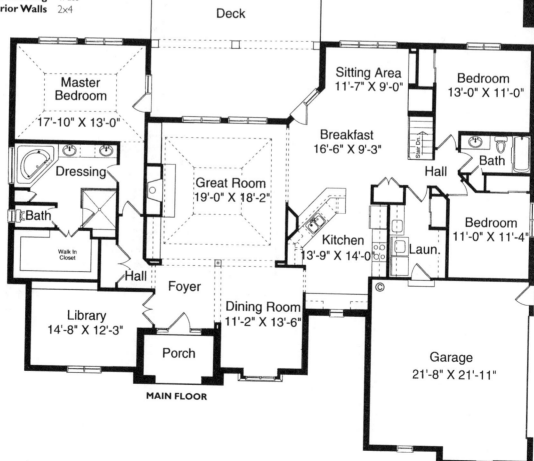

Deck

Master Bedroom
17'-10" X 13'-0"

Sitting Area
11'-7" X 9'-0"

Bedroom
13'-0" X 11'-0"

Breakfast
16'-6" X 9'-3"

Stair Dn.

Dressing

Hall

Bath

Great Room
19'-0" X 18'-2"

Bath

Walk In Closet

Kitchen
13'-9" X 14'-0"

Laun.

Bedroom
11'-0" X 11'-4"

Hall

Foyer

Library
14'-8" X 12'-3"

Dining Room
11'-2" X 13'-6"

Porch

Garage
21'-8" X 21'-11"

MAIN FLOOR

Design 99469

Units	Single
Price Code	F
Total Finished	2,538 sq. ft.
Main Finished	2,538 sq. ft.
Garage Unfinished	755 sq. ft.
Dimensions	68'8"x64'8"
Foundation	Basement
Bedrooms	3
Full Baths	2
Half Baths	1
Main Ceiling	8'
Max Ridge Height	24'6"
Roof Framing	Stick
Exterior Walls	2x4

* Alternate foundation options available at an additional charge.
Please call 1-800-235-5700 for more information.

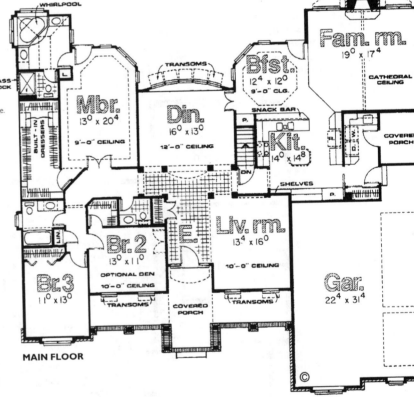

MAIN FLOOR

Design 93035

Units	Single
Price Code	F
Total Finished	2,545 sq. ft.
Main Finished	2,545 sq. ft.
Garage Unfinished	436 sq. ft.
Porch Finished	96 sq. ft.
Dimensions	69'x63'6"
Foundation	Crawlspace
	Slab
Bedrooms	4
Full Baths	2
Half Baths	1
Max Ridge Height	23'
Roof Framing	Stick
Exterior Walls	2x4

HERS   HIS

SLOPE CLG   SLOPE CLG

KS

MSTR BATH

ARCH   SEAT

SLOPE CLG   SLOPE CLG

FP

PATIO

BRKFST
9-6x9-6
10 FT CLG

FAMILY RM
13-4x14-8
10 FT CLG

MSTR BEDRM
14-4x17-4
CATHEDRAL CLG

BEDRM 2
14-8x11-0

42" LEDGE

LIVING RM
17-0x18-8
12 FT CLG

KITCHEN
13-8x12-6
10 FT CLG

PWDR

UTILITY

BATH 2

PAN

OPTIONAL FR DOORS

SLOPE CLG

FOYER
DN

DINING RM
11-8x13-4
12 FT CLG

GARAGE

BEDRM 3
11-0x11-6

DN

DN

SLOPE CLG

STUDY/
BEDRM 4
11-6x13-0
COFFERED CLG

PORCH

MAIN FLOOR

Merillat.

Visit us at www.merillat.com

Units	Single
Price Code	H
Total Finished	2,555 sq. ft.
Main Finished	2,555 sq. ft.
Garage Unfinished	640 sq. ft.
Dimensions	70'6"x76'6"
Foundation	Crawlspace
Bedrooms	3
Full Baths	2
Half Baths	I
Max Ridge Height	28'4"
Exterior Walls	2x6

* Alternate foundation options available at an additional charge.
Please call 1-800-235-5700 for more information.

MAIN FLOOR

Design 69109

Units	Single
Price Code	F
Total Finished	2,556 sq. ft.
Main Finished	2,556 sq. ft.
Garage Unfinished	520 sq. ft.
Dimensions	74'x82'
Foundation	Basement
	Crawlspace
Bedrooms	3
Full Baths	2
Half Baths	1
Main Ceiling	9'
Vaulted Ceiling	19'4"
Max Ridge Height	24'
Roof Framing	Truss
Exterior Walls	2x6

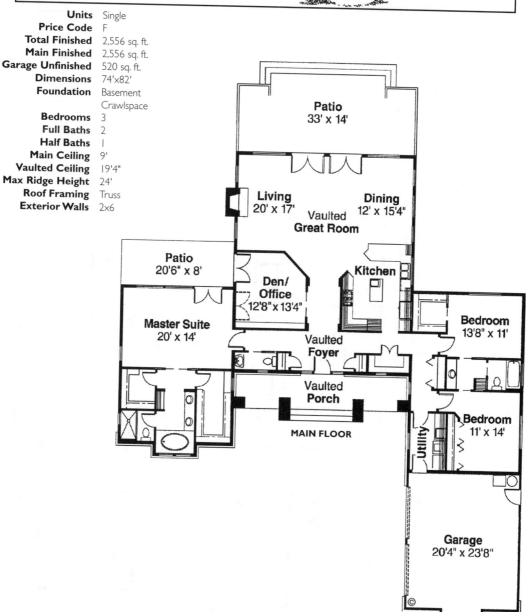

Patio 33' x 14'

Living 20' x 17'

Dining 12' x 15'4"

Vaulted Great Room

Kitchen

Patio 20'6" x 8'

Den/Office 12'8" x 13'4"

Bedroom 13'8" x 11'

Master Suite 20' x 14'

Vaulted Foyer

Vaulted Porch

Bedroom 11' x 14'

Utility

MAIN FLOOR

Garage 20'4" x 23'8"

Design 94640

Units	Single
Price Code	F
Total Finished	2,558 sq. ft.
Main Finished	2,558 sq. ft.
Garage Unfinished	549 sq. ft.
Porch Unfinished	151 sq. ft.
Dimensions	63'6"x71'6"
Foundation	Crawlspace
	Slab
Bedrooms	4
Full Baths	3
Main Ceiling	9'
Max Ridge Height	21'6"
Roof Framing	Stick
Exterior Walls	2x4

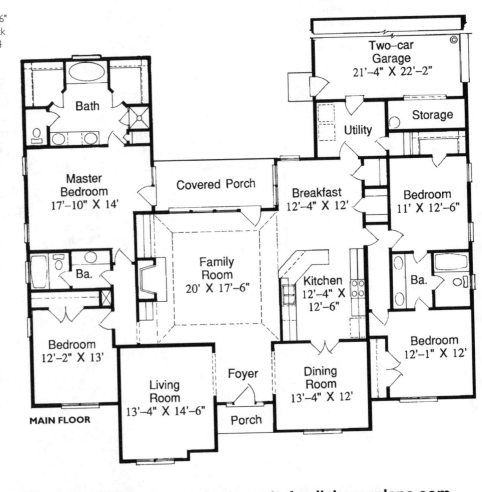

MAIN FLOOR

Design 92418

Units	Single
Price Code	F
Total Finished	2,564 sq. ft.
Main Finished	2,564 sq. ft.
Bonus Unfinished	302 sq. ft.
Dimensions	72'x66'
Foundation	Basement
Bedrooms	3
Full Baths	2
Half Baths	1
Main Ceiling	9'
Vaulted Ceiling	14'
Max Ridge Height	22'4"
Roof Framing	Stick
Exterior Walls	2x4

MAIN FLOOR

Units	Single
Price Code	F
Total Finished	2,569 sq. ft.
Main Finished	2,569 sq. ft.
Bonus Unfinished	352 sq. ft.
Garage Unfinished	702 sq. ft.
Deck Unfinished	132 sq. ft.
Porch Unfinished	62 sq. ft.
Dimensions	68'10"x74'7"
Foundation	Slab
Bedrooms	4
Full Baths	3
Main Ceiling	10'
Max Ridge Height	31'6"
Roof Framing	Stick
Exterior Walls	2x4

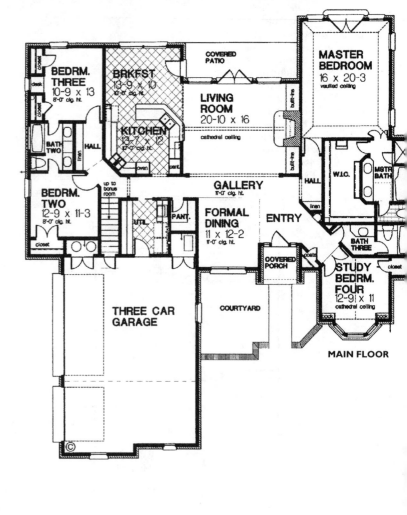

MAIN FLOOR

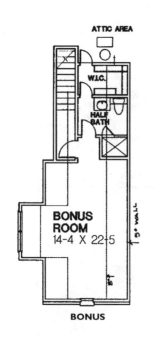

BONUS

Design 99194

Units	Single
Price Code	F
Total Finished	2,570 sq. ft.
Main Finished	2,570 sq. ft.
Garage Unfinished	808 sq. ft.
Dimensions	79'x63'
Foundation	Basement
Bedrooms	4
Full Baths	2
3/4 Baths	1
Main Ceiling	9'
Max Ridge Height	28'
Roof Framing	Truss
Exterior Walls	2x6

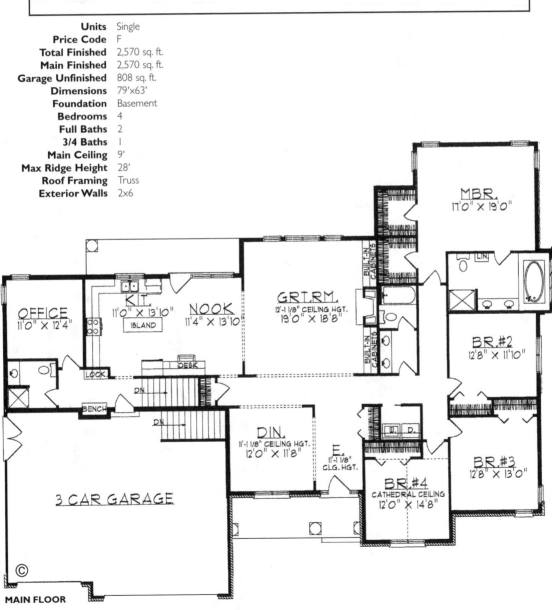

MAIN FLOOR

Units	Single
Price Code	F
Total Finished	2,579 sq. ft.
Main Finished	2,579 sq. ft.
Garage Unfinished	630 sq. ft.
Dimensions	60'x70'
Foundation	Slab
Bedrooms	4
Full Baths	3
Max Ridge Height	26'6"
Roof Framing	Stick
Exterior Walls	2x4

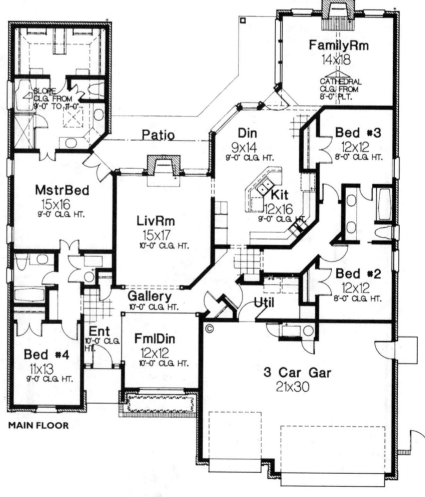

MAIN FLOOR

Design 62003

2,501-3,000 sq. ft. HOME PLANS

Units	Single
Price Code	F
Total Finished	2,582 sq. ft.
Main Finished	2,582 sq. ft.
Garage Unfinished	552 sq. ft.
Porch Unfinished	365 sq. ft.
Dimensions	77'x57'8"
Foundation	Crawlspace
	Slab
Bedrooms	4
Full Baths	2
Half Baths	1
Main Ceiling	9'
Roof Framing	Stick
Exterior Walls	2x4

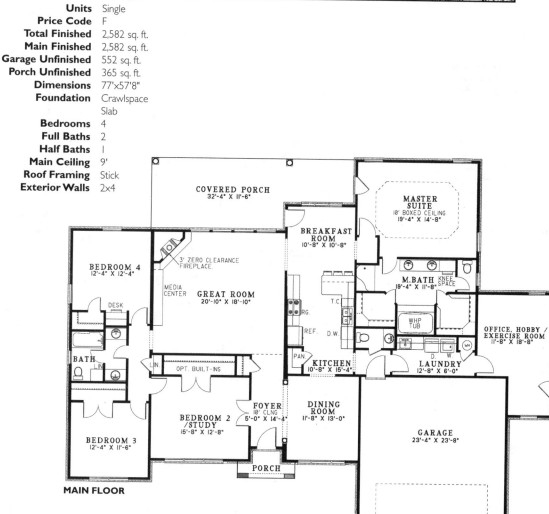

MAIN FLOOR

Visit us at www.merillat.com

Merillat

Design 96938

Units	Single
Price Code	F
Total Finished	2,585 sq. ft.
Main Finished	2,585 sq. ft.
Bonus Unfinished	519 sq. ft.
Basement Unfinished	2,609 sq. ft.
Garage Unfinished	607 sq. ft.
Dimensions	61'x80'
Foundation	Basement
	Crawlspace
Bedrooms	3
Full Baths	2
Half Baths	1
Main Ceiling	9'
Vaulted Ceiling	12'
Tray Ceiling	10'6"
Max Ridge Height	31'
Roof Framing	Stick
Exterior Walls	2x4

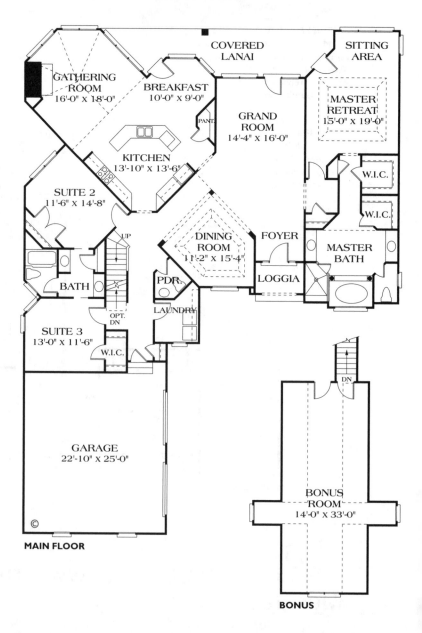

COVERED LANAI

SITTING AREA

GATHERING ROOM
16'-0" x 18'-0"

BREAKFAST
10'-0" x 9'-0"

GRAND ROOM
14'-4" x 16'-0"

MASTER RETREAT
15'-0" x 19'-0"

KITCHEN
13'-10" x 13'-6"

PANT.

W.I.C.

SUITE 2
11'-6" x 14'-8"

W.I.C.

DINING ROOM
11'-2" x 15'-4"

FOYER

MASTER BATH

BATH

UP

PDR.

LOGGIA

OPT. DN

LAUNDRY

SUITE 3
13'-0" x 11'-6"

W.I.C.

GARAGE
22'-10" x 25'-0"

MAIN FLOOR

DN

BONUS ROOM
14'-0" x 33'-0"

BONUS

Design 99678

Units	Single
Price Code	F
Total Finished	2,585 sq. ft.
Main Finished	2,585 sq. ft.
Bonus Unfinished	160 sq. ft.
Basement Unfinished	2,585 sq. ft.
Garage Unfinished	520 sq. ft.
Porch Unfinished	292 sq. ft.
Dimensions	72'x69'10"
Foundation	Basement
	Crawlspace
	Slab
Bedrooms	3
Full Baths	2
3/4 Baths	1
Max Ridge Height	24'
Roof Framing	Stick
Exterior Walls	2x4

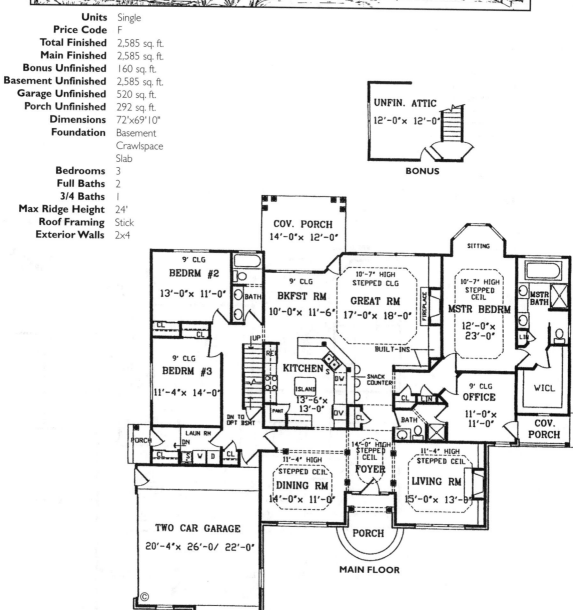

UNFIN. ATTIC
12'-0" x 12'-0"

BONUS

MAIN FLOOR

Design 97472

Units	Single
Price Code	F
Total Finished	2,586 sq. ft.
Main Finished	2,586 sq. ft.
Garage Unfinished	757 sq. ft.
Deck Unfinished	311 sq. ft.
Dimensions	72'8"x64'8"
Foundation	Basement
Bedrooms	3
Full Baths	2
Half Baths	1
Main Ceiling	9'
Max Ridge Height	29'6"
Roof Framing	Stick
Exterior Walls	2x4

* Alternate foundation options available at an additional charge.
Please call 1-800-235-5700 for more information.

WHIRLPOOL

Sit.
12⁰ x 6⁸
10'-0"
CEIL.

Mbr.
13⁰ x 13⁶

Liv.
16⁰ x 13⁰
13'-0"
CEIL.

Bfst.
12⁴ x 11⁸

SNACK BAR

Fam.Rm.
19⁰ x 17⁴
CATHEDRAL CEIL.

W. D.

COV'D PORCH

Kit.
14⁰ x 15⁰

R.

DN

P.

STOR.

L.

Br.2
11⁰ x 14⁰

Br.3
13⁰ x 11⁸
11'-0"
CEIL.

E.

Din.
13⁰ x 13⁰
11'-0"
CEIL.

Gar.
22⁴ x 31⁴

MAIN FLOOR

COVERED PORCH

©

Design 98246

PHOTOGRAPHY: COURTESY OF THE DESIGNER

Units	Single
Price Code	G
Total Finished	2,588 sq. ft.
Main Finished	2,588 sq. ft.
Basement Unfinished	2,588 sq. ft.
Garage Unfinished	469 sq. ft.
Porch Unfinished	150 sq. ft.
Dimensions	77'x52'6"
Foundation	Basement
Bedrooms	4
Full Baths	2
3/4 Baths	1
Half Baths	1
Main Ceiling	8'
Vaulted Ceiling	12'
Max Ridge Height	22'
Roof Framing	Stick
Exterior Walls	2x4

Please note: The photographed home may have been modified to suit homeowner preferences. If you order plans, have a builder or design professional check them against the photograph to confirm actual construction details.

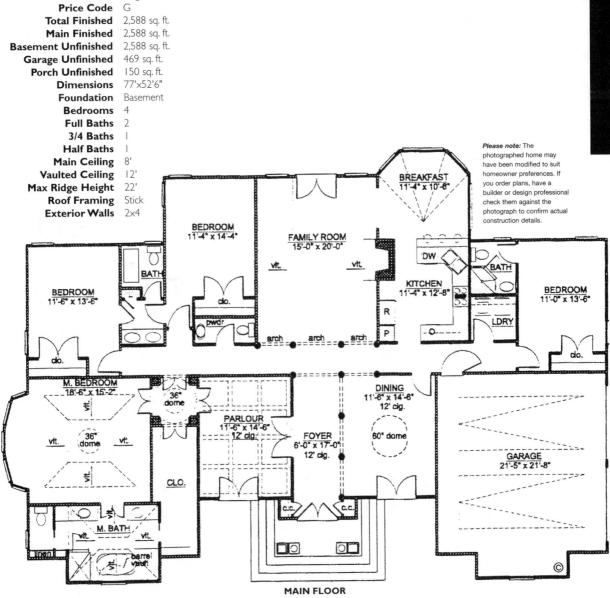

MAIN FLOOR

PHOTOGRAPHER: LAURIE BLACK

Units	Single
Price Code	F
Total Finished	2,591 sq. ft.
Main Finished	2,591 sq. ft.
Garage Unfinished	528 sq. ft.
Dimensions	84'x70'
Foundation	Crawlspace
Bedrooms	3
Full Baths	2
Half Baths	1
Main Ceiling	9'
Vaulted Ceiling	12'4"
Max Ridge Height	18'
Roof Framing	Truss
Exterior Walls	2x6

Please note: The photographed home may have been modified to suit homeowner preferences. If you order plans, have a builder or design professional check them against the photograph to confirm actual construction details.

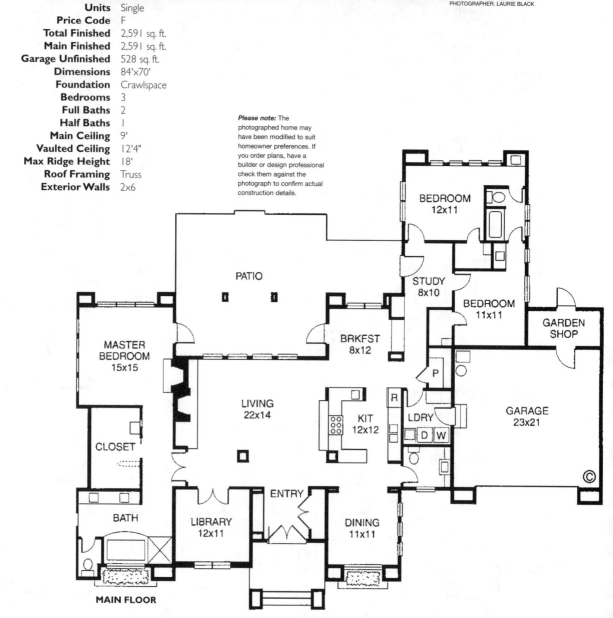

MAIN FLOOR

Design 66091

Units	Single
Price Code	F
Total Finished	2,606 sq. ft.
Main Finished	2,606 sq. ft.
Garage Unfinished	292 sq. ft.
Deck Unfinished	224 sq. ft.
Dimensions	79'7"×55'10"
Foundation	Slab
Bedrooms	3
Full Baths	2
Half Baths	1
Main Ceiling	9'
Max Ridge Height	26'6"
Roof Framing	Stick
Exterior Walls	2x4

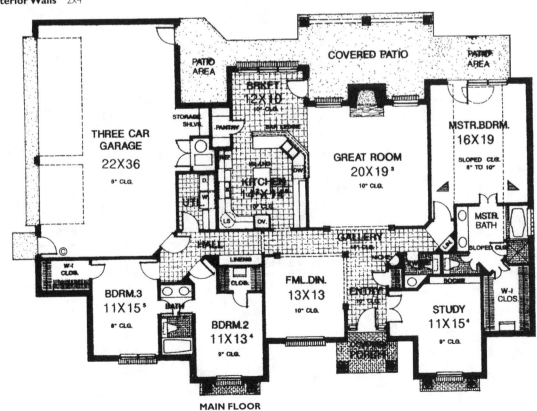

MAIN FLOOR

Units	Single
Price Code	F
Total Finished	2,613 sq. ft.
Main Finished	2,613 sq. ft.
Garage Unfinished	612 sq. ft.
Deck Unfinished	322 sq. ft.
Porch Unfinished	48 sq. ft.
Dimensions	67'11"x76'2"
Foundation	Slab
Bedrooms	4
Full Baths	3
Main Ceiling	8'-10'
Max Ridge Height	28'6"
Roof Framing	Stick
Exterior Walls	2x4

MAIN FLOOR

Design 98978

2,501-3,000 sq. ft. HOME PLANS

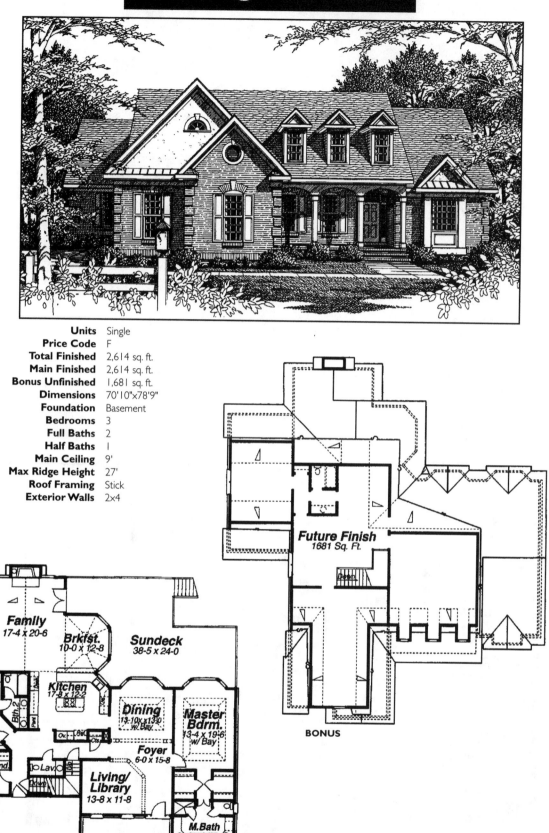

Units	Single
Price Code	F
Total Finished	2,614 sq. ft.
Main Finished	2,614 sq. ft.
Bonus Unfinished	1,681 sq. ft.
Dimensions	70'10"x78'9"
Foundation	Basement
Bedrooms	3
Full Baths	2
Half Baths	1
Main Ceiling	9'
Max Ridge Height	27'
Roof Framing	Stick
Exterior Walls	2x4

Future Finish
1681 Sq. Ft.

BONUS

Family
17-4 x 20-6

Brkfst.
10-0 x 12-8

Sundeck
38-5 x 24-0

Bdrm.3
13-8 x 11-6

Kitchen
17-8 x 12-2

Dining
13-10 x 13-10
w/ Bay

Master
Bdrm.
13-4 x 19-6
w/ Bay

Bdrm.2
13-8 x 11-6

Foyer
6-0 x 15-8

Living/
Library
13-8 x 11-8

M.Bath

Double Garage
21-4 x 27-8

MAIN FLOOR

Units	Single
Price Code	F
Total Finished	2,615 sq. ft.
Main Finished	2,615 sq. ft.
Garage Unfinished	713 sq. ft.
Dimensions	87'4"x65'7"
Foundation	Slab
Bedrooms	4
Full Baths	2
3/4 Baths	1
Max Ridge Height	25'
Roof Framing	Stick
Exterior Walls	2x4

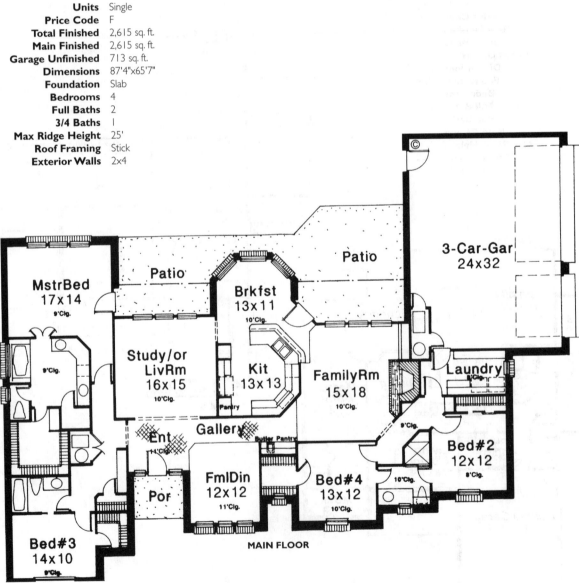

MAIN FLOOR

Design 98547

Units	Single
Price Code	F
Total Finished	2,626 sq. ft.
Main Finished	2,626 sq. ft.
Garage Unfinished	506 sq. ft.
Deck Unfinished	156 sq. ft.
Porch Unfinished	42 sq. ft.
Dimensions	65'x66'10"
Foundation	Slab
Bedrooms	4
Full Baths	2
3/4 Baths	1
Max Ridge Height	24'6"
Roof Framing	Stick
Exterior Walls	2x4

MAIN FLOOR

Merillat.

Visit us at www.merillat.com

Units	Single
Price Code	F
Total Finished	2,629 sq. ft.
Main Finished	2,629 sq. ft.
Basement Unfinished	2,629 sq. ft.
Dimensions	65'x72'
Foundation	Basement
Bedrooms	3
Full Baths	2
Half Baths	1
Max Ridge Height	27'5"
Roof Framing	Truss
Exterior Walls	2x6

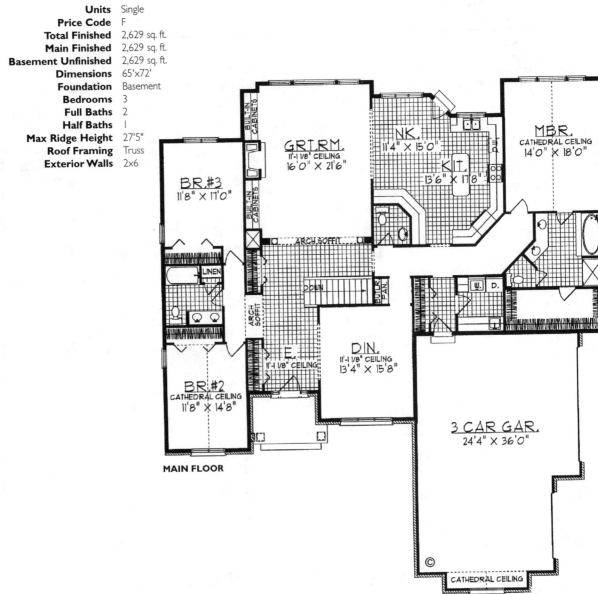

MAIN FLOOR

BR.#3
11'8" X 17'0"

BUILT-IN CABINETS

GRT.RM.
11'-1 1/8" CEILING
16'0" X 21'6"

NK.
11'4" X 15'0"

KIT.
13'6" X 17'8"

MBR.
CATHEDRAL CEILING
14'0" X 18'0"

ARCH SOFFIT

LINEN

ARCH SOFFIT

DOWN

F.
11'-1 1/8" CEILING

DIN.
11'-1 1/8" CEILING
13'4" X 15'8"

W. D.

BR.#2
CATHEDRAL CEILING
11'8" X 14'8"

3 CAR GAR.
24'4" X 36'0"

CATHEDRAL CEILING

Design 93252

Units	Single
Price Code	F
Total Finished	2,644 sq. ft.
Main Finished	2,644 sq. ft.
Basement Unfinished	2,644 sq. ft.
Dimensions	82'4"x65'
Foundation	Basement
Bedrooms	4
Full Baths	2
Half Baths	1
Max Ridge Height	31'
Roof Framing	Stick
Exterior Walls	2x4

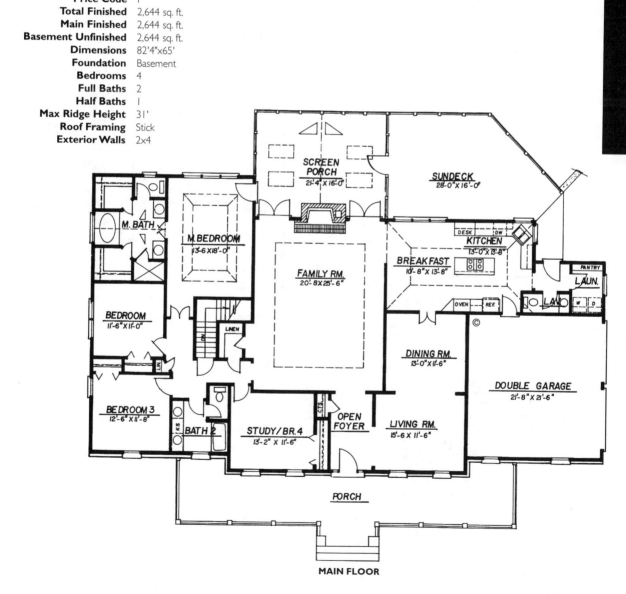

MAIN FLOOR

Units	Single
Price Code	F
Total Finished	2,647 sq. ft.
Main Finished	1,431 sq. ft.
Lower Finished	1,216 sq. ft.
Basement Unfinished	215 sq. ft.
Dimensions	52'x49'
Foundation	Basement
Bedrooms	4
Full Baths	3
Max Ridge Height	23'
Roof Framing	Truss

MAIN FLOOR

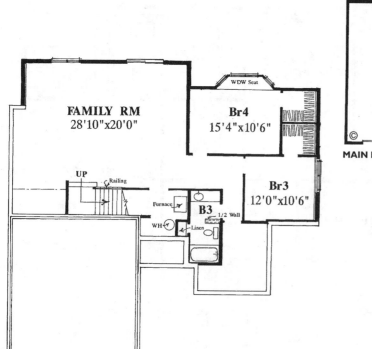

LOWER FLOOR

Design 68085

2,301-3,000 sq. ft. HOME PLANS

Units	Single
Price Code	F
Total Finished	2,650 sq. ft.
Main Finished	2,650 sq. ft.
Garage Unfinished	771 sq. ft.
Deck Unfinished	58 sq. ft.
Dimensions	76'x60'8"
Foundation	Basement
	Crawlspace
	Slab
Bedrooms	3
Full Baths	2
Half Baths	1
Main Ceiling	9'
Max Ridge Height	27'9"
Roof Framing	Stick
Exterior Walls	2x4

* Alternate foundation options available at an additional charge.
Please call 1-800-235-5700 for more information.

WHIRLPOOL

COVERED PORCH

Bfst.
11⁴ x 8⁰

Mbr.
15⁰ x 18⁰

13'-9"
CEIL.

10'-0"
CEIL.

Fam.Rm.
18⁸ x 15³

Kit.
13⁷ x 14⁰

Din.
15⁰ x 15⁰

R.

P.

P.

BOOKS

BOOKS

Sitting
11⁰ x 11⁸

DISPLAY

DN

L.

12'-0"
CEIL.

BOOKS

E.

Den
11⁴ x 14⁸

Gar.
21⁴ x 31⁴

W

D

COVERED STOOP

Br.2
12⁰ x 12⁰

Br.3
15⁰ x 11⁰

STORAGE

©

MAIN FLOOR

Units	Single
Price Code	F
Total Finished	2,654 sq. ft.
Main Finished	2,654 sq. ft.
Garage Unfinished	745 sq. ft.
Dimensions	73'x68'
Foundation	Crawlspace
Bedrooms	4
Full Baths	2
Half Baths	1
Main Ceiling	9'
Vaulted Ceiling	13'
Tray Ceiling	10'2"
Max Ridge Height	23'
Roof Framing	Truss
Exterior Walls	2x6

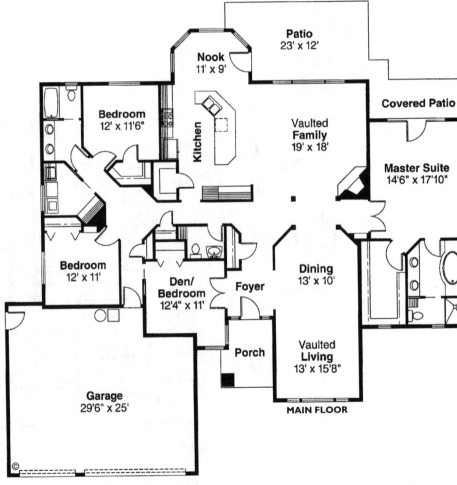

Patio 23' x 12'

Nook 11' x 9'

Covered Patio

Bedroom 12' x 11'6"

Kitchen

Vaulted Family 19' x 18'

Master Suite 14'6" x 17'10"

Bedroom 12' x 11'

Den/ Bedroom 12'4" x 11'

Foyer

Dining 13' x 10'

Garage 29'6" x 25'

Porch

Vaulted Living 13' x 15'8"

MAIN FLOOR

Design 63033

2,501-3,000 sq.ft. HOME PLANS

Units	Single
Price Code	F
Total Finished	2,660 sq. ft.
Main Finished	2,660 sq. ft.
Garage Unfinished	539 sq. ft.
Porch Unfinished	465 sq. ft.
Dimensions	66'4"x73'4"
Foundation	Slab
Bedrooms	4
Full Baths	3
Main Ceiling	10'
Max Ridge Height	25'
Roof Framing	Truss
Exterior Walls	2x4

Covered Patio

Family Room
20⁰ · 16⁰
10⁰ Clg.

fireplace

shelves

Breakfast

Sitting Rm
23⁰ · 15⁰
10⁰ Clg.

Bath

Living Room
15⁰ · 13⁴
12⁰ Clg.

Kitchen

dw

desk

Bedroom 2
12⁰ · 11⁰
10⁰ Clg.

ref

pantry

Master Bedroom

Bath

lin

Bath

w.i.c.

Den Study
Bedroom 4
11⁰ · 11⁰
10⁰ Clg.

Foyer

Entry

Dining
11⁰ · 11⁰
14⁰ Clg.

linen

Utility

d w

Bedroom 3
12⁰ · 11⁰
10⁰ Clg.

ac

ac

wh

MAIN FLOOR

Double Garage

©

Units	Single
Price Code	F
Total Finished	2,675 sq. ft.
Main Finished	2,675 sq. ft.
Garage Unfinished	638 sq. ft.
Dimensions	69'x59'10"
Foundation	Slab
Bedrooms	4
Full Baths	2
3/4 Baths	1
Max Ridge Height	28'
Roof Framing	Stick
Exterior Walls	2x4

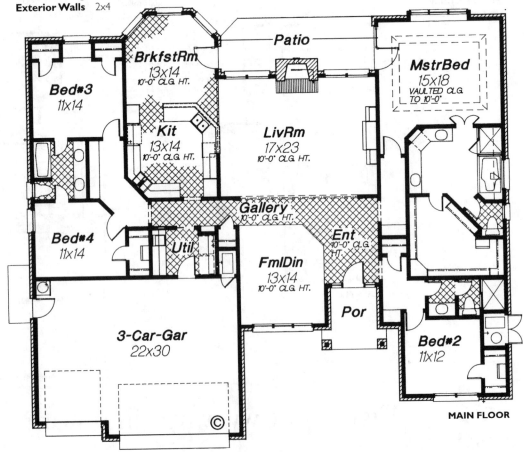

MAIN FLOOR

Design 65632

Units	Single
Price Code	G
Total Finished	2,682 sq. ft.
Main Finished	2,682 sq. ft.
Dimensions	74'10"x75'
Foundation	Crawlspace
	Slab
Bedrooms	4
Full Baths	3
Half Baths	I
Main Ceiling	9'
Max Ridge Height	30'
Roof Framing	Stick
Exterior Walls	2x4

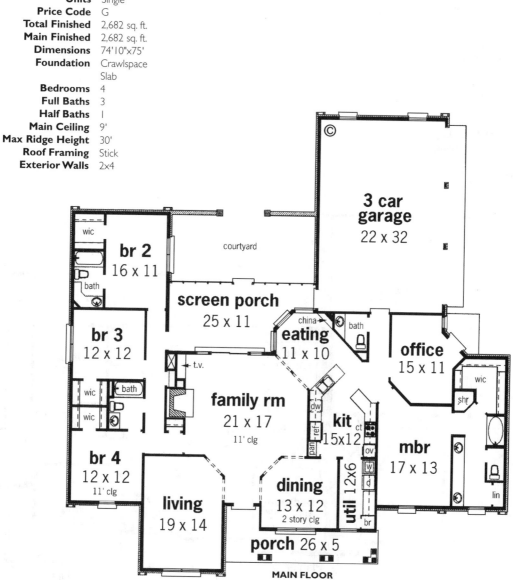

MAIN FLOOR

Units	Single
Price Code	F
Total Finished	2,692 sq. ft.
Main Finished	2,692 sq. ft.
Garage Unfinished	736 sq. ft.
Dimensions	88'x62'
Foundation	Crawlspace
Bedrooms	3
Full Baths	2
Half Baths	1
Main Ceiling	9'
Second Ceiling	12'
Tray Ceiling	10'
Max Ridge Height	22'
Roof Framing	Truss
Exterior Walls	2x6

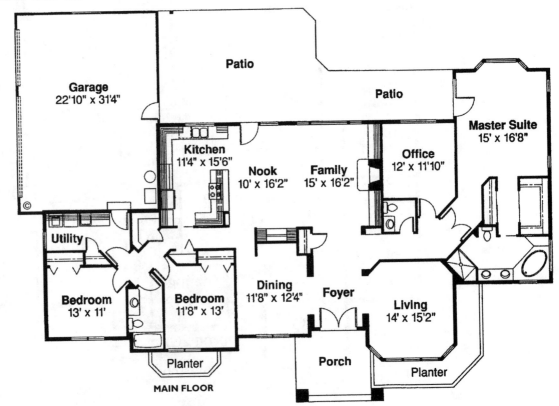

MAIN FLOOR

Design 91841

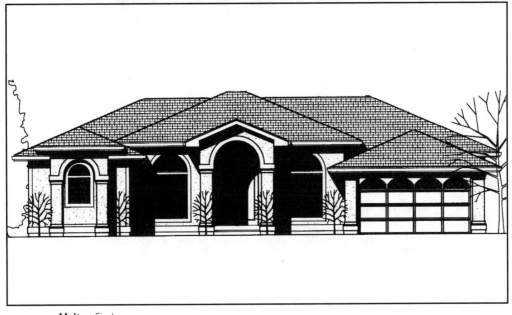

Units	Single
Price Code	F
Total Finished	2,710 sq. ft.
Main Finished	2,710 sq. ft.
Garage Unfinished	402 sq. ft.
Dimensions	64'x80'
Foundation	Basement
	Crawlspace
	Slab
Bedrooms	3
Full Baths	2
Half Baths	1
Main Ceiling	10'
Max Ridge Height	19'6"
Exterior Walls	2x4

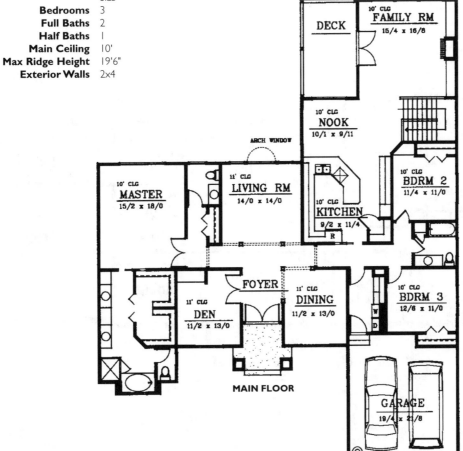

MAIN FLOOR

Units	Single
Price Code	F
Total Finished	2,719 sq. ft.
Main Finished	2,719 sq. ft.
Dimensions	96'x43'
Foundation	Crawlspace
	Slab
Bedrooms	4
Full Baths	2
Half Baths	1
Main Ceiling	8'
Max Ridge Height	26'
Roof Framing	Stick
Exterior Walls	2x6

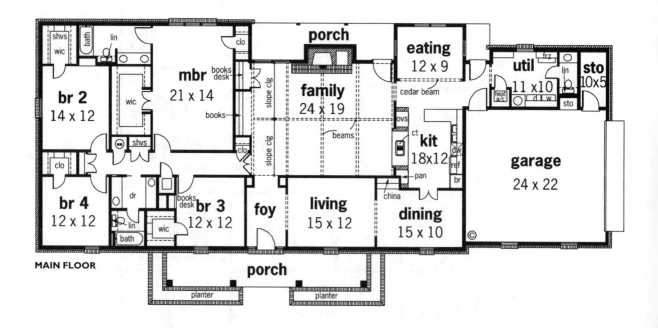

MAIN FLOOR

Design 99162

Units	Single
Price Code	F
Total Finished	2,730 sq. ft.
Main Finished	2,730 sq. ft.
Basement Unfinished	2,730 sq. ft.
Garage Unfinished	707 sq. ft.
Dimensions	72'x81'8"
Foundation	Basement
Bedrooms	3
Full Baths	2
Half Baths	1
Max Ridge Height	26'
Roof Framing	Truss
Exterior Walls	2x6

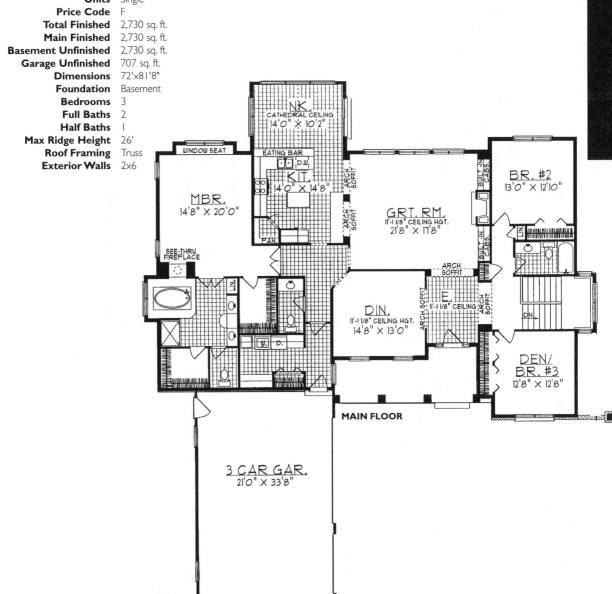

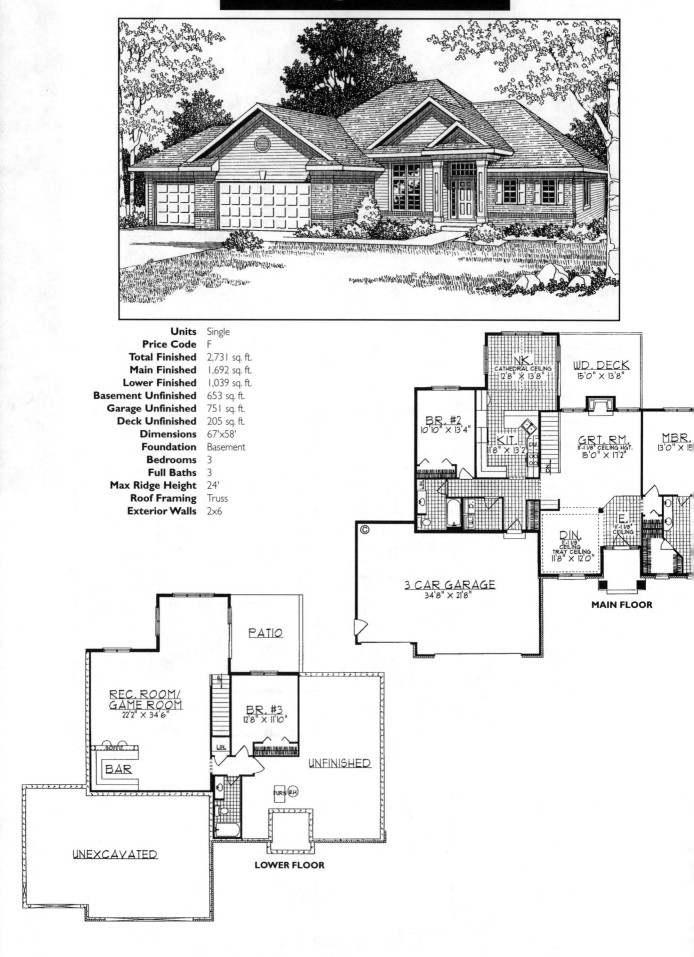

Units	Single
Price Code	F
Total Finished	2,731 sq. ft.
Main Finished	1,692 sq. ft.
Lower Finished	1,039 sq. ft.
Basement Unfinished	653 sq. ft.
Garage Unfinished	751 sq. ft.
Deck Unfinished	205 sq. ft.
Dimensions	67'x58'
Foundation	Basement
Bedrooms	3
Full Baths	3
Max Ridge Height	24'
Roof Framing	Truss
Exterior Walls	2x6

NK.
CATHEDRAL CEILING
12'8" X 13'8"

WD. DECK
15'0" X 13'8"

BR. #2
10'10" X 13'4"

KIT.
11'8" X 13'2"

GRT. RM.
11'-1 1/8" CEILING HGT.
15'0" X 17'2"

MBR.
13'0" X 15'

DIN.
11'-1 1/8"
CEILING
TRAY CEILING
11'8" X 12'0"

11'-1 1/8"
CEILING

3 CAR GARAGE
34'8" X 21'8"

MAIN FLOOR

PATIO

REC. ROOM/
GAME ROOM
22'2" X 34'6"

BR. #3
12'8" X 11'10"

BAR

LIN.

UNFINISHED

FURN. W.H.

UNEXCAVATED

LOWER FLOOR

Design 63034

Units	Single
Price Code	F
Total Finished	2,746 sq. ft.
Main Finished	2,746 sq. ft.
Garage Unfinished	459 sq. ft.
Porch Unfinished	244 sq. ft.
Dimensions	65'x70'
Foundation	Slab
Bedrooms	4
Full Baths	2
3/4 Baths	I
Main Ceiling	10'
Max Ridge Height	25'
Roof Framing	Truss
Exterior Walls	2x4

MAIN FLOOR

Units	Single
Price Code	F
Total Finished	2,750 sq. ft.
Main Finished	2,750 sq. ft.
Garage Unfinished	695 sq. ft.
Dimensions	66'8"x72'8"
Foundation	Basement
Bedrooms	4
Full Baths	3
Half Baths	I
Main Ceiling	9'
Max Ridge Height	26'6"
Roof Framing	Stick
Exterior Walls	2x4

* Alternate foundation options available at an additional charge.
Please call 1-800-235-5700 for more information.

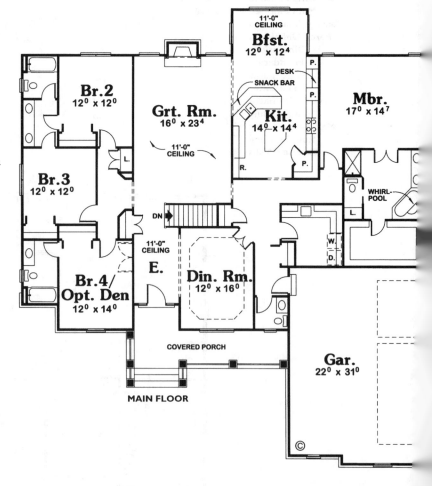

Design 20407

Units	Single
Price Code	G
Total Finished	2,753 sq. ft.
Main Finished	2,753 sq. ft.
Garage Unfinished	440 sq. ft.
Dimensions	65'2"x74'
Foundation	Crawlspace
Bedrooms	3
Full Baths	2
Half Baths	1
Max Ridge Height	27'
Roof Framing	Stick
Exterior Walls	2x4, 2x6

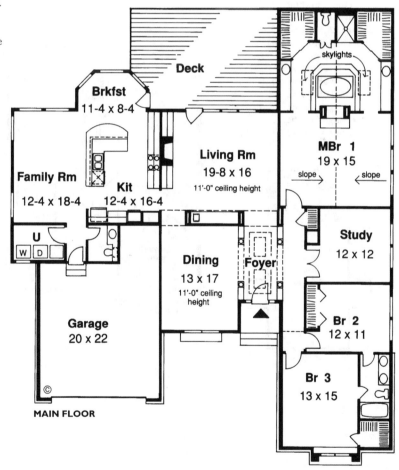

Deck

Brkfst 11-4 x 8-4

skylights

MBr 1 19 x 15

slope → ← slope

Family Rm 12-4 x 18-4

Kit 12-4 x 16-4

Living Rm 19-8 x 16
11'-0" ceiling height

Study 12 x 12

U
W D

Dining 13 x 17
11'-0" ceiling height

Foyer

Br 2 12 x 11

Garage 20 x 22

Br 3 13 x 15

MAIN FLOOR

Units	Single
Price Code	G
Total Finished	2,755 sq. ft.
Main Finished	2,755 sq. ft.
Bonus Unfinished	440 sq. ft.
Garage Unfinished	724 sq. ft.
Porch Unfinished	419 sq. ft.
Dimensions	73'x82'8"
Foundation	Slab
Bedrooms	4
Full Baths	2
3/4 Baths	1
Max Ridge Height	22'
Roof Framing	Truss

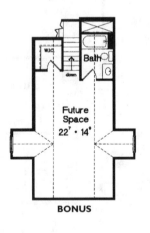

BONUS

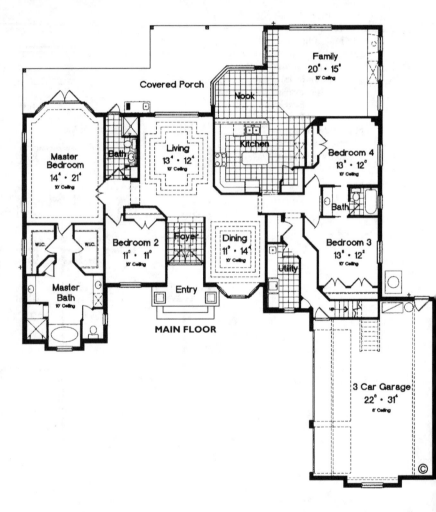

MAIN FLOOR

Design 97776

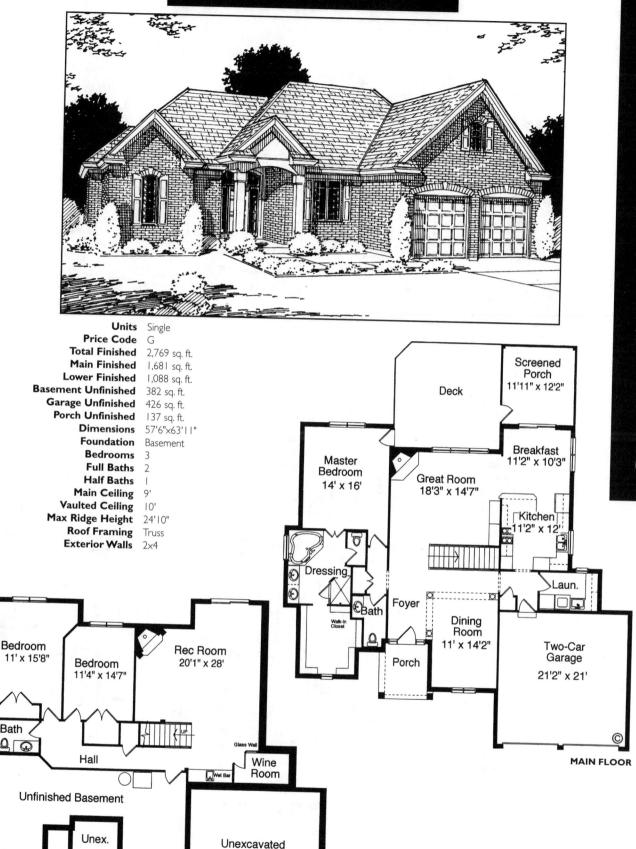

Units	Single
Price Code	G
Total Finished	2,769 sq. ft.
Main Finished	1,681 sq. ft.
Lower Finished	1,088 sq. ft.
Basement Unfinished	382 sq. ft.
Garage Unfinished	426 sq. ft.
Porch Unfinished	137 sq. ft.
Dimensions	57'6"x63'11"
Foundation	Basement
Bedrooms	3
Full Baths	2
Half Baths	1
Main Ceiling	9'
Vaulted Ceiling	10'
Max Ridge Height	24'10"
Roof Framing	Truss
Exterior Walls	2x4

Main Floor

Deck

Screened Porch 11'11" x 12'2"

Master Bedroom 14' x 16'

Great Room 18'3" x 14'7"

Breakfast 11'2" x 10'3"

Kitchen 11'2" x 12'

Dressing

Bath

Walk-In Closet

Foyer

Laun.

Dining Room 11' x 14'2"

Porch

Two-Car Garage 21'2" x 21'

Lower Floor

Bedroom 11' x 15'8"

Bedroom 11'4" x 14'7"

Rec Room 20'1" x 28'

Bath

Hall

Glass Wall

Wet Bar

Wine Room

Unfinished Basement

Unex.

Unexcavated

Units	Single
Price Code	G
Total Finished	2,775 sq. ft.
Main Finished	2,775 sq. ft.
Garage Unfinished	763 sq. ft.
Dimensions	74'x68'
Foundation	Basement
Bedrooms	4
Full Baths	2
Half Baths	1
Main Ceiling	8'
Max Ridge Height	26'
Roof Framing	Stick
Exterior Walls	2x4

* Alternate foundation options available at an additional charge.
Please call 1-800-235-5700 for more information.

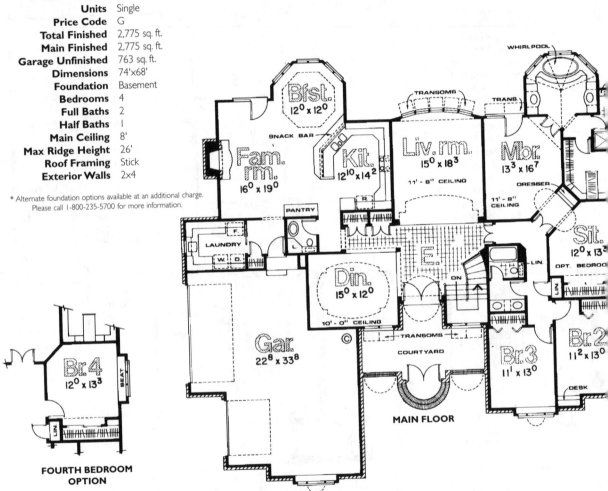

FOURTH BEDROOM
OPTION

MAIN FLOOR

Design 93068

Units	Single
Price Code	G
Total Finished	2,777 sq. ft.
Main Finished	2,777 sq. ft.
Garage Unfinished	501 sq. ft.
Porch Unfinished	88 sq. ft.
Dimensions	88'4"x54'9"
Foundation	Slab
Bedrooms	3
Full Baths	2
Half Baths	1
Main Ceiling	10'8"
Max Ridge Height	21'8"
Roof Framing	Stick
Exterior Walls	2x4

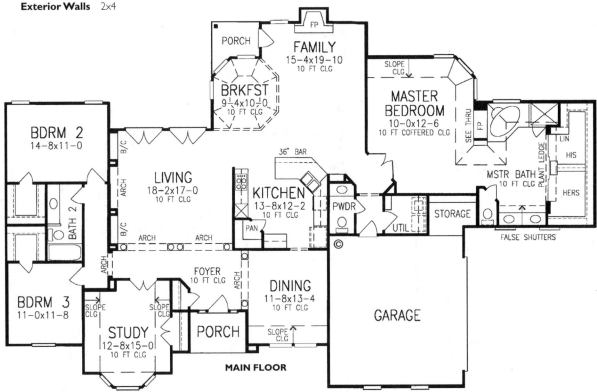

MAIN FLOOR

Units	Single
Price Code	F
Total Finished	2,781 sq. ft.
Main Finished	2,781 sq. ft.
Bonus Unfinished	319 sq. ft.
Garage Unfinished	623 sq. ft.
Porch Unfinished	361 sq. ft.
Dimensions	64'10"x76'9"
Foundation	Slab
Bedrooms	4
Full Baths	3

Master Bedroom 14'4"x 18'4"

Covered Porch 21'5"x 10'6"

Breakfast 14'x 11'4"

Bedroom 12'6"x 11'6"

Walk-In Closet

Walk-In Closet

Living 21'6"x 23'

Kitchen 14'x 13'

Bath

Master Bath

Dressing

Bath

Foyer

Dining 14'5"x 14'

Utility

Bedroom 12'x 12'

w d

Bedroom 11'10"x 13'

Porch

Unfinished Gameroom 11'4"x 26'

Two Car Garage 21'2"x 26'

BONUS

MAIN FLO

Units	Single
Price Code	G
Total Finished	2,791 sq. ft.
Main Finished	2,791 sq. ft.
Dimensions	84'x54'
Foundation	Crawlspace
	Slab
Bedrooms	4
Full Baths	2
Main Ceiling	8'-12'
Max Ridge Height	29'
Exterior Walls	2x4

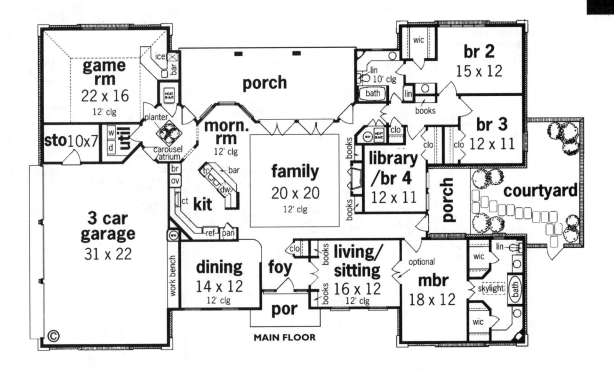

MAIN FLOOR

Merillat.

Visit us at www.merillat.com

Units	Single
Price Code	F
Total Finished	2,828 sq. ft.
Main Finished	2,828 sq. ft.
Garage Unfinished	862 sq. ft.
Deck Unfinished	72 sq. ft.
Porch Unfinished	72 sq. ft.
Dimensions	74'x82'4"
Foundation	Slab
Bedrooms	4
Full Baths	2
3/4 Baths	1
Half Baths	1
Main Ceiling	9'
Max Ridge Height	32'
Roof Framing	Stick
Exterior Walls	2x4

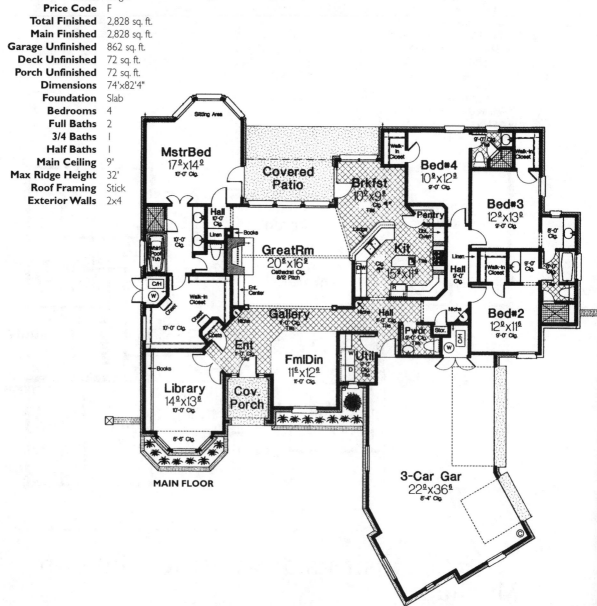

MAIN FLOOR

Design 93119

Units	Single
Price Code	G
Total Finished	2,837 sq. ft.
Main Finished	2,837 sq. ft.
Basement Unfinished	2,837 sq. ft.
Garage Unfinished	724 sq. ft.
Dimensions	85'4"x61'
Foundation	Basement
Bedrooms	3
Full Baths	2
Main Ceiling	9'
Max Ridge Height	23'
Roof Framing	Truss
Exterior Walls	2x6

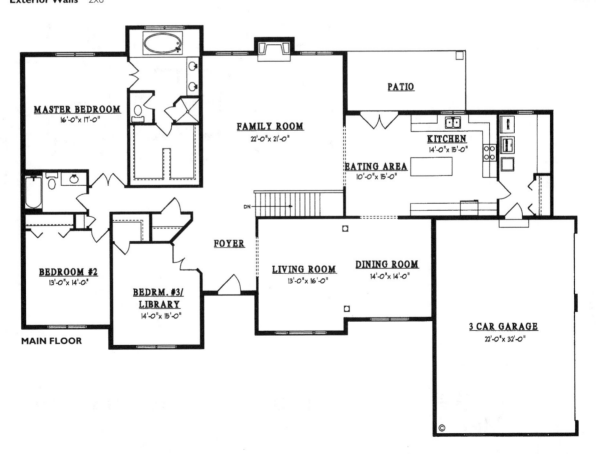

MASTER BEDROOM
16'-0" x 17'-0"

FAMILY ROOM
22'-0" x 21'-0"

PATIO

KITCHEN
14'-0" x 15'-0"

EATING AREA
10'-0" x 15'-0"

DN

FOYER

BEDROOM #2
13'-0" x 14'-0"

BEDRM. #3/
LIBRARY
14'-0" x 15'-0"

LIVING ROOM
13'-0" x 16'-0"

DINING ROOM
14'-0" x 14'-0"

3 CAR GARAGE
22'-0" x 32'-0"

MAIN FLOOR

Design 97532

Units	Single
Price Code	G
Total Finished	2,838 sq. ft.
Main Finished	2,838 sq. ft.
Garage Unfinished	722 sq. ft.
Dimensions	96'1"x95'1"
Foundation	Slab
Bedrooms	4
Full Baths	3
Main Ceiling	9'-11'
Max Ridge Height	25'
Roof Framing	Stick
Exterior Walls	2x4

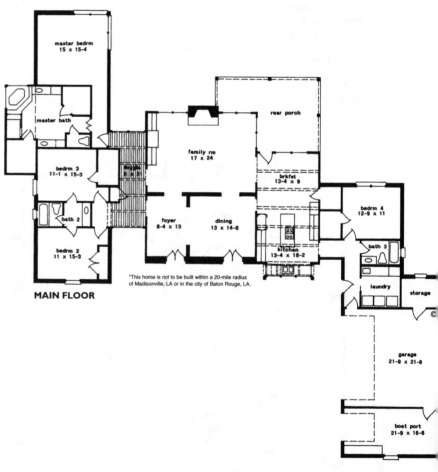

master bedrm
15 x 15-4

master bath

bedrm 3
11-1 x 15-3

bath 2

bedrm 2
11 x 15-3

family rm
17 x 24

rear porch

brkfst
13-4 x 9

foyer
8-4 x 13

dining
13 x 14-8

kitchen
13-4 x 18-2

bedrm 4
12-9 x 11

bath 3

laundry

storage

garage
21-9 x 21-8

boat port
21-9 x 16-8

MAIN FLOOR

*This home is not to be built within a 20-mile radius of Madisonville, LA or in the city of Baton Rouge, LA.

Design 98332

Units	Single
Price Code	G
Total Finished	2,847 sq. ft.
Main Finished	2,847 sq. ft.
Basement Unfinished	2,847 sq. ft.
Garage Unfinished	484 sq. ft.
Deck Unfinished	324 sq. ft.
Dimensions	66'x76'4"
Foundation	Basement
Bedrooms	4
Full Baths	3
Half Baths	1
Max Ridge Height	22'6"
Roof Framing	Truss
Exterior Walls	2x4

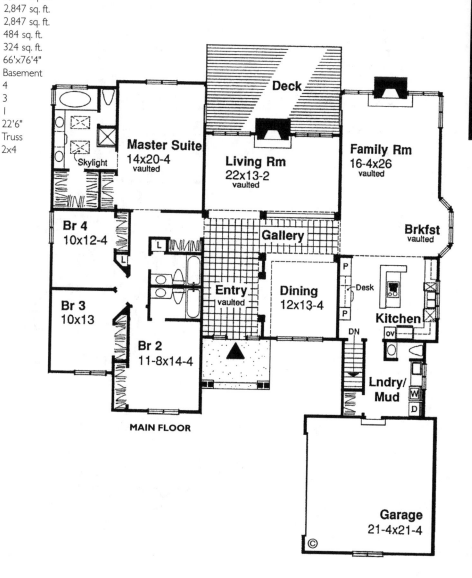

Deck

Master Suite
14x20-4
vaulted

Skylight

Living Rm
22x13-2
vaulted

Family Rm
16-4x26
vaulted

Br 4
10x12-4

Gallery

Brkfst
vaulted

Br 3
10x13

Desk

Entry
vaulted

Dining
12x13-4

Kitchen

Br 2
11-8x14-4

DN

ov

Lndry/
Mud

W D

MAIN FLOOR

Garage
21-4x21-4

Units	Single
Price Code	H
Total Finished	2,850 sq. ft.
Main Finished	2,850 sq. ft.
Garage Unfinished	588 sq. ft.
Dimensions	63'4"x86'
Foundation	Slab
Bedrooms	3
Full Baths	2
Half Baths	1
Main Ceiling	10'
Max Ridge Height	33'6"
Exterior Walls	2x4

* Alternate foundation options available at an additional charge.
Please call 1-800-235-5700 for more information.

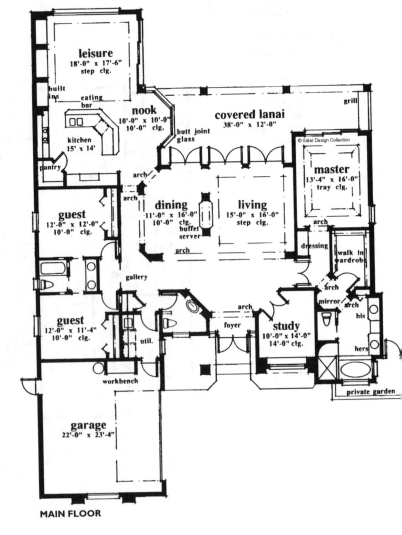

MAIN FLOOR

Design 92298

Units	Duplex
Price Code	G
Total Finished	2,865 sq. ft.
Main Finished	1,406 sq. ft. (unit A)
Main Finished	1,459 sq. ft. (unit B)
Dimensions	70'x60'
Foundation	Slab
Bedrooms	4
Full Baths	3
3/4 Baths	1
Main Ceiling	8'
Max Ridge Height	22'
Roof Framing	Stick
Exterior Walls	2x4

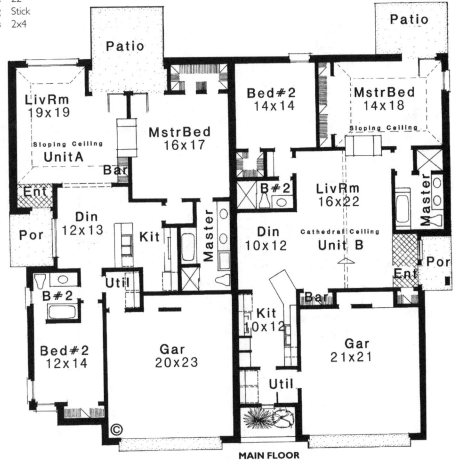

MAIN FLOOR

Units	Single
Price Code	G
Total Finished	2,896 sq. ft.
Main Finished	2,896 sq. ft.
Dimensions	80'8"x69'
Foundation	Basement
Bedrooms	3
Full Baths	2
3/4 Baths	1
Half Baths	1
Max Ridge Height	27'
Exterior Walls	2x6

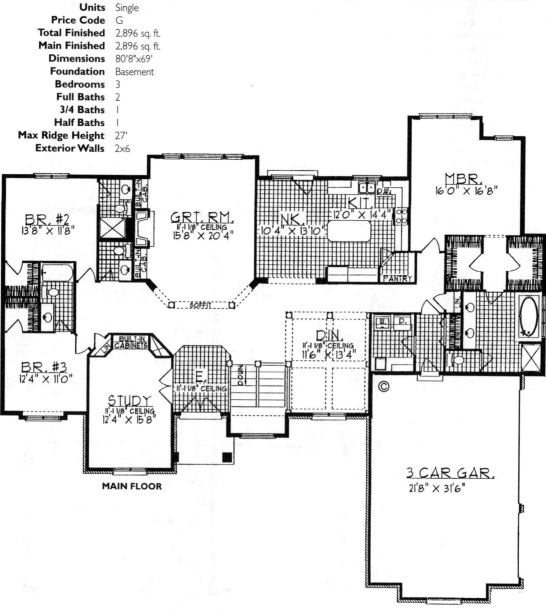

MAIN FLOOR

Design 63036

Units	Single
Price Code	G
Total Finished	2,920 sq. ft.
Main Finished	2,920 sq. ft.
Garage Unfinished	692 sq. ft.
Dimensions	70'x84'8"
Foundation	Slab
Bedrooms	3
Full Baths	2
3/4 Baths	1
Max Ridge Height	23'
Roof Framing	Truss
Exterior Walls	2x4

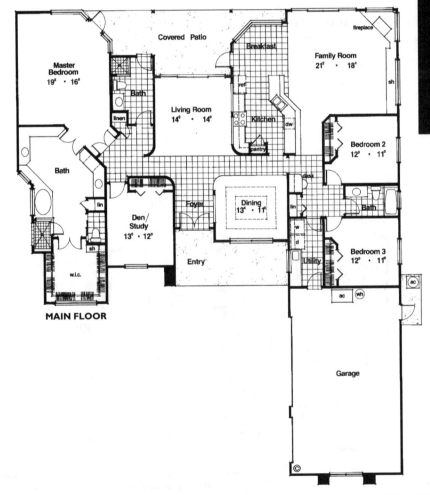

MAIN FLOOR

Units	Single
Price Code	G
Total Finished	2,927 sq. ft.
Main Finished	2,927 sq. ft.
Garage Unfinished	729 sq. ft.
Dimensions	105'x60'2"
Foundation	Crawlspace
Bedrooms	3
Full Baths	3
Main Ceiling	9'
Vaulted Ceiling	16'
Tray Ceiling	10'7½"
Max Ridge Height	23'10"
Roof Framing	Truss
Exterior Walls	2x6

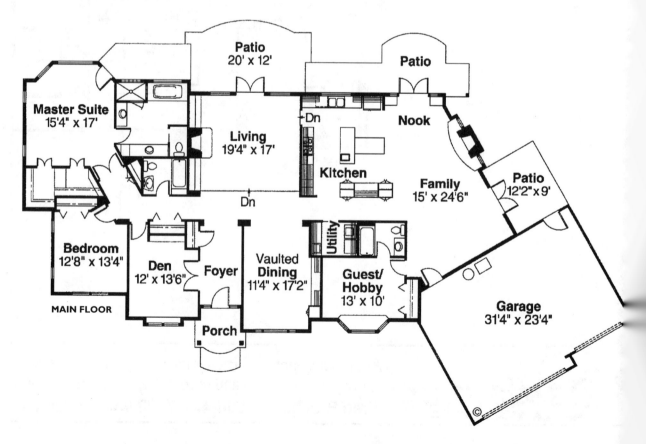

Master Suite 15'4" x 17'

Patio 20' x 12'

Patio

Living 19'4" x 17'

Nook

Kitchen

Family 15' x 24'6"

Patio 12'2" x 9'

Bedroom 12'8" x 13'4"

Den 12' x 13'6"

Foyer

Vaulted Dining 11'4" x 17'2"

Utility

Guest/ Hobby 13' x 10'

Garage 31'4" x 23'4"

MAIN FLOOR

Porch

Dn

Dn

Design 63063

2,501–3,000 sq. ft. HOME PLANS

Units	Single
Price Code	G
Total Finished	2,962 sq. ft.
Main Finished	2,962 sq. ft.
Garage Unfinished	737 sq. ft.
Dimensions	70'8"x76'8"
Foundation	Slab
Bedrooms	4
Full Baths	2
3/4 Baths	1
Main Ceiling	8'
Vaulted Ceiling	14'
Max Ridge Height	24'4"
Roof Framing	Truss

MAIN FLOOR

Visit us at www.merillat.com

Merillat.

Units	Single
Price Code	G
Total Finished	2,991 sq. ft.
Main Finished	2,991 sq. ft.
Dimensions	93'x65'
Foundation	Basement
Bedrooms	3
Full Baths	2
Half Baths	1
Max Ridge Height	27'
Roof Framing	Truss
Exterior Walls	2x6

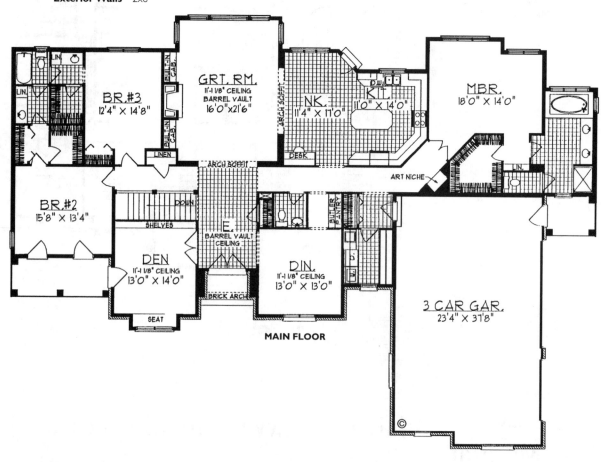

MAIN FLOOR

Design 66092

Units	Single
Price Code	I
Total Finished	3,002 sq. ft.
Main Finished	3,002 sq. ft.
Bonus Unfinished	455 sq. ft.
Dimensions	78'x75'7"
Foundation	Slab
Bedrooms	4
Full Baths	2
3/4 Baths	I
Half Baths	I
Main Ceiling	9'
Max Ridge Height	29'
Roof Framing	Stick
Exterior Walls	2x4

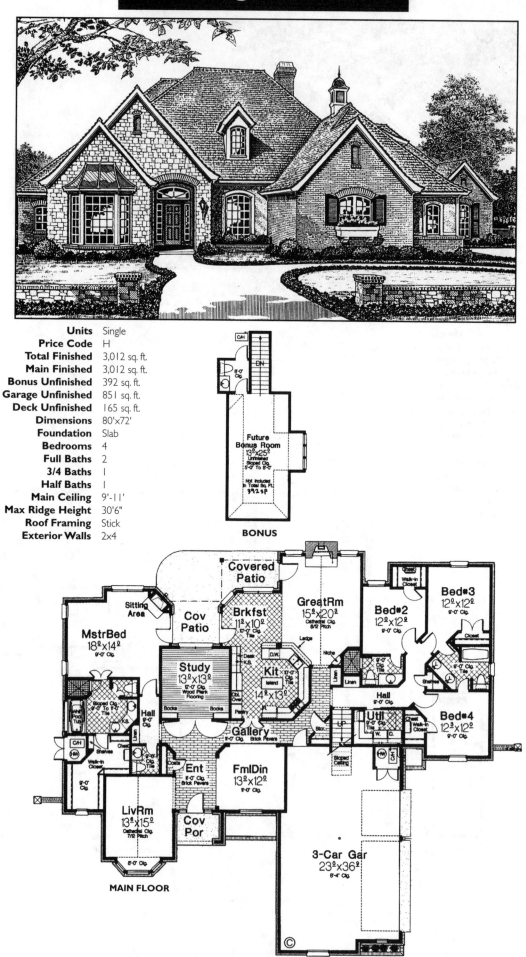

Units	Single
Price Code	H
Total Finished	3,012 sq. ft.
Main Finished	3,012 sq. ft.
Bonus Unfinished	392 sq. ft.
Garage Unfinished	851 sq. ft.
Deck Unfinished	165 sq. ft.
Dimensions	80'x72'
Foundation	Slab
Bedrooms	4
Full Baths	2
3/4 Baths	1
Half Baths	1
Main Ceiling	9'-11'
Max Ridge Height	30'6"
Roof Framing	Stick
Exterior Walls	2x4

BONUS

MAIN FLOOR

Design 92130

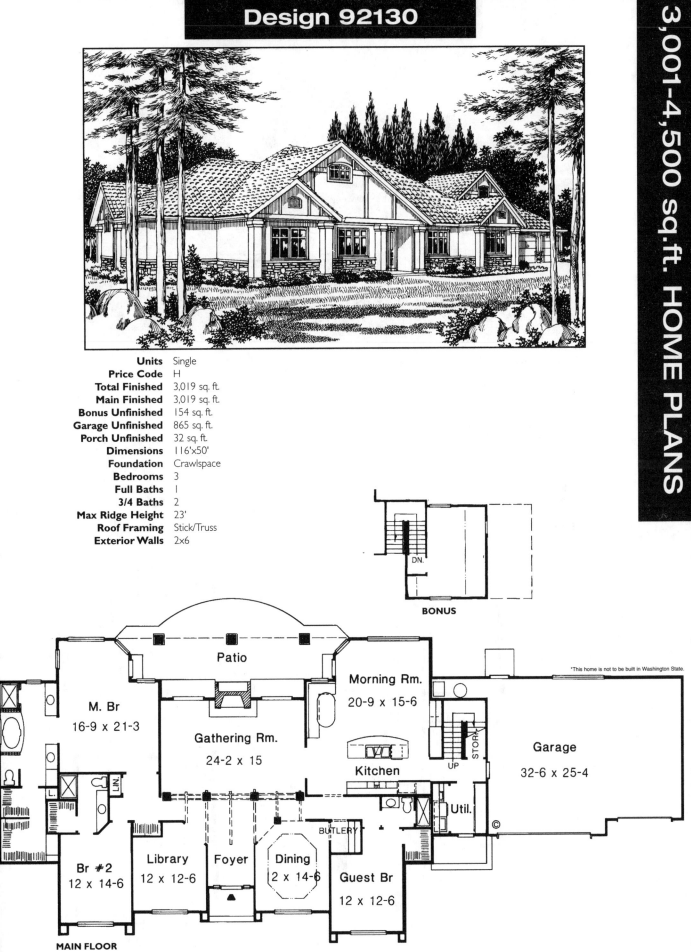

Units	Single
Price Code	H
Total Finished	3,019 sq. ft.
Main Finished	3,019 sq. ft.
Bonus Unfinished	154 sq. ft.
Garage Unfinished	865 sq. ft.
Porch Unfinished	32 sq. ft.
Dimensions	116'x50'
Foundation	Crawlspace
Bedrooms	3
Full Baths	1
3/4 Baths	2
Max Ridge Height	23'
Roof Framing	Stick/Truss
Exterior Walls	2x6

DN.

BONUS

*This home is not to be built in Washington State.

Patio

Morning Rm.
20-9 x 15-6

M. Br
16-9 x 21-3

Gathering Rm.
24-2 x 15

Kitchen

UP

STOR.

Garage
32-6 x 25-4

Util.

LIN.

BUTLERY

Br #2
12 x 14-6

Library
12 x 12-6

Foyer

Dining
2 x 14-6

Guest Br
12 x 12-6

©

MAIN FLOOR

Units	Single
Price Code	H
Total Finished	3,020 sq. ft.
Main Finished	3,020 sq. ft.
Garage Unfinished	469 sq. ft.
Porch Unfinished	95 sq. ft.
Dimensions	78'8"x79'9"
Foundation	Slab
Bedrooms	4
Full Baths	3
Main Ceiling	10'-12'
Max Ridge Height	30'7"
Roof Framing	Stick
Exterior Walls	2x4

MAIN FLOOR

*This home is not to be built within a 20-mile radius of Madisonville, LA or in the city of Baton Rouge, LA.

Design 10601

Units	Single
Price Code	H
Total Finished	3,025 sq. ft.
Main Finished	3,025 sq. ft.
Garage Unfinished	722 sq. ft.
Dimensions	98'10"x56'6"
Foundation	Slab
Bedrooms	4
Full Baths	3
Max Ridge Height	19'
Roof Framing	Stick
Exterior Walls	2x6

MAIN FLOOR

Design 97373

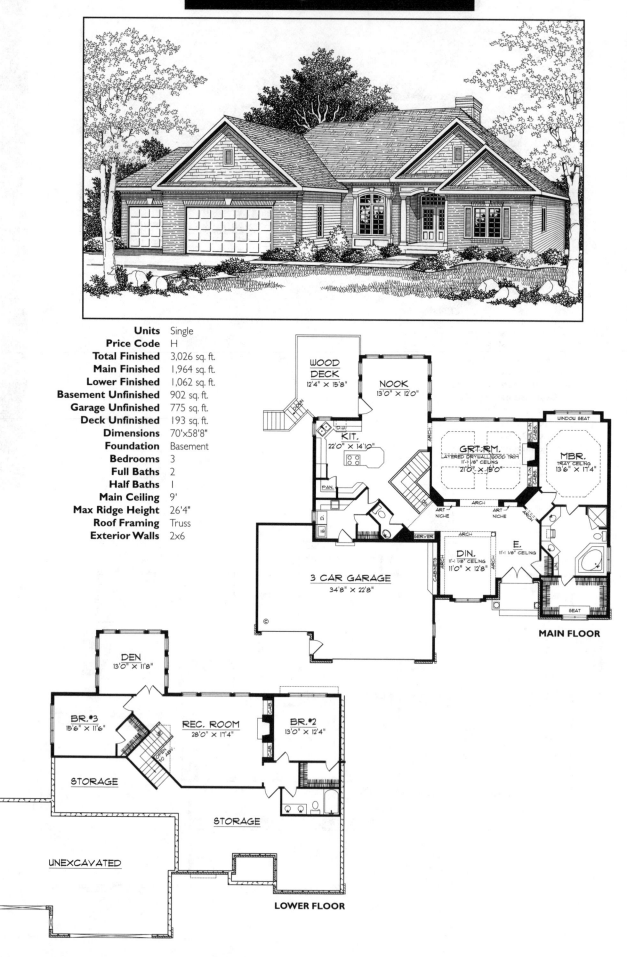

Units	Single
Price Code	H
Total Finished	3,026 sq. ft.
Main Finished	1,964 sq. ft.
Lower Finished	1,062 sq. ft.
Basement Unfinished	902 sq. ft.
Garage Unfinished	775 sq. ft.
Deck Unfinished	193 sq. ft.
Dimensions	70'x58'8"
Foundation	Basement
Bedrooms	3
Full Baths	2
Half Baths	1
Main Ceiling	9'
Max Ridge Height	26'4"
Roof Framing	Truss
Exterior Walls	2x6

WOOD DECK
12'4" X 15'8"

NOOK
13'0" X 12'0"

WINDOW SEAT

KIT.
22'0" X 14'10"

GRT. RM.
LAYERED DRYWALL/WOOD TRIM
11'-1 1/8" CEILING
21'0" X 19'0"

MBR.
TRAY CEILING
13'6" X 17'4"

PAN.

BUILT-IN CABS.

BUILT-IN CABS.

ART NICHE   ART NICHE

ARCH

ARCH

SERVER

CABINETS

DIN.
11'-1 1/8" CEILING
11'0" X 12'8"

E.
11'-1 1/8" CEILING

3 CAR GARAGE
34'8" X 22'8"

SEAT

MAIN FLOOR

DEN
13'0" X 11'8"

BR. #3
15'6" X 11'6"

REC. ROOM
28'0" X 17'4"

BR. #2
13'0" X 12'4"

CAB.

CAB.

STORAGE

STORAGE

UNEXCAVATED

LOWER FLOOR

To order blueprints, call **800-235-5700** or visit us on the web, **familyhomeplans.com**

Design 98723

Units	Single
Price Code	H
Total Finished	3,027 sq. ft.
Main Finished	3,027 sq. ft.
Garage Unfinished	560 sq. ft.
Dimensions	99'x62'
Foundation	Slab
Bedrooms	5
Full Baths	3
Half Baths	1
Max Ridge Height	28'
Roof Framing	Stick/Truss
Exterior Walls	2x6

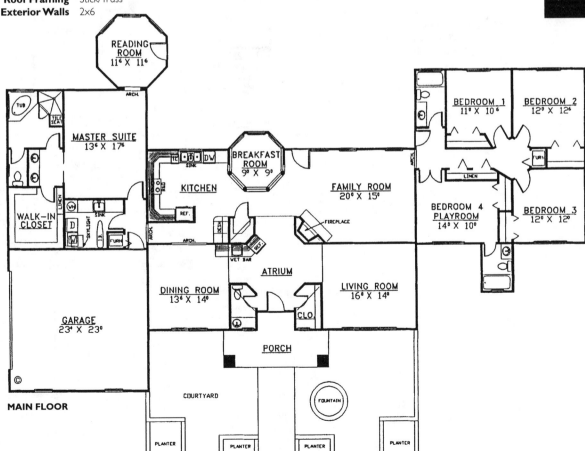

PHOTOGRAPHY: LAURIE BLACK

Units	Single
Price Code	H
Total Finished	3,028 sq. ft.
Main Finished	3,028 sq. ft.
Garage Unfinished	672 sq. ft.
Porch Unfinished	756 sq. ft.
Dimensions	86'x92'
Foundation	Crawlspace
Bedrooms	3
Full Baths	2
Half Baths	I
Main Ceiling	9'
Tray Ceiling	14'
Max Ridge Height	23'4"
Roof Framing	Stick
Exterior Walls	2x6

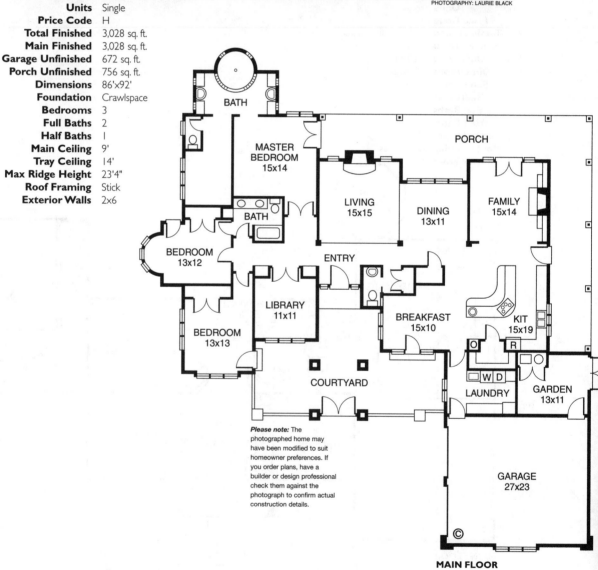

Please note: The photographed home may have been modified to suit homeowner preferences. If you order plans, have a builder or design professional check them against the photograph to confirm actual construction details.

MAIN FLOOR

Design 97511

Units	Single
Price Code	H
Total Finished	3,032 sq. ft.
Main Finished	3,032 sq. ft.
Garage Unfinished	594 sq. ft.
Porch Unfinished	401 sq. ft.
Dimensions	73'x87'8"
Foundation	Slab
Bedrooms	3
Full Baths	2
3/4 Baths	1
Main Ceiling	10'-14'
Max Ridge Height	26'
Roof Framing	Stick
Exterior Walls	2x4

*This home is not to be built within a 20-mile radius of Madisonville, LA or in the city of Baton Rouge, LA.

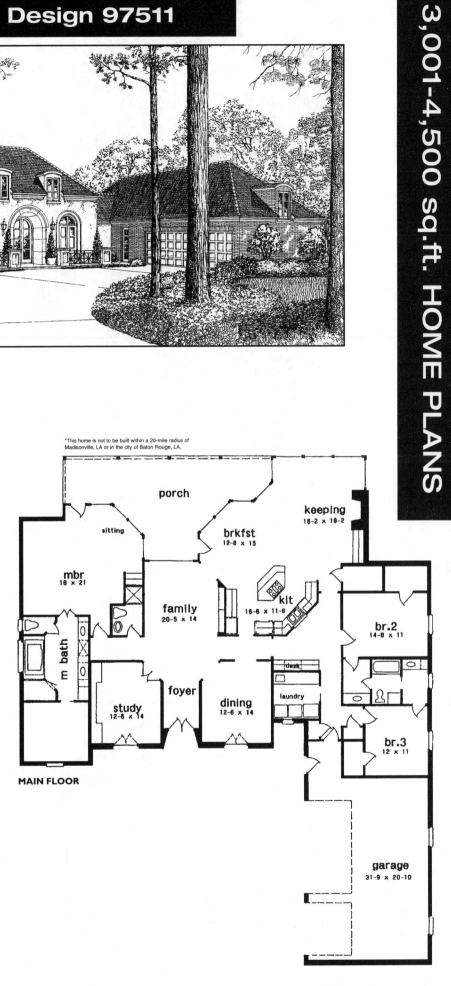

MAIN FLOOR

Design 61056

Units	Single
Price Code	H
Total Finished	3,034 sq. ft.
Main Finished	3,034 sq. ft.
Garage Unfinished	556 sq. ft.
Porch Unfinished	205 sq. ft.
Dimensions	74'4"x67'
Foundation	Basement
	Crawlspace
	Slab
Bedrooms	3
Full Baths	2
Half Baths	1
Exterior Walls	2x4

MAIN FLOOR

Design 97524

Units	Single
Price Code	H
Total Finished	3,039 sq. ft.
Main Finished	3,039 sq. ft.
Garage Unfinished	503 sq. ft.
Porch Unfinished	305 sq. ft.
Dimensions	73'8"×93'3"
Foundation	Slab
Bedrooms	4
Full Baths	3
Max Ridge Height	33'3"
Roof Framing	Stick
Exterior Walls	2×4

*This home is not to be built within a 20-mile radius of Madisonville, LA or in the city of Baton Rouge, LA.

keeping
14 x 15-10

brkfst
10 x 15-6

porch

kit
11-4 x 16

laundry

family
20 x 21

mbr
16 x 15

br.3
11-8 x 13-4

master bath

dining
12-4 x 14

foyer
12-4 x 7-6

br.2
(opt study)
12-8 x 13-3

br.4
12 x 12

garage
21 x 22

MAIN FLOOR

Units	Single
Price Code	I
Total Finished	3,064 sq. ft.
Main Finished	3,064 sq. ft.
Bonus Unfinished	366 sq. ft.
Garage Unfinished	716 sq. ft.
Dimensions	79'6"x91'
Foundation	Slab
Bedrooms	3
Full Baths	1
3/4 Bath	2
Main Ceiling	10'-12'
Second Ceiling	8'
Max Ridge Height	24'4"
Roof Framing	Truss

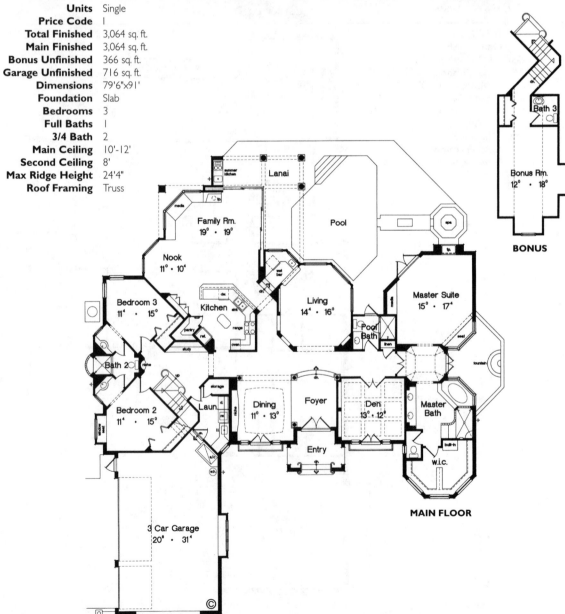

BONUS

MAIN FLOOR

Design 92279

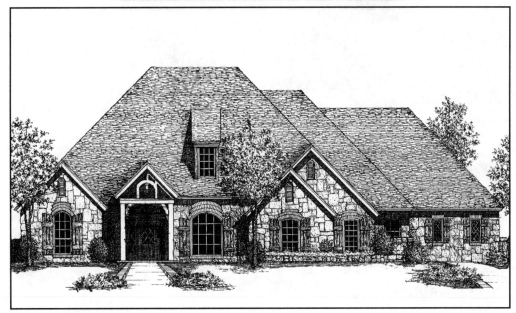

Units	Single
Price Code	H
Total Finished	3,079 sq. ft.
Main Finished	3,079 sq. ft.
Garage Unfinished	630 sq. ft.
Dimensions	80'x74'10"
Foundation	Slab
Bedrooms	4
Full Baths	2
3/4 Baths	1
Half Baths	1
Max Ridge Height	31'6"
Roof Framing	Stick
Exterior Walls	2x4

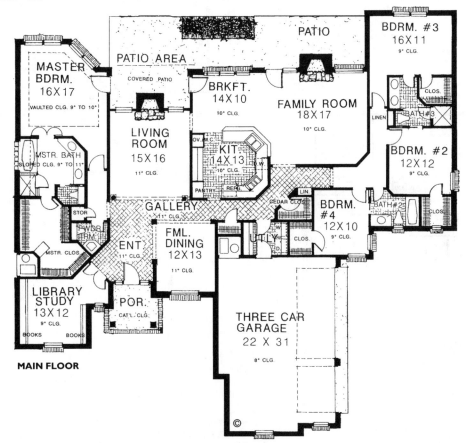

MAIN FLOOR

Design 99158

Units	Single
Price Code	H
Total Finished	3,080 sq. ft.
Main Finished	2,230 sq. ft.
Lower Finished	850 sq. ft.
Basement Unfinished	2,230 sq. ft.
Garage Unfinished	875 sq. ft.
Deck Unfinished	265 sq. ft.
Porch Unfinished	195 sq. ft.
Dimensions	71'x73'
Foundation	Basement
Bedrooms	4
Full Baths	2
3/4 Baths	1
Max Ridge Height	26'6"
Roof Framing	Truss
Exterior Walls	2x4

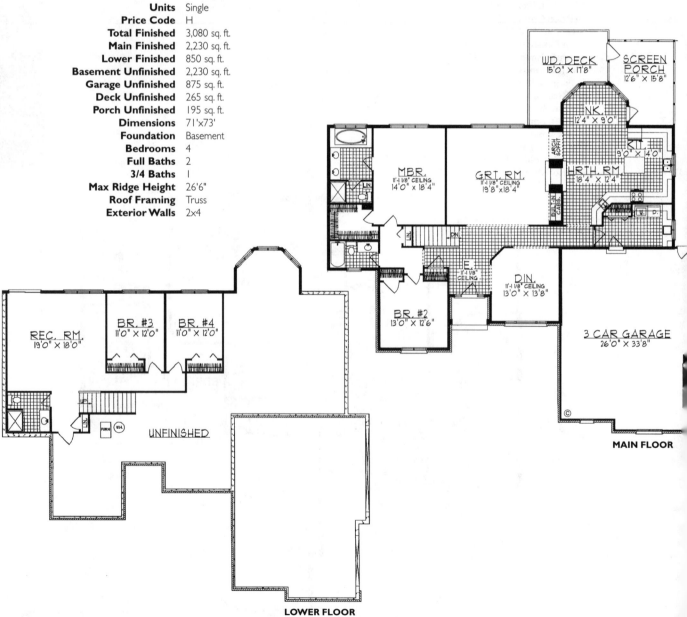

WD. DECK 15'0" X 17'8"

SCREEN PORCH 12'6" X 15'8"

NK. 12'4" X 9'0"

KIT. 9'0" X 14'0"

MBR. 14'0" X 18'4" 11'-1 1/8" CEILING

GRT. RM. 19'8" X 18'4" 11'-1 1/8" CEILING

HRTH. RM. 18'4" X 12'4"

BR. #2 13'0" X 12'6"

DIN. 13'0" X 13'8" 11'-1 1/8" CEILING

3 CAR GARAGE 26'0" X 33'8"

MAIN FLOOR

REC. RM. 19'0" X 18'0"

BR. #3 11'0" X 12'0"

BR. #4 11'0" X 12'0"

UNFINISHED

LOWER FLOOR

Design 66056

Units	Single
Price Code	G
Total Finished	3,080 sq. ft.
Main Finished	3,080 sq. ft.
Garage Unfinished	675 sq. ft.
Deck Unfinished	245 sq. ft.
Dimensions	77'x74'5"
Foundation	Slab
Bedrooms	3
Full Baths	2
3/4 Baths	1
Half Baths	1
Main Ceiling	9'-11'
Max Ridge Height	29'
Roof Framing	Stick
Exterior Walls	2x4

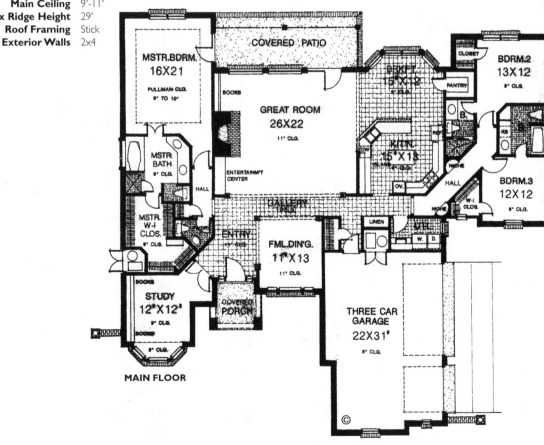

MAIN FLOOR

Design 96521

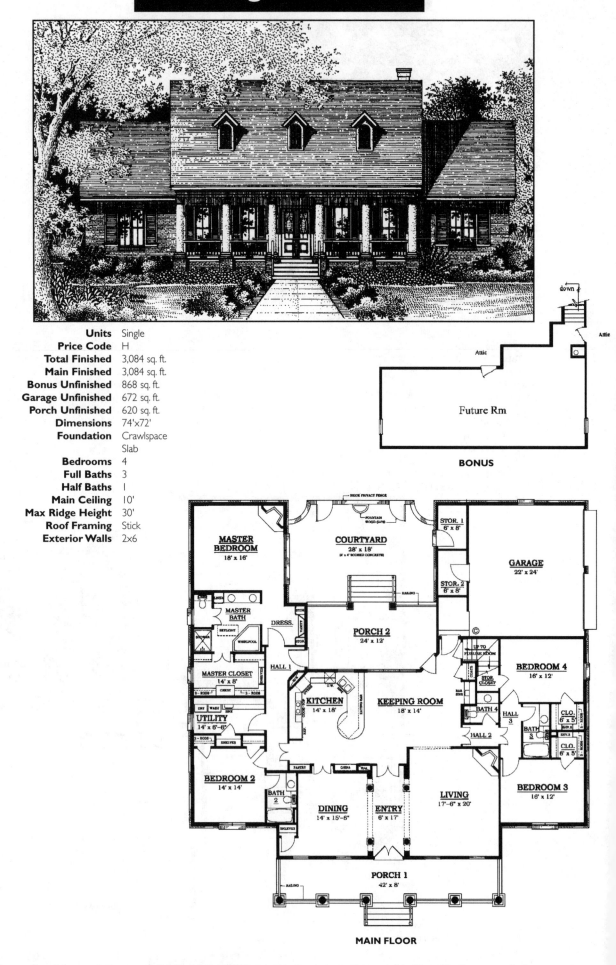

Units	Single
Price Code	H
Total Finished	3,084 sq. ft.
Main Finished	3,084 sq. ft.
Bonus Unfinished	868 sq. ft.
Garage Unfinished	672 sq. ft.
Porch Unfinished	620 sq. ft.
Dimensions	74'x72'
Foundation	Crawlspace
	Slab
Bedrooms	4
Full Baths	3
Half Baths	1
Main Ceiling	10'
Max Ridge Height	30'
Roof Framing	Stick
Exterior Walls	2x6

BONUS

MAIN FLOOR

Design 99159

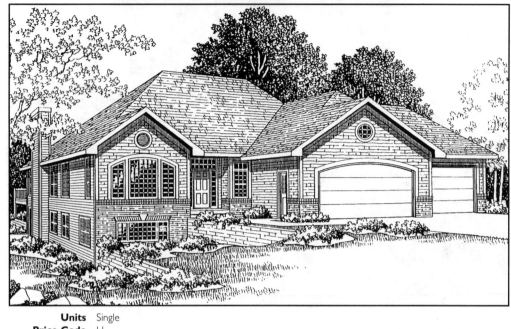

Units	Single
Price Code	H
Total Finished	3,086 sq. ft.
Main Finished	2,263 sq. ft.
Lower Finished	823 sq. ft.
Dimensions	63'x63'8"
Foundation	Basement
Bedrooms	4
Full Baths	3
Max Ridge Height	25'6"
Roof Framing	Truss
Exterior Walls	2x6

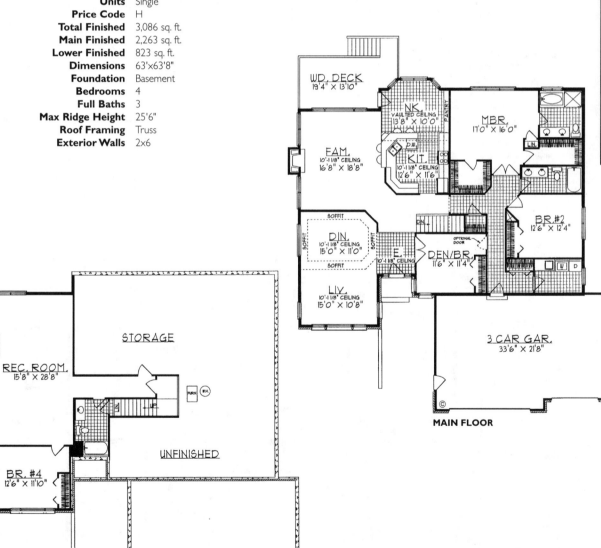

MAIN FLOOR

LOWER FLOOR

Units	Single
Price Code	H
Total Finished	3,089 sq. ft.
Main Finished	3,089 sq. ft.
Garage Unfinished	660 sq. ft.
Deck Unfinished	98 sq. ft.
Porch Unfinished	60 sq. ft.
Dimensions	91'x71'9"
Foundation	Slab
Bedrooms	4
Full Baths	3
Half Baths	I
Max Ridge Height	27'
Roof Framing	Stick
Exterior Walls	2x4

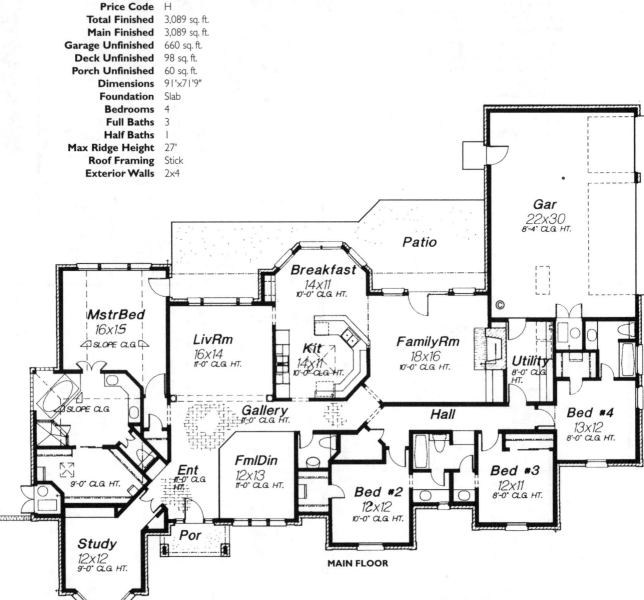

MAIN FLOOR

Design 63065

Units	Single
Price Code	H
Total Finished	3,091 sq. ft.
Main Finished	3,091 sq. ft.
Garage Unfinished	698 sq. ft.
Dimensions	62'x82'4"
Foundation	Slab
Bedrooms	4
Full Baths	2
3/4 Baths	1
Main Ceiling	12'
Max Ridge Height	26'8"
Roof Framing	Truss
Exterior Walls	2x4

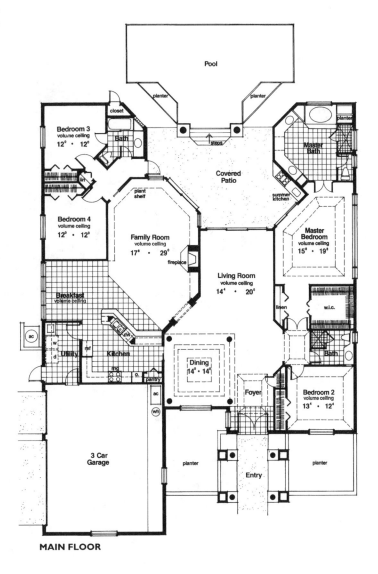

MAIN FLOOR

Design 97811

Units	Single
Price Code	H
Total Finished	3,093 sq. ft.
Main Finished	3,093 sq. ft.
Garage Unfinished	802 sq. ft.
Porch Unfinished	62 sq. ft.
Dimensions	77'x72'4"
Foundation	Slab
Bedrooms	3
Full Baths	2
3/4 Baths	1
Half Baths	1
Main Ceiling	10'
Max Ridge Height	33'
Roof Framing	Stick
Exterior Walls	2x4

MAIN FLOOR

Design 63019

Units	Single
Price Code	H
Total Finished	3,119 sq. ft.
Main Finished	3,119 sq. ft.
Garage Unfinished	142 sq. ft.
Dimensions	60'x90'
Foundation	Slab
Bedrooms	4
Full Baths	2
3/4 Baths	2
Main Ceiling	10'
Max Ridge Height	23'8"
Roof Framing	Truss

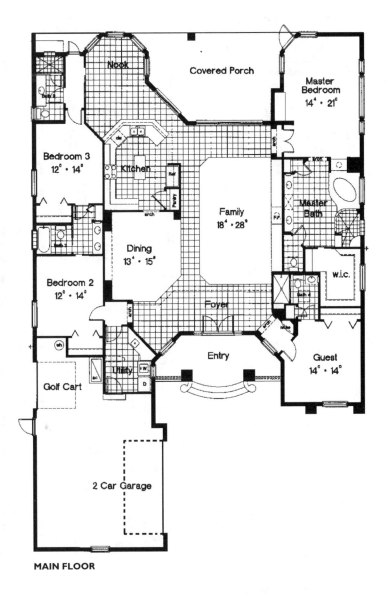

MAIN FLOOR

Design 92221

Units	Duplex
Price Code	G
Total Finished	3,121 sq. ft.
Main Finished	3,121 sq. ft.
Garage Unfinished	1,034 sq. ft.
Porch Unfinished	122 sq. ft.
Dimensions	64'x81'7"
Foundation	Slab
Bedrooms	5
Full Baths	4
Main Ceiling	8'
Max Ridge Height	22'
Roof Framing	Stick
Exterior Walls	2x4

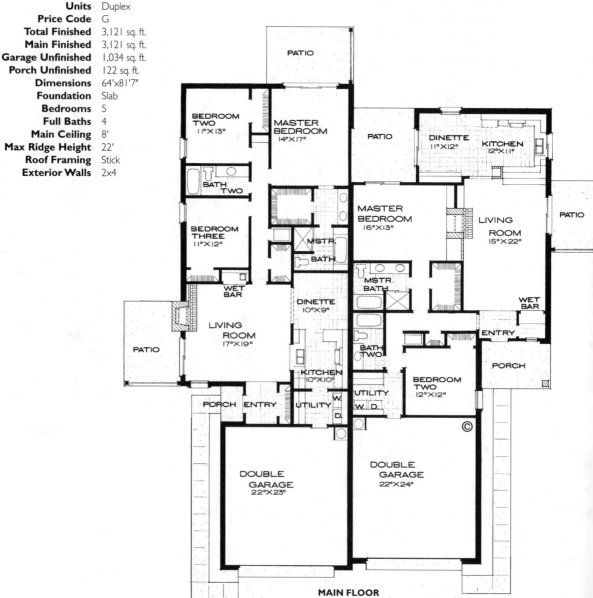

MAIN FLOOR

To order blueprints, call **800-235-5700** or visit us on the web, **familyhomeplans.com**

Design 61031

Units	Single
Price Code	H
Total Finished	3,124 sq. ft.
Main Finished	3,124 sq. ft.
Dimensions	70'x88'2"
Foundation	Crawlspace
	Slab
Bedrooms	3
Full Baths	2
3/4 Baths	1
Half Baths	1
Main Ceiling	9'
Roof Framing	Stick
Exterior Walls	2x4

MAIN FLOOR

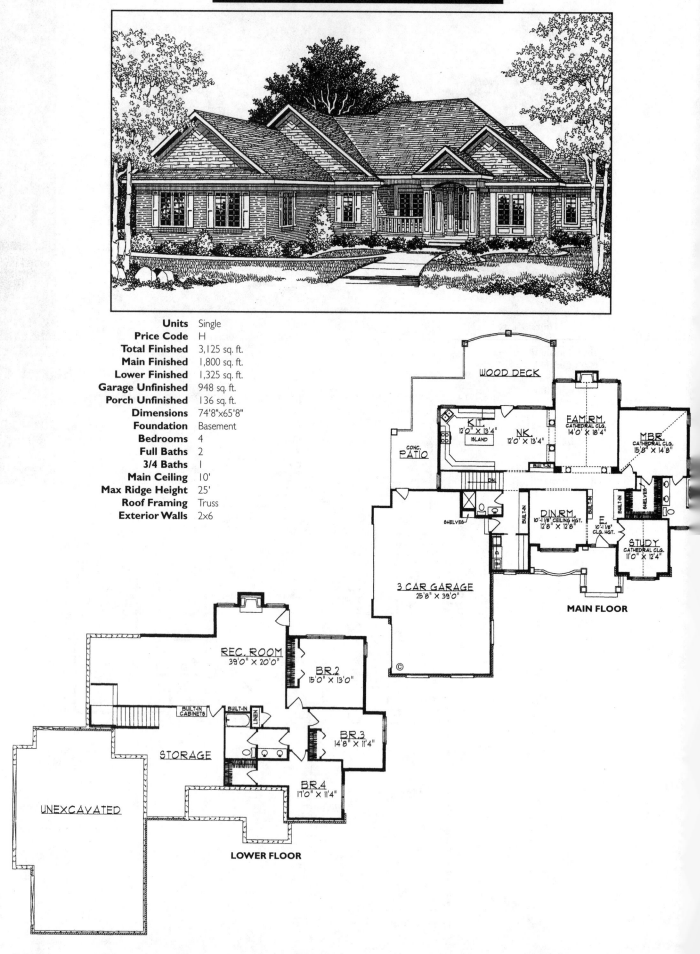

Units	Single
Price Code	H
Total Finished	3,125 sq. ft.
Main Finished	1,800 sq. ft.
Lower Finished	1,325 sq. ft.
Garage Unfinished	948 sq. ft.
Porch Unfinished	136 sq. ft.
Dimensions	74'8"x65'8"
Foundation	Basement
Bedrooms	4
Full Baths	2
3/4 Baths	1
Main Ceiling	10'
Max Ridge Height	25'
Roof Framing	Truss
Exterior Walls	2x6

WOOD DECK

KIT.
12'0" X 13'4"
ISLAND

NK.
12'0" X 13'4"

FAM. RM.
CATHEDRAL CLG.
14'0" X 18'4"

MBR
CATHEDRAL CLG.
15'8" X 14'8"

CONC.
PATIO

BUILT-IN

DN.

SHELVES

DIN. RM.
10'-1 1/8" CEILING HGT.
12'8" X 12'8"

BUILT-IN

BUILT-IN

E.
10'-1 1/8"
CLG. HGT.

BUILT-IN

SHELVES

STUDY
CATHEDRAL CLG.
11'0" X 12'4"

3 CAR GARAGE
25'8" X 39'0"

MAIN FLOOR

REC. ROOM
39'0" X 20'0"

BR.2
15'0" X 13'0"

BUILT-IN
CABINETS

BUILT-IN

LINEN

STORAGE

BR.3
14'8" X 11'4"

BR.4
17'0" X 11'4"

UNEXCAVATED

LOWER FLOOR

To order blueprints, call **800-235-5700** or visit us on the web, **familyhomeplans.com**

Design 92214

Units	Single
Price Code	H
Total Finished	3,140 sq. ft.
Main Finished	3,140 sq. ft.
Dimensions	74'x88'10"
Foundation	Basement
	Crawlspace
	Slab
Bedrooms	4
Full Baths	2
3/4 Baths	I

MAIN FLOOR

Design 97793

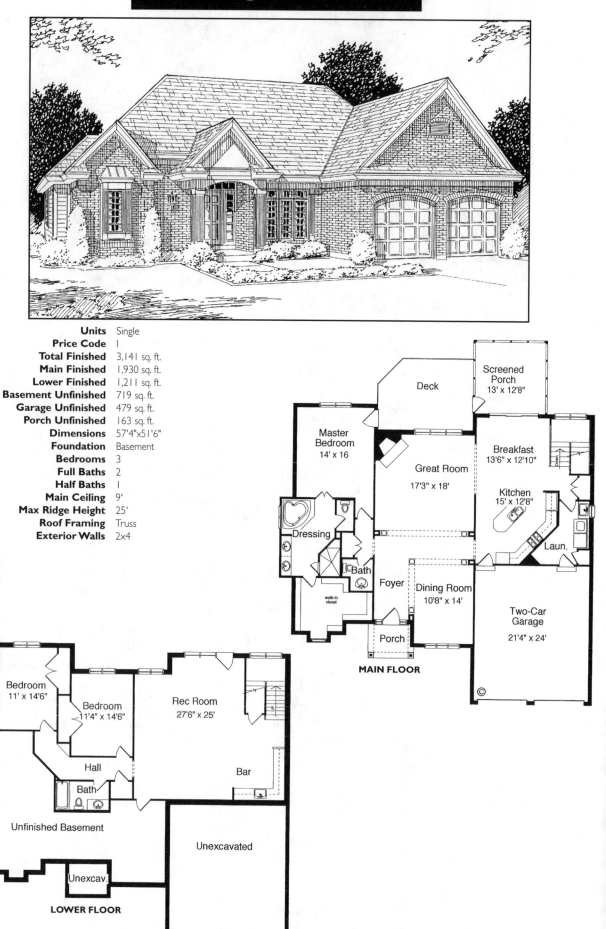

Units	Single
Price Code	I
Total Finished	3,141 sq. ft.
Main Finished	1,930 sq. ft.
Lower Finished	1,211 sq. ft.
Basement Unfinished	719 sq. ft.
Garage Unfinished	479 sq. ft.
Porch Unfinished	163 sq. ft.
Dimensions	57'4"x51'6"
Foundation	Basement
Bedrooms	3
Full Baths	2
Half Baths	I
Main Ceiling	9'
Max Ridge Height	25'
Roof Framing	Truss
Exterior Walls	2x4

Main Floor

- Deck
- Screened Porch 13' x 12'8"
- Master Bedroom 14' x 16
- Great Room 17'3" x 18'
- Breakfast 13'6" x 12'10"
- Kitchen 15' x 12'8"
- Dressing
- Bath
- walk-in closet
- Foyer
- Dining Room 10'8" x 14'
- Laun.
- Two-Car Garage 21'4" x 24'
- Porch

Lower Floor

- Bedroom 11' x 14'6"
- Bedroom 11'4" x 14'6"
- Rec Room 27'6" x 25'
- Hall
- Bath
- Bar
- Unfinished Basement
- Unexcavated
- Unexcav.

Units	Single
Price Code	H
Total Finished	3,157 sq. ft.
Main Finished	3,157 sq. ft.
Dimensions	91'10"x93'10"
Foundation	Slab
Bedrooms	3
Full Baths	2
Half Baths	1
Max Ridge Height	30'
Roof Framing	Stick
Exterior Walls	2x4

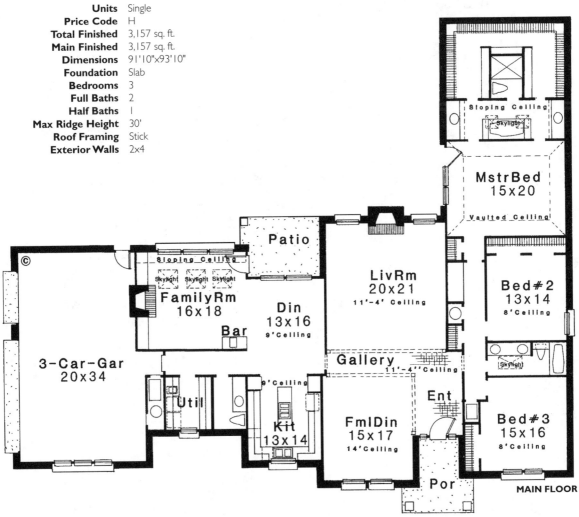

MAIN FLOOR

Merillat.

Visit us at www.merillat.com

Units	Single
Price Code	H
Total Finished	3,160 sq. ft.
Main Finished	3,160 sq. ft.
Dimensions	84'x90'
Foundation	Crawlspace
Bedrooms	3
Full Baths	2
Half Baths	1
Max Ridge Height	29'
Roof Framing	Stick
Exterior Walls	2x4

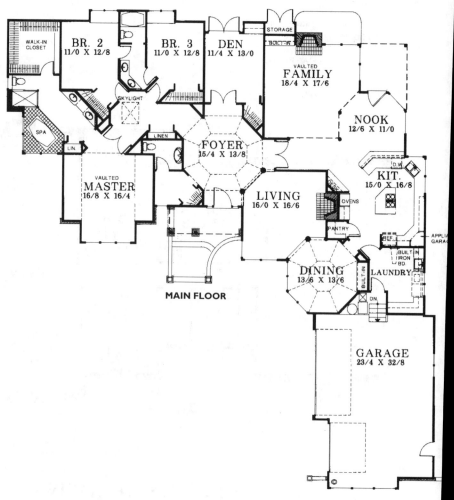

MAIN FLOOR

Design 66000

Units	Single
Price Code	H
Total Finished	3,162 sq. ft.
Main Finished	3,162 sq. ft.
Garage Unfinished	662 sq. ft.
Deck Unfinished	240 sq. ft.
Porch Unfinished	62 sq. ft.
Dimensions	85'10"x66'3"
Foundation	Slab
Bedrooms	4
Full Baths	2
3/4 Baths	1
Half Baths	1
Max Ridge Height	31'
Roof Framing	Stick
Exterior Walls	2x4

MAIN FLOOR

Units	Single
Price Code	H
Total Finished	3,168 sq. ft.
Main Finished	3,168 sq. ft.
Porch Unfinished	130 sq. ft.
Dimensions	107'10"x78'10"
Foundation	Crawlspace
Bedrooms	3
Full Baths	2
Half Baths	1
Max Ridge Height	23'
Roof Framing	Truss
Exterior Walls	2x6

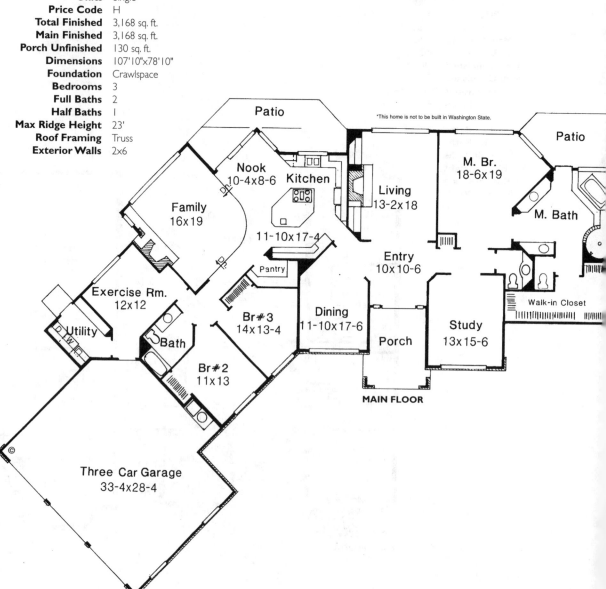

*This home is not to be built in Washington State.

MAIN FLOOR

Design 99195

Units	Single
Price Code	H
Total Finished	3,172 sq. ft.
Main Finished	2,037 sq. ft.
Lower Finished	1,135 sq. ft.
Basement Unfinished	2,037 sq. ft.
Garage Unfinished	731 sq. ft.
Deck Unfinished	124 sq. ft.
Porch Unfinished	126 sq. ft.
Dimensions	72'4"×57'
Foundation	Basement
Bedrooms	3
Full Baths	2
Half Baths	1
Main Ceiling	9'
Vaulted Ceiling	11'
Tray Ceiling	10'
Max Ridge Height	28'4"
Roof Framing	Truss
Exterior Walls	2x6

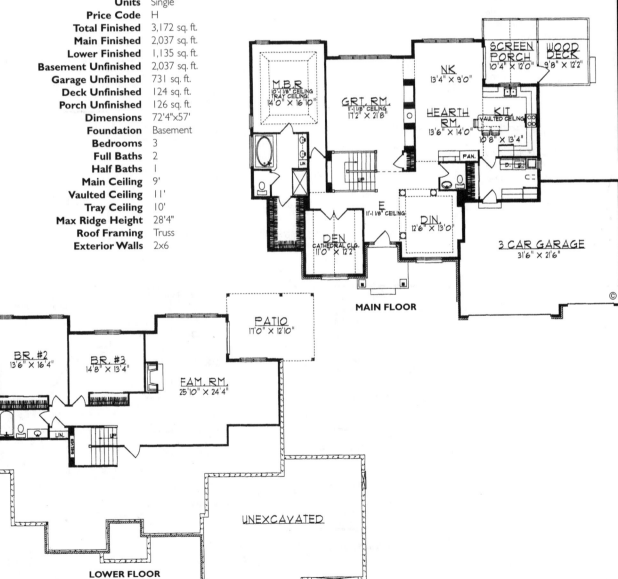

MAIN FLOOR

LOWER FLOOR

Units	Single
Price Code	H
Total Finished	3,183 sq. ft.
Main Finished	3,183 sq. ft.
Garage Unfinished	752 sq. ft.
Porch Unfinished	565 sq. ft.
Dimensions	82'4"x81'6"
Foundation	Basement
	Crawlspace
	Slab
Bedrooms	4
Full Baths	2
Half Baths	1
Main Ceiling	9'
Roof Framing	Stick
Exterior Walls	2x4

MAIN FLOOR

Design 52003

Units	Single
Price Code	H
Total Finished	3,190 sq. ft.
Main Finished	3,190 sq. ft.
Bonus Unfinished	305 sq. ft.
Basement Unfinished	3,190 sq. ft.
Garage Unfinished	696 sq. ft.
Dimensions	74'x84'6"
Foundation	Basement
	Crawlspace
Bedrooms	4
Full Baths	3
Half Baths	1
Main Ceiling	9'
Max Ridge Height	26'
Roof Framing	Stick
Exterior Walls	2x4

CAD FILES AVAILABLE
For more information call
800-235-5700

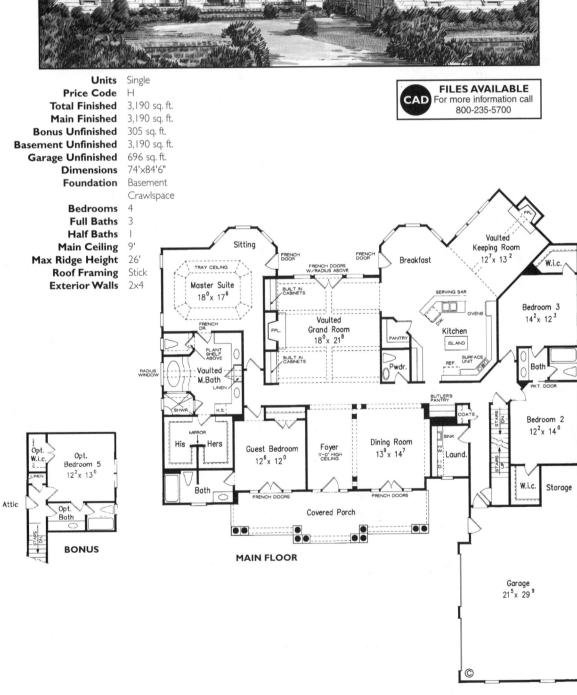

BONUS

MAIN FLOOR

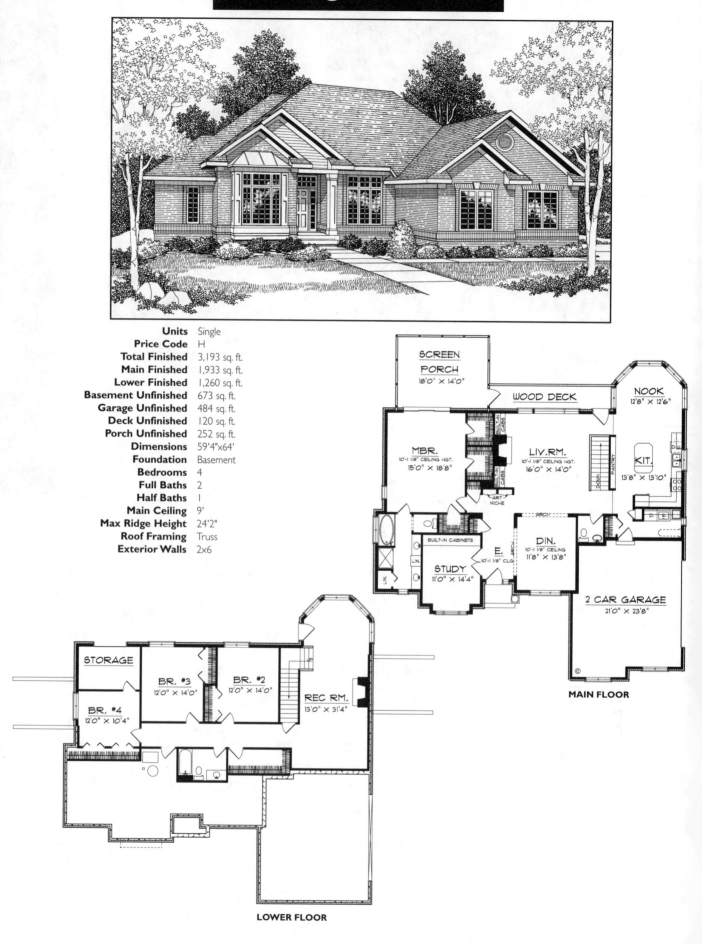

Units	Single
Price Code	H
Total Finished	3,193 sq. ft.
Main Finished	1,933 sq. ft.
Lower Finished	1,260 sq. ft.
Basement Unfinished	673 sq. ft.
Garage Unfinished	484 sq. ft.
Deck Unfinished	120 sq. ft.
Porch Unfinished	252 sq. ft.
Dimensions	59'4"x64'
Foundation	Basement
Bedrooms	4
Full Baths	2
Half Baths	1
Main Ceiling	9'
Max Ridge Height	24'2"
Roof Framing	Truss
Exterior Walls	2x6

SCREEN PORCH 18'0" X 14'0"

WOOD DECK

NOOK 12'8" X 12'6"

MBR. 10'-1 1/8" CEILING HGT. 15'0" X 18'8"

BUILT-IN CABS.

LIV. RM. 10'-1 1/8" CEILING HGT. 16'0" X 14'0"

KIT. 13'8" X 13'10"

PANTRY

DOWN

ART NICHE

BUILT-IN CABINETS

LIN.

STUDY 11'0" X 14'4"

E. 10'-1 1/8" CLG.

ARCH

DIN. 10'-1 1/8" CEILING 11'8" X 13'8"

ARCH

2 CAR GARAGE 21'0" X 23'8"

MAIN FLOOR

STORAGE

BR. #3 12'0" X 14'0"

BR. #2 12'0" X 14'0"

BR. #4 12'0" X 10'4"

REC RM. 13'0" X 31'4"

LOWER FLOOR

Design 63104

Units	Single
Price Code	H
Total Finished	3,212 sq. ft.
Main Finished	3,212 sq. ft.
Garage Unfinished	684 sq. ft.
Dimensions	84'x96'
Foundation	Slab
Bedrooms	3
Full Baths	2
Half Baths	1
Max Ridge Height	26'10"
Roof Framing	Truss
Exterior Walls	2x4

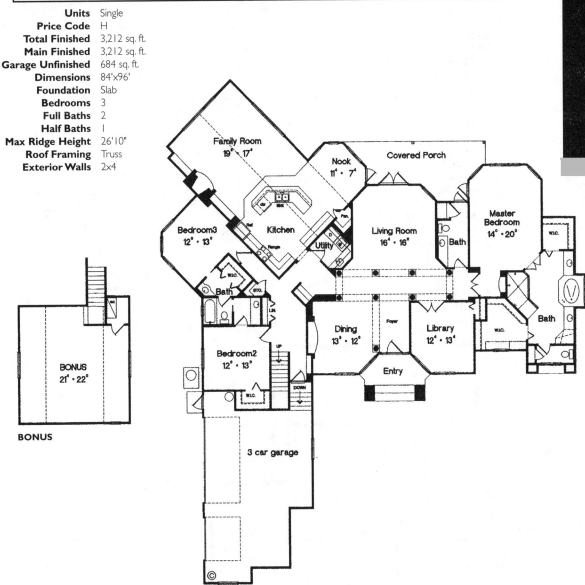

BONUS

MAIN FLOOR

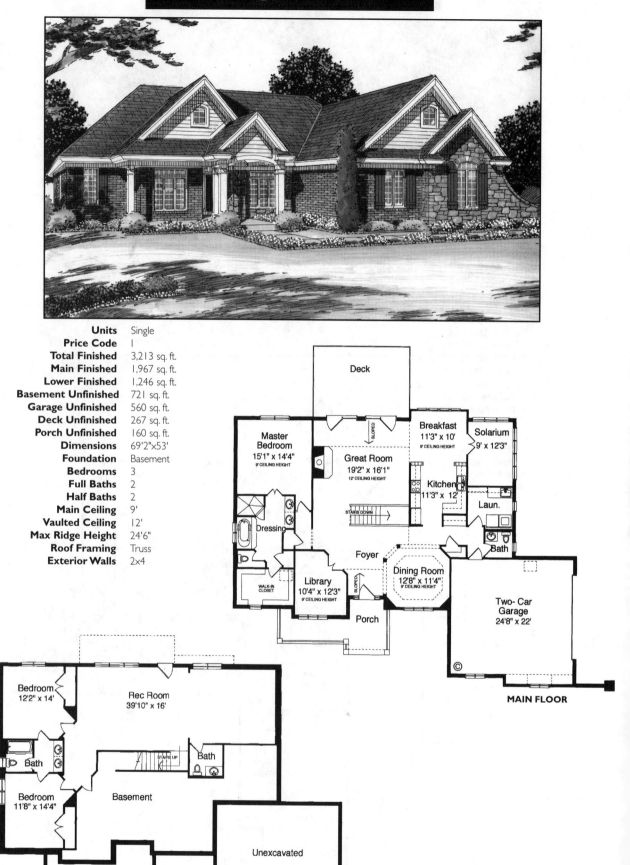

Units	Single
Price Code	I
Total Finished	3,213 sq. ft.
Main Finished	1,967 sq. ft.
Lower Finished	1,246 sq. ft.
Basement Unfinished	721 sq. ft.
Garage Unfinished	560 sq. ft.
Deck Unfinished	267 sq. ft.
Porch Unfinished	160 sq. ft.
Dimensions	69'2"×53'
Foundation	Basement
Bedrooms	3
Full Baths	2
Half Baths	2
Main Ceiling	9'
Vaulted Ceiling	12'
Max Ridge Height	24'6"
Roof Framing	Truss
Exterior Walls	2x4

Deck

Master Bedroom
15'1" x 14'4"
9' CEILING HEIGHT

Great Room
19'2" x 16'1"
12' CEILING HEIGHT

Breakfast
11'3" x 10'
9' CEILING HEIGHT

Solarium
9' x 12'3"

Kitchen
11'3" x 12'

Laun.

SLOPED

Dressing

STAIRS DOWN

Bath

WALK-IN CLOSET

Library
10'4" x 12'3"
9' CEILING HEIGHT

Foyer

Dining Room
12'8" x 11'4"
9' CEILING HEIGHT

SLOPED

Porch

Two-Car Garage
24'8" x 22'

©

MAIN FLOOR

Bedroom
12'2" x 14'

Rec Room
39'10" x 16'

Bath

STAIRS UP

Bath

Bedroom
11'8" x 14'4"

Basement

Unexcavated

Unexcavated

LOWER FLOOR

Design 97513

Units	Single
Price Code	H
Total Finished	3,230 sq. ft.
Main Finished	3,230 sq. ft.
Garage Unfinished	729 sq. ft.
Porch Unfinished	212 sq. ft.
Dimensions	94'8"x88'5"
Foundation	Slab
Bedrooms	4
Full Baths	3
Main Ceiling	10'-12'
Max Ridge Height	30'6"
Roof Framing	Stick
Exterior Wall	2x4

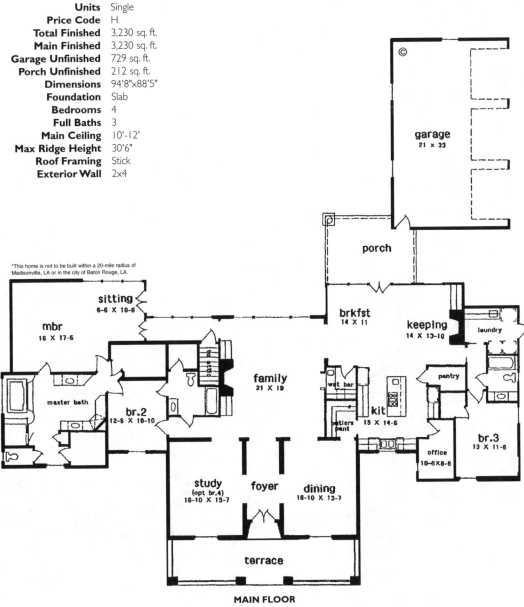

*This home is not to be built within a 20-mile radius of Madisonville, LA or in the city of Baton Rouge, LA.

MAIN FLOOR

Units	Single
Price Code	H
Total Finished	3,239 sq. ft.
Main Finished	3,239 sq. ft.
Garage Unfinished	748 sq. ft.
Deck Unfinished	184 sq. ft.
Porch Unfinished	64 sq. ft.
Dimensions	118'9"x55'1"
Foundation	Slab
Bedrooms	3
Full Baths	2
3/4 Baths	1
Main Ceiling	9'-11'
Max Ridge Height	27'
Roof Framing	Stick
Exterior Walls	2x4

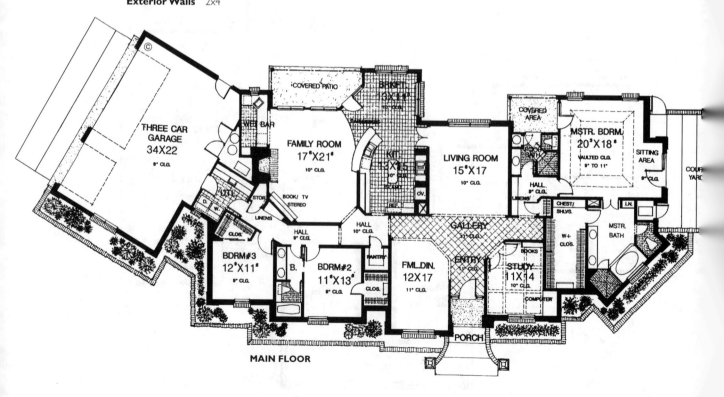

MAIN FLOOR

Design 10497

Units	Single
Price Code	I
Total Finished	3,409 sq. ft.
Main Finished	2,014 sq. ft.
Lower Finished	1,395 sq. ft.
Basement Unfinished	619 sq. ft.
Garage Unfinished	722 sq. ft.
Dimensions	63'8"x52'
Foundation	Basement
Bedrooms	4
Full Baths	3

DECK

SUN PORCH
16'-2" X 7'-0"

GARDEN AREA

MAST. BEDROOM
16'-4" X 13'-10"

C.

B.

BREAKFAST AREA

BAR

GREAT ROOM
17'-0" X 25'-2"

BEDROOM 2
11'-0" X 13'-4"

KITCHEN

ISLAND

16'-4" X 19'-4"

Q.

P.

H.

LAUND.

B.

H.

C.

DW

R

H.

DINING ROOM
14'-1" X 13'-4"

DOWN

FOYER

C.

3-CAR GARAGE
33'-4" X 21'-8"

P.

MAIN FLOOR

DRIVE

PATIO

WD. STOVE

BEDROOM 3
12'-1" X 13'-4"

BEDROOM 4
12'-1" X 13'-4"

RECREATION ROOM
34'-2" X 29'-10"

C.

C.

F.

WH

BAR

L.

H.

UP

B.

STUDY / T.V.
12'-4" X 8'-6"

STORAGE
25'-0" X 27'-0"

LOWER FLOOR

Design 93170

Units	Single
Price Code	H
Total Finished	3,241 sq. ft.
Main Finished	1,938 sq. ft.
Lower Finished	1,303 sq. ft.
Basement Unfinished	635 sq. ft.
Porch Unfinished	168 sq. ft.
Dimensions	70'x60'4"
Foundation	Basement
Bedrooms	4
Full Baths	3
Half Baths	1
Max Ridge Height	22'6"
Roof Framing	Stick
Exterior Walls	2x6

Design 94280

Units	Single
Price Code	H
Total Finished	3,244 sq. ft.
Main Finished	3,244 sq. ft.
Garage Unfinished	810 sq. ft.
Dimensions	90'x105'
Foundation	Slab
Bedrooms	3
Full Baths	2
3/4 Baths	1
Half Baths	1
Main Ceiling	10'
Tray Ceiling	13'
Max Ridge Height	29'
Roof Framing	Truss
Exterior Walls	2x4

* Alternate foundation options available at an additional charge.
Please call 1-800-235-5700 for more information.

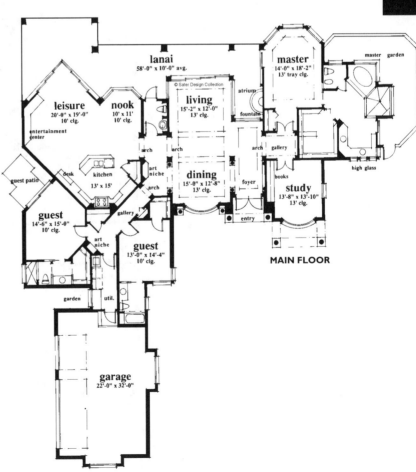

MAIN FLOOR

Units	Single
Price Code	I
Total Finished	3,250 sq. ft.
Main Finished	3,250 sq. ft.
Dimensions	65'x88'
Foundation	Slab
Bedrooms	3
Full Baths	2
3/4 Baths	1
Half Baths	1
Main Ceiling	10'
Roof Framing	Truss
Exterior Walls	2x8

* Alternate foundation options available at an additional charge.
Please call 1-800-235-5700 for more information.

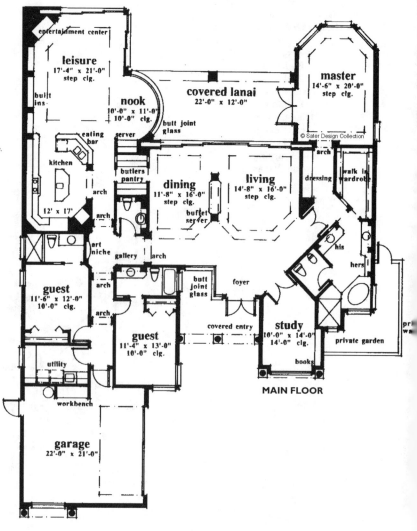

MAIN FLOOR

Design 98513

Units	Single
Price Code	I
Total Finished	3,352 sq. ft.
Main Finished	3,352 sq. ft.
Garage Unfinished	672 sq. ft.
Deck Unfinished	462 sq. ft.
Porch Unfinished	60 sq. ft.
Dimensions	91'x71'9"
Foundation	Slab
Bedrooms	4
Full Baths	2
3/4 Baths	I
Half Baths	I
Main Ceiling	9'-11'
Max Ridge Height	28'2"
Roof Framing	Stick
Exterior Walls	2x4

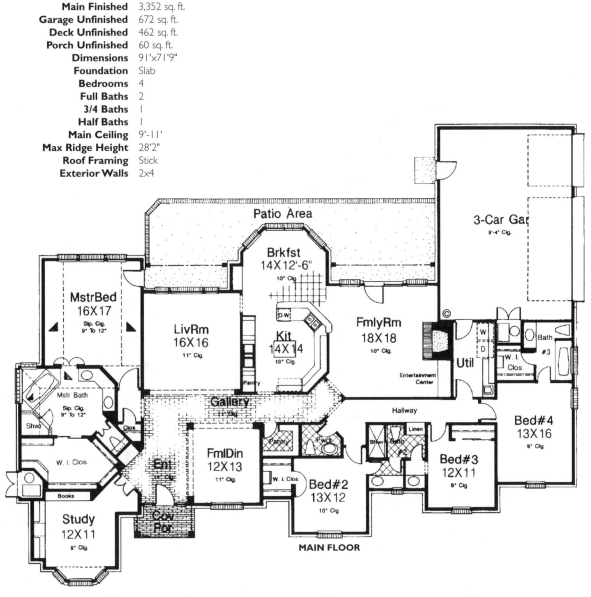

MAIN FLOOR

Units	Single
Price Code	I
Total Finished	3,254 sq. ft.
Main Finished	3,254 sq. ft.
Garage Unfinished	588 sq. ft.
Deck Unfinished	274 sq. ft.
Porch Unfinished	60 sq. ft.
Dimensions	80'x69'11"
Foundation	Slab
Bedrooms	4
Full Baths	2
3/4 Baths	I
Max Ridge Height	24'
Roof Framing	Stick
Exterior Walls	2x4

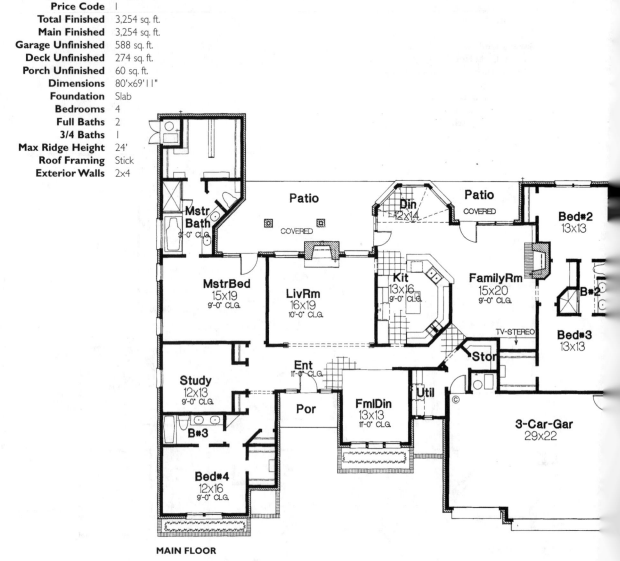

MAIN FLOOR

Units	Single
Price Code	G
Total Finished	3,119 sq. ft.
Main Finished	3,119 sq. ft.
Garage Unfinished	742 sq. ft.
Porch Unfinished	340 sq. ft.
Dimensions	60'x90'
Foundation	Slab
Bedrooms	4
Full Baths	2
3/4 Baths	2
Main Ceiling	10', 12', 14'
Vaulted Ceiling	12'
Max Ridge Height	23'
Roof Framing	Truss

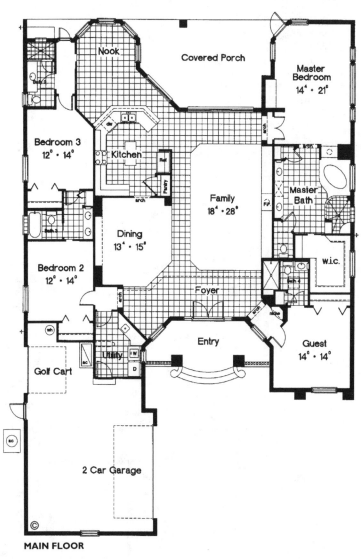

MAIN FLOOR

Design 97880

Units	Single
Price Code	I
Total Finished	3,262 sq. ft.
Main Finished	3,262 sq. ft.
Garage Unfinished	632 sq. ft.
Deck Unfinished	320 sq. ft.
Porch Unfinished	48 sq. ft.
Dimensions	79'8"x65'4"
Foundation	Slab
Bedrooms	4
Full Baths	3
Half Baths	I
Main Ceiling	10'
Max Ridge Height	31'
Roof Framing	Stick
Exterior Walls	2x4.

MAIN FLOOR

Design 97307

Units	Single
Price Code	I
Total Finished	3,386 sq. ft.
Main Finished	3,386 sq. ft.
Basement Unfinished	3,386 sq. ft.
Garage Unfinished	739 sq. ft.
Dimensions	95'x73'8"
Foundation	Basement
Bedrooms	3
Full Baths	2
3/4 Baths	I
Main Ceiling	9'1⅛"
Max Ridge Height	27'8"
Roof Framing	Truss
Exterior Walls	2x6

MAIN FLOOR

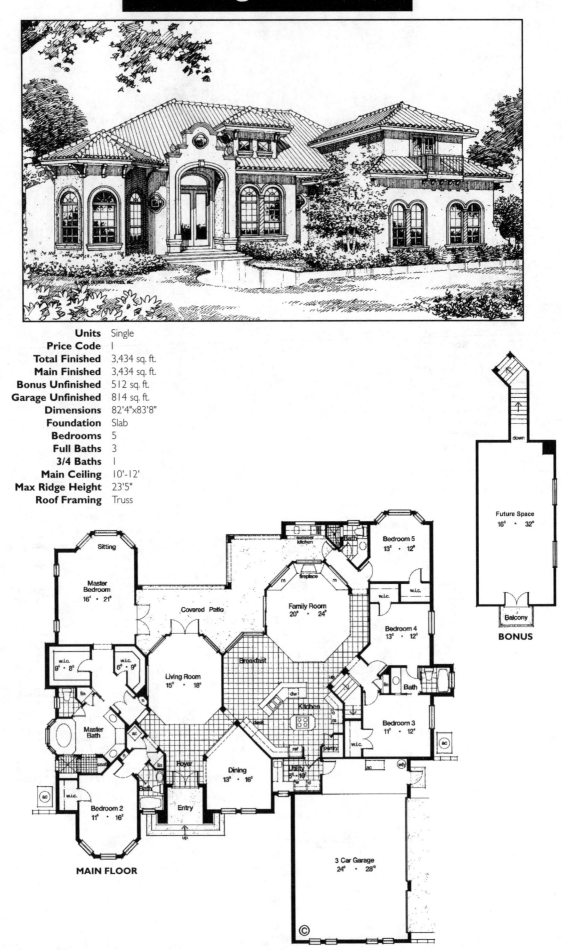

Units	Single
Price Code	I
Total Finished	3,434 sq. ft.
Main Finished	3,434 sq. ft.
Bonus Unfinished	512 sq. ft.
Garage Unfinished	814 sq. ft.
Dimensions	82'4"x83'8"
Foundation	Slab
Bedrooms	5
Full Baths	3
3/4 Baths	I
Main Ceiling	10'-12'
Max Ridge Height	23'5"
Roof Framing	Truss

BONUS

MAIN FLOOR

Design 92291

Units	Duplex
Price Code	G
Total Finished	3,434 sq. ft.
Main Finished	3,434 sq. ft.
Garage Unfinished	966 sq. ft.
Dimensions	62'10"x81'7"
Foundation	Slab
Bedrooms	6
Full Baths	4
Main Ceiling	8'
Max Ridge Height	25'
Roof Framing	Stick
Exterior Walls	2x4

MAIN FLOOR

PHOTOGRAPHY: COURTESY OF THE DESIGNER

Units	Single
Price Code	I
Total Finished	3,477 sq. ft.
Main Finished	3,477 sq. ft.
Garage Unfinished	771 sq. ft.
Porch Unfinished	512 sq. ft.
Dimensions	95'x88'8"
Foundation	Slab
Bedrooms	3
Full Baths	2
3/4 Baths	I
Half Baths	I
Main Ceiling	14'
Vaulted Ceiling	14'
Tray Ceiling	12'
Max Ridge Height	35'6"
Roof Framing	Stick

* Alternate foundation options available at an additional charge.
Please call 1-800-235-5700 for more information.

MAIN FLOOR

Design 50001

Units	Single
Price Code	I
Total Finished	3,488 sq. ft.
Main Finished	1,916 sq. ft.
Lower Finished	1,572 sq. ft.
Basement Unfinished	696 sq. ft.
Garage Unfinished	538 sq. ft.
Deck Unfinished	267 sq. ft.
Porch Unfinished	156 sq. ft.
Dimensions	68'6"x53'2"
Foundation	Basement
Bedrooms	4
Full Baths	3
Half Baths	I
Exterior Walls	2x4

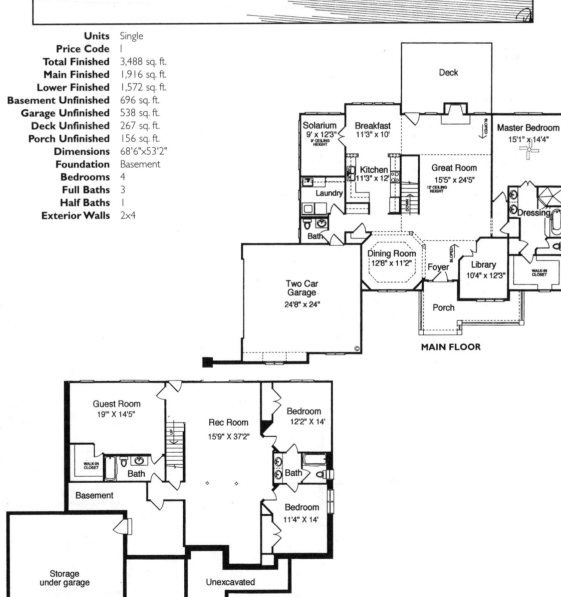

Design 97306

Units	Single
Price Code	I
Total Finished	3,499 sq. ft.
Main Finished	3,499 sq. ft.
Basement Unfinished	3,499 sq. ft.
Garage Unfinished	847 sq. ft.
Deck Unfinished	246 sq. ft.
Porch Unfinished	221 sq. ft.
Dimensions	92'x74'8"
Foundation	Basement
Bedrooms	3
Full Baths	I
3/4 Baths	I
Half Baths	I
Main Ceiling	9'1⅛"
Max Ridge Height	26'1"
Roof Framing	Truss
Exterior Walls	2x6

MAIN FLOOR

Design 68098

3,001-4,000 sq.ft. HOME PLANS

Units	Duplex
Price Code	J
Total Finished	3,503 sq. ft.
Main Finished	1,825 sq. ft. (unit a)
Main Finished	1,678 sq. ft. (unit b)
Dimensions	111'4"x50'
Foundation	Basement
Bedrooms	3
Full Baths	2
Main Ceiling	9'
Max Ridge Height	20'8"
Roof Framing	Stick
Exterior Walls	2x4

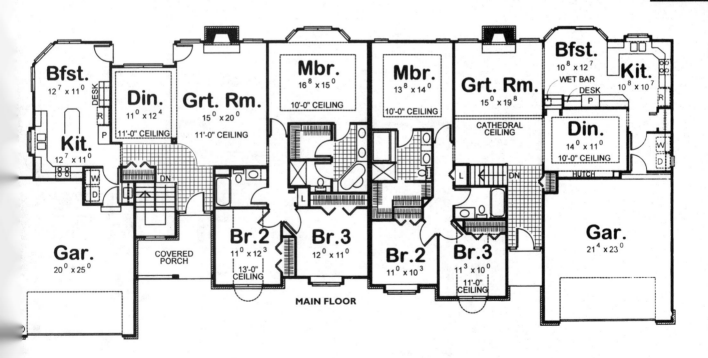

MAIN FLOOR

Units	Single
Price Code	J
Total Finished	3,510 sq. ft.
Main Finished	3,510 sq. ft.
Garage Unfinished	704 sq. ft.
Deck Unfinished	320 sq. ft.
Porch Unfinished	62 sq. ft.
Dimensions	91'x72'10"
Foundation	Slab
Bedrooms	4
Full Baths	2
3/4 Baths	1
Half Baths	1
Main Ceiling	10'
Max Ridge Height	33'
Roof Framing	Stick
Exterior Walls	2x4

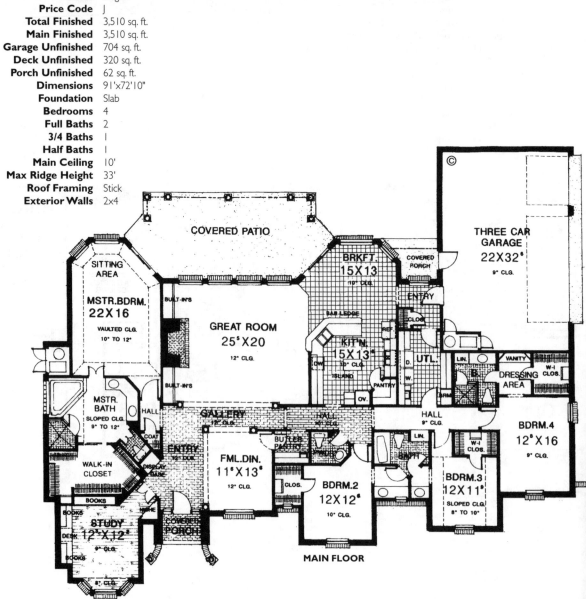

MAIN FLOOR

Design 68097

3,001-4,000 sq.ft. HOME PLANS

Units	Duplex
Price Code	J
Total Finished	3,570 sq. ft.
Main Finished	1,802 sq. ft. (unit A)
Main Finished	1,768 sq. ft. (unit B)
Garage Unfinished	445 sq. ft. (unit A)
Garage Unfinished	542 sq. ft. (unit B)
Dimensions	109'4"x59'4"
Foundation	Basement
Bedrooms	6
Full Baths	4
Main Ceiling	9'
Max Ridge Height	22'
Roof Framing	Stick
Exterior Walls	2x4

* Alternate foundation options available at an additional charge.
Please call 1-800-235-5700 for more information.

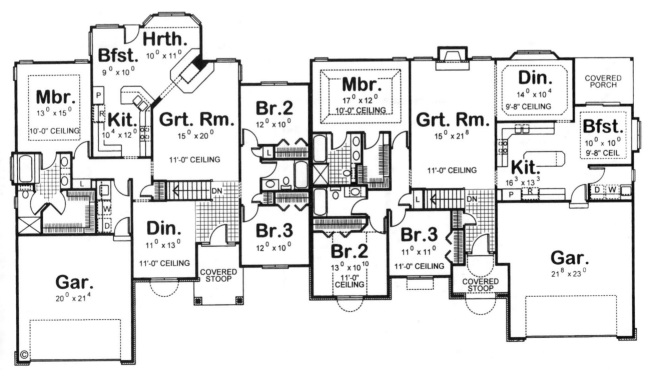

MAIN FLOOR

Design 97714

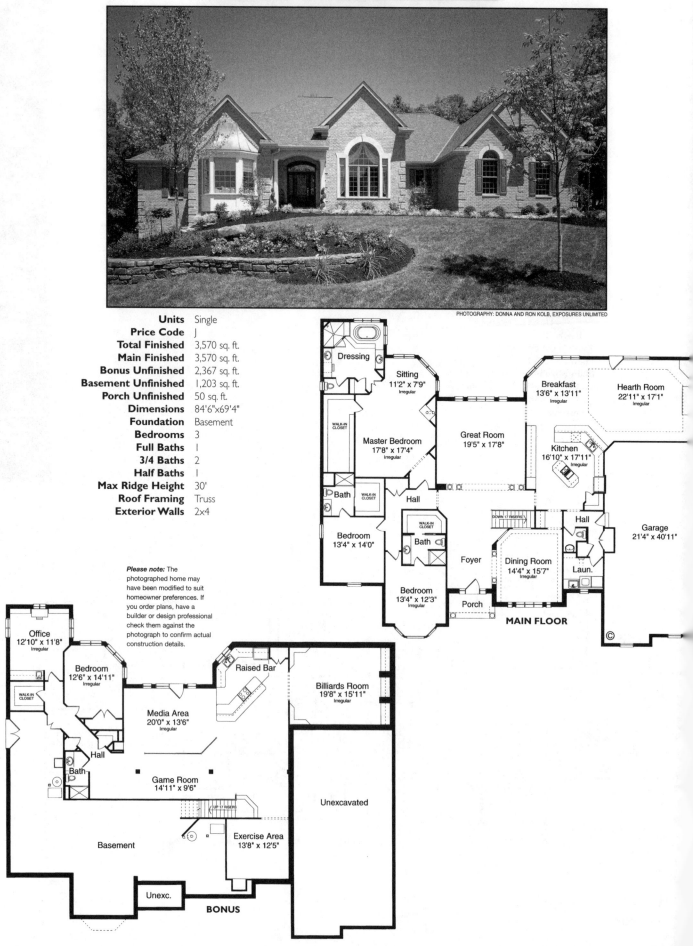

PHOTOGRAPHY: DONNA AND RON KOLB, EXPOSURES UNLIMITED

Units	Single
Price Code	J
Total Finished	3,570 sq. ft.
Main Finished	3,570 sq. ft.
Bonus Unfinished	2,367 sq. ft.
Basement Unfinished	1,203 sq. ft.
Porch Unfinished	50 sq. ft.
Dimensions	84'6"x69'4"
Foundation	Basement
Bedrooms	3
Full Baths	1
3/4 Baths	2
Half Baths	1
Max Ridge Height	30'
Roof Framing	Truss
Exterior Walls	2x4

Please note: The photographed home may have been modified to suit homeowner preferences. If you order plans, have a builder or design professional check them against the photograph to confirm actual construction details.

MAIN FLOOR

Dressing

Sitting
11'2" x 7'9"
Irregular

WALK-IN CLOSET

Master Bedroom
17'8" x 17'4"
Irregular

Bath

WALK-IN CLOSET

Hall

Bedroom
13'4" x 14'0"

WALK-IN CLOSET

Bath

Bedroom
13'4" x 12'3"
Irregular

Foyer

Porch

Great Room
19'5" x 17'8"

Breakfast
13'6" x 13'11"
Irregular

Hearth Room
22'11" x 17'1"
Irregular

Kitchen
16'10" x 17'11"
Irregular

DOWN 17 RISERS

Dining Room
14'4" x 15'7"
Irregular

Hall

Laun.

Garage
21'4" x 40'11"

BONUS

Office
12'10" x 11'8"
Irregular

Bedroom
12'6" x 14'11"
Irregular

WALK-IN CLOSET

Hall

Bath

Raised Bar

Media Area
20'0" x 13'6"
Irregular

Billiards Room
19'8" x 15'11"
Irregular

Game Room
14'11" x 9'6"

UP 17 RISERS

Unexcavated

Basement

Exercise Area
13'8" x 12'5"

Unexc.

Design 93154

Units	Single
Price Code	J
Total Finished	3,578 sq. ft.
Main Finished	2,443 sq. ft.
Lower Finished	1,135 sq. ft.
Basement Unfinished	1,308 sq. ft.
Porch Unfinished	196 sq. ft.
Dimensions	82'4"x71'
Foundation	Basement
Bedrooms	3
Full Baths	3
Max Ridge Height	23'
Roof Framing	Stick
Exterior Walls	2x6

Units	Single
Price Code	J
Total Finished	3,578 sq. ft.
Main Finished	3,578 sq. ft.
Bonus Unfinished	522 sq. ft.
Garage Unfinished	864 sq. ft.
Deck Unfinished	222 sq. ft.
Porch Unfinished	264 sq. ft.
Dimensions	100'x72'8"
Foundation	Basement
	Crawlspace
	Slab
Bedrooms	4
Full Baths	3
Half Baths	1
Main Ceiling	10'
Second Ceiling	8'
Max Ridge Height	31'
Roof Framing	Stick
Exterior Walls	2x4

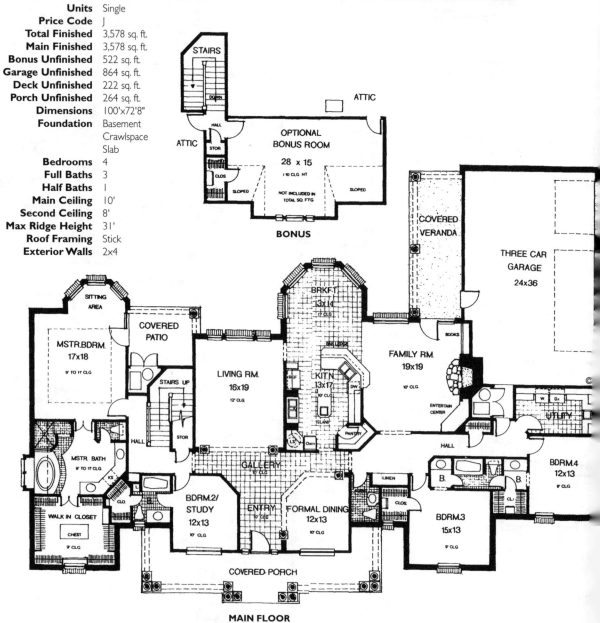

MAIN FLOOR

Design 32600

PHOTOGRAPHER: LANGDON CLAY, JEFF BLANTON

Units	Single
Price Code	J
Total Finished	3,594 sq. ft.
Main Finished	3,594 sq. ft.
Dimensions	80'2"x94'8"
Foundation	Basement
	Slab
Bedrooms	3
Full Baths	1
3/4 Baths	1
Half Baths	1
Max Ridge Height	33'
Roof Framing	Truss
Exterior Walls	2x6

Please note: The photographed home may have been modified to suit homeowner preferences. If you order plans, have a builder or design professional check them against the photograph to confirm actual construction details.

M BDRM

BRKFS

FR
27'x16'

LR
17'x17'

K
17'x16

BDRM
13'x12'

LBRY
14' 5"x12'

DR
12'x16'

BDRM
13'x13'

MAIN FLOOR

G
24'x24

BONUS
RM ABOVE

Design 98582

Units	Single
Price Code	J
Total Finished	3,741 sq. ft.
Main Finished	3,741 sq. ft.
Bonus Unfinished	536 sq. ft.
Garage Unfinished	672 sq. ft.
Deck Unfinished	182 sq. ft.
Porch Unfinished	48 sq. ft.
Dimensions	90'x76'1"
Foundation	Slab
Bedrooms	4
Full Baths	3
Half Baths	1
Max Ridge Height	32'
Roof Framing	Stick
Exterior Walls	2x4

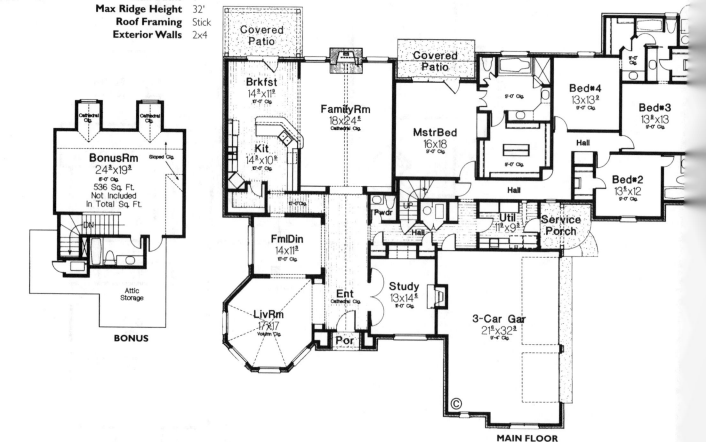

BONUS

MAIN FLOOR

Design 63070

Units	Single
Price Code	J
Total Finished	3,743 sq. ft.
Main Finished	3,743 sq. ft.
Garage Unfinished	775 sq. ft.
Dimensions	86'8"x94'8"
Foundation	Slab
Bedrooms	4
Full Baths	2
3/4 Baths	1
Half Baths	1
Max Ridge Height	27'10"
Roof Framing	Truss

MAIN FLOOR

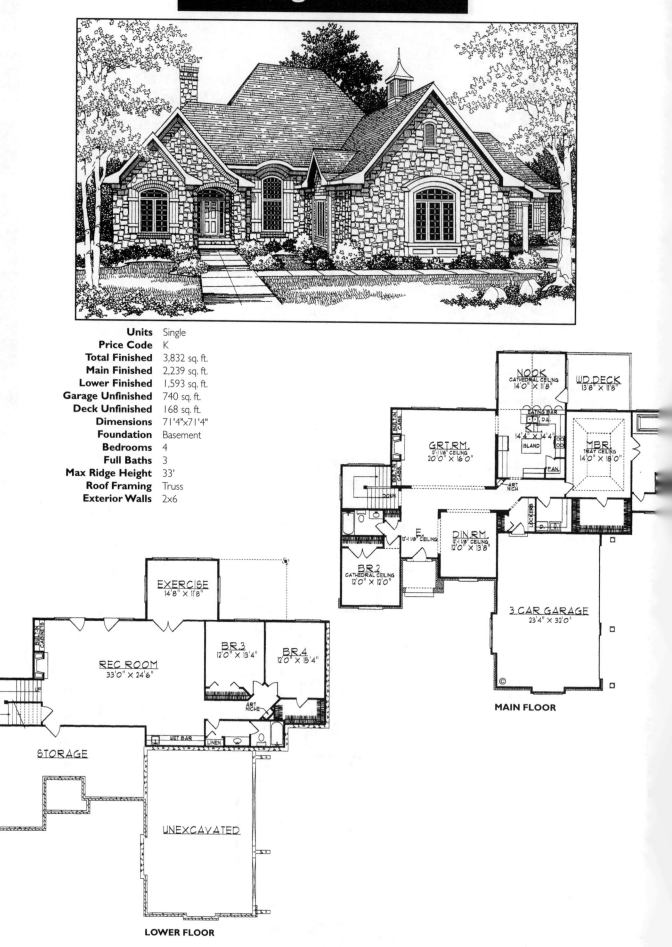

Units	Single
Price Code	K
Total Finished	3,832 sq. ft.
Main Finished	2,239 sq. ft.
Lower Finished	1,593 sq. ft.
Garage Unfinished	740 sq. ft.
Deck Unfinished	168 sq. ft.
Dimensions	71'4"x71'4"
Foundation	Basement
Bedrooms	4
Full Baths	3
Max Ridge Height	33'
Roof Framing	Truss
Exterior Walls	2x6

NOOK
CATHEDRAL CEILING
14'0" X 11'8"

WD. DECK
13'8" X 11'8"

GRT. RM.
12'-11/8" CEILING
20'0" X 16'0"

KIT.
14'4" X 14'4"
ISLAND

MBR.
TRAY CEILING
14'0" X 18'0"

DIN. RM.
12'-11/8" CEILING
12'0" X 13'8"

BR. 2
CATHEDRAL CEILING
12'0" X 12'0"

3 CAR GARAGE
23'4" X 32'0"

MAIN FLOOR

EXERCISE
14'8" X 11'8"

REC ROOM
33'0" X 24'6"

BR. 3
12'0" X 13'4"

BR. 4
12'0" X 15'4"

ART NICHE

STORAGE

WET BAR

LINEN

UNEXCAVATED

LOWER FLOOR

Design 97329

Units	Single
Price Code	K
Total Finished	3,839 sq. ft.
Main Finished	2,370 sq. ft.
Lower Finished	1,469 sq. ft.
Basement Unfinished	838 sq. ft.
Garage Unfinished	781 sq. ft.
Dimensions	75'4"x54'
Foundation	Basement
Bedrooms	5
Full Baths	2
3/4 Baths	2
Main Ceiling	9'
Max Ridge Height	29'2"
Roof Framing	Truss
Exterior Walls	2x6

MAIN FLOOR

LOWER FLOOR

Units	Single
Price Code	K
Total Finished	3,891 sq. ft.
Main Finished	3,891 sq. ft.
Garage Unfinished	813 sq. ft.
Dimensions	86'8"x96'4"
Foundation	Slab
Bedrooms	4
Full Baths	2
3/4 Baths	1
Half Baths	1
Main Ceiling	10'-12'
Max Ridge Height	24'8"
Roof Framing	Truss
Exterior Walls	2x4

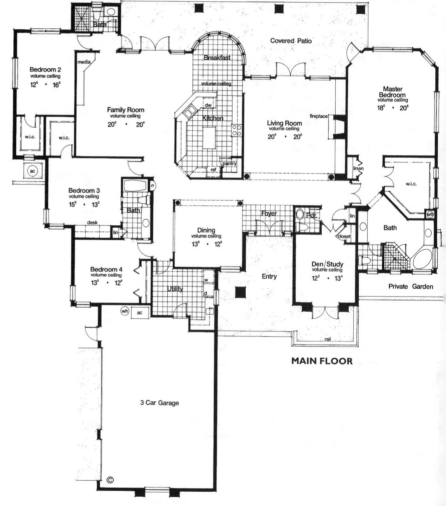

MAIN FLOOR

Design 65653

Units	Single
Price Code	K
Total Finished	3,960 sq. ft.
Main Finished	3,960 sq. ft.
Dimensions	98'x90'
Foundation	Basement
	Crawlspace
	Slab
Bedrooms	4
Full Baths	4
Half Baths	I
Max Ridge Height	29'
Roof Framing	Stick
Exterior Walls	2x6

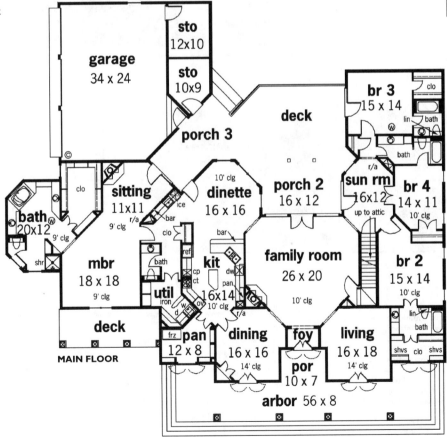

MAIN FLOOR

Design 94224

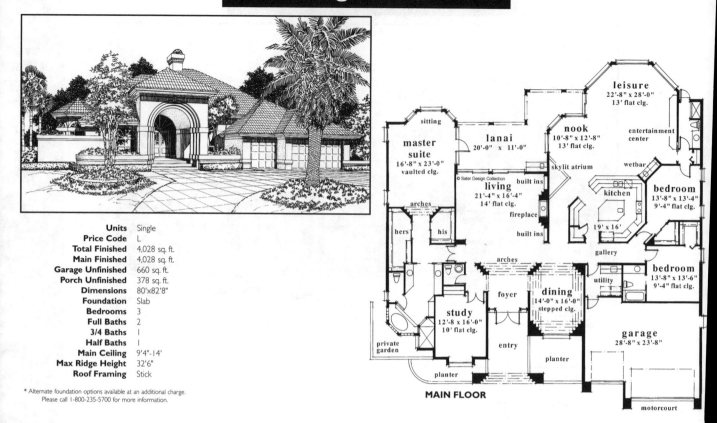

Units	Single
Price Code	L
Total Finished	4,028 sq. ft.
Main Finished	4,028 sq. ft.
Garage Unfinished	660 sq. ft.
Porch Unfinished	378 sq. ft.
Dimensions	80'x82'8"
Foundation	Slab
Bedrooms	3
Full Baths	2
3/4 Baths	1
Half Baths	1
Main Ceiling	9'4"-14'
Max Ridge Height	32'6"
Roof Framing	Stick

* Alternate foundation options available at an additional charge.
Please call 1-800-235-5700 for more information.

MAIN FLOOR

Design 24802

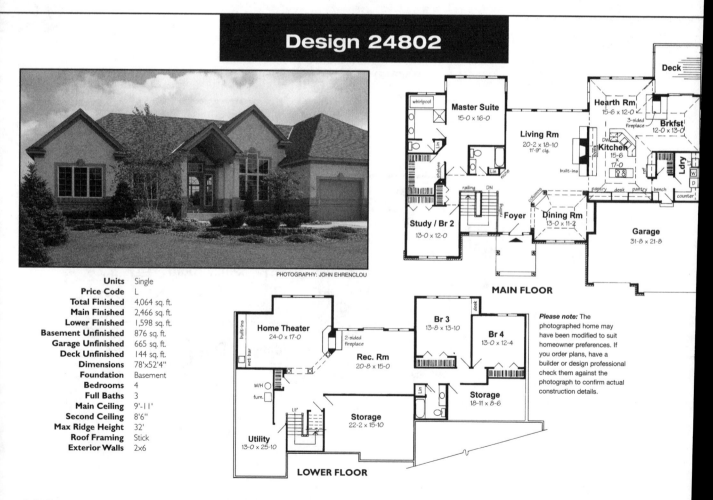

PHOTOGRAPHY: JOHN EHRENCLOU

Units	Single
Price Code	L
Total Finished	4,064 sq. ft.
Main Finished	2,466 sq. ft.
Lower Finished	1,598 sq. ft.
Basement Unfinished	876 sq. ft.
Garage Unfinished	665 sq. ft.
Deck Unfinished	144 sq. ft.
Dimensions	78'x52'4"
Foundation	Basement
Bedrooms	4
Full Baths	3
Main Ceiling	9'-11'
Second Ceiling	8'6"
Max Ridge Height	32'
Roof Framing	Stick
Exterior Walls	2x6

MAIN FLOOR

Please note: The photographed home may have been modified to suit homeowner preferences. If you order plans, have a builder or design professional check them against the photograph to confirm actual construction details.

LOWER FLOOR

PHOTOGRAPHY: DONNA & RON KOLB, EXPOSURES UNLIMITED

Units	Single
Price Code	L
Total Finished	4,328 sq. ft.
Main Finished	2,582 sq. ft.
Lower Finished	1,746 sq. ft.
Basement Unfinished	871 sq. ft.
Deck Unfinished	1,074 sq. ft.
Porch Unfinished	80 sq. ft.
Dimensions	70'8"x64'4"
Foundation	Basement
Bedrooms	3
Full Baths	2
3/4 Baths	1
Half Baths	1
Main Ceiling	9'1"-13'6"
Max Ridge Height	26'5"
Roof Framing	Truss
Exterior Walls	2x4, 2x6

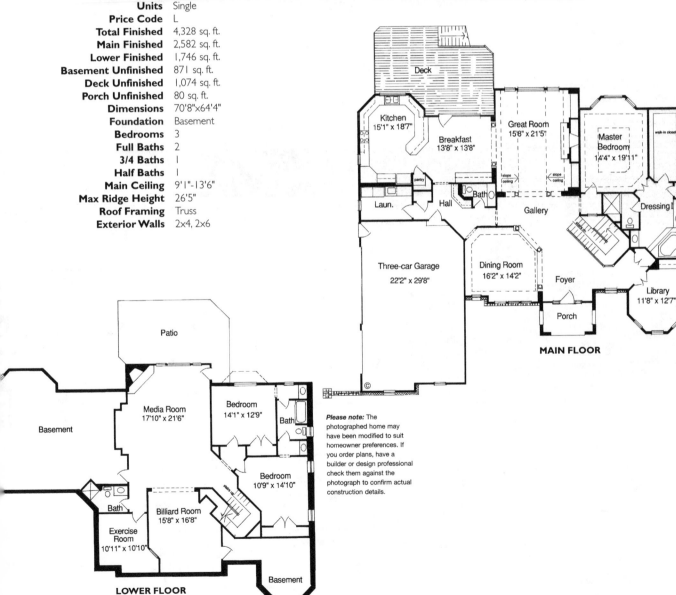

Please note: The photographed home may have been modified to suit homeowner preferences. If you order plans, have a builder or design professional check them against the photograph to confirm actual construction details.

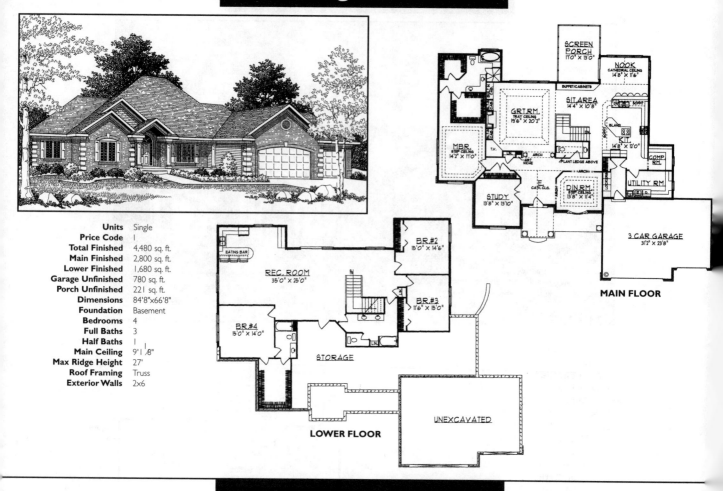

MAIN FLOOR

LOWER FLOOR

Units	Single
Price Code	I
Total Finished	4,480 sq. ft.
Main Finished	2,800 sq. ft.
Lower Finished	1,680 sq. ft.
Garage Unfinished	780 sq. ft.
Porch Unfinished	221 sq. ft.
Dimensions	84'8"x66'8"
Foundation	Basement
Bedrooms	4
Full Baths	3
Half Baths	1
Main Ceiling	9'1.8"
Max Ridge Height	27'
Roof Framing	Truss
Exterior Walls	2x6

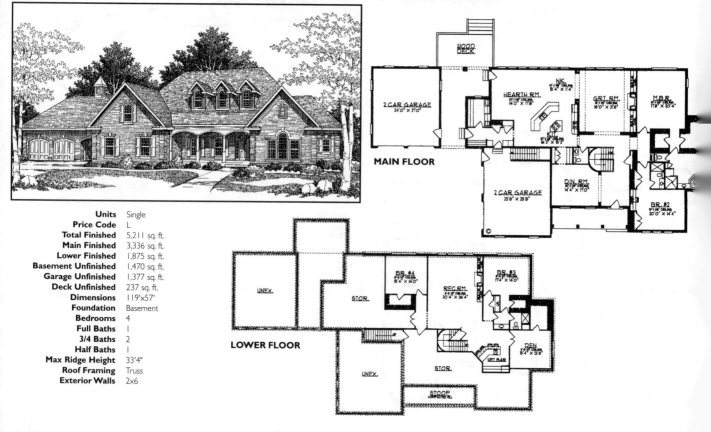

MAIN FLOOR

LOWER FLOOR

Units	Single
Price Code	L
Total Finished	5,211 sq. ft.
Main Finished	3,336 sq. ft.
Lower Finished	1,875 sq. ft.
Basement Unfinished	1,470 sq. ft.
Garage Unfinished	1,377 sq. ft.
Deck Unfinished	237 sq. ft.
Dimensions	119'x57'
Foundation	Basement
Bedrooms	4
Full Baths	1
3/4 Baths	2
Half Baths	1
Max Ridge Height	33'4"
Roof Framing	Truss
Exterior Walls	2x6

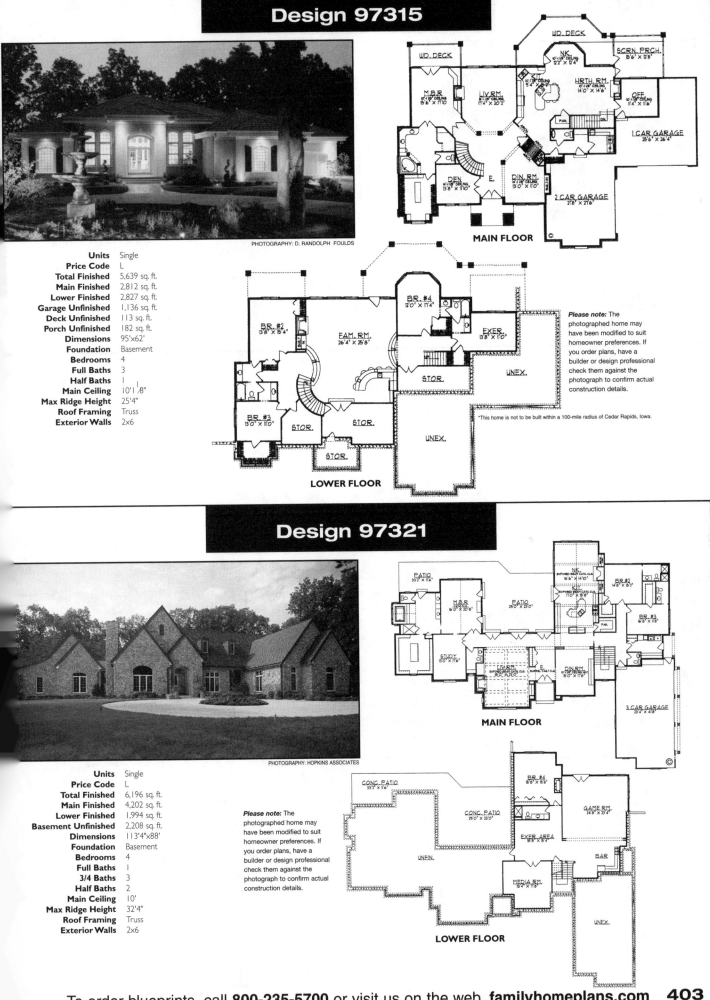

Design 97315

PHOTOGRAPHY: D. RANDOLPH FOULDS

MAIN FLOOR

WD. DECK

WD. DECK

NK.
12'2" X 12'4"

SCRN. PRCH.
13'6" X 17'8"

M.B.R.
15'6" X 17'10"

LIV. RM.
17'4" X 20'2"

HRTH. RM.
14'0" X 14'6"

OFF.
11'4" X 11'6"

1 CAR GARAGE
25'6" X 26'4"

DEN
13'8" X 11'0"

DIN. RM.
13'0" X 11'0"

2 CAR GARAGE
27'8" X 21'8"

Units	Single
Price Code	L
Total Finished	5,639 sq. ft.
Main Finished	2,812 sq. ft.
Lower Finished	2,827 sq. ft.
Garage Unfinished	1,136 sq. ft.
Deck Unfinished	113 sq. ft.
Porch Unfinished	182 sq. ft.
Dimensions	95'x62'
Foundation	Basement
Bedrooms	4
Full Baths	3
Half Baths	1
Main Ceiling	10'1 1/8"
Max Ridge Height	25'4"
Roof Framing	Truss
Exterior Walls	2x6

BR. #4
12'0" X 11'4"

BR. #2
13'8" X 15'4"

FAM. RM.
26'4" X 25'8"

EXER.
13'8" X 11'0"

UNEX.

STOR.

BR. #3
13'0" X 11'0"

STOR.

STOR.

UNEX.

STOR.

LOWER FLOOR

Please note: The photographed home may have been modified to suit homeowner preferences. If you order plans, have a builder or design professional check them against the photograph to confirm actual construction details.

*This home is not to be built within a 100-mile radius of Cedar Rapids, Iowa.

Design 97321

PHOTOGRAPHY: HOPKINS ASSOCIATES

MAIN FLOOR

PATIO
33'2" X 11'6"

NK.
EXPOSED BEAM CATH. CLG.
16'6" X 14'10"

BR. #2
12'6" X 15'2"

M.B.R.
16'6" X 20'8"

PATIO
29'0" X 23'0"

KIT.
EXPOSED BEAM CATH. CLG.
11'0" X 15'8"

BR. #3
16'8" X 11'8"

STUDY
13'0" X 11'6"

LIV. RM.
EXPOSED BEAM CATH. CLG.
BARREL VAULT CLG.

DIN. RM.
15'0" X 11'8"

3 CAR GARAGE
23'4" X 41'8"

Units	Single
Price Code	L
Total Finished	6,196 sq. ft.
Main Finished	4,202 sq. ft.
Lower Finished	1,994 sq. ft.
Basement Unfinished	2,208 sq. ft.
Dimensions	113'4"x88'
Foundation	Basement
Bedrooms	4
Full Baths	1
3/4 Baths	3
Half Baths	2
Main Ceiling	10'
Max Ridge Height	32'4"
Roof Framing	Truss
Exterior Walls	2x6

Please note: The photographed home may have been modified to suit homeowner preferences. If you order plans, have a builder or design professional check them against the photograph to confirm actual construction details.

CONC. PATIO
33'2" X 11'6"

BR. #4
15'8" X 15'8"

GAME RM.
24'6" X 23'4"

CONC. PATIO
29'0" X 23'0"

EXER. AREA
15'8" X 15'4"

UNFIN.

BAR

MEDIA RM.
15'4" X 11'8"

UNEX.

LOWER FLOOR

Design 97157

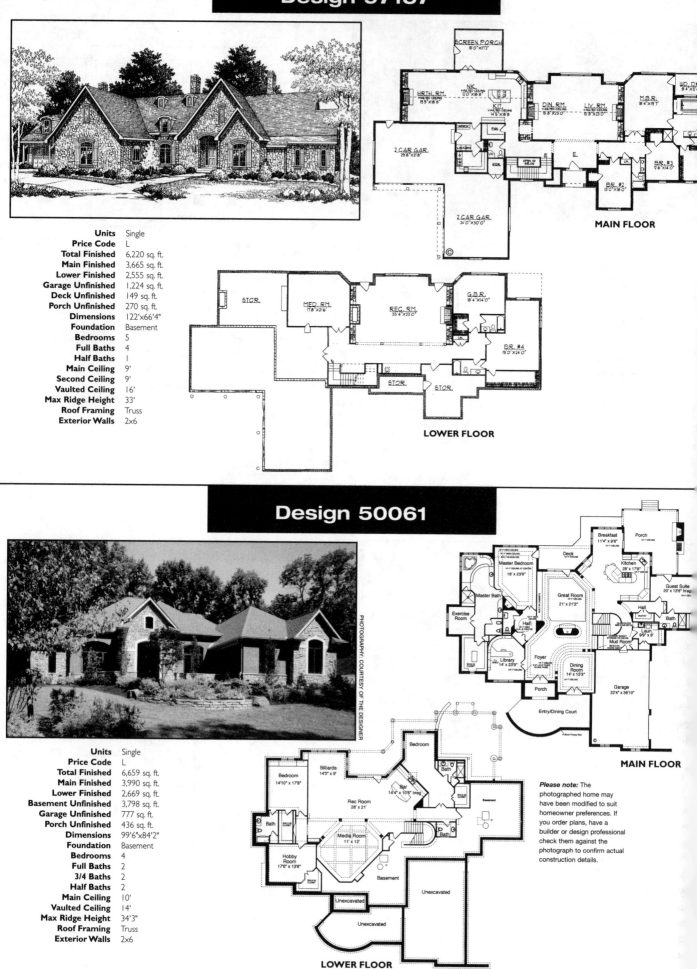

MAIN FLOOR

LOWER FLOOR

Units	Single
Price Code	L
Total Finished	6,220 sq. ft.
Main Finished	3,665 sq. ft.
Lower Finished	2,555 sq. ft.
Garage Unfinished	1,224 sq. ft.
Deck Unfinished	149 sq. ft.
Porch Unfinished	270 sq. ft.
Dimensions	122'x66'4"
Foundation	Basement
Bedrooms	5
Full Baths	4
Half Baths	1
Main Ceiling	9'
Second Ceiling	9'
Vaulted Ceiling	16'
Max Ridge Height	33'
Roof Framing	Truss
Exterior Walls	2x6

Design 50061

MAIN FLOOR

LOWER FLOOR

Units	Single
Price Code	L
Total Finished	6,659 sq. ft.
Main Finished	3,990 sq. ft.
Lower Finished	2,669 sq. ft.
Basement Unfinished	3,798 sq. ft.
Garage Unfinished	777 sq. ft.
Porch Unfinished	436 sq. ft.
Dimensions	99'6"x84'2"
Foundation	Basement
Bedrooms	4
Full Baths	2
3/4 Baths	2
Half Baths	2
Main Ceiling	10'
Vaulted Ceiling	14'
Max Ridge Height	34'3"
Roof Framing	Truss
Exterior Walls	2x6

Please note: The photographed home may have been modified to suit homeowner preferences. If you order plans, have a builder or design professional check them against the photograph to confirm actual construction details.

PHOTOGRAPHY: COURTESY OF THE DESIGNER

Exterior Elevations

These front, rear, and sides of the home include information pertaining to the exterior finish materials, roof pitches, and exterior height dimensions.

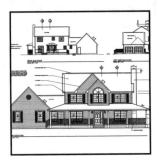

Cabinet Plans

These plans, or in some cases elevations, will detail the layout of the kitchen and bathroom cabinets at a larger scale. Available for most plans.

Typical Wall Section

This section will address insulation, roof components, and interior and exterior wall finishes. Your plans will be designed with either 2x4 or 2x6 exterior walls, but if you wish, most professional contractors can easily adapt the plans to the wall thickness you require.

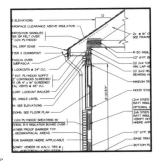

Fireplace Details

If the home you have chosen includes a fireplace, a fireplace detail will show typical methods of constructing the firebox, hearth, and flue chase for masonry units, or a wood frame chase for zero-clearance units. Available for most plans.

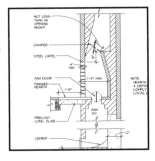

Foundation Plan

These plans will accurately show the dimensions of the footprint of your home, including load-bearing points and beam placement if applicable. The foundation style will vary from plan to plan. **(Please note: There may be an additional charge for optional foundation plan. Please call for details.)**

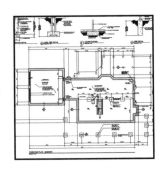

Roof Plan

The information necessary to construct the roof will be included with your home plans. Some plans will reference roof trusses, while many others contain schematic framing plans. These framing plans will indicate the lumber sizes necessary for the rafters and ridgeboards based on the designated roof loads.

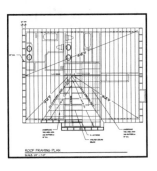

Typical Cross Section

A cut-away cross section through the entire home shows your building contractor the exact correlation of construction components at all levels of the house. It will help to clarify the load bearing points from the roof all the way down to the basement. Available for most plans.

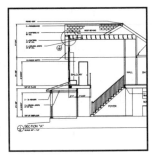

Detailed Floor Plans

The floor plans of your home accurately depict the dimensions of the positioning of all walls, doors, windows, stairs, and permanent fixtures. They will show you the relationship and dimensions of rooms, closets, and traffic patterns. The schematic of the electrical layout may be included in the plan.

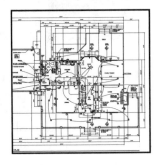

Stair Details

If the design you have chosen includes stairs, the plans will show the information that you need in order to build them— either through a stair cross section or on the floor plans.

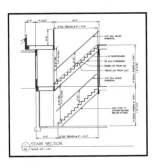

Garlinghouse Options & Extras

Reversed Plans can Make Your Dream Home Just Right!

You could have exactly the home you want by flipping it end-for-end. Simply order your plans "reversed." We'll send you one full set of mirror-image plans (with the writing backwards) as a master guide for you and your builder.

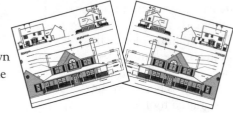

The remaining sets of your order will come as shown in this book so the dimensions and specifications are easily read on the job site. Most plans in our collection come stamped "reversed" so there is no construction confusion.

We can only send reversed plans with multiple-set orders. There is a $50 charge for this service.

Some plans in our collection are available in "Right Reading Reverse." Right Reading Reverse plans will show your home in reverse. This easy-to-read format will save you valuable time and money. Please contact our Sales Department at 800-235-5700 to check for Right Reading Reverse availability. There is a $135 charge for this service. **RRR**

Remember to Order Your Materials List

Available at a modest additional charge, the Materials List gives the quantity, dimensions, and specifications for the major materials needed to build your home. You will get faster, more accurate bids from your contractors and building suppliers—and avoid paying for unused materials and waste. **Materials Lists are available for all home plans except as otherwise indicated, but can only be ordered with a set of home plans.** Due to differences in regional requirements and homeowner or builder preferences, electrical, plumbing and heating/air conditioning equipment specifications are not designed specifically for each plan. **ML**

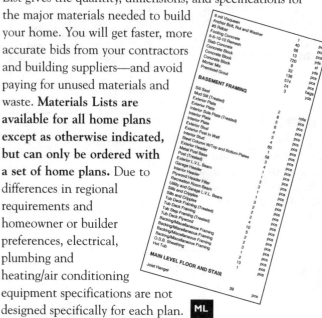

What Garlinghouse Offers

Home Plan Blueprint Package

By purchasing a multiple-set package of blueprints or a Vellum from Garlinghouse, you not only receive the physical blueprint documents necessary for construction, but you are also granted a license to build one (and only one) home. You can also make simple modifications, including minor non-structural changes and material substitutions, to our design as long as these changes are made directly on the blueprints purchased from Garlinghouse and no additional copies are made.

Home Plan Vellums

By purchasing Vellums for one of our home plans, you receive the same construction drawings found in the blueprints, but printed on vellum paper. Vellums can be erased and are perfect for making design changes. They are also semi-transparent, making them easy to duplicate. But most importantly, the purchase of home plan Vellums comes with a broader license that allows you to make changes to the design (i.e., create a hand drawn or CAD derivative work), to make copies of the plan, and to build one home from the plan.

License to Build Additional Homes

With the purchase of a blueprint package or Vellums, you automatically receive a license to build one home and only one home. If you want to build more homes than you are licensed to build through your purchase of a plan, then additional licenses must be purchased at reasonable costs from Garlinghouse. Inquire for more information.

Modifying Your Favorite Design Made Easy

MODIFICATION PRICING GUIDE

CATEGORIES	AVERAGE COST from... to
Adding or removing living space (square footage)	Quote required
Adding or removing a garage	$400-$680
Garage: Front entry to side load or vice versa	Starting at $300
Adding a screened porch	$280-$600
Adding a bonus room in the attic	$450-$780
Changing full basement to crawlspace or vice versa	Starting at $220
Changing full basement to slab or vice versa	Starting at $260
Changing exterior building material	Starting at $200
Changing roof lines	$360-$630
Adjusting ceiling heights	$280-$500
Adding, moving or removing an exterior opening	$55 per opening
Adding or removing a fireplace	$90-$200
Modifying a non-bearing wall or room	$55 per room
Changing exterior walls from 2''x4'' to 2''x6''	Starting at $200
Redesigning a bathroom or a kitchen	$120-$280
Reverse plan right reading	Quote required
Adapting plans for local building code requirements	Quote required
Engineering stamp only	Quote required
Any other engineering services	Quote required
Adjust plan for handicapped accessibility	Quote required
Interactive Illustrations (choices of exterior materials)	Quote required
Metric conversion of home plan	$400

Please remember that figures shown are average costs. Your quote may be higher or lower depending upon your specific requirements.

#1 Modifying Your Garlinghouse Home Plan

Simple modifications to your dream home, including minor non-structural changes and material substitutions, can be made by you and your builder with the consent of your local building official, by marking the changes directly on your blueprints. However, if you are considering making significant changes to your chosen design, we recommend that you use the services of The Garlinghouse Design Staff. We will help take your ideas and turn them into a reality, just the way you want. Here's our procedure:

Call 800-235-5700 and order your modification estimate. The fee for this estimate is $50. We will review your plan changes and provide you with an estimate to draft your specific modifications before you purchase the vellums. *Please note: A vellum must be purchased to modify a home plan design.*

After you receive your estimate, if you decide to have Garlinghouse do the changes, the $50 estimate fee will be deducted from the cost of your modifications. If, however, you chose to use a different service, the $50 estimate fee is non-refundable. *(Note: Personal checks cannot be accepted for the estimate.)*

A 75% deposit is required before we begin making the actual modifications to your plans.

Once the design changes have been completed to your vellum plan, a representative will call to inform you that your modified vellum plan is complete and will be shipped as soon as the final payment has been made. For additional information, call us at 1-800-235-5700. Please refer to the Modification Pricing Guide for estimated modification costs.

#2 Reproducible Vellums for Local Modification Ease

If you decide not to use Garlinghouse for your modifications, we recommend that you follow our same procedure of purchasing vellums. You then have the option of using the services of the original designer of the plan, a local professional designer, or an architect to make the modifications.

With a vellum copy of our plans, a design professional can alter the drawings just the way you want, then you can print as many copies of the modified plans as you need to build your house. And, since you have already started with our complete detailed plans, the cost of those expensive professional services will be significantly less than starting from scratch. Refer to the price schedule for vellum costs.

Ignoring Copyright Laws Can Be
A $100,000 MISTAKE

S. copyright laws allow for statutory penalties of up to $100,000 per incident for copyright infringement involving any of the copyrighted plans found in this publication. The law can be confusing. So, for your own protection, take the time to understand what you can and cannot do when it comes to home plans.

What You Can't Do

You Cannot Duplicate Home Plans
Purchasing a set of blueprints and making additional sets by reproducing the original is illegal. If you need more than one set of a particular home plan, you must purchase them.

You Cannot Copy Any Part of a Home Plan to Create Another
Creating your own plan by copying even part of a home design found in this publication without permission is called "creating a derivative work" and is illegal.

You Cannot Build a Home Without a License
You must have specific permission or a license to build a home from a copyrighted design, even if the finished home has been changed from the original plan. It is illegal to build one of the homes found in this publication without a license.

How to obtain a construction cost calculation based on labor rates and building material costs in your zip code area.

ZIP QUOTE has the answer! *What will your dream home cost?*

How does Zip Quote actually work? When you call to order, you must choose from the options available for your specific home in order for us to process your order. Once we receive your Zip Quote order, we process your specific home plan building materials list through our Home Cost Calculator which contains up-to-date rates for all residential labor trades and building material costs in your zip code area. The result? A calculated cost to build your dream home in your zip code area. This calculation will help you (as a consumer or a builder) evaluate your building budget.

All database information for our calculations is furnished by Marshall & Swift, L.P. For over 60 years, Marshall & Swift L.P. has been a leading provider of cost data to professionals in all aspects of the construction and remodeling industries.

Zip Quote can be purchased in two separate formats, either an itemized or a bottom-line format.

Option 1 The **Itemized Zip Quote** is a detailed building materials list. Each building materials list line item will separately state the labor cost, material cost, and equipment cost (if applicable) for the use of that building material in the construction process. This building materials list will be summarized by the individual building categories and will have additional columns where you can enter data from your contractor's estimates for a cost comparison between the different suppliers and contractors who will actually quote you their products and services.

Option 2 The **Bottom-Line Zip Quote** is a one line summarized total cost for the home plan of your choice. This cost calculation is also based on the labor cost, material cost, and equipment cost (if applicable) within your zip code area. Bottom-Line Zip Quote is available for most plans. Please call for availability.

Cost The price of your Itemized Zip Quote is based upon the pricing schedule of the plan you have selected, in addition to the price of the materials list. Please refer to the pricing schedule on our order form. The price of your initial Bottom-Line Zip Quote is $29.95. Each additional Bottom-Line Zip Quote ordered in conjunction with the initial order is only $14.95. A Bottom-Line Zip Quote may be purchased separately and does NOT have to be purchased in conjunction with a home plan order.

FYI An Itemized Zip Quote Home Cost Calculation can ONLY be purchased in conjunction with a Home Plan order. The Itemized Zip Quote can not be purchased separately. If you find within 60 days of your order date that you will be unable to build this home, then you may apply the price of the plans and the materials list towards the price of a new set of plans (see order info pages for plan exchange policy). The Itemized Zip Quote and the Bottom-Line Zip Quote are NOT returnable. The price of the initial Bottom-Line Zip Quote order can be credited toward the purchase of an Itemized Zip Quote order, only if available. Additional Bottom-Line Zip Quote orders, within the same order can not be credited. Please call our Sales Department for more information.

An Itemized Zip Quote is available for plans where you see this symbol. **ZIP**

A Bottom-Line Zip Quote is available for all plans under 4,000 sq. ft. or where you see this symbol. **BL** Please call for current availability.

Some More Information The Itemized and Bottom-Line Zip Quotes give you approximated costs for constructing the particular house in your area. These costs are not exact and are only intended to be used as a preliminary estimate to help determine the affordability of a new home and/or as a guide to evaluate the general competitiveness of actual price quotes obtained through local suppliers and contractors. **Land, landscaping, sewer systems, site work, contractor overhead and profit, and other expenses are not included in our building cost figures. Excluding land and landscaping, you may incur an additional 20% to 40% in costs from the original estimate.** Garlinghouse and Marshall & Swift L.P. cannot guarantee any level of data accuracy or correctness in Zip Quote and disclaim all liability for loss with respect to the same, in excess of the original purchase price of the Zip Quote product. All Zip Quote calculations are based upon the actual blueprints and do not reflect any differences or options that may be shown on the published house renderings, floor plans or photographs.

CAD Files Now Available

A CAD file is available for plans where you see this symbol.

Cad files are available in .dc5 or .dxf format or .dwg formats (R12, R13, R14, R2000). Please specify the file format at the time of your order. You will receive one bond set along with the CAD file when you place your order. **NOTE: CAD files are NOT returnable and can not be exchanged.**

Your Blueprints Can Be Sealed by A Registered Architect

We can have your home plan blueprints sealed by an architect that is registered in most states. Please call our Order Department for details. Although an architect's seal will not guarantee approval of your home plan blueprints, a seal is sometimes required by your state or local building department in order to get a building permit. Please talk to your local building officials, before you order your blueprints, to determine if a seal is needed in your area. You will need to provide the county and state of your building site when ordering an architect's seal on your blueprints, and please allow additional time to process your order (an additional five to fifteen working days, at least). Seals are available for plans numbered 0-15,999, 17,000-18,999, 20,000 - 31,999, and 34,000 - 34,999.

State Energy Certificates

A few states require that an energy certificate be prepared for your new home to their specifications before a building permit can be issued. Again, your local building official can tell you if one is required in your state. You will first need to fill out the energy certificate checklist available to you when your order is placed. This list contains questions about type of heating used, siding, windows, location of home, etc. This checklist provides all the information needed to prepare your state energy certificate. **Please note: energy certificates are only available on orders for blueprints with an architect's seal.** Certificates are available for plans numbered 0-15,999, 17,000-18,999, 20,000 - 31,999, and 34,000 - 34,999.

Specifications & Contract Form

We send this form to you free of charge with your home plan order. The form is designed to be filled in by you or your contractor with the exact materials to use in the construction of your new home. Once signed by you and your contractor it will provide you with peace of mind throughout the construction process.

Detail Plans
Valuable Information About Construction Techniques—Not Plan Specific

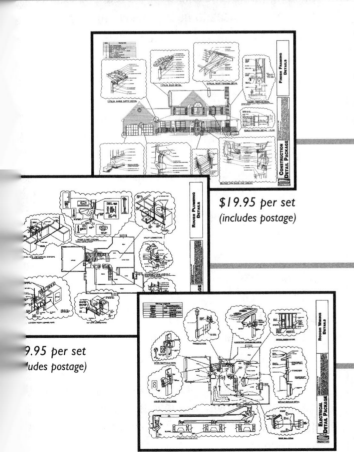

$19.95 per set
(includes postage)

$19.95 per set
(includes postage)

$19.95 per set
(includes postage)

PLEASE NOTE: The detail plans are not specific to any one home plan and should be used only as a general reference guide. Because local codes and requirements vary greatly, we recommend that you obtain drawings and bids from licensed contractors to do your mechanical plans. However, if you want to know more about techniques — and deal more confidently with subcontractors — we offer these remarkably useful detail sheets. These detail sheets will aid in your understanding of these technical subjects.

RESIDENTIAL CONSTRUCTION DETAILS

Ten sheets that cover the essentials of stick-built residential home construction. Details foundation options — poured concrete basement, concrete block, or monolithic concrete slab. Shows all aspects of floor, wall and roof framing. Provides details for roof dormers, overhangs, chimneys and skylights. Conforms to requirements of Uniform Building code or BOCA code. Includes a quick index and a glossary of terms.

RESIDENTIAL PLUMBING DETAILS

Eight sheets packed with information detailing pipe installation methods, fittings, and sized. Details plumbing hook-ups for toilets, sinks, washers, sump pumps, and septic system construction. Conforms to requirements of National Plumbing code. Color coded with a glossary of terms and quick index.

RESIDENTIAL ELECTRICAL DETAILS

Eight sheets that cover all aspects of residential wiring, from simple switch wiring to service entrance connections. Details distribution panel layout with outlet and switch schematics, circuit breaker and wiring installation methods, and ground fault interrupter specifications. Conforms to requirements of National Electrical Code. Color coded with a glossary of terms.

Questions?
Call our customer service number at 1-800-235-5700.

The Garlinghouse Company

Order Form

BEST PLAN VALUE IN THE INDUSTRY!

Order Code No. H4RHP

_____ foundation

_____ set(s) of blueprints for plan # _____ $ _____

_____ Vellum for plan # _____ $ _____

_____ Additional set(s) @ $50 each for plan # _____ $ _____
(Not available for 1 set-study set)

_____ Mirror Image Reverse @ $50 each $ _____

_____ Right Reading Reverse @ $135 each $ _____

_____ Materials list for plan # _____ $ _____

_____ Detail Plans (Not plan specific) @ $19.95 each
❏ Construction ❏ Plumbing ❏ Electrical $ _____

_____ Bottom-Line Zip Quote @ $29.95 for plan # _____ $ _____

_____ Additional Bottom-Line Zip Quotes
@ $14.95 for plan(s) # _____ $ _____

Zip code where building _____

_____ Itemized Zip Quote for plan(s) # _____ $ _____

Shipping $ _____

Subtotal $ _____

Sales Tax (VA residents add 4.5% sales tax. Not required for other states) $ _____

TOTAL AMOUNT ENCLOSED $ _____

Send your check, money order, or credit card information to:
(No C.O.D.'s Please)

Please submit all United States & other nations orders to:
The Garlinghouse Co.
Attn: Order Fulfillment Dept.
4125 Lafayette Rd. Ste. 100
Chantilly, VA. 20151
CALL: (800) 235-5700

VISA   _MasterCard_

Please Submit all Canadian plan orders to:
Garlinghouse Company
102 Ellis Street
Penticton, BC V2A 4L5
CALL: (800) 361-7526   FAX: (250) 493-7526

ADDRESS INFORMATION:

NAME: _____

STREET: _____

CITY: _____

STATE: _____ **ZIP:** _____

DAYTIME PHONE: _____

E-MAIL ADDRESS: _____

Credit Card Information

Charge To: ❏ Visa   ❏ Mastercard

Card # | | | | | | | | | | | | | | | | |

Signature _____ Exp. _____ / _____

To order your plan on-line now
using our secure server, visit:
www.garlinghouse.com

CUSTOMER SERVICE	**TO PLACE ORDERS**
Questions on existing orders?	• To order your home plans • Questions about a plan
➡ **1-800-895-3715**	➡ **1-800-235-5700**

Privacy Statement (please read)

Dear Valued Garlinghouse Customer,

Your privacy is extremely important to us. We'd like to take a little of your time to explain our privacy policy.

As a service to you, we would like to provide your name to companies such as the following:

• Building material manufacturers that we are affiliate with, who would like to keep you current with their product line and specials.

• Building material retailers that would like to offer yo competitive prices to help you save money.

• Financing companies that would like to offer you competitive mortgage rates.

In addition, as our valued customer, we would like to send you newsletters to assist in your building experience. _We_ would also appreciate _your_ feedback b filling out a customer service survey aimed to improve our operations.

You have total control over the use of your contac information. You let us know exactly how you want to contacted. Please check all boxes that apply.
Thank you.

☐ Don't mail
☐ Don't call
☐ Don't E-mail
☐ Only send Garlinghouse newsletters
   and customer service surveys

In closing, we hope this shows Garlinghouse's firm commitment to providing superior customer service a protection of your privacy. We thank you for your time and consideration.

Sincerely,

The Garlinghouse Company

For Our USA Customers:
Order Toll Free: 1-800-235-5700
Monday-Friday 8:00 a.m. to 8:00 p.m. Eastern Time

CUSTOMER SERVICE	TO PLACE ORDERS
Questions on existing orders?	• To order your home plans • Questions about a plan
➡ 1-800-895-3715	➡ 1-800-235-5700

For Our Canadian Customers:
Order Toll Free: 1-800-361-7526
Monday-Friday 8:00 a.m. to 5:00 p.m. Pacific Time
or FAX your Credit Card order to 1-250-493-7526
Customer Service: 1-250-493-0942

Please have ready: 1. Your credit card number 2. The plan number 3. The order code number ➡ H4RHP

Garlinghouse 2004 Blueprint Price Code Schedule
Prices subject to change without notice.

	1 Set Study Set	4 Sets	8 Sets	Vellums	ML	Bottom-Line ZIP Quote	CADD Files
A	$395	$435	$485	$600	$60	$29.95	$1,250
B	$425	$465	$515	$630	$60	$29.95	$1,300
C	$450	$490	$540	$665	$60	$29.95	$1,350
D	$490	$530	$580	$705	$60	$29.95	$1,400
E	$530	$570	$620	$750	$70	$29.95	$1,450
F	$585	$625	$675	$800	$70	$29.95	$1,500
G	$630	$670	$720	$850	$70	$29.95	$1,550
H	$675	$715	$765	$895	$70	$29.95	$1,600
I	$700	$740	$790	$940	$80	$29.95	$1,650
J	$740	$780	$830	$980	$80	$29.95	$1,700
	$805	$845	$895	$1,020	$80	$29.95	$1,750
	$825	$865	$915	$1,055	$80	$29.95	$1,800

Shipping — (Plans 1-35999)

	1-3 Sets	4-6 Sets	7+ & Vellums
Standard Delivery (UPS 2-Day)	$25.00	$30.00	$35.00
Overnight Delivery	$35.00	$40.00	$45.00

Shipping — (Plans 36000-99999)

	1-3 Sets	4-6 Sets	7+ & Vellums
Ground Delivery (7-10 Days)	$15.00	$20.00	$25.00
Express Delivery (3-5 Days)	$20.00	$25.00	$30.00

International Shipping & Handling

	1-3 Sets	4-6 Sets	7+ & Vellums
Regular Delivery Canada (10-14 Days)	$30.00	$35.00	$40.00
Express Delivery Canada (7-10 Days)	$60.00	$70.00	$80.00
Overseas Delivery Airmail (3-4 Weeks)	$50.00	$60.00	$65.00

Additional sets with original order $50

IMPORTANT INFORMATION TO READ BEFORE YOU PLACE YOUR ORDER

How Many Sets of Plans Will You Need?

The Standard 8-Set Construction Package
Our experience shows that you'll speed up every step of construction and avoid costly building errors by ordering enough sets to go around. Each tradesperson wants a set—the general contractor and all subcontractors: foundation, electrical, plumbing, heating/air conditioning, and framers. Don't forget your lending institution, building department, and, of course, a set for yourself. * Recommended For Construction *

The Minimum 4-Set Construction Package
If you're comfortable with arduous follow-up, this package can save you a few dollars by giving you the option of passing down plan sets as work progresses. You might have enough copies to go around if work goes exactly as scheduled and no plans are lost or damaged by subcontractors. But for only $60 more, the 8-set package eliminates these worries. * Recommended For Bidding *

The 1 Set-Study Set
We offer this set so you can study the blueprints to plan your dream home in detail. They are stamped "study set only—not for construction" and you cannot build a home from them. In pursuant to copyright laws, it is *illegal* to reproduce any blueprint. 1 set-study sets cannot be ordered in a reversed format.

To Reorder, Call 800-235-5700
If you find after your initial purchase that you require additional sets of plans, a materials list, or other items, you may purchase them from us at special reorder prices (please call for pricing details) provided that you reorder within six months of your original order date. There is a $28 reorder processing fee that is charged on all reorders. For more information on reordering plans, please contact our Sales Department.

Customer Service/Exchanges Call 800-895-3715
If for some reason you have a question about your existing order, please call 800-895-3715. Your plans are custom printed especially for you once you place your order. For that reason we cannot accept any returns. If for some reason you find that the plan you have purchased from us does not meet your needs, then you may exchange that plan for any other plan in our collection. We allow you 60 days from your original invoice date to make an exchange. At the time of the exchange, you will be charged a processing fee of 20% of the total amount of your original order, plus the difference in price between the plans (if applicable), plus the cost to ship the new plans to you. Call our Customer Service Department for more information. Please Note: Reproducible Vellums can only be exchanged if they are unopened.

Important Shipping Information
Please refer to the shipping charts on the order form for service availability for your specific plan number. Our delivery service must have a street address or Rural Route Box number—never a post office box. (PLEASE NOTE: Supplying a P.O. Box number will *only* will delay the shipping of your order.) Use a work address if someone is home during the day. Orders being shipped to APO or FPO must go via First Class Mail. Please include the proper postage.
For our International Customers, only Certified bank checks and money orders are accepted and must be payable in U.S. currency. For speed, we ship international orders Air Parcel Post. Please refer to the chart for the correct shipping cost.

Important Canadian Shipping Information
To our friends in Canada, we have a plan design affiliate in Penticton, BC. This relationship will help you avoid the delays and charges associated with shipments from the United States. Moreover, our affiliate is familiar with the building requirements in your community and country. We prefer payments in U.S. currency. If you however are sending Canadian funds, please add 45% to the prices of the plans and shipping fees.

Important Note About Building Code Requirements
All plans are drawn to conform to one or more of the industry's major national building standards. However, due to the variety of local building regulations, your home may need to be modified to comply with local requirements—snow loads, energy loads, seismic zones, etc. Do check them fully and consult your local building officials.
A few states require that all building plans used be drawn by an architect registered in that state. While having your plans reviewed and stamped by such an architect may be prudent, laws requiring non-conforming plans like ours to be completely redrawn forces you to unnecessarily pay very large fees. If your state has such a law, we strongly recommend you contact your state representative to protest.
The rendering, floor plans, and technical information contained within this publication are not guaranteed to be totally accurate. Consequently, no information in this publication should be used either as a guide to constructing a home or for estimating the cost of building a home. Complete blueprints must be purchased for such purposes.

Index

Option Key

BL Bottom-Line Zip Quote   **ML** Materials List BL/ML   **ZIP** Itemized Zip Quote   **RRR** Right Reading Reverse   **DUP** Duplex

Index

Option Key

BL Bottom-Line Zip Quote **ML** Materials List BL/ML **ZIP** Itemized Zip Quote **RRR** Right Reading Reverse **DUP** Duplex

TOP SELLING
GARAGE PLANS

Save money by Doing-It-Yourself using our Easy-To-Follow plans. Whether you intend to build your own garage or contract it out to a building professional, the Garlinghouse garage plans provide you with everything you need to price out your project and get started. Put our 90+ years of experience to work for you. Order now!!

No. 06016C $24.95

Cape Cod Style Apartment Garage With One Bedroom

- 28' x 24' Overall Dimensions
- 544 Square Foot Apartment
- 12/12 Gable Roof with Dormers
- Slab or Stem Wall Foundation Options

No. 06015C $24.95

Apartment Garage With Two Bedrooms

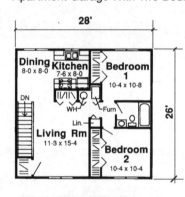

- 28' x 26' Overall Dimensions
- 728 Square Foot Apartment
- 4/12 Pitch Gable Roof
- Slab or Stem Wall Foundation Options

No. 06012C $16.95

30' Deep Gable &/or Eave Entry Jumbo Garages

- 4/12 Pitch Gable Roof
- Available Options for Extra Tall Walls, Garage & Personnel Doors, Foundation, Window, & Sidings
- Package contains 4 Different Sizes
- 30' x 28'   • 30' x 32'   • 30' x 36'   • 30' x 40'

No. 06013C $16.95

Two-Car Eave Entry Garage With Mudroom/Breezeway

- Attaches to Any House
- 36' x 24' Eave Entry
- Available Options for Utility Room with Bath, Mudroom, Screened-In Breezeway, Roof, Foundation, Garage & Personnel Doors, Window, & Sidings

No. 06001C $14.95

12', 14' & 16' Wide-Gable Entry 1-Car Garages

- Available Options for Roof, Foundation, Window, Door, & Sidings
- Package contains 8 Different Sizes
- 12' x 20' Mini-Garage • 14' x 22' • 16' x 20' • 16' x 24'
- 14' x 20' • 14' x 24' • 16' x 22' • 16' x 26'

No. 06003C $14.95

24' Wide-Gable Entry 2-Car Garages

- Available Options for Side Shed, Roof, Foundation, Garage & Personnel Doors, Window, & Sidings
- Package contains 5 Different Sizes
- 24' x 22' • 24' x 28' • 24' x 36'
- 24' x 24' • 24' x 32'

No. 06007C $16.95

Gable 2-Car Gable Entry Gambrel Roof Garages

- Rear Stairs to Loft Workshop
- Front Loft Cargo Door With Pulley Lift
- Available Options for Foundation, Garage & Personnel Doors, Window, & Sidings
- Package contains 5 Different Sizes
- 22' x 26' • 22' x 28' • 24' x 28' • 24' x 30' • 24' x 32'

No. 06006C $16.95

22' & 24' Deep Eave Entry 2 & 3-Car Garages

- Can Be Built Stand-Alone or Attached to House
- Available Options for Roof, Foundation, Garage & Personnel Doors, Window, & Sidings
- Package contains 6 Different Sizes
- 22' x 28' • 22' x 32' • 24' x 32'
- 22' x 30' • 24' x 30' • 24' x 36'

No. 06002C $14.95

20' & 22' Wide-Gable Entry 2-Car Garages

- Available Options for Roof, Foundation, Garage & Personnel Doors, Window, & Sidings
- Package contains 7 Different Sizes
- 20' x 20' • 20' x 24' • 22' x 22' • 22' x 28'
- 20' x 22' • 20' x 28' • 22' x 24'

No. 06008C $16.95

Eave Entry 2 & 3-Car Clerestory Roof Garages

- Interior Side Stairs to Loft Workshop
- Available Options for Engine Lift, Foundation, Garage & Personnel Doors, Window, & Sidings
- Package contains 4 Different Sizes
- 24' x 26' • 24' x 28' • 24' x 32' • 24' x 36'

Order Code No: **H4RHP**

Garage Order Form

Please send me 1 complete set of the following
GARAGE PLAN BLUEPRINTS:

Item no. & description _____	Price	
Additional Sets	$ _____	
(@ $10.00 EACH)	$ _____	
Garage Vellum		
(@ $200.00 EACH)	$ _____	

Shipping Charges: **UPS Ground (3-7 days within the US)** $ _____
 1-3 plans $7.95
 4-6 plans $9.95
 7-10 plans $11.95
 11 or more plans $17.95

Subtotal: $ _____

Resident sales tax: $ _____
(VA residents add 4.5%. Not required for other states.)

Total Enclosed: $ _____

My Billing Address is:

Name: _____

Address: _____

City: _____

State: _____ Zip:_____

Daytime Phone No. (_____) _____

My Shipping Address is:

Name: _____

Address: _____
 (UPS will not ship to P.O. Boxes)

City: _____

State: _____ Zip: _____

For Faster Service...Charge It!
U.S. & Canada Call
1(800)235-5700

All foreign residents call 1(860)659-5667

M A S T E R C A R D, V I S A

Card # | | | | | | | | | | | | | | | | | | |

Signature _____ Exp.___/___

If paying by credit card, to avoid delays:
billing address must be as it appears on credit card statement

Here's What You Get

- One complete set of drawings for each plan ordered
- Detailed step-by-step instructions with easy-to-follow diagrams on how to build your garage (not available with apartment garages)
- For each garage style, a variety of size and garage door configuration options
- Variety of roof styles and/or pitch options for most garages
- Complete materials list
- Choice between three foundation options: Monolithic Slab, Concrete Stem Wall or Concrete Block Stem Wa
- Full framing plans, elevations and cross-sectionals for each garage size and configuration

Garage Plan Blueprints

All blueprint garage plan orders contain one complete se of drawings with instructions and are priced as listed ne> to the illustration. **These blueprint garage plans can no be modified.** Additional sets of plans may be obtained fo $10.00 each with your original order. UPS shipping used unless otherwise requested. Please include th proper amount for shipping.

Garage Plan Vellums

By purchasing vellums for one of our garage plans, yo receive one vellum set of the same construction drawin found in the blueprints, but printed on vellum pap Vellums can be erased and are perfect for making desi changes. They are also semi-transparent making the easy to duplicate. But most importantly, the purchase garage plan vellums comes with a broader license th allows you to make changes to the design (ie, create hand drawn or CAD derivative work), to make copies the plan and to build one garage from the plan.

Send your order to:
(With check or money order payable in U.S. funds only)
The Garlinghouse Company
Attn: Order Fulfillment Dept.
4125 Lafayette Rd. Ste. 100
Chantilly, Va. 20151

No C.O.D. orders accepted; U.S. funds only. UPS will not ship to Po: Office boxes, FPO boxes, APO boxes, Alaska or Hawaii.

Canadian orders:
UPS Ground (5-10 days within Canada)
 1-3 plans $15.95
 4-6 plans $17.95
 7-10 plans $19.95
 11 or more plans $24.95
Prices subject to change without notice.